Pass the Plate

The Collection From Christ Church

Originally Published by

Episcopal Churchwomen
and Friends of
Christ Episcopal Church
New Bern,
North Carolina 28560
1981

Pass the Plate

1st Printing	November 1981
2nd Printing	January 1983
3rd Printing	July 1984
4th Printing	December 1986
5th Printing	August 1989
6th Printing	January 2002
7th Printing	February 2005

ISBN 1-931294-20-8
Library of Congress Number: 84-152512

Manufactured in China
Cookbook Resources, LLC
541 Doubletree Drive
Highland Village, Texas 75077
Toll free 866-229-2665

www.cookbookresources.com

Pass the Plate

COOKBOOK COMMITTEE

Co-chairmen

Mrs. James R. Stewart
Mrs. T. Reed Underhill

Steering Committee

Mrs. J. Muse McCotter
Mrs. Ben W. Parrish
Mrs. John T. Taylor, Jr.
Mrs. J. Brooks McIntyre
Mrs. Wm. Edward Stewart
Mrs. William B. Anderson, V
Mrs. Robert D. Darden
Mrs. Earl Applegate
Mrs. Robert R. Emory, Jr.

Cover Art and Illustrations

Mrs. Stewart H. Smith
Mrs. Kenneth Williams

Many thanks go to those special people who have made contributions toward the completion of this cookbook. We are particularly grateful to Mr. Earl Applegate, Major James R. Stewart and Dr. T. Reed Underhill, to all those who dutifully typed and retyped copy and to our many proofreaders.

The Women of Christ Episcopal Church have carefully edited and tested the recipes contained in this cookbook. We regret that due to space limitations, it was impossible to use all recipes which were submitted. Multiple listing of contributors after a recipe indicates that recipes submitted were similar, not necessarily identical.

It has been our attempt throughout this cookbook to be as specific as possible. Where generalities exist, measurements are left to the cook's taste and good judgment.

A few words of explanation:

1. *Flour* is all-purpose flour. Any other flour is specified.
2. *Sugar* is granulated. Any other sugar is specified.
3. *Confectioners' sugar* and *powdered sugar* are the same sugar. The difference between 4X and 10X confectioners' sugar is the number of times it has been sifted. If you are making decorator cake icing, you would want to use 10X sugar for an ultra-smooth product.
4. *Margarine* and *butter* may be used interchangeably in most recipes. Butter will be specified if it is mandatory.
5. *Vegetable oil* is not interchangeable with butter, margarine or other solid shortening.
6. *Condensed milk* is a sweetened milk product and is *not* interchangeable with *evaporated milk*.
7. Dairy *sour cream* and a non-dairy canned product are interchangeable.
8. *Pepper* indicates black pepper.

TABLE OF CONTENTS

CHRIST CHURCH PARISH—AN HISTORICAL SKETCH

New Bern was settled in 1710 by a colony of Swiss and German Palatines under the leadership of Baron Christopher deGraffenried. The baron named the settlement to honor his native Bern, Switzerland. The majority of the New Bern colonists were formerly Calvinist and Lutheran by religious persuasion, and Baron deGraffenried wrote the Bishop of London in 1711 to request the reception of the colonists into the Church of England.

Craven Parish was one of nine parishes in the Province of North Carolina provided for by "An Act for Establishing the Church and Appointing Select Vestrys" in 1715. This act marks the beginning of Christ Church in New Bern.

A lot for a church was given in 1723 by Colonel Thomas Pollock, Proprietary Governor. This lot was sold because it was considered "insufficient and not so commodious," and the vestry purchased four lots on the north side of Pollock Street between Middle and Craven Streets for a Church, churchyard and other parish purposes. This site has been used by the parish for more than two centuries.

The Craven Parish vestrymen laid a tax on all tithables in New Bern in 1739 for the construction of a church. The small colonial brick church was completed in 1750. The church was erected at the corner of Pollock and Middle Streets, and it was later torn down to be replaced by a larger structure. The site and the floor plan of the colonial church are preserved by a brick wall which has been erected over the original brick and ballast foundations and is presently being used as an outdoor chapel.

In response to an appeal of the Christ Church vestrymen to the Bishop of London, the Reverend James Reed came to New Bern in 1753 as the first rector of the parish. Mr. Reed also served the Carteret Parish and eight chapels at remote points. The Society for the Propagation of the Gospel in Foreign Parts enrolled him in 1758 as a regular Missionary.

In 1752, before the arrival of the first rector, King George II presented the parish a silver Communion Service, a Bible and a Book of Common Prayer. These gifts are still in the possession of the parish. The Communion Service, in regular use in the parish to this day, consists of a chalice, paten, two large flagons, and a large basin. Each piece of the set bears four hallmarks and the Royal Arms of Great Britain, which includes initials of the reigning monarch—"GR" for George Rex. The hallmarks are as follows: the initials "MF" are the maker's mark denoting Mordecai Fox as the manufacturer; the date letter "r" superimposed on a shield indicates that the silver pieces were made in 1752; the crowned leopard's head is the town mark for London; and the "lion passant gardant" is the assay mark which guarantees that the purity of the silver is 92.5 per cent as required by law. A small hole made by boring for assaying or testing is also found in each piece of the Communion Service.

The outside covers of the George II Bible and Prayer Book are inscribed with the royal coat of arms. The Bible was printed in Oxford in 1717, and the Prayer Book was printed in 1752 at Cambridge.

The first rector of Christ Church, The Reverend Mr. Reed, was keenly interested in education, and he was instrumental in the establishment of North Carolina's first incorporated school. The local school was incorporated in 1766 by the General Assembly, and Mr. Reed was named one of the trustees. It was the second private secondary school to receive a charter in English America.

The Reverend James Reed, a Royalist and one of the outstanding ministers in Colonial America, died in May, 1777, before the close of the Revolutionary War. His body was interred in the graveyard near Middle Street where his grave is appropriately marked and identified.

Richard Dobbs Spaight and William Blount, signers of the Federal Constitution in 1787, were two of the prominent communicants of Christ Church in these early days. Spaight was a member of Congress, and he served in 1792-95 as the first native-born Governor of North Carolina. William Blount later served as Governor of the Territory South of the River Ohio and as Senator from Tennessee.

John Hawks, supervising architect of Governor Tyron's Palace in the late 1760's, was another prominent communicant of Christ Church. His grandson, William N. Hawks, served as rector of the parish from 1847-1853.

John Wright Stanly, also an Eighteenth Century member of this church, was an illustrious patriot who spent a considerable personal fortune in support of the revolutionary cause. He was buried in the churchyard, and his restored home is considered one of the most beautiful buildings in New Bern and America.

The organizing convention of the Diocese of North Carolina was held in Christ Church on April 24, 1817. This new diocese of the Protestant Episcopal Church in the United States of America was placed under the care of the Bishop of Virginia until it could elect its own bishop.

A new church was constructed on Pollock Street to replace the smaller Colonial structure at the corner of the lot. This second church was consecrated February 1, 1824 by the Right Reverend John Stark Ravenscroft, who became the first bishop of North Carolina one year earlier. The church burned in January, 1871, but a large portion of the thick brick walls remained. Christ Church was rebuilt in 1873, and the old walls were incorporated in the structure. The church was consecrated in 1875 by Bishop Thomas A. Atkinson.

The organization of the Diocese of East Carolina was accomplished at its first convention which met in Christ Church December 12-13, 1883. This was the second diocese to be organized in this church. Dr. Alfred Augustine Watson, a former rector of the parish, was elected the first bishop of the new diocese.

A centennial celebration commemorating the organization of the Diocese of North Carolina was held May 17, 1917 in Christ Church. The three bishops of the Dioceses of East Carolina and North Carolina and the Missionary District of Asheville attended the service, and a bronze tablet was presented which commemorated the 100th anniversary celebration. This tablet is on the west wall of the church.

On May 17-18, 1933, the Convention of the Diocese of East Carolina met in Christ Church to celebrate the Golden Jubilee anniversary of the organization of the diocese. A tablet was unveiled to mark this event and placed near the earlier commemorative tablet on the west wall.

The 250th anniversary of the founding of the parish was celebrated at a service in October, 1965, with the Right Reverend Bernard Markham, Bishop of Nassau and the Bahamas, as speaker. Bishop Markham brought greeting from the Church of England which nurtured Christ Church in its early years until the American Revolution.

On April 5, 1970, while guests of the Tryon Palace Commission, Lord and Lady Tryon of Great Durnford, near historic Salisbury, England, attended Christ Church's regular Sunday morning service.

Taken from the works of Miss Gertrude S. Carraway, eminent historian of New Bern and Christ Church

CHRIST CHURCH NEWCOMER'S DINNER

Mixmaster Cheese Biscuits
Wayco Country Ham
Berne Restaurant Fried Chicken
Broccoli Casserole
Congealed Mixed Fruit Salad
Pickles and Relishes
Hot Rolls and Butter
Tea and Coffee
Parkhill Jarvis' Rum Cake

MIXMASTER CHEESE BISCUITS

Stores well
Can be frozen

½ pound Fleischmann's margarine, softened
½ pound Cracker Barrel Extra Sharp cheese, grated
2 cups flour
½ teaspoon cayenne pepper
1 teaspoon salt
1 teaspoon lemon juice

Preheat oven to 300 degrees. Allow margarine and grated cheese to reach room temperature in a large mixing bowl. Blend with mixmaster for a few minutes. Add flour, cayenne and salt which have been sifted together. When this is well-blended, add lemon juice. Cream for 20 minutes. Drop by teaspoonfuls onto a cookie sheet and bake for 20 to 25 minutes. Place another cookie sheet or pan under the rack holding the biscuits while they are cooking. This keeps them from browning. Cool on paper towels and store in an airtight container.
Yield: about 75 biscuits

Dora Winters Taylor (Mrs. John T., Jr.)

BROCCOLI CASSEROLE

4 (10-ounce) packages frozen broccoli spears
2 (10¾-ounce) cans cream of chicken soup
1 cup Miracle Whip
4 teaspoons lemon juice
1 cup Pepperidge Farm Herb Dressing, crushed
4 tablespoons butter
Sharp Cheddar cheese, grated

Cook broccoli as directed on package. Cut cooked broccoli into bite-sized pieces and arrange in 9x13-inch Pyrex casserole dish. Mix cream of chicken soup with Miracle Whip and lemon juice and pour over broccoli. Brown crushed herb dressing in butter and sprinkle on top of broccoli and soup mixture. Sprinkle grated cheese on top and bake at 350 degrees 20-30 minutes until bubbly.
Yield: 20 servings

Frances Mason Clement (Mrs. Donald H.)

CONGEALED FRUIT SALAD

4 (16-ounce) cans grapefruit sections
2 (20-ounce) cans pineapple slices, cut up
2 (11-ounce) cans mandarin oranges
1 (6-ounce) jar maraschino cherries
1½-2 cups pecans, chopped
2 (6-ounce) packages lemon Jello
Juice of 2 lemons

Drain fruits and reserve juices. Dissolve Jello in four cups of boiling water. Add 2 cups of fruit juice and juice of 2 lemons. Add drained fruits and put in one 9x13-inch container and one 8- or 9-inch square container. Refrigerate until congealed.
Yield: 20 servings

Margaret Gibbs Dunn (Mrs. John G., Jr.)

PARKHILL JARVIS' RUM CAKE

Cake:

1 cup pecans or walnuts, chopped
1 (18½-ounce) package yellow cake mix
1 (3¾-ounce) package vanilla instant pudding mix
½ cup Bacardi dark rum, 80 proof
4 eggs
½ cup cold water
½ cup Wesson oil

Preheat oven to 325 degrees. Grease and flour 10-inch tube or 12-cup Bundt pan. Sprinkle nuts in bottom. Mix cake ingredients and pour over nuts. Bake 1 hour. Cool. Invert cake on serving plate.

Glaze:

½ cup butter
¼ cup water
1 cup sugar
½ cup Bacardi dark rum

Melt butter in saucepan. Stir in water and sugar. Boil 5 minutes, stirring constantly. Remove from heat. Add rum. Prick top and drizzle glaze evenly over top and sides. Allow cake to absorb glaze. Repeat until glaze is used up.

Christ Church Communion Service

King George II presented the silver communion service to the parish in 1752. Made by London silversmith Mordecai Fox, the chalice, paten, two flagons, and basin are still in use in Christ Church today. During the War Between the States, when the Union army occupied New Bern, the silver was hidden, first in Wilmington and later in a closet full of rubbish in Fayetteville.

First Baptist Church **239 Middle Street**

In 1809 John Brinson, Elijah Clark, and Mary Mitchell met in Sheriff Clark's house on Middle Street to organize New Bern's first Baptist congregation. By 1811 the first simple frame church was ready for use. The present impressive brick building was dedicated July 2, 1848. Thomas Meredith, who founded the "Biblical Recorder" and for whom Meredith College in Raleigh, N.C., is named, and William Hopper, who founded Wake Forest College, were ministers here.

FIRST BAPTIST CHRISTMAS DINNER

Baked Ham
Baked Turkey with Giblet Gravy
Asparagus Casserole
Sweet Potato Soufflé
Grape-Cranberry Salad
Dinner Rolls
Pecan Pie
Peach and Coconut Cake

ASPARAGUS CASSEROLE

½ cup margarine
½ cup flour
1 (14-ounce) can asparagus, reserve liquid
1 (10-ounce) can asparagus, reserve liquid
½ cup milk
½ cup grated cheese
5 hard-boiled eggs
20 saltine crackers, crushed

Preheat oven to 350 degrees. Butter 7x5x3-inch casserole dish. Melt margarine; add flour to make a thick paste. Add liquid from both cans of asparagus; add milk and cook over low heat stirring constantly until thick. Stir in grated cheese. Add asparagus and stir until asparagus comes to pieces. Add chopped boiled eggs. Pour into casserole and cover with cracker crumbs. Bake until crumbs are brown or about 20 minutes.

Miss Margie Ragsdale

SWEET POTATO SOUFFLÉ

3 cups sweet potatoes, cooked and mashed
1 cup sugar
½ teaspoon salt
2 eggs, beaten lightly
⅓ stick butter, melted
1 cup milk
1 teaspoon vanilla

Topping:
⅓ cup butter
1 cup brown sugar
⅓ cup flour
1 cup pecans, chopped
1 cup coconut

Preheat oven to 350 degrees. Mix together sweet potatoes and sugar. Add salt and eggs; stirring well. Add butter, milk and vanilla; stir well. Pour into greased baking dish and bake for 35 minutes. Remove from oven. Melt butter for topping. Add sugar, flour, pecans and coconut. Mix well. Spread on the top of the baked sweet potatoes and return to oven for 20 additional minutes. Yield: 6 servings

Bee Garris King (Mrs. Robert, Jr.)
Carey's grandmother

GRAPE-CRANBERRY SALAD

½ box cranberries, crushed
¼ cup sugar
1 cup Tokay grapes, cut and seeded
1 cup miniature marshmallows
½ cup pecans, chopped
½ pint whipping cream, whipped
¼ cup sugar

Sweeten cranberries with ¼ cup sugar and sweetened whipping cream with ¼ cup sugar. Combine all ingredients and refrigerate until serving time.

Pat Farrell Thompson (Mrs. T. R.)

DINNER ROLLS

2 packages dry yeast
2 cups warm water
7 cups flour
½ cup sugar
1 teaspoon salt
¼ cup oil
1 egg

Dissolve yeast in warm water. Add 3 cups of flour, sugar and salt. Mix well. Add oil and egg. Mix well. Add 4 more cups flour gradually. Knead until firm either on counter or in bowl. Use additional oil to coat bowl and turn dough in bowl to coat with oil. Cover with damp towel. Let rise until double. Make into favorite shape dinner rolls or divide dough and roll out thinly in rectangle. Spread with soft butter, cinnamon-sugar, nuts or raisins. Roll as for jellyroll and cut in ½-¾-inch rounds. Place on greased cookie sheet. Let rise until double. Bake in preheated 400 degree oven for cinnamon rolls; 450 degrees for dinner rolls for 10 minutes.

Judith Branch Blythe (Mrs. Charles B.)
owner of Branch's Office Supply

PECAN PIE

3 eggs
1 cup light brown sugar
1 tablespoon butter
1 cup light Karo syrup
1 cup pecans
1 teaspoon salt
1 teaspoon vanilla
Unbaked pie shell

Preheat oven to 300 degrees. Beat eggs and sugar until thick. Add Karo, nuts, vanilla, butter and salt. Pour into pie shell and bake for one hour.

Julia Woodson Hudson (Mrs. John S., Jr.)

PEACH AND COCONUT CAKE

May be prepared ahead
Can freeze
Stores well

Cake:
2 cups sugar
1 cup butter
4 eggs
1 cup milk
3½ cups flour
1 teaspoon baking powder
1 teaspoon vanilla

Preheat oven to 400 degrees. Grease six 10-inch layer pans or be prepared to bake layers and regrease as necessary for the number of pans you have in order to make 6 layers. Cream sugar and butter thoroughly; add eggs one at the time. Sift flour and baking powder 3 times and add alternately with milk to creamed mixture; add vanilla. Bake 6 layers for 15 minutes. Layers will be very thin. As each layer comes from oven spread with filling.

Filling:
1 (28-ounce) and 1 (16-ounce) can peaches
2 tablespoons cornstarch
½ cup water
26-ounces coconut (canned, frozen or fresh)

Put peaches plus juice in blender and blend until smooth; then pour purée into saucepan and heat. Mix cornstarch with water and add to peach mixture; stir constantly until thick. Cool. As each layer is taken out of oven, spread with peach mixture and sprinkle coconut over as you layer cake. Pat coconut on sides and lots on top. This cake tastes better as days go by and freezes beautifully.

Betty Jones Kilby (Mrs. Earle)

First Church of Christ Scientist 406 Middle Street

This is the oldest Christian Science Church in North Carolina. Its cornerstone was laid December 31, 1903. Mrs. Mary Baker Eddy, discoverer of Christian Science, made a financial contribution to this church. Next door to the church is the church reading room.

Centenary United Methodist Church 416 Middle Street

Methodists organized in New Bern in 1802. Their present structure, which was dedicated on October 22, 1905, is their third location in New Bern. The architects were Charles Granville Jones of New York City and Herbert Woodley Simpson of New Bern. The bell which is now located in the side yard of the church was taken from the belfry of the second Methodist church building and was returned during the late 1960's to Centenary United Methodist Church.

CENTENARY LUNCHEON BUFFET

Congealed Cranberry Salad
Chicken Breast with Wine
Broccoli-Cheese Casserole
Buttermilk Refrigerator Rolls
Old-Fashioned Lemon Pie
Knobby Apple Cake
Frozen Rum Custard
Chocolate-Peanut Butter Dainties

CRANBERRY SALAD

1½ cups fresh cranberries, ground
½ cup sugar
2 (3-ounce) packages orange or lemon Jello
¼ teaspoon salt
2 cups boiling water
1½ cups cold water
1 tablespoon lemon juice
¼ teaspoon cinnamon
⅛ teaspoon cloves
1 orange, sectioned and diced
½ cup almonds or walnuts, chopped

Combine cranberries and sugar and set aside. Dissolve Jello and salt in boiling water. Add cold water, lemon juice, cinnamon and cloves. Chill until thickened. Fold in cranberries, orange pieces and nuts. Spoon into a 6-cup mold. Chill until firm, about 4 hours. Unmold. Garnish with crisp salad greens.
Yield: 12 servings

Joan Serrins Respess (Mrs. William A.)

CHICKEN BREAST WITH WINE

1 (10½-ounce) can cream of mushroom soup
1 (10½-ounce) can cream of chicken soup
½ soup can Sauterne wine
½ green pepper, chopped
1 (8-ounce) can water chestnuts, slivered
Salt
Pepper
6 chicken breast halves

Preheat oven to 350 degrees. Butter a shallow flat casserole and lay chicken breasts in bottom. Combine remaining ingredients and pour over chicken. Cover with foil or a top to casserole. Bake for 1 hour with lid on; remove lid and brown for a short period of time.
Yield: 6 servings

Joan Serrins Respess (Mrs. William A.)

BROCCOLI-CHEESE CASSEROLE

Gals especially like this, making it great for a bridge luncheon!

3 eggs, beaten
1 (8-ounce) carton cottage cheese
Dash or two of pepper
1 cup Cheddar cheese, shredded
3 tablespoons flour
2 teaspoons salt
2 (10-ounce) packages frozen chopped broccoli, thawed

Preheat oven to 350 degrees. In large bowl beat eggs slightly; beat in both cheeses, flour, salt and pepper. Drain broccoli well, patting dry with paper towels. Stir into egg mixture. Pour into greased 9x9 baking dish, spreading evenly with spoon. Bake for 30-35 minutes until mixture is firm and pulls away from sides of pan. Loosen edges with spatula, slice and serve.
Yield: 6-8 servings

Dorothy Lee Taylor Jernigan (Mrs. Curtis D.)

BUTTERMILK REFRIGERATOR ROLLS

2 packages dry yeast
4 tablespoons warm water
3/4 cup shortening, melted
1/4 cup sugar
2 cups buttermilk
5 cups self-rising flour

Dissolve yeast in warm water. Add other ingredients. Mix thoroughly by hand. Add more flour if needed. Cover and refrigerate. Use as needed. About 1½ hours before baking, roll pieces of dough into 1-inch balls and put three in muffin tin. Prepare as many rolls as needed and refrigerate remaining dough. Cover rolls and let rise in warm place for 1 hour before baking. Bake in preheated 425 degree oven until brown, about 12 minutes.

Ellen Johnson Pauling (Mrs. Tom)

OLD-FASHIONED LEMON PIE

1½ cups sugar
1½ cups water
1 tablespoon butter
2 tablespoons cornstarch
1/3 teaspoon cream of tartar
3 eggs
2 lemons, juiced and rinds grated
1 pie shell, baked

Mix 1 cup sugar and 1 cup water and butter. Let boil 3 minutes. Add cornstarch mixed with remaining ½ cup water. Stir well. Add grated rind of lemons and juice. Add egg yolks and stir well until mixture thickens. Remove from heat and let cool. Beat egg whites until very stiff; add remaining ½ cup sugar a little at a time to egg whites and fold 1/3 egg white mixture into pie filling. Pour into pie shell. Add cream of tartar to remainder of egg white mixture to form meringue; cover pie with meringue. Bake 15 minutes in oven preheated to 400 degrees and TURNED OFF before placing pie inside. Let pie remain in oven until meringue is golden brown.

Marjorie Stephens Carawon (Mrs. Tuck)

CHOCOLATE-PEANUT BUTTER DAINTIES

½ (13½-ounce) box graham cracker crumbs
1 (18-ounce) jar crunchy peanut butter
1 (3½-ounce) can Baker's Angel Coconut
1 cup butter, melted
1 (16-ounce) box powdered sugar
1½ cups pecans, chopped
1 (12-ounce) bag Nestle's chocolate bits
¾ bar of paraffin

Put paraffin and chocolate bits in top of double boiler and melt. Mix all other ingredients together and make into small balls. Dip them into the paraffin-chocolate and put on waxed paper to harden. Store them in a tight container.

Linda Peterson Jones (Mrs. Michael D.)

KNOBBY APPLE CAKE

3 tablespoons butter or margarine
1 cup sugar
2 eggs, beaten
½ teaspoon cinnamon
½ teaspoon nutmeg
½ teaspoon salt
1 teaspoon soda
1 cup sifted flour
3 cups apples, diced
¼ cup nuts, chopped
1 teaspoon vanilla

Preheat oven to 350 degrees. Grease 8x8-inch baking dish. Cream butter and sugar; add eggs, mixing well. Sift dry ingredients together. Add to creamed mixture. Stir in diced apples, nuts and vanilla. Pour into prepared pan and bake 40-45 minutes. Serve hot or cold with or without whipped cream or ice cream.
Yield: 8-9 servings

Elsie Lamm Mayo (Mrs. Alfred)

All Saints Chapel **809 Pollock Street**

The chapel was built in 1895 on a lot on Pollock Street that was bequeathed to the Diocese by Rev. Edward M. Forbes. Mrs. Margaret D. Nelson donated the structure and presented the belfry and the bell. All Saints Chapel was closed November of 1931, but in 1938 the vestry of Christ Church approved its use for a nursery school for underprivileged children. It was deconsecrated at that time.

First Presbyterian Church **412 New Street**

In 1807 subscription was announced for the Presbyterian Meeting House. In 1819 the lot was purchased and building began. Uriah Sandy, the builder, achieved a classic simplicity of design which makes this one of New Bern's loveliest churches. The church was dedicated on January 6, 1822.

FIRST PRESBYTERIAN CHURCH WOMEN OF THE CHURCH LUNCHEON

Chicken Casserole
Strawberry Salad
Minted Peas
Carrot Cake
Tea

FIVE CAN CHICKEN CASSEROLE

Can be made ahead

This dish was originally made by opening five cans, dumping them together, heating and then serving. The cost of canned chicken is greater than stewing your own so we switched.

1 (3-pound) chicken, cooked, meat removed from bone and cut up OR canned equivalent
1 (10¾-ounce) can cream of celery soup
1 (10¾-ounce) can cream of chicken soup
1 (6-ounce) can evaporated milk
1 can Chinese noodles

Choice of seasonings: chopped onion, pimiento, Worcestershire sauce, soy sauce, etc.
Mix chicken, soups and milk together. Fold in ¾ can of Chinese noodles. Add whatever seasonings you like. Pour into flat baking dish and top with remaining noodles. Bake at 350 degrees until bubbly.

Introduced to WOC of First Presbyterian Church by Mrs. Al Kolb

BETTY MARSHBURN'S STRAWBERRY SALAD

This may be used as a salad or dessert.

1 (15-ounce) can crushed pineapple and juice
1 (3-ounce) package strawberry gelatin
1 (8-ounce) carton Trim cottage cheese
1 (8-ounce) container Cool Whip

In a saucepan, heat pineapple and gelatin to boiling. Make sure all the gelatin has dissolved. Cool to room temperature. Add cottage cheese and Cool Whip. Pour into 9x13-inch glass dish. Refrigerate. Salad will congeal in 4-6 hours.

MINTED PEAS

1 (10-ounce) package Dulany tiny peas
½ cup water
1 teaspoon dried mint leaves
Lump of butter
Pinch of sugar
Salt to taste
Pepper to taste

In a saucepan put water, mint, sugar, salt and pepper. Bring to a boil. Add peas and cook 2-3 minutes. Drain slightly and add butter.

Gretchen Deichmann Speer (Mrs. Howard)

CARROT CAKE

2 cups flour, sifted
2 cups sugar
¼ teaspoon salt
1 teaspoon baking powder
1 teaspoon baking soda
1 teaspoon cinnamon
4 eggs
1½ cups vegetable oil
2 cups carrots, grated

Preheat oven to 350 degrees. Grease and flour three 9-inch layer cake pans. Sift dry ingredients together. Blend together eggs and vegetable oil. Add dry ingredients, mixing thoroughly. Stir in carrots. Pour into prepared pans and bake 30-40 minutes.

Icing:
1 (8-ounce) package cream cheese, softened
½ cup butter or margarine
1 teaspoon vanilla extract
1 (16-ounce) package confectioners' sugar
1 cup pecans, chopped

Cream together softened cream cheese and butter. Add vanilla and sugar. Frost cake and sprinkle with chopped nuts.
Yield: 12 servings

Margaret Williford Smith (Mrs. J. Murphy)

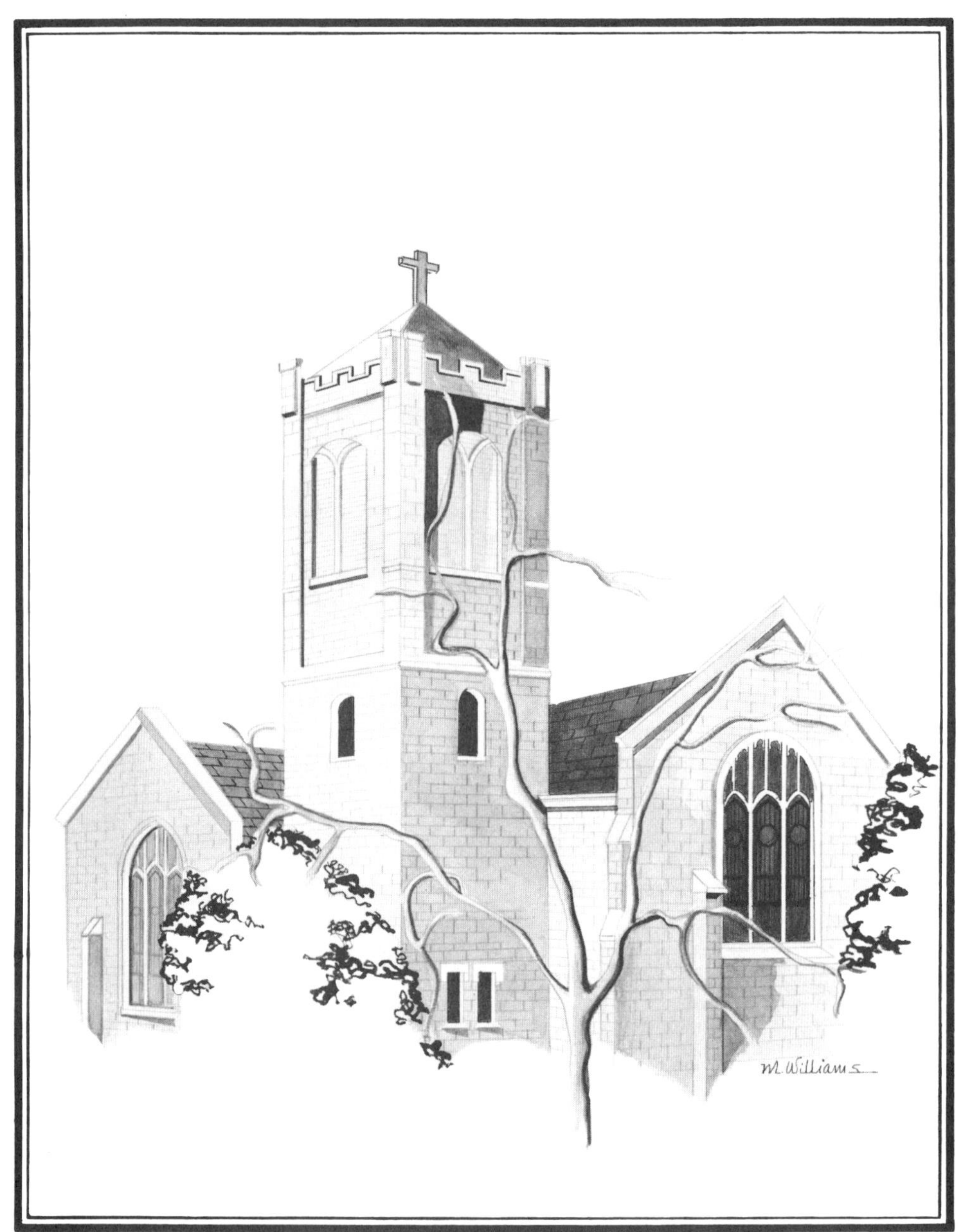

St. Cyprian's Episcopal Church **613 Queen Street**

The building was completed in 1812 as a Baptist meeting house. The Episcopal congregation was transferred to St. Cyprian's from Christ Church on June 20, 1866 with the Rev. H. A. Skinner as rector. The building is presently being restored.

ST. CYPRIAN'S SUMMER LUNCHEON

Candied Pecans
Crab Delight with Sliced Tomatoes
Five Cup Salad on Lettuce Leaf
Quick Ginger Bread
Tea and Coffee

CANDIED PECANS

1 (16-ounce) package light brown sugar
½ cup water
4 cups pecans halves
2 teaspoons cinnamon
1 teaspoon vanilla

In a medium saucepan, combine sugar and cinnamon; add water. Cook until this reaches a soft ball stage (about 235 degrees on candy thermometer) when dropped into cold water. Let cook 15 minutes; add vanilla and pecan halves. Stir quickly until pecans are coated and syrup starts to thicken. Pour quickly onto waxed paper and separate halves immediately. Store in airtight container.

Ruth Herring Miller (Mrs. Charles A.)

CRAB DELIGHT

2 tablespoons green pepper, chopped
2 tablespoons butter
2 tablespoons flour
1 cup tomatoes, strained
1 cup cheese, grated
⅔ cup milk, scalded
Cayenne
½ teaspoon mustard
¼ teaspoon salt
½ teaspoon Worcestershire sauce
1 egg, slightly beaten
1 cup crabmeat, flaked
6 patty shells or toast rounds

Brown green pepper in butter; add flour. Mix until smooth. Combine seasoning, tomatoes, cheese and egg. Add to the first mixture. Cook over hot water in the top of double boiler for 10 minutes. Stir constantly while slowly adding milk. Add crabmeat and heat thoroughly. Serve on patty shells or toast rounds.
Yield: 6 servings

Naomi Webb Ryder (Mrs. W. W.)

FIVE OR SIX CUP SALAD

1 cup mandarin oranges
1 cup chunk pineapple
1 cup shredded coconut
1 cup miniature marshmallows
1 cup sour cream
1 cup pecans (optional)

Mix all ingredients and chill. Serve on crisp lettuce leaves.

Naomi Webb Ryder (Mrs. W. W.)

QUICK GINGERBREAD

2 cups sifted flour
½ cup sugar
½ teaspoon soda
1 teaspoon baking powder
1 teaspoon salt
1½ teaspoons ginger
1 teaspoon cinnamon
¼ teaspoon cloves
1 cup molasses
½ cup shortening, melted
1 egg, unbeaten
½ cup sour milk
¼ cup hot water
1 cup raisins (optional)

Grease and lightly flour a 9-inch square pan. Sift dry ingredients into mixing bowl. Stir in molasses, shortening, egg and milk. Add hot water and raisins if desired. Pour into prepared pan and bake 45 mintues at 350 degrees. Yield: 9 servings

Helen Hargett Henry (Mrs. Robert)

Temple Chester B'Nai Sholem **505 Middle Street**

The Jewish congregation was in existence before 1824. Chester B'Nai Sholem temple was built in 1908. The congregation is a member of the Union of American Hebrew Congregations. In 1977 the N.C. Museum of Art held a Judaic Art Exhibit here showing many ceremonial and religious objects of art.

TEMPLE CHESTER B'NAI SHOLEM

"Moses, I have a precious gift in my treasury whose name is the Sabbath and I want to give it to Israel. Go and tell them."

The Sabbath, for Jews on Saturday, is a festive day; a day of spiritual refreshment. According to tradition, three meals should be eaten on the Sabbath. The most important meal is at the beginning of the Sabbath, sundown, Friday. Before the family sits down to eat, the mistress of the house lights at least two Sabbath candles. One candle is to "remember the Sabbath day" (Exodus 20:8) and the other "to observe the Sabbath day" (Deuteronomy 5:12). She places two loaves of bread, traditionally Challah, a braided egg bread, on the table to correspond to the double portion of manna for the Sabbath. (Exodus 16:22-26) The parents then bless the children and the father recites the Kiddush (grace). Even in the poorest families it has been traditional for Jews to reserve the most festive meal for Friday night; to use the best of whatever is in their possession; to dress in their cleanest, finest clothes. The following are some dishes which might be used for a traditional Friday meal.

SABBATH MEAL

Challah*
Gefilte Fish*
Matzo Balls*
Chicken Soup
Cabbage Rolls*
Noodle Pudding*
Roast Chicken
Dilled Green Beans
Green Salad with Delicious Dressing*
Jewish Apple Cake*
Jellyroll*
Mandelbröt*
Teiglach*
*Indicates recipes found in this section.

CHALLAH

This is a traditional bread which may be braided for daily use or is coiled by one snake-like rope into a beehive for Rosh Hashanah.

8 cups flour
1 package dry yeast
½ cup warm water
2 eggs
1 tablespoon salt
⅓ cup sugar
⅓ cup oil
1⅓-1½ cups warm water
1 egg yolk

In a large bowl with flour poured in, form a "well" in the flour and sprinkle yeast in middle. Pour ½ cup warm water over yeast to dissolve. Sprinkle sugar and salt around edge. Beat eggs in "well." Add oil and beat. Break "well" mixing all the time, adding water gradually. Knead carefully and cover in greased bowl. Place in warm spot to rise a little more than twice its size. Knead again a bit. Cut into 6 equal balls. Roll each ball out like a rope. Using three balls per loaf, form into braid and place on well-greased baking sheet to rise to double volume. Bake at 350 degrees about 45 mintues after brushing with egg yolk to glaze. If bread is to be for Rosh Hashanah, divide dough into two balls and roll out into two large ropes. Coil each into a beehive-like mound on well-greased baking sheet and brush with egg after second rising. Bake as above.
Yield: 2 loaves

Miriam Schulman Allenson (Mrs. Andrew J.)

MATZO BALLS

Batter must be prepared in advance

2 eggs
2 tablespoons ice water
1½ tablespoons cold rendered chicken fat
½ cup matzo meal
½ teaspoon salt
⅛ teaspoon pepper
1 quart boiling water *OR* chicken soup

Beat eggs and water. Add fat and beat. Stir in matzo meal and seasonings. Cover and refrigerate for *one hour.* Make 12 balls and drop them into boiling water or chicken soup. Cover and simmer 20-30 minutes.
Yield: 12 balls

Carol Yudell Goldman (Mrs. Raymond)

GEFILTE FISH

5 pounds white fish *OR* any fatty fish
2 pounds yellow pike
3 medium onions
1 large egg to each pound of ground fish
1 tablespoon coarse salt to each pound ground fish
2 teaspoons white pepper
1/3 cup cold water
1 tablespoon sugar
2 onions
Lots of sliced carrots

Have the fishmonger filet the fish. Reserve the bones, head and skins. Grind fish in a meat grinder with the onions. Add the water and mix again until thickened. For one-half hour, boil the skins, bones, heads and onions. Strain. Meanwhile form the fish mixture into balls approximately the size of tennis balls. They can be round or oblong. Be sure to wet your hands from time to time to keep fish mixture from sticking to you. Drop the fish balls into the fish stock. Make sure stock is sufficient to almost cover balls. Now add sliced carrots and sugar. Cover the pot, and bring to a fast boil. Boil for about 15 minutes; lower heat and cook for about one hour. It is very important that the pot is large enough for the fish to expand. Run a knife around the edge of the pot occasionally, to keep the fish from sticking. Do not stir. Remove from heat. Allow fish to cool for about 30 minutes. Pry apart very carefully. Remove fish to platter. Spoon a little sauce over the balls; garnish with carrots. Refrigerate until very cold. Serve with lots of red horseradish. The fish will be better if it stands at room temperature for a short time before serving.

Helen Konigsberg Schulman (Mrs. Herman M.)

DELICIOUS DRESSING

1/4 cup cider vinegar
4 teaspoons Dijon mustard
2 tablespoons onion, grated
1/4 teaspoon dried thyme
1/4 teaspoon salt
1/4 teaspoon ground pepper
1/2 cup olive oil
1/4 cup parsley, chopped

Combine vinegar, mustard, onion, thyme, salt and pepper in quart bowl. Gradually add oil beating constantly with wire whip until thick. Stir in parsley. Yield: 1 1/2 cups

Miriam Schulman Allenson (Mrs. Andrew J.)

CABBAGE ROLLS

May be frozen

2 pounds ground beef
3 large eggs
1 small onion, grated
⅓ cup regular rice
Salt to taste
Pepper to taste
Garlic powder to taste
2 large, firm heads cabbage, as perfect as possible
1 pound dark brown sugar
2 (15-ounce) cans tomato sauce
2 (29-ounce) cans tomatoes
Sour salt*
Water
4-6 beef knee bones
½ cup Crisco
2 large onions, diced
Boiling water

*Sour salt can be found in communities with Jewish or Hungarian populations. White vinegar may be used as a substitute and measured by the capful.

Combine ground beef, eggs, small grated onion, rice, salt, pepper and garlic powder. Refrigerate until needed. Turn cabbages stem-side up and with a very sharp, small knife, make an incision across the base of the outermost leaf. Peel away. Repeat this process until leaves can no longer be removed without tearing. Make slits around the stem to sever the next top-most leaves. Place cabbages stem-side up in a clean sink or in a deep container; pour boiling water over cabbage, making sure to try to get water in the incisions. Let sit. Boil more water and make more incisions if necessary to remove all leaves. Repeat until you are left with the innermost leaves and heart. Leaves removed should be soft enough to fold without cracking. Cut off spines from each leaf and reserve. Take out meat mixture and with a leaf in your hand, place a tablespoon of the meat mixture on leaf. Roll from the base and when halfway rolled fold in left side. Roll the rest of the way. You now have a close-ended cylinder. Carefully stuff the open end in with your fingers and the roll will stay closed by itself. Repeat until you've used up all the meat. In each of two large pots melt ¼ cup Crisco. Add diced onion to each pot and some cabbage scraps. Sauté until soft. Add to each one large can tomatoes and two or three knee bones. Lay cabbage rolls around pot in concentric circles. Pour some tomato sauce over rolls and add layers until each pot contains 30 or less pieces adding additional sauce between layers. Add water just to cover. Cook over medium heat covered for 30 minutes. Add brown sugar and two or three good-sized crystals of sour salt. Taste occasionally and adjust seasonings. If liquid is markedly sweet and sour, the rolls will be also. Cook 2-3 hours. Shake the pot occasionally to make sure nothing sticks. The longer this cooks, the better it is.
Yield: 50-65 rolls

Miriam Schulman Allenson (Mrs. Andrew J.)

NOODLE PUDDING

1 pound medium egg noodles
1 onion, diced
1 (4-ounce) can mushrooms, drained
4 eggs, beaten
Salt
Pepper

Cook noodles as directed on package. Rinse and drain. Set aside. Sauté the onion until tender. Add mushrooms. In a large bowl combine noodles, onion-mushroom mixture and remaining ingredients. Place in a greased 9x13-inch Pyrex pan. Bake at 350 degrees for 45 minutes to 1 hour or until brown on top.
Yield: 8-10 servings

Muriel Ertischek Steinberg (Mrs. Louis)

JEWISH APPLE CAKE

4 large eggs
2¼ cups sugar
3 cups flour
½ teaspoon salt
3 teaspoons baking powder
1 cup vegetable oil
⅓ cup orange juice
2½ teaspoons vanilla extract
6 medium apples, peeled, cored and thinly sliced
2 teaspoons cinnamon
3 tablespoons sugar, plus enough flour to coat apples

Preheat oven to 350 degrees. Grease and flour 10-inch tube pan. Beat eggs and sugar until smooth. Add dry ingredients alternately with liquid ingredients. Mix apples, cinnamon, 3 tablespoons sugar and small amount of flour in another bowl. Pour half the batter in the tube pan. Add half apple mix. Repeat another layer of each. Bake in the middle of the oven 1-1½ hours.
Yield: 1 (10-inch) cake

Donna Browdy Goldman (Mrs. E. Dale)

JELLYROLL

4 eggs, separated
1¼ cups sugar
1½ cups flour
1 teaspoon baking powder
⅔ cup warm water
1 teaspoon vanilla
Powdered sugar

Preheat oven to 350 degrees. Line 15½x10½-inch jellyroll pan with waxed paper. Set aside. Beat egg yolks and sugar together; add all ingredients and blend well. Set aside. Beat whites in another bowl until stiff and glossy peaks form. Fold whites into egg yolk mixture until blended. Pour into jellyroll pan. Bake for 20 minutes. Meanwhile sprinkle a clean cloth towel with powdered sugar. When the jellyroll is done, invert immediately onto towel. Peel off waxed paper; roll cake starting at a long side. Cool for ten minutes. Then unroll and spread with your favorite jelly. Roll again, making sure seam side is down when placed on platter. Frost top with more jelly and sprinkle with nuts.

Ethel Kolodny Elden (Mrs. Lou)

MANDELBRÖT

This recipe is easily doubled and should be if to be served to company. These little toasts become addictive!

3¼ cups flour
2 level teaspoons baking powder
3 eggs
1 cup sugar
1 teaspoon vanilla extract
1 teaspoon maple syrup
2 tablespoons lemon juice
2 tablespoons orange juice
1 cup almonds or walnuts, chopped
1 cup vegetable oil
Cinnamon

Mix all ingredients together except cinnamon. Form loaves a little longer than your hand. Place on Teflon cookie sheet and sprinkle tops with cinnamon. Bake at 350 degrees for 20-25 mintues until brown on the edges. Take off sheet and cool for a little while on board. Then cut into strips about one-inch thick across each loaf. Place slices on sides on a cookie sheet and toast, turning on reverse side until golden.
Yield: approximately 3 dozen

Miriam Schulman Allenson (Mrs. Andrew J.)

TEIGLACH

3 eggs
2 teaspoons sugar
2 tablespoons Mazola oil
¼ teaspoon ginger
1¾ to 2 cups flour
⅓ cup raisins, cut in pieces
¼ cup nuts, chopped
1 cup sugar
1 cup honey
2 teaspoons ginger
½ cup boiling water

Mix first five ingredients to form a soft dough. Add raisins and chopped nuts. Divide dough into four parts. Roll each part into long roll about ¾-inch in diameter. Cut into one-inch pieces. In large pan bring to boil honey and 1 cup sugar. Turn to low heat and keep boiling slowly. Drop pieces of dough into boiling honey. Cover and boil 25 minutes. Do NOT peep! Should be golden brown by this time. Stir with wooden spoon and listen for hollow sound. Sprinkle 2 teaspoons ginger on mixture then add ½ cup boiling water and stir. Cool to warm; pour into jar and cover when completely cooled.

Isobel Vatz (Mrs. Harry L.)

St. Paul's Catholic Church **510 Middle Street**

St. Paul's, the oldest Catholic Church in North Carolina, was constructed in 1839 from a design suggested by Bishop John England of Charleston, S.C. On May 24, 1821, in the parlor of Judge William Gaston's house, Bishop England celebrated the first Mass in North Carolina by a Roman Catholic Bishop.

ST. PAUL'S LENTEN SUPPER

Clam Chowder
Southern Spoon Bread
Spinach Salad with Korean Dressing
Moby Dick's Delight
Dutch Baked Filet of Fish
Zucchini Provençal
Lebanese String Beans
Norwegian Apple Tart
Baklava

NEW ENGLAND CLAM CHOWDER

2 dozen large clams *OR* 2 (10½-ounce) cans minced clams
1 quart water
¼ pound salt pork, diced
1 cup onion, chopped
3 large potatoes, pared and diced
¼ teaspoon thyme leaves, crumbled
½ teaspoon salt
⅛ teaspoon pepper
2 cups milk
2 cups light cream
2 tablespoons butter or margarine

If using fresh clams, scrub and run under cold water. Cook in water; covered. Discard any that do not open. Remove clams from shells with small knife, working over bowl so you can catch all juices. Remove and discard dark parts of clams; chop clams coarsely. Strain broth from kettle into bowl containing clam juice. Add water if needed to make 4 cups of liquid. If using canned clams, drain them; measure juice. Add water to make 4 cups. Cook salt pork in heavy kettle 5 minutes or until bits are crisp and golden. Remove with slotted spoon. Drain on paper towels. Cook onion in fat left in pan until soft. Add clam broth and water mixture, salt pork bits, potatoes, thyme, salt and pepper. Cover. Simmer 10 minutes or until potatoes are tender but not soft. Add clams. Stir in milk and cream slowly. Add butter or margarine. Bring just to boiling but do NOT boil. Spoon into serving bowl.
Yield: 8 servings

Linda Rice Morris (Mrs. Kenneth)

SOUTHERN SPOON BREAD

3 cups milk
1 cup white corn meal
1 teaspoon butter, melted
1 teaspoon sugar
1 teaspoon salt
3 egg yolks, beaten
3 egg whites, stiffly beaten

Preheat oven to 350 degrees. Grease a 9x9-inch baking dish and set aside. Beat egg yolks; set aside. Beat egg whites until stiff; set aside. Scald milk in top of double boiler; add corn meal gradually and cook 5 minutes, stirring until very smooth. Cool slightly and add butter, sugar and salt. Add egg yolks; fold in egg whites. Pour into prepared baking dish and bake 45 minutes.

Elizabeth McCormick Rice (Mrs. Clyde G.)

SANDY SLAUGHTER'S KOREAN DRESSING

4 slices bacon, fried crisp
2 eggs, hard-boiled and chopped
⅔ cup salad oil
¼ cup sugar
½ cup catsup
¼ cup vinegar
1 onion, sliced
Pinch of salt
Spinach, cleaned

Combine oil, sugar, catsup, vinegar, onion and salt in a jar. Shake well. Serve over spinach salad and sprinkle with bacon bits and chopped egg.

Linda Rice Morris (Mrs. Kenneth)

MOBY DICK'S DELIGHT

Can make ahead
Can freeze

1½ pounds shrimp, shelled, deveined and cooked
1 cup fresh crabmeat *OR* 1 (7½-ounce) can crabmeat, drained boned and flaked
1 (5-ounce) can water chestnuts, drained and sliced
½ cup pimiento, coarsely chopped
2 tablespoons butter
3 tablespoons onion, finely chopped
¼ cup green pepper, finely chopped
1 (4-ounce) can mushrooms, sliced and drained
2 tablespoons butter
2 tablespoons flour
3 cups light cream
1 teaspoon salt
½ cup dry sherry
1 (8-ounce) package egg noodles, cooked and drained

Cook egg noodles according to package directions; drain and set aside. Combine shrimp, crabmeat, water chestnuts and pimiento in a bowl. Heat 2 tablespoons butter in a medium saucepan; add onion, green pepper and mushrooms. Sauté gently 5 minutes or until tender. Add vegetables to seafood mixture. Melt 2 tablespoons butter in same saucepan; stir in flour and salt. Cook 1 minute. Remove pan from heat. Stir in sherry and cream gradually. Cook over medium heat, stirring constantly until sauce thickens slightly and comes to a boil. Add to vegetable-seafood mixture. Fold in noodles. Spoon into lightly buttered 2½-quart baking dish. To use immediately bake in preheated 400 degree oven 25 minutes until bubbly. To use later the same day, refrigerate until 1 hour before serving. Remove from refrigerator and preheat oven to 400 degrees. Bake 25 minutes until bubbly. To freeze, wrap UNBAKED in casserole. Thaw completely and bake as above.
Yield: 8-10 servings

Eileen Connell Cella (Mrs. E. J.)

DUTCH BAKED FILET OF FISH

4 flounder filets or other fish
1 tablespoon butter or margarine
2 teaspoons lemon juice
Salt to taste
Pepper to taste

Season filets with salt and pepper and sprinkle with lemon juice. Roll each up neatly and put into buttered ovenproof dish. Dot each filet with butter; cover and bake at 350 degrees for 15 minutes. While fish is baking, prepare the following sauce. When fish has completed baking, remove from oven and reserve stock which has formed during baking.

Sauce:
4 ounces Gouda cheese, grated
1 cup milk
Rind of half a lemon
2 peppercorns
½ bay leaf
Few parsley stalks
1 tablespoon butter or margarine
1 tablespoon flour
1 egg yolk
Pinch nutmeg
Salt to taste
Pepper to taste

Place lemon rind, bay leaf, peppercorns and parsley stalks in the milk. Simmer milk and herbs in saucepan gently for 10 minutes; strain. Make sauce by melting butter in saucepan; add flour and cook a few minutes. Gradually add the milk and cook stirring until thickened. Add grated cheese leaving a little to sprinkle over top. Add egg yolk and fish stock reserved from cooked filets. Season well with salt and pepper and nutmeg. Pour sauce over cooked fish. Sprinkle with reserved cheese and brown in 400 degree oven for 20-30 minutes or until golden brown. Garnish with additional parsley if desired and serve at once.
Yield: 4 servings

Pauline Roy Wheeler (Mrs. Frederick)

ZUCCHINI PROVENÇAL

6 cups zucchini, sliced
8 tomatoes, peeled, cored and diced
2 teaspoons salt
1 teaspoon sugar OR 1/8 teaspoon sugar substitute
2 cloves garlic, crushed
1/4 teaspoon thyme
1/8 teaspoon basil
1/8 teaspoon pepper

Mix and simmer very slowly in large covered skillet or saucepan, until the zucchini is just tender, about 40 minutes. 60 caloires per serving.
Yield: 8 servings

Mary Bray Mullineaux

LEBANESE STRING BEANS

1/2 cup Wesson oil
1 cup onion, finely chopped or sliced
1 cup fresh or canned tomatoes, drained
1 pound string beans, cut lengthwise
2 cups water
Salt to taste
Pepper to taste

Heat oil in large saucepan; add onions. Sauté 15 minutes. Add remaining ingredients. Cover and simmer 1 1/2 hours. Serve hot or cold.

Idell Shapou Zaytoun (Mrs. John)

NORWEGIAN APPLE TART

1 (9-inch) pie crust
1 pound cooking apples, peeled and cored
3 tablespoons sugar
¼ teaspoon cinnamon
4 tablespoons sugar
2 tablespoons raisins
Grated rind from ½ lemon
2 eggs

Stew peeled and cored apples with 3 tablespoons sugar, cinnamon, raisins and lemon rind. Add egg yolks. Pour apple mixture into shell. Make meringue with egg whites and 4 tablespoons sugar. Pile over pie filling spreading to edges of crust and bake at 250 degrees for 30-45 minutes, until set.

Pauline Roy Wheeler (Mrs. Frederick)

BAKLAVA

Delicious, delicate dessert.

Pour cooled syrup on hot pastry OR hot syrup on cooled pastry so pastry does not become soggy.

1¾ cup walnuts, finely chopped
¾ cup sugar
1 teaspoon ground cinnamon
¼ teaspoon ground cloves
½ cup butter, melted (unsalted preferred)
1 (16-ounce) package filo or strudel dough
½ cup water
1 cup sugar
2 teaspoons lemon OR lime juice
1 tablespoon Flower water or Orange water (optional)

Thaw filo in the refrigerator overnight. Mix walnuts, ¾ cup sugar, cinnamon and cloves together for nut filling and set aside. Melt butter and set aside. Grease 9x13-inch baking dish and place 4-5 sheets of filo into the greased pan, folding filo ends to fit. Sprinkle a few tablespoons of the nut mixture on the filo. Repeat alternating filo and nut mixture until all have been used. Cut through all layers diagonally with a sharp knife. (I use an electric knife.) Pour melted butter evenly on top. Bake at 350 degrees for 1 hour or until brown. While pastry is baking prepare the syrup by stirring 1 cup sugar into ½ cup water and cooking until sugar melts. Add lime or lemon juice and orange water. Cook syrup until it reaches soft-boil stage of 230 degrees and mixture begins to thicken.
Yield: 2 dozen pieces

Maggie Michel Costandy (Mrs. Nabil T.)

Christ Church Steeple **320 Pollock Street**

Christ Church's steeple has long been a landmark for the whole area. Until recent years it was the highest point in the city. There was a weathervane atop the first Christ Church, built in 1752, and also on the 1824 church. The crown, symbolic of the Kingship of Christ, or, perhaps, the Crown of Life, is appropriate to surmount the church.

Tryon Palace

Tryon Palace served as both the official governmental building of colonial North Carolina when New Bern was the colonial capital and the residence of the governor and his family. After the American Revolution it was the site of many legislative meetings and the inaugurations of four early state governors. In 1794, the new capital was established in Raleigh, and in 1798, the main building of Tryon Palace was destroyed by fire. Reconstruction of the Palace began in 1952, and it opened officially to the public on April 8, 1959. Tryon Palace was known in colonial times as the most beautiful building in America. Restored to its former splendor, the Palace is today a living example of the fashionable taste Governor William Tryon brought with him from England. Tryon Palace and its lovely gardens are the nucleus of a unique restoration complex in the heart of historic New Bern.

ARTICHOKE SPREAD

Passes for crabmeat!

1 (16-ounce) can artichoke hearts
1 cup mayonnaise
3 ounces Parmesan cheese

Preheat oven to 350 degrees. Drain artichokes well, then mash them with fork or potato masher. Add mayonnaise and cheese. Bake in a greased baking dish uncovered for 25 minutes. Serve hot and spread on crackers.
Yield: 12 servings

Patricia Byrum McCotter (Mrs. C. Kennedy, Jr.)

MARY'S ARTICHOKES

Can be frozen

2 (6-ounce) jars marinated artichokes
1 small onion, chopped fine
1 clove garlic, minced
¼ cup fine bread crumbs
⅛ teaspoon salt
⅛ teaspoon pepper
Tabasco to taste
¼ teaspoon oregano
½ pound sharp Cheddar cheese, grated
2 eggs
2 tablespoons parsley

Drain marinade from 1 jar of artichokes into a frying pan. Chop artichokes. To liquid add onion, garlic and sauté. Beat eggs in bowl; add bread crumbs and seasonings. Stir in cheese, parsley, artichokes and sautéed mixture. Turn into greased 7x11-inch baking dish and bake at 325 degrees for 30 minutes. Let stand 5 minutes after baking and cut into small squares. May be wrapped in foil and frozen at this point for later use. To serve when frozen, thaw and reheat in foil 15 minutes at 325 degrees.

Barbara Straub Stewart

ASPARAGUS BLUE CHEESE APPETIZERS

May freeze

1 (16-ounce) loaf soft white bread (crusts removed)
1 (5-ounce) jar pasteurized cheese spread with blue cheese
1 (10½-ounce) can asparagus tips, drained
½ cup butter or margarine

Roll each slice of bread flat with a rolling pin. Spread each slice with about 1 teaspoon of cheese spread. Put an asparagus tip along one edge and roll up bread with asparagus inside. Cut each bread roll in thirds crosswise. Melt butter in a small saucepan or skillet over moderately high heat and remove from heat. Dip each roll in the melted butter and place, seam side down, on the baking sheet. Cover and refrigerate about 1 hour. (At this point rolls may be wrapped and frozen until ready to heat.) Heat oven to 375 degrees. Bake 5 minutes; turn and bake 3 minutes longer, until crisp and brown. Serve immediately.
Yield: 50 appetizers

Patricia L. Woodard

MARINATED VEGETABLES

Do a day ahead
Do not freeze

4 cups vegetables of your choice (carrots, broccoli, cauliflower, green beans, green peppers, celery, mushrooms, etc.) cut into two-bite pieces
⅔ cup light oil
⅓ cup vinegar
1 clove garlic, crushed
⅛ teaspoon salt
Pepper to taste
¼ teaspoon mustard
1 small onion, finely chopped
¼ teaspoon basil
¼ teaspoon dill
1 teaspoon parsley, finely chopped

Simmer carrots. Simmer or steam other vegetables, covered, for 10 minutes. Drain immediately and rinse with cold water to preserve color. Combine remaining ingredients, pour over vegetables and chill 12-24 hours. Drain well before serving.
Yield: appetizer for 4-6 persons

Pauline Morris Blair (Mrs. Robert G.)

CUCUMBER CASES STUFFED WITH SPINACH

Can do ahead

6 (3-inch) cucumbers
½ cup spinach, finely chopped (1 package thawed, squeezed dry)
3 small green onions, minced
⅓ cup mayonnaise *(or less)*
¾ teaspoon salt
Freshly ground pepper
3 tablespoons lemon juice
Yolk of 1 hard-boiled egg, mashed

Peel and cut cucumber into ¾-1-inch thick pieces and scoop out the seeds from one end of each cucumber piece, leaving the other end closed to form a little case. Chill and dry these cucumber cases. Fill with spinach mixed with remaining ingredients and chill again after filling. These may be filled an hour or two before serving. Mixture can be made early in the day and cucumbers readied for stuffing later.
Yield: 2½ dozen servings

Carol Webb Pullen (Mrs. John S.)

PHYLLIS' BLUE CHEESE TOMATOES

May do ahead

1 pint cherry tomatoes
2 (3-ounce) packages cream cheese
2-ounces blue cheese, crumbled
2 tablespoons dairy sour cream
2 tablespoons celery, finely chopped
1 tablespoon onion, finely chopped
½ cup pecans, chopped

Wash tomatoes and cut off tops to make caps. Scoop out pulp from caps and bottoms. Beat together cream cheese, blue cheese, and sour cream until blended. Stir in celery, onion and nuts. Fill tomato shells with cheese mixture, mounding slightly. Replace tomato tops; secure with wooden picks. Garnish with sprigs of parsley if tomato stems are missing.

Eugenia Hofler Clement (Mrs. Robert L.)

ORGANIZED OLIVES

Make ahead
May be frozen

1 (16-ounce) can pitted ripe olives
2-3 tablespoons minced onion, fresh or frozen
1 cup sharp Cheddar cheese, grated
½ cup sifted flour
¼ teaspoon salt
⅛-½ teaspoon dry mustard to taste
3 tablespoons butter
1 teaspoon milk
1-2 drops Tabasco sauce
Hot mustard

Remove 25 olives from can and drain. Stuff center of olive with onion piece. Combine dry ingredients and add cheese. Stir in mixture of cooled, melted butter, milk and Tabasco. Mix well. Taste to decide if more Tabasco is needed. Wrap 1 teaspoon dough around each olive. Bake on lightly greased cookie sheet in preheated 400 degree oven for 10-12 minutes. When cooled, olives may be frozen in plastic bags for later use. To warm after freezing, thaw olives and preheat oven to 400 degrees. Bake on lightly greased cookie sheet 5 minutes. Olives may be served with hot mustard.
Yield: 25 olives

Jane Potter Jones (Mrs. Richard S.)

MUSHROOM ROLL-UPS

3 tablespoons butter
4 onions, sliced
1 (8-ounce) package cream cheese, softened
King-size loaf bread, thin sliced, fresh
1 pound fresh mushrooms
Few drops Tabasco
Melted butter

Fry onions in butter. Slice mushrooms; add to onions and fry until tender. Remove from heat. Chop together in bowl. Add cream cheese and Tabasco. Remove crusts from bread and roll each slice with a rolling pin. Spread thin layer of mushroom mixture on each slice of bread and roll up jellyroll fashion. Put on baking sheet and brush roll with melted butter. Bake for 20 minutes at 350 degrees.

Joan Brooks Kunkel (Mrs. Cooper D.)

SPANISH OLIVES

1 (9-ounce) jar green olives, stuffed with pimiento
½ cup red wine vinegar
¼ cup olive oil
1 green chili pepper, chopped
1 clove garlic, minced
1 teaspoon oregano

Put olives with liquid into a large jar. Add remaining ingredients and shake well. Refrigerate several days before serving. Good with drinks or sandwiches.

Elizabeth Reese Ward (Mrs. David L., Jr.)

MARINATED MUSHROOMS

Mushrooms
White onions
⅔ cup tarragon vinegar
½ cup salad oil
1 clove garlic, pressed
1 tablespoon sugar
1½ teaspoons salt
2 tablespoons water
Dash of ground pepper
Dash of Tabasco

Clean mushrooms in water. Combine in bowl with thinly sliced small white onions. Mix vinegar, oil, garlic, sugar, salt, water, pepper and Tabasco. Pour over the mushrooms and onions. Marinate in refrigerate for several hours.

Virginia McGehee Borowicz (Mrs. Ronald R.)

STUFFED MUSHROOMS

1 (16-ounce) box fresh mushrooms, washed and stems removed
½ teaspoon cooking oil
1 tablespoon onion, chopped
1 tablespoon mushroom stems, chopped
¼ cup hard salami, chopped
¼ cup Cheeze-Whiz
1 tablespoon catsup

Prepare mushrooms and set aside. In a saucepan combine oil, onion and mushroom stems and cook until onion is tender. Add salami, Cheeze-Whiz, catsup and cook until mixture is smooth. Stuff in mushroom caps and bake 8 minutes at 425 degrees.

Anne Fowler Hiller (Mrs. Carl J.)

BOURSIN CHEESE

Mix can be stored in refrigerator
Must do ahead
Can freeze

2 cloves garlic
8 ounces unsalted whipped butter
16 ounces cream cheese
½ teaspoon salt
½ teaspoon basil
½ teaspoon marjoram
½ teaspoon chives
¼ teaspoon thyme
¼ teaspoon pepper
1 teaspoon dill

Crush garlic in blender or food processor, add butter, softened cheese and spices. Mix and store in refrigerator overnight before serving.

Use cottage cheese in dips rather than sour cream to save calories.

DILL VEGETABLE DIP

Easy
Do ahead
Stores well in refrigerator
Can be halved

2 cups mayonnaise
2 cups commercial sour cream
3 tablespoons fresh parsley*
3 tablespoons onion, grated
3 tablespoons dill weed
1½ tablespoons seasoned salt
2 tablespoons thyme (optional)

*If dried parsley is used, reduce amount to 1 tablespoon.
Blend together all ingredients; chill several hours. Serve with raw vegetables such as whole cherry tomatoes, bite-sized pieces of cauliflower, celery and carrot strips. Dip may be made several days ahead of time.
Yield: 4½ cups

Sharon Nichols Hobson (Mrs. Steve R.)

VEGETABLE DIP

1 (5-ounce) jar pimiento cheese spread
1 (2½-ounce) can deviled ham
2 tablespoons parsley, finely snipped
2 tablespoons mayonnaise
1 teaspoon onion, grated
3-4 drops bottled hot pepper sauce

Combine cheese spread, deviled ham, parsley, mayonnaise, onion and hot pepper sauce. Beat until creamy and chill.

Lindy Allmond Emory (Mrs. Robert R., Jr.)

BENEDICTINE DIP

Keeps well

2 (8-ounce) packages cream cheese, softened
1 large cucumber, minced
1 medium onion, minced
1 tablespoon mayonnaise
¾ teaspoon salt

Beat cream cheese until smooth. Stir in the remaining ingredients blending well. Chill. Serve with fresh vegetables.
Yield: 4 cups

Caroline Ashford Smith

CHEDDAR-BEER SPREAD

1 pound Cheddar cheese
¾ cup beer or white wine
½ teaspoon salt

In large bowl, with spoon, stir finely shredded cheese (about four cups), beer or wine and salt. Mix well. Serve with crackers.
Yield: 2½ cups

Grace Green Burnette (Mrs. A. W., Jr.)

BLUE CHEESE PUFFS

1 (10-ounce) package large refrigerator buttermilk biscuits
1 (4-ounce) package blue cheese
½ cup margarine
Caraway seeds or sesame seeds

Preheat oven to 400 degrees. Cut buttermilk biscuits into fourths. Roll into balls and roll balls in caraway seeds. Place balls in 7x11-inch baking dish. Melt margarine and blue cheese together in a saucepan and pour over balls. Bake 10-15 minutes turning balls over at 7 minutes.
Yield: 40 puffs

Jane Johnson Straub (Mrs. Robert L.)

CURRY BITES

Easy
Do early in the day

1 cup sharp Cheddar cheese, shredded
¼ cup mayonnaise
¼ cup ripe olives, chopped
2 tablespoons green onions, chopped
¼ teaspoon curry powder
4 English muffins

Split English muffins. Mix all ingredients and spread generously on muffins. Cut into fourths and broil two minutes or until hot and bubbly.
Yield: 32 squares

Lee Thompson McIntyre (Mrs. J. Brooks)

BACON-CHEESE FINGERS

10 slices Roman Meal Bread (cut into thirds)
1 cup Cheddar cheese, grated
8 slices bacon, cooked and crumbled
3 or 4 tablespoons mayonnaise
1 tablespoon onion, grated
½ teaspoon celery salt

Mix together the last 5 ingredients. Spread on bread slices and bake at 325 degrees for 10 minutes.

Greta Black Mitchell (Mrs. Thomas J.)

CHEESE PUFFS

Make a day ahead
Can be frozen

1 loaf firm, unsliced white bread, crusts removed
3 ounces cream cheese
¼ pound sharp Cheddar cheese
½ cup butter or margarine
2 egg whites, stiffly beaten

Preheat oven to 400 degrees before baking. Cut trimmed bread into 1-inch cubes. Melt cheeses and butter in top of double boiler until of rarebit consistency. Remove from heat. Cool slightly. Fold in stiffly beaten egg whites. Dip bread cubes into cheese mixture until well coated. Place on cookie sheet. Refrigerate overnight or freeze. Bake 12 to 15 minutes or until puffy and golden brown. Yield: about 4 dozen.

Muriel Meier Coombs (Mrs. Bruce)

Soak fruits to be used in a watermelon fruit boat in champagne overnight for extra flavor. Drain fruit before adding to boat.

HERBED PARTY TRIANGLES

Can be made in advance

1 (8-ounce) package cream cheese, softened
¾ cup almonds, finely chopped
¼ cup green pepper, chopped
¼ cup onion, chopped
3 tablespoons pimiento, chopped
1 tablespoon catsup
¾ teaspoon salt
¾ teaspoon pepper
1 loaf Pepperidge Farm Very Thin Rye Bread

Combine cream cheese, almonds, green pepper, onion, pimiento, catsup, salt and pepper. Chill. Cut rye bread into halves forming triangles. Remove crusts from bread. Spread chilled mixture to edges of bread before serving. Yield: 4-5 dozen

Beverly Moore Perdue (Mrs. Gary R.)
N. C. Governor

HOT SHOTS

Part made ahead

⅓ cup grated Parmesan cheese
¾ cups mayonnaise
½ teaspoon onion, chopped
Dash Worcestershire sauce
Salt
Pepper
1 loaf Pepperidge Farm Party Rye Bread

Combine Parmesan cheese, mayonnaise, onion, Worcestershire, salt and pepper to taste. Cover and refrigerate until needed. At serving time spread mixture on party rye slices fairly thickly. Place slices of bread on cookie sheet and broil several minutes until topping is golden and bubbly. Leftover mixture can be refrigerated several days or used on hot vegetables.

Barbara Johnson Potter (Mrs. Carlton F.)

Hors d'oeuvres can be created at the drop of a hat with a package of cream cheese, a box of crackers and a lively spread. Mix Catalina Salad Dressing with softened cream cheese or spread Chutney, Hot Pepper Jelly or Pickapeppa Sauce on top of cream cheese block, and pass the crackers.

PENANCE COOKIES

These cookies are prepared for the Rector as a "PENANCE."

1 pound sharp Cheddar cheese
1 pound butter or margarine
1 pound flour (about 4 cups)
¼ teaspoon red pepper

Grate the cheese and add margarine several hours or overnight before you plan to make cookies. When cheese and margarine have reached room temperature, mix thoroughly . . . hands work best. Gradually add the flour and red pepper. Using your hands, work into a soft dough. If the dough is too sticky, add enough flour to make it manageable. Put dough in press and squeeze onto an ungreased cookie sheet. Dough may be formed into a roll, chilled, and sliced thinly. Bake at 375 degrees 10-12 minutes.
Yield: 12 dozen

Sarah "Johnny" Greene

DEVILED HAM PUFFS

1 (8-ounce) package cream cheese, softened
1 egg yolk, beaten
1 teaspoon onion juice
½ teaspoon baking powder
Salt to taste
¼ teaspoon horseradish
¼ teaspoon Tabasco
2 (2¼-ounce) cans deviled ham
24 (1-inch) bread rounds

Combine cream cheese, egg yolk, onion juice, baking powder, salt, horseradish, Tabasco. Blend until smooth. Stir in ham. Toast bread rounds lightly on one side; spoon about 1 teaspoon of ham mixture on untoasted side of bread. Bake on cookie sheet in 375 degree oven for 10-12 minutes or until puffed and lightly browned. Serve hot.
Yield: 2 dozen

Anne Fowler Hiller (Mrs. Carl J.)

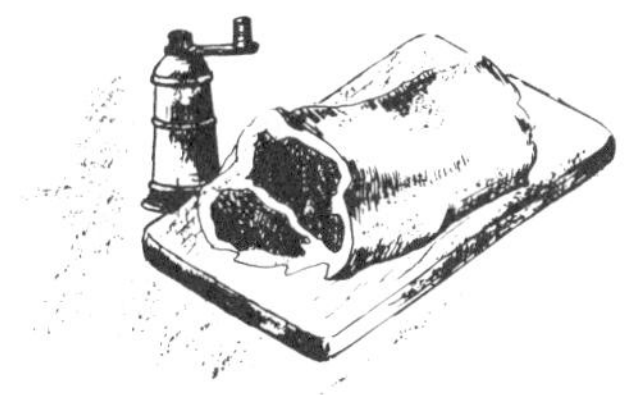

DEVILED HAM AND CHEESE LOG

Prepare in advance
Flavor improves if made several days in advance

1 (4½-ounce) can deviled ham
½ cup nuts, finely chopped
1 (8-ounce) package cream cheese, softened
½ teaspoon garlic salt
½ teaspoon Worcestershire sauce
¼ teaspoon Tabasco sauce
Paprika

Blend all ingredients, except paprika in large mixing bowl. Chill several hours or overnight. Shape into roll about 7x½-inch. Sprinkle paprika on waxed paper and roll log evenly. Wrap in waxed paper and keep refrigerated until ready to use. Serve with Ritz crackers.
Yield: 1 cheese log

Carolyn Brown Latham (Mrs. Edward B.)

APPETIZER HAM BALL

2 (4½-ounce) cans deviled ham
3 tablespoons stuffed green olives, chopped
1 tablespoon prepared mustard
Hot pepper sauce to taste
1 (3-ounce) package cream cheese, softened
2 teaspoons milk
Parsley
Assorted crackers

Blend ham, olives, mustard and pepper sauce to taste. Form in ball on serving dish; chill. Combine cream cheese and milk. Use as frosting on ham ball. Chill; remove from refrigerator 15 minutes before serving. Garnish with parsley. Serve with assorted crackers.

Shirley Taylor Pridgen (Mrs. Lonnie E., Jr.)

BEEF-PECAN SPREAD

½ cup pecans, chopped
2 tablespoons butter
½ teaspoon salt
1 (8-ounce) package cream cheese, softened
½ cup sour cream
2 tablespoons milk
1 (5-ounce) jar dried beef
¼ cup green pepper, chopped
2 tablespoons onion flakes
½ teaspoon garlic salt

Preheat oven to 350 degrees. In small frying pan, heat pecans in butter and salt. Blend cream cheese with milk in bowl. Stir in dried beef, green pepper, onion flakes and garlic salt until all ingredients are combined. Fold in sour cream. Turn into an 8-inch pie plate; top with pecans. Bake for 20 minutes. Serve warm with crackers or party rye. If you find this too salty, and I do, rinse dried beef or eliminate the salt.

Rena Terrell Knott (Mrs. Edmund T.)

CHIPPED BEEF DIP

8 ounces cream cheese
8 ounces sour cream
1 teaspoon onion, minced
2½ ounces chipped beef, diced
1 cup pecans, chopped

Slowly heat cream cheese to melt. Add sour cream, mixing well. Stir in onions and diced chipped beef. Place in chafing dish and top with pecans. Serve hot with crackers.

Susanne Darby Thompson (Mrs. Michael B.)

BEEF-OLIVE SPREAD

Can keep for 1 week in refrigerator

1 (2½-ounce) package smoked beef, chopped or cut up fine
1 (8-ounce) package cream cheese, softened
1 teaspoon dried onion
1 tablespoon sherry
2 tablespoons mayonnaise
¼ cup stuffed olives, chopped

Soak onion in sherry for 5 minutes. Add the softened cream cheese and mayonnaise and beat until smooth. Add chopped beef and olives. Keep in refrigerator until 1 hour before serving with crackers.

Frances Mason Clement (Mrs. Donald H.)

COCKTAIL MEDALLIONS

Make ahead
Can freeze

1 (15-ounce) can pineapple chunks
3 tablespoons soy sauce
1 tablespoon wine vinegar
1 tablespoon brown sugar
¼ teaspoon ginger
¼ teaspoon salt
1 pound chicken livers (about 30)
2 (5-ounce) cans water chestnuts
30 bacon strips

Count the pineapple chunks and add to marinade made of the next 5 ingredients. Cut in half chicken livers so that there is a number equal to number of pineapple chunks. Drain water chestnuts and cut into same number of pieces. Add livers and water chestnuts to marinade. Cover and refrigerate several hours. Cut 30 bacon strips in half lengthwise. Using a small wooden skewer for each medallion, skewer one end of a bacon strip; then add a piece of pineapple, piece of liver and piece of water chestnut. Wrap other end of bacon around, skewering it to hold. Place all medallions in flat freezer container and pour marinade over them. Freeze. To serve, defrost, drain marinade and reserve the liquid. Arrange skewers on broiler pan and broil about 4 inches from heat, turning once, until livers are done and bacon is crisp, 4-5 minutes. Brush once or twice with marinade. Keep hot on hot tray or in chafing dish.
Yield: 4½ dozen

Ann Harris Bustard (Mrs. Victor W.)

LIVER PÂTÉ PINEAPPLE

May do ahead

2 cups butter or margarine
2 pounds chicken livers
1 teaspoon curry powder
¼ teaspoon salt
¼ teaspoon pepper
⅓ cup Cognac
1 small bottle of stuffed olives
1 top from a fresh pineapple*

*To remove the top from the pineapple, twist it. Do not cut it or there will be a point on the bottom.

Sauté chicken livers in butter. Add curry powder, salt and pepper. Cook 9 minutes, stirring constantly. Blend mixture in electric blender until smooth. Add Cognac and chill to consistency of modeling clay. Mold into pineapple shape. Cover with sliced olives to look like scales on a pineapple. Make small indentations with thumb in top of pineapple mold. Set pineapple top in place. Voilà! You have a pineapple.

Charlotte Duffy Williams (Mrs. E. R.)

HOT SAUCY SWEDISH MEATBALLS

4 (4x4-inch) sandwich slices white bread
¼ cup cream
1½ pounds ground round
1 tablespoon onion, minced
½ teaspoon salt
2 eggs, slightly beaten
5 tablespoons butter
3 tablespoons flour
2 cups beef bouillon
½ teaspoon Tabasco sauce
1 tablespoon dry mustard
1 tablespoon white horseradish
¼ teaspoon celery salt

Trim crusts from the bread and soak slices in cream for approximately 4 minutes. Mix the softened bread with the ground round, onion, salt, and eggs. Form into 1-inch balls. Melt the butter in a skillet and sauté the meatballs until they are brown. Reserve pan drippings. To prepare the sauce, combine the flour with the beef bouillon in a large saucepan. Bring the mixture to a boil, stirring constantly, until smooth. Add the Tabasco, mustard, horseradish and celery salt; stir. Add the meatballs with pan drippings to the sauce. Simmer gently for 3 minutes. Transfer the meatballs and sauce to a chafing dish and serve hot.

Yield: 5 dozen

Melanie Applegate (Mrs. Earl)

SURPRISE COCKTAIL MEATBALLS

5 slices white bread, crumbled
1 cup milk
2 tablespoons soy sauce
1 teaspoon garlic salt
½ teaspoon onion powder
1 pound ground beef
1 pound sausage
2 (5-ounce) cans water chestnuts

Mix together all ingredients except water chestnuts. Cut water chestnuts in quarters. Roll meat into balls around pieces of chestnuts. Bake at 350 degrees 18-20 minutes. Drain and serve warm in chafing dish.
Yield: enough hors d'oeuvres for twenty

Anne Fowler Hiller (Mrs. Carl J.)

SWEDISH SWEET-SOUR COCKTAIL MEATBALLS

A real standby
Can do ahead
Keeps in refrigerator at least one week

2 pounds ground round beef
2 eggs
⅓ cup dried parsley flakes
2 tablespoons instant minced onion
1 cup Corn Flake Crumbs
2 tablespoons soy sauce
⅓ cup catsup
½ teaspoon garlic powder
¼ teaspoon pepper (or suit your taste)
1 (16-ounce) can jellied cranberry sauce
1 (12-ounce) bottle chili sauce
2 tablespoons dark brown sugar, firmly packed
1 tablespoon bottled lemon juice

Preheat oven to 350 degrees. Combine first nine ingredients and blend well—it does better if you get your hands in it! Form into small meatballs about the size of walnuts and arrange in baking pan about 15x10-inch. Combine remaining ingredients in medium-sized saucepan. Cook over moderate heat stirring frequently, until mixture is smooth and cranberry sauce is melted. Pour over meatballs and bake uncovered for 30 minutes. Serve in chafing dish with toothpicks.
Yield: about 60 meatballs

Terry Trippe Brubaker (Mrs. William J.)
Jean Schocke McCotter (Mrs. Clifton L.)

BACON ROLL-UPS

May do ahead
Can freeze

2 (3-ounce) containers cream cheese with chives
25 slices mixed grain sandwich bread, crust removed and cut in half
25 slices bacon, cut in half
Parsley sprigs (optional), for garnish

Spread 1 scant teaspoon of cream cheese mixture on each slice of bread and roll tightly. Wrap each roll up with bacon securing with a toothpick. Place roll ups on a broiler pan; bake at 350 degrees for 30 minutes turning if necessary. Roll ups may be assembled ahead and frozen. To serve, thaw overnight in refrigerator and bake at 350 degrees for 30-40 minutes.

Eugenia Hofler Clement (Mrs. Robert L.)

CROCKPOT HOT DOGS

Easy
Economical
Last minute
Serve immediately

1 package hot dogs
1 (10-ounce) jar currant, grape or apple jelly
1 (6-ounce) jar mustard

In crockpot melt jelly and mustard together on medium heat. Cut each hot dog into 4 pieces. Once jelly and mustard are blended add hot dogs and cook for 20 minutes before serving. Serve hot dogs hot; leave crockpot on low heat. This may also be done in a saucepan or chafing dish.
Yield: 20 servings

Laura Hall Courter (Mrs. Kim)
Susan Lee Thomas (Mrs. John G.)

DATE-NUT SAUSAGE BALLS

Can freeze

1 (16-ounce) package sausage
3 cups Bisquick
1 (10-ounce) package Cheddar cheese, grated
1 cup English walnuts, chopped
1 cup dates, chopped

Preheat oven to 325 degrees. Combine sausage, Bisquick and cheese until thoroughly blended. Knead in remaining ingredients. With hands, roll dough into marble-sized pieces and place on cookie sheet. Bake for 13 minutes. Cool. Store in airtight container or freeze.
Yield: 6-8 dozen

Pat Arant Minschew (Mrs. Erick)
Jean Arant Blanchard (Mrs. Joe)

SAUSAGE BALLS IN PASTRY BLANKETS

Can freeze

1 pound bulk sausage
2 teaspoons curry powder
½ teaspoon nutmeg
¼ teaspoon powdered sage
½ pound sharp cheese, greated
½ cup butter, softened
1½ cups flour, sifted
¼ teaspoon salt
1 teaspoon paprika

Combine first 4 ingredients and form into small balls about ½ tablespoon each. Fry out some of the fat and drain balls on absorbent paper. Prepare pastry by blending cheese, butter, flour, salt and paprika. Shape 1 tablespoon dough around each sausage ball. Freeze. To serve, place thawed balls on ungreased baking sheet. Bake in preheated 400 degree oven for 12-15 minutes.
Yield: 65 balls

Ann Harris Bustard (Mrs. Victor W.)

SAUSAGE BALLS

Can freeze

3 cups Bisquick baking mix
1 pound Jesse Jones "Hot" sausage
1 (10-ounce) package sharp Cheddar cheese

Mix sausage meat with Bisquick, thoroughly. Grate and melt cheese and pour over meat and cheese already prepared. Mix these ingredients well. Make up ball in sizes desired and place in freezer until needed. Cook in 350 degree oven until sausage balls are browned on top. Length of time depends on size.
Yield: 3 dozen

Anna Gillikin Lamm (Mrs. Ronald A.)
Laura Hall Courter (Mrs. Kim)
Susan Lee Thomas (Mrs. John G.)

SAUSAGE PINWHEELS

2 boxes of Flako pie crust mix
1 pound bulk hot sausage

Make up pie crust, 1 box at a time according to the directions on the package. Let sausage get soft. Roll out crust into a large square. Spread ½ pound sausage over crust almost to the edges. Roll into log. Wrap in waxed paper. Freeze. Take out of the freezer and slice while still frozen and bake at 350 degrees for 10-12 minutes. Drain on a paper towel. (Make up the other box of Flako the same way.)
Yield: Makes 2 rolls (each roll makes around 50)

Becky Elmore Clement (Mrs. Joseph M.)

SAUSAGE ROLL-UPS

1 can biscuits
⅓ pound hot sausage

Preheat oven to 350 degrees. Flatten each biscuit until it is about 3-inches in diameter. Place layer of hot sausage on top of biscuit and roll up. Slice in ½-inch wheels. Place on baking sheet and bake 8-10 minutes or until brown.

Becky Melton Kafer (Mrs. C. William)

TUNA CROUSTADE

French bread in poor boy or small loaves
1 (9¼-ounce) can tuna
1 (8-ounce) package cream cheese
1 tablespoon lemon juice
2 teaspoons onion, grated
1 teaspoon horseradish
¼ teaspoon salt
¼ teaspoon liquid smoke

Hollow out loaves of bread. Mix together tuna and rest of ingredients. Fill holes in bread. Slice thinly to serve.

Carol Coleman Pursell (Mrs. Elliott D.)

CLAM SPREAD

1 (6½-ounce) can minced clams
1 (8-ounce) package cream cheese
2 tablespoons mayonnaise
Dash of Worcestershire sauce
½ small onion, minced fine
Salt to taste
Pepper to taste
Garlic salt to taste

Drain clams and save juice. Chop clams fine and add remaining ingredients and clam juice as needed for spreading consistency. Season to taste. Chill and serve with crackers.

Florence Richardson Pollock (Mrs. Raymond)

CLAM-CHEESE DIP

1 (7-7½-ounce) can minced clams
2 (3-ounce) packages cream cheese, softened
¼ teaspoon salt
2 teaspoons onion, grated
1 teaspoon Worcestershire sauce
3 drops Tabasco sauce
1 teaspoon chopped parsley
2 teaspoons lemon juice

Drain clams; reserve liquid. Combine all ingredients except clam liquid; blend into paste. Add liquid 1 tablespoon at a time until desired consistency. Chill. Yields: 1 pint

Karen Dunn Mason (Mrs. John B.)

BERT'S HOT CLAM SPREAD

2 (6½-ounce) cans minced clams, drained
2 teaspoons lemon juice
1 medium onion, finely minced
2 teaspoons dry parsley
½ cup butter, melted
1 teaspoon oregano
Pepper
2-4 drops Tabasco sauce
¾ cup dry seasoned bread crumbs, preferably Italian-style
Parmesan cheese
1½ cups sharp Cheddar cheese, shredded
Crackers, preferably Triscuits
Paprika

Preheat oven to 350 degrees. Mix the first 9 ingredients and put in a 9-inch greased pie plate. Sprinkle with Parmesan cheese, 1½ cups shredded sharp cheese, and paprika. Bake for 20 minutes. Serve with crackers.

Birdsall S. Viault

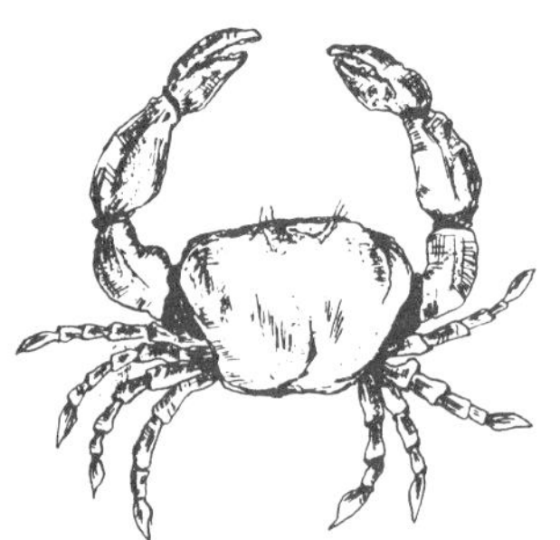

CRAB BITES

May be served as an hors d'oeuvre or a luncheon sandwich

1 (7-ounce) can Harris claw crab
1 cup margarine or butter, softened
1 (5-ounce) jar sharp Old English cheese, softened
½ teaspoon garlic salt or seasoned salt
2 tablespoons mayonnaise (not homemade)
2 dashes Worcestershire
6 English Muffins, split

Blend crab, butter, cheese, seasoning, mayonnaise and Worcestershire into a paste. Spread on split muffins. Each muffin may be cut into eight bite-sized pieces or left whole and frozen. Bake thawed in a preheated 400 degree oven 10-15 minutes or until browned.
Yield: 96 hors d'oeuvre bites or 12 sandwich halves

Sarah Reed Underhill (Mrs. Gary M.)

SWISS CRAB DELIGHTS

1 (6½-ounce) can crabmeat, drained and flaked
1 tablespoon green onion, sliced
4 ounces Swiss cheese, shredded
½ cup mayonnaise
1 teaspoon lemon juice
¼ teaspoon curry powder
1 (10-ounce) can flaky refrigerator rolls
Water chestnuts, sliced
Paprika

Preheat oven to 400 degrees. Combine crabmeat, onion, cheese, mayonnaise, lemon and curry. Take one package of a dozen refrigerator rolls and separate each roll into three layers. Place on ungreased baking sheet and spoon on crab mixture. Top each with a few slices of water chestnuts and sprinkle with paprika. Bake 10-12 minutes or until golden brown.
Yield: 3 dozen

Patricia Byrum McCotter (Mrs. C. Kennedy, Jr.)

CRAB PUFFS SUPREME

May be made ahead and frozen

1 (6½-ounce) can crabmeat, drained and flaked
½ cup sharp Cheddar cheese, grated
3 green onions, chopped
1 teaspoon Worcestershire sauce
1 teaspoon dry mustard
1 cup water
½ cup butter or margarine
¼ teaspoon salt
1 cup flour
4 eggs

Preheat oven to 400 degrees. Combine crab, cheese, onions, Worcestershire, and mustard and mix well. Combine water, butter and salt in large saucepan and bring to a boil. Remove from heat and immediately add flour, beating until mixture leaves sides of pan and forms a ball. Add eggs, one at a time, beating thoroughly after each addition. Thoroughly blend in crab mixture. Drop by small teaspoonfuls onto ungreased baking sheet. Bake 15 minutes, then reduce heat to 350 degrees and bake 10 minutes more. Unbaked puffs may be frozen on baking sheet and transferred to plastic bags. Bake without thawing at 375 degrees until crisp.
Yield: 4 dozen

Pat Best Woodward (Mrs. J. Arthur)

CRAB DIP

1 (8-ounce) package cream cheese, softened
½ cup mayonnaise
2 tablespoons catsup
3 tablespoons French dressing
1 (7½-ounce) can crab, drained and flaked
2 tablespoons onion, finely chopped

Blend all ingredients together well and chill.
Yields: 2 cups

Ann Holmes Novak (Mrs. David W.)

CRAB HORS D'OEUVRE

1 pound deluxe backfin crabmeat
1 tablespoon capers
1 cup mayonnaise
Dash lemon juice
Dash Tabasco
Saltines
Sharp cheese, grated

Mix crab, capers, mayonnaise, lemon juice and Tabasco. Sprinkle crushed saltines and sharp cheese on top. Put in preheated 350 degree oven until cheese melts. Serve in chafing dish with crackers.

Becky Elmore Clement (Mrs. Joseph)

CRABMEAT DIP

Easy
Serve immediately

1 pound crabmeat
3 (5-ounce) jars Kraft cream cheese and chives
½ cup butter
Worcestershire or Tabasco to taste

Heat combined ingredients. Serve in chafing dish with melba toast.
Yield: 16 servings

Sandra Phillips Moore (Mrs. William M., Jr.)

HOT CRAB DIP

1 (8-ounce) package cream cheese
2 tablespoons onion, minced
1 teaspoon horseradish
¼ teaspoon salt
½ cup almonds, sliced or chopped
1 cup fresh crabmeat *OR* (6½-ounce) can crab

Mix all ingredients and bake 20-25 minutes at 350 degrees. Serve hot with choice of dippers or crackers.

Muriel Meier Coombs (Mrs. Bruce)

GRETCHEN'S HOT CRAB DIP

Can be made ahead and placed in refrigerator

2 tablespoons green pepper, finely chopped
2 tablespoons butter
2 tablespoons flour
½ teaspoon prepared mustard
¼ teaspoon salt
Dash cayenne pepper
1 cup canned, stewed tomatoes, drained
1 teaspoon sugar
1 cup Kraft American Cheese, grated
1 egg yolk, slightly beaten
1 cup hot milk
1 pound crabmeat

Cook green pepper in butter for 5 minutes. Blend in flour, mustard, salt, dash of cayenne, tomatoes and sugar. Add cheese and egg. Cook for a few minutes. Add hot milk and crabmeat. Delicious served on toast triangles or small crackers from chafing dish.
Yield: 75 servings

Borrowed From: Gretchen Deichmann Speer (Mrs. Howard)
Margaret Gibbs Dunn (Mrs. John G., Jr.)

ANGELS ON HORSEBACK

12 slices bacon, cut to match number of oysters
1 pint oysters, well-drained
Toothpicks
Salt, pepper and paprika to taste
Parsley

Wrap bacon around oysters. Secure with toothpicks. Sprinkle each oyster with salt, pepper and paprika. Place a rack on a shallow baking pan. Brown slowly at 350 degrees for about 15-20 minutes. Serve on a bed of parsley.

Melinda Renuart (Mrs. John R.)

MOTHER'S PICKLED OYSTERS

1 quart select oysters
1 cup vinegar
1 teaspoon pickling spice
1 blade mace or 1/4 teaspoon ground mace
1 pod red pepper
1 teaspoon salt
1 teaspoon cloves
1 bay leaf

Cook oysters in their own juice until thoroughly curled. In separate saucepan heat vinegar and all other ingredients to boiling and simmer several minutes. When both oysters and vinegar mixture are thoroughly cooled, pour together and chill in refrigerator overnight. Serve with thin slices of lemon floating on top.

Leah Jones Ward (Mrs. David L.)
Matilda Hancock Turner

MY AUNT'S PICKLED OYSTERS

1 quart oysters
2 cups vinegar
1 teaspoon red pepper
6 teaspoons peppercorns
1 teaspoon pickling spices
2 tablespoons whole mace
2 teaspoons salt
1 teaspoon ground pepper

Combine all ingredients except oysters in a saucepan. Cover and bring to a boil. Put oysters in and bring to a boil again. Simmer until gills of oysters curl. Cool. Refrigerate at least 24 hours before serving.

John Cotton Tayloe

SMOKED OYSTER DIP

Keeps well

1 (8-ounce) package cream cheese, softened
1½ cups mayonnaise
4 dashes hot sauce
1 tablespoon lemon juice
1 (4-ounce) can chopped black olives
1 (3.66-ounce) can smoked oysters, drained and chopped

Combine the first four ingredients, mixing well. Stir in olives and oysters. Serve with raw vegetables or crackers.
Yield: 2 cups

Karen Hansen Norman (Mrs. Joseph H., IV)

LOBSTER DELIGHT

2 tablespoons green peppers, finely chopped
2 tablespoons onion, finely chopped
2 tablespoons butter
2 tablespoons flour
½ tablespoon prepared mustard
¾ cup canned tomatoes
½ pound cheese, grated
1 egg
¾ cup milk
1 can lobster or 1 small cooked frozen lobster tail

Cook pepper and onion in butter, add flour, mustard, cheese, tomatoes and milk. Cook until slightly thickened. Add lobster. Last, add egg and cook on low heat until slightly thick and smooth. Serve on crackers or in pastry shells.

Margaret L. Scott (Mrs. James H.)

CHEESE SHRIMP DIP

1 (3-ounce) can shrimp
1 cup mayonnaise
Dash garlic powder
½ pound Colby cheese, grated
1 teaspoon Worcestershire sauce
1 medium onion, minced

Mix all together. Chill for a few hours to let flavors blend.

Elizabeth Harrell Disosway (Mrs. Jack)

LOW-CALORIE SHRIMP DIP

12 ounces cottage cheese
½ teaspoon lemon peel, grated
1½ teaspoons lemon juice
½ teaspoon dill weed
¼ teaspoon salt
⅛ teaspoon Tabasco
¼ cup celery, minced
1 teaspoon parsley, minced
¾ cup cooked shrimp, cut up and veined

Blend the cottage cheese, lemon peel and juice, dill, salt, and Tabasco in a blender until smooth. Stir in remaining ingredients. Serve sprinkled with additional cut-up parsley.
Yield: 2 cups

Rees Hamilton Carter (Mrs. Fredrick A.)

Large scooped-out vegetables, round loaves of bread hollowed-out or foil-lined flower pots make good servers for dips.

KATY'S SHRIMP DIP

Must do ahead

1 (8-ounce) package cream cheese
Dry sherry
Clove of garlic
1 pound shrimp, cut into bite-sized pieces
"Old Bay" Seasoning

Thin cream cheese with dry sherry to the consistency of sour cream. Toss cooked and cleaned shrimp with "Old Bay" seasoning—use just a small amount sprinkled over shrimp. Mix shrimp with cream cheese and add clove garlic. Let stand overnight to blend. When ready to serve, remove clove garlic and serve with crackers.

Eugenia Hofler Clement (Mrs. Robert L.)

CREAMY SHRIMP SANDWICHES

Time consuming, but worth the effort!

2 pounds shrimp, cooked, cleaned and chopped
½ cup butter, in pieces
½ teaspoon dry mustard
1 teaspoon Worcestershire sauce
¼ teaspoon lemon juice
1 small onion, chopped
1 tablespoon sherry
Tabasco, 5 drops or so to taste
Whipped butter
Bread (frozen white sandwich bread)

Combine chopped shrimp, onion, sherry, lemon juice and Tabasco. Blend small amounts of this mixture in a blender until all is well-minced. Add the remaining ingredients and butter. You may wish to use more butter. When mixture is well-blended, spread on lightly buttered white sandwich bread and cut sandwiches into quarters. I use whipped butter and spread on frozen bread so it doesn't fall apart. Cut off crusts.

Margaret Manning Preston (Mrs. Ronald A.)

PARTY MOLD

Make ahead

2 (8-ounce) packages cream cheese
¼ pound sharp cheese, grated
1 small wedge Roquefort cheese
1 teaspoon garlic salt
½ teaspoon curry powder
2 teaspoons Worcestershire sauce
1 pound crab, shrimp or lobster or all three
1 teaspoon paprika
1 tablespoon mayonnaise
1 tablespoon lemon juice

Have all ingredients at room temperature. Mix, adding cream if necessary in order to blend. Grease cold 1-quart mold or bowl with salad oil. Fill with mixture and allow to chill overnight, if possible. Unmold by shaking. Decorate with paprika and hard-boiled egg yolk pressed through a sieve, or with chopped parsley, pimiento and stuffed olives. Excellent on crackers or dark bread. Cover in the refrigerator; it will keep for several days.
Yields: 20 servings

Mary Sutherland Hasell (Mrs. Thomas M., Jr.)

SASSY SHRIMP MOLD

This always brings raves and a request for the recipe!

5 (8-ounce) cans shrimp, drained
2 onions, finely grated
2 lemons, juiced
4 cups mayonnaise
1 tablespoon horseradish
3 envelopes Knox gelatine
2 cups cold water

Mash up the shrimp with a fork or a food processor. Add onions, lemon juice, mayonnaise, and horseradish. Dissolve gelatine in the cold water, then place the gelatine in the top of a double boiler and heat. Remove and cool to room temperature. Add to other ingredients and stir well. Spray an 11-cup mold with Pam, add the ingredients and chill until firm. Serve with Pepperidge Farm Party Rye or crackers. Half of the recipe fills a 5½ cup fish mold perfectly for a nice hors d'oeuvre for 10 to 12 people.

Alice Graham Underhill (Mrs. T. Reed)

PICKLED SHRIMP AND MUSHROOMS

Quick and elegant appetizer for parties
Easy
Do a day ahead

2½ pounds shrimp
1¼ cups oil
¾ cup white vinegar
1½ teaspoons salt
2 teaspoons celery seed
7-8 bay leaves
Dash Tabasco
1 large onion, sliced
1 can button mushrooms
McCormick's Shrimp Boil
2½ teaspoons capers and juice (optional)

Cook shrimp as directed on McCormick's Shrimp Boil. In a large bowl alternate cleaned shrimp, sliced onions and mushrooms. Make a sauce by combining oil, vinegar, salt, celery seed, Tabasco and bay leaves. Pour over shrimp mixture and refrigerate at least 24 hours. Add capers and juice, if desired.

Nancy Springett Wetherington (Mrs. John S.)

PICKLED SHRIMP

Must do ahead

3 onions, sliced
2 pounds shrimp, cooked
2 tablespoons sugar
1 teaspoon salt
½ teaspoon dry mustard
Dash Tabasco
2 tablespoons Worcestershire sauce
½ cup catsup
⅓ cup vinegar
¾ cup salad oil

Slice onions and soak in cool water for one hour. Cook shrimp and allow to cool. Drain onions and mix with shrimp. Combine sugar, salt, mustard, Tabasco, Worcestershire sauce, catsup, vinegar and salad oil. Pour ingredients over shrimp and onions and marinate in refrigerator for at least eight hours or overnight.

Mary Ann Southern (Mrs. Thomas L.)

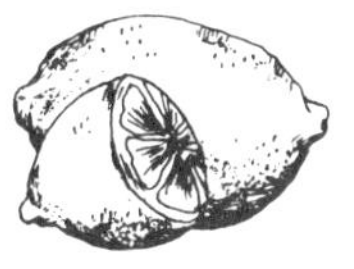

SEASIDE SHRIMP

4 pounds raw shrimp, cleaned
6 tablespoons onion, minced
1 tablespoon salt
2 cups beer*
2 bay leaves
½ cup butter
¼ cup flour
2 teaspoons Tabasco
¼ cup lemon juice
¼ cup parsley, minced

*I use only 1½ cups.
Melt butter in large skillet, add onions and shrimp. Cook 2 minutes stirring once or twice. Stir in flour, salt, Tabasco, beer, lemon juice and bay leaves. Simmer, stirring occasionally, 5 minutes. Remove bay leaves. Place shrimp and sauce in chafing dish. Sprinkle with parsley. Serve with toothpicks.

Anne Bratton Allen (Mrs. H. Eldridge Allen)

APPETIZER ROLL-UPS

Men love this!

Easy—can make ahead of time

1 (6½-ounce) can tuna fish
1 (6-ounce) package Swiss cheese
1 (8-ounce) package hard salami
½ teaspoon parsley flakes
½ teaspoon lemon juice
2 to 3 teaspoons mayonnaise
Salt to taste
Pepper to taste

Mix tuna, parsley, lemon juice, mayonnaise and salt and pepper together. Arrange one slice of cheese on salami round and trim to fit. Place one teaspoonful of tuna mixture on cheese and salami. Roll up, jellyroll fashion, and secure with two toothpicks. Repeat until cheese, salami and tuna are gone. Refrigerate at least two hours. Before serving, cut each roll in half being sure a toothpick is in each half.

Marilyn Miller Smith (Mrs. Stewart H.)

ROASTED PEANUTS—TRADITIONAL RECIPE

In the shell: Place peanuts one or two layers deep in 9x13-inch baking pans. (Two of these pans can hold up to 5 pounds of peanuts in the shell.) Roast at 350 degrees for 25-35 minutes, stirring occasionally. Shell and sample during the last few minutes to assure the desired doneness. REMEMBER, peanuts will continue cooking internally a little bit after removal from the oven. Cool and store at room temperature for up to a week or in a cool, dry place for a prolonged period of time.

Already shelled: Place raw, shelled peanuts one layer deep in a 9x13-inch baking pan. Roast at 350 degrees for 15 to 20 minutes until golden brown. Stir for even roasting. Garnish, if desired with melted butter and salt. Cool and store for several months in a closed container in the refrigerator. All peanuts keep indefinitely when frozen.

These are quick, easy, economical variations which afford a much better flavor than purchased roasted peanuts, which, due to long storage, have already lost many B vitamins.

Peggy Witmeyer Bernard

SALMON BALL

Can do ahead

2 cups canned salmon, drained
1 (8-ounce) package cream cheese, softened
1 tablespoon lemon juice
1 teaspoon prepared horseradish
1 tablespoon onion, minced
¼ teaspoon salt
Worcestershire sauce, to taste
Parsley flakes

Mix all ingredients together except parsley flakes. Chill 4-8 hours. Shape into a ball and roll in parsley flakes. Serve with crackers.

Dorothy Elizabeth Selak

ROLLED GRAPE LEAVES

1 pound ground round steak (*NOT* hamburger)
1 pound lamb meat (ground once by butcher)
1 quart grape leaves*
1 teaspoon salt
1 teaspoon pepper
1 cup long-cooking rice, uncooked

*These can be found in the gourmet section of most supermarkets.
Mix ground round, ground lamb, salt, pepper and raw rice together. Rinse grape leaves in cold water, being careful not to tear leaves. Separate each leaf and lay flat on table. Place 1 tablespoon of mixture of above ingredients across top of each leaf and roll leaf tightly. Place each roll neatly and snugly in Dutch oven, seam-side down. Cover with 1 cup water and cook slowly for 1 hour on top of the stove.
Yield: about 8 dozen

Aggie Shapou Derda (Mrs. Cletus F.)

PRAIRIE FIRE

Men like this!

1 (16-ounce) can refried beans
1/4 cup butter
1/3 pound Cheddar cheese, grated
2 Jalapeño peppers, chopped
1 teaspoon Jalapeño pepper juice
1 medium onion, grated fine
Corn chips

Heat all ingredients except corn chips in a double boiler until cheese is melted and ingredients are thoroughly blended. Serve in chafing dish with corn chips. Yield: 6-8 servings

Sherwood Wright Crawford (Mrs. Thomas R.)

SUPER NACHO

This is a real conversation piece!

Part made ahead

1 pound ground beef
1 large onion, chopped
1 (15-ounce) can refried beans
1 pound sharp Cheddar cheese, grated
1 (8-ounce) bottle taco sauce, mild or hot
1/2 head lettuce, shredded
2 cups sour cream
1 1/2 cups guacamole
1 (2 1/4-ounce) can chopped ripe olives
Doritos

Brown beef with onion; drain. Spread beans on the bottom of a 13- or 14-inch pizza pan; spread meat mixture over beans and pat down. Pat cheese onto meat. Drizzle taco sauce over all. May be refrigerated up to 48 hours at this point. When ready to serve, heat oven to 375 degrees and bake 18-20 minutes. Remove from oven and sprinkle with lettuce. Add sour cream on top of lettuce and guacamole on sour cream. Sprinkle drained olives over all. Serve with Doritos for dipping.

Carolyn Angell Corliss (Mrs. G. A.)

CHILI CON QUESO

1 tablespoon bacon fat
1 small onion, chopped
1 heaping tablespoon flour
1 (10-ounce) can Valley or Old El Paso Tomatoes and Green Chilies
1 pound Velveeta cheese, chopped
Evaporated milk
Fritos or Tostitos

Sauté chopped onion in bacon fat; add flour and stir well. Add tomatoes and green chilies and heat over low heat until thick. Add chopped cheese and stir continuously until cheese has melted. Mixture will be quite thick. Thin to dunking consistency with evaporated milk. Keep warm during serving. Serve with Fritos or Tostitos. Potato chips do NOT dip well with this.
Yield: 4 cups

Anne Bratton Allen (Mrs. H. Eldridge)

ANTIPASTO

Keeps well for four to six months

3 large onions, chopped
3 green peppers, chopped
3 carrots, very thinly sliced
3 (7-ounce) cans white tuna
4 sweet pickles, chopped
2 (8-ounce) cans mushrooms
1 (24-ounce) bottle catsup
15 peppercorns
4 bay leaves
2 (8-ounce) cans tomato sauce
2 teaspoons Worcestershire sauce
1 teaspoon vinegar
1 cup olive oil, or ½ olive oil and ½ vegetable oil
Garlic salt to taste

Cook carrots in a small amount of water for 10 minutes. Drain. In a large pot, such as a Dutch oven, cook onions and peppers in oil until onions are soft; add tomato sauce, vinegar, catsup, Worcestershire sauce and simmer for 5 minutes. Add rest of the ingredients and cook slowly for 15 minutes. Let it cool; place in glass jars, and put in the refrigerator. Serve on crackers, preferably Triscuits.

Alice Graham Underhill (Mrs. T. Reed)

PEANUT-BUTTER CRISPS

Can be frozen

1 loaf Pepperidge Farm Thin-sliced Bread
12 ounces peanut butter
12 ounces vegetable oil
Parsley flakes
Crazy salt
Seasoned salt

Remove crusts from each slice of bread and cut slices into 4 strips. Place all strips on one cookie sheet and all crusts and heels on another cookie sheet. Place both cookie sheets in the oven and bake at 250 degrees for an hour. When toasted, remove crusts to blender container and make crumbs with them. Mix oil and peanut butter until smooth. Mix crumbs with parsley flakes, crazy salt, seasoned salt *OR* any other flavored salt or herb of your choice. Use a light touch with the salt as it is easy to get crumbs too salty. Dip strips first into oil mixture, then roll in crumbs. Let dry on waxed paper. Store in tightly covered container or freeze.

Jane Johnson Straub (Mrs. Robert L.)

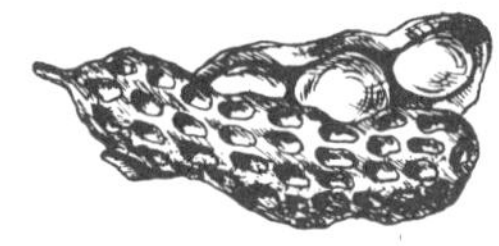

TINY PIZZAS

Easy
Do early in the day
Can double

Wonder brown and serve rolls
1 (8-ounce) can tomato sauce
Oregano
Parmesan cheese
Olive halves or flat anchovies

Preheat oven to 400 degrees. Slice cold rolls from top to bottom (about 5 slices to a roll). Top with tomato sauce, covering the whole slice. Sprinkle with oregano and Parmesan cheese. Garnish with olive halves or flat anchovy pieces. Bake 10-12 minutes or until roll is brown. If prepared early, place on cookie sheet, refrigerate and heat when ready.

Florence Woods Christie (Mrs. Charles W.)

PIZZA ROUNDS

Can freeze

1 pound hamburger
1 pound sausage
1 teaspoon basil
1 teaspoon oregano leaves
½ teaspoon garlic powder
1 pound Velveeta cheese
2 loaves Pepperidge Farm Party Rye

Brown and drain hamburger and sausage. Add other ingredients and stir over low heat. Spread on bread. Freeze on cookie sheets at this point and transfer to plastic bags later. When ready to serve, heat under broiler until bubbly.
Yield: About 4 dozen rounds

Rena Terrell Knott (Mrs. Edmund T.)

BAMBINI

1 cup ricotta cheese
½ cup Mozzarella, coarsely grated
¼ cup Parmesan cheese
1 (10-ounce) package large flaky refrigerator biscuits
20 very thin slices pepperoni

Combine ricotta, Mozzarella and Parmesan in bowl, mixing thoroughly. Halve each biscuit horizontally forming 20 thin biscuits. Shape dough into ovals. Place pepperoni slightly off center on dough. Top with about 1 tablespoon of cheese mixture. Fold dough over to enclose filling. Place on lightly greased baking sheet and bake at 350 degrees for 15-20 minutes.
Yield: 20 pieces

Joyce Bell Straub (Mrs. Terence M.)

GERALD COLVIN'S EASY ONION SQUARES

Will keep a long time if stored in tight tin box

1 loaf Pepperidge Farm Thin-sliced White Bread
½ cup butter
1 package Lipton's Onion Soup Mix

Remove crust and cut bread slices into squares. Combine softened butter and soup mix. Spread thinly on bread squares and bake at 200 degrees for 1 hour.

Genevieve Tolson Dunn (Mrs. Mark S.)

Jerkins-Duffy House **301 Johnson Street**

This Federal design house was built about 1819 by Captain Thomas Jerkins. On the roof may be seen a "Captain's Walk," sometimes called a "Widow's Walk." These were built by sea captains so that ships might be sighted coming up the river. During the War Between the States, this house was occupied by Union Staff officers. This house was restored in 1957 by Mr. and Mrs. Robert Lee Stallings.

Beverages

COFFEE PUNCH

Delicious with hot coffee cake!

Part done ahead

1 pot of coffee (8 cups)
½ gallon vanilla ice cream
½ pint whipping cream

Make a pot of coffee and *cool overnight* in refrigerator. Sweeten coffee to taste. 15 minutes before serving pour cold coffee over ½ gallon vanilla ice cream and let melt until slushy. Whip ½ pint whipping cream and put dollop on top of each cup as it is served.

Mary Stallings Parrish (Mrs. Ben W.)

HOW TO SPICE UP COFFEE

Dutch Coffee
To 1 cup of hot coffee add:
Cinnamon stick
1 tablespoon whipped cream
1 pat butter

Mexican coffee
¼ teaspoon cinnamon
Dollop whipped cream
Sprinkle of nutmeg

Italian Coffee
Equal parts of hot chocolate and hot coffee
Dollop of whipped cream
Grated semi-sweet chocolate

Irish Coffee
¾ cup coffee
2 teaspoons sugar
2 tablespoons Irish whiskey

Stir above together and add a large swirl of whipped cream.

VIENNESE ICED COFFEE

Can be made ahead and assembled before serving

¼ cup instant coffee
2½ tablespoons sugar
8 whole cloves
1 (3-inch) stick cinnamon
3 cups water
Crushed ice
1 pint vanilla ice cream
½ cup heavy cream, whipped
Ground cinnamon

Combine coffee, sugar, cloves, stick cinnamon and water. Cover, bring to a boil. Remove from heat and let stand, covered for 5 minutes to steep. Strain. Chill well. Fill four chilled tall glasses one-fourth full with crushed ice. Add a scoop of ice cream to each. Pour in coffee and mix with ice cream. Top each with whipped cream and a dash of cinnamon.
Yield: 4 servings

Carol Webb Pullen (Mrs. John S.)

DELICIOUS DIET SMOOTHIE

1 firm to ripe banana
¾ cup low-calorie cranberry juice
¼ cup orange juice

Combine all ingredients together in a blender and mix well. Add a few ice cubes and blend a little more, until frothy. Serve immediately. Can be stored in the refrigerator in blender container overnight, which simplifies morning preparation. This doubles easily.
Yield: 1 serving

Alice Graham Underhill (Mrs. T. Reed)

CRANBERRY PUNCH

2 (28-ounce) bottles ginger ale
1 (46-ounce) can pineapple juice
1 quart cranberry juice
1 quart pineapple sherbet

Chill all ingredients. Mix in a punch bowl. Makes a delicious light pink punch. Good for weddings and parties.
Yield: Serves 30

Karen Brannock Askew (Mrs. M. H., III)

GINGER PEACH FROTH

This is an original recipe.

Easy
Quick
Economical

4 pitted, peeled peaches*
6 cups milk
½ teaspoon ginger
2 tablespoons honey

*One can of peaches in natural juice (drained) can be substituted for the fresh peaches, adjusting the honey to taste.
Put all ingredients in a blender and mix to froth. Serve at once. This is an easy, quick, economical recipe that is especially appealing served at a summer brunch or luncheon (perhaps with cucumber sandwiches and mixed nuts).

*Hint: Whenever adding honey to other ingredients in a blender either heat the honey (putting jar in pot of hot water) or add the honey while the blender is in operation.
Yield: 8 servings

Peggy Witmeyer Bernard

SLUSH PUNCH

Part must be made ahead

1 (6-ounce) can frozen orange juice
1 (6-ounce) can frozen limeade or lemonade
5 cans water
¾ cup pineapple juice
3 teabags
¾ cup sugar
Ginger ale

In large mixing bowl suitable for freezing, mix orange juice, limeade, 5 cans water and pineapple juice. In small saucepan boil 1 cup water and add teabags steeping 5 minutes. Add sugar and stir until dissolved. Combine tea and fruit juice mix and freeze. Remove punch every 2 hours and beat . . . this gives the slushy texture. When ready to serve mix with equal parts of ginger ale.
Yield: 6½ cups punch concentrate

Mary Stallings Parrish (Mrs. Ben W.)

KOOL-AID PUNCH

4 (.14-ounce) packages lemon-lime Kool-Aid
4 cups sugar
2 gallons water
1 (46-ounce) can unsweetened orange juice
1 (46-ounce) can unsweetened pineapple juice
3 (12-ounce) cans frozen lemonade, not diluted

Mix Kool-Aid, sugar and water. Freeze part of the Kool-Aid in a bowl or ring mold to use in the punch bowl for ice. Add remaining ingredients and chill.
Yield: 3 gallons, 50 servings

Mavis Coley Lee (Mrs. W. D., Jr.)
Susan Lee Thomas (Mrs. John G.)

ORANGE PUNCH

2 bottles (28-ounce) ginger ale
1 (46-ounce) can orange juice
1 (46-ounce) can pineapple juice
Sugar to taste

Mix all the ingredients together and serve over a ring made from frozen juices, so the punch will not be diluted.
Yield: 35 (4-ounce) servings

Susan Lee Thomas (Mrs. John G.)

7-UP SHERBET PUNCH

2 quarts sherbet
6 (28-ounce) bottles of 7-Up

Put the sherbet in a large punch bowl and let stand at room temperature until mushy. Add chilled 7-Up. Stir several times. Suggested flavors are raspberry, pineapple, lemon, lime, orange, or cranberry. Try using one quart lemon sherbet with one quart of any other flavor.
Yield: 50 servings

Marian Bartlett Stewart (Mrs. Wm. Edward)

SUMMER COOLER

Can do ahead
Keeps well in the refrigerator

2 cups sugar
2½ cups water
Juice of 6 lemons
Juice of 2 oranges
Grated orange rind of 2 oranges
1 cup mint leaves

Boil sugar and water for 5 minutes. Cool and add juices and rind and pour over mint leaves. Strain into quart mason jar and keep in the refrigerator. When serving, fill glass ⅓ full with mixture, then add ice and water to fill glass.

Alice Smith Flood (Mrs. Robert)

HOT CHOCOLATE MIX

Delicious and great for gift-giving!

1 (8-quart box Carnation Instant Milk
1 (16-ounce) jar Coffeemate
1 (2-pound) box Nestle's Quik
1 (1-pound) box confectioners' sugar

Mix all the ingredients together, sifting the sugar. Store in airtight containers. To prepare, fill mug half full of mix and add boiling water.

Nancy Stilley Turner (Mrs. Charles H., Jr.)

WASSAIL

This is an original recipe.

Can be doubled

4 quarts (1 gallon) apple cider
4 (6-ounce) cans frozen lemonade
1 tablespoon ground cloves
4 sticks cinnamon
½ teaspoon ground allspice

Heat ingredients and let boil 10-15 minutes. Serve hot.
Yield: 20 servings

Billie Ruth Stewart Sudduth (Mrs. W. Douglas)

CUP O' CHEER

Can do ahead
Keeps well

½ cup water
1 cup granulated sugar
2 sticks cinnamon
12 whole cloves
6 cups grapefruit juice
1 quart cider
3 cups orange juice

Bring to boil the sugar, cloves and cinnamon in ½ cup water. Reduce heat and simmer 20 minutes. Add the fruit juices. The beauty of this recipe is it can be served either hot or cold—just add fruit slices for garnish. Also it can be made 2 weeks ahead, and if served hot, may be reheated over and over.
Yield: Makes 26 punch cups

Jean Schocke McCotter (Mrs. Clifton L.)

ORDINATION PUNCH

This is an adaptation of Carrie Duffy Ward's Frozen Punch, as prepared by Frances Clement and Bay McCotter for Michael Thompson's Ordination in February 1981.

48 tea bags—12 quarts water
2 (8-ounce) bottles of lemon juice
5 pounds sugar
2 level tablespoons citric acid (Available at drugstores)
2 (46-ounce) cans unsweetened orange juice
2 (46-ounce) cans unsweetened grapefruit juice
2 (46-ounce) cans unsweetened pineapple juice
4 packages frozen strawberries, sliced
4 (6-ounce) cans frozen orange juice concentrate

Make tea. Add juices, sugar, citric acid. Freeze in 1 gallon containers. When serving, take punch from freezer about 4 hours before using. Mash up with potato masher. Add 1 package thawed strawberries, and 1 undiluted orange juice to 1 gallon batch of punch mix. Add only to the first 4 batches of punch you make. Add 2 quarts of ginger ale to each gallon of punch mix. We used 16 quarts of ginger ale to 6 gallons of punch.
Yield: 200 servings (Makes 6 gallons plus 1 quart)

FROZEN WINE PUNCH

Freeze

1 Fifth Lambrusco wine*
1 (48-ounce) can unsweetened pineapple juice
1 (32-ounce) jar cranberry juice cocktail
1 (28-ounce) bottle 7-Up
2 tablespoons lemon juice

*Any semi-sweet red wine will do
Mix all ingredients. Pour into 12- or 16-ounce containers. Freeze. Thaw to "slushy" stage to serve. Mixture can be refrozen.
Yield: 15 generous servings, 28 (5½-ounce) servings

June Reasons (Mrs. W. E.)

FROZEN MARGARITAS SUPREME

Lime wedge
Coarse salt
1 (6-ounce) can frozen limeade concentrate, thawed and undiluted
¾ cup tequila
¼ cup Triple Sec or other orange-flavored liqueur
Crushed ice
Lime slices (optional)

Rub the rim of 4 cocktail glasses with wedge of lime. Place salt in saucer; spin rim of each glass in salt. Set prepared glasses aside. Combine limeade, tequila, and Triple Sec in container of electric blender; blend well. Add crushed ice to fill blender three-fourths full; blend well. Pour beverage into prepared glasses; garnish with a slice of lime, if desired.
Yield: 4 servings

SANGRÍA

2 (6-ounce) cans frozen limeade concentrate, thawed
1 quart dry red wine, chilled
1 (28-ounce) bottle club soda
1 tray ice cubes
1 orange

Reconstitute limeade according to label directions. Combine limeade, wine and club soda. Pour over ice cubes in a small punch bowl. Garnish with thinly sliced orange. Serve in chilled punch cups.
Yield: approximately 30 servings

Mary Ann Psychas Dunn (Mrs. John G. III)

VENETIAN COFFEE

Easy

½ teaspoon sugar
2½ ounces coffee
1 jigger "Christian Brothers" Brandy (80 proof)
Whipped cream

Place sugar in cup, add coffee, brandy and float whipped cream on top. Serve immediately. Delish!
Yield: 1 cup

Marian Bartlett Stewart (Mrs. Wm. Edward)

BEER PUNCH

1 cup sugar
1 cup water
1½-2 tablespoons lemon rind
1 cup lemon juice
½ cup grapefruit juice
1 (12-ounce) beer

Mix first three ingredients, boil and then cool. After the first mixture has cooled add the next three ingredients. Serve over ice with clove studded lemon slice.
Yield: 4 servings

Diane Gough Fowler (Mrs. Phillip L.)

BOBBIE BELL'S CHAMPAGNE PUNCH

This punch was served at Assistant Rector F. Clayton Matthew's Farewell Party in December 1979.

1 fifth Champagne, chilled
1 (48-ounce) jug apple cider
1 quart ginger ale
Ice ring

Make ice ring with cherries, mint leaves and/or lemon slices. Use apple cider rather than water to fill mold so it won't dilute the punch. Have all ingredients chilled. Pour over unmolded ice ring in punch bowl.
Yield: about 20 servings

Jo Simmons Aiken (Mrs. Hovey E.)

FRENCH MINT TEA

13 tea bags
¼ cup fresh mint leaves (lightly packed)
Water
Juice from 2 fresh-squeezed lemons
1 (6-ounce) can frozen orange juice concentrate
1 cup sugar
Mint sprigs (garnish)

Combine tea, mint leaves and 1 quart water in large saucepan. Cover, bring to boil and immediately remove from heat. Let steep 30 minutes. Add lemon juice, orange juice concentrate, sugar, and additional water to make 2 quarts liquid. Strain and chill. Serve over ice and garnish with mint.
Yield: 2 quarts

Gail R. Austin (Mrs. W. Joseph)

A special cold weather treat for grown-ups is prepackaged hot chocolate mixture made according to package directions which has had Peppermint Schnapps added to taste and whipped cream spooned on top.

SPICED TEA

1 cup water
¾ cup sugar
3 teaspoons tea
1 teaspoon allspice
1½ cups of orange juice
½ cup lemon juice
½ cup pineapple juice (optional)

Boil water with sugar five minutes. Remove from heat and add tea and allspice. Cover and let stand for 15 minutes. Strain into a pitcher. Add orange juice, lemon juice and two quarts of water. Pineapple juice may be added—in a larger quantity than stated above, if desired. Can be used for either hot or cold tea and keeps for several days.
Yield: Makes about 14 cups of tea

Miss Gertrude S. Carraway

RUSSIAN TEA

Easy
Stores well
Great Christmas gift

2 cups Tang
1 cup instant tea (lemon flavored NOT sweetened)
2 cups sugar
½ teaspoon cinnamon
½ teaspoon ground cloves

Mix all ingredients in large jar or bowl and shake or stir to mix well. Store in airtight containers. Use 2 teaspoons to 1 cup boiling water.

Patricia Byrum McCotter (Mrs. C. Kennedy, Jr.)

APRICOT FROST

May double

1 (6-ounce) can frozen lemonade concentrate
1 lemonade can vodka
1 (17-ounce) can apricots*
Ice cubes

*Each can contains 8-10 apricot halves which is enough to double this recipe. Mix lemonade, vodka, 4-5 apricot halves and ice in blender container. Serve in daiquiri glasses. Adjust the amount of ice used to suit your taste. Sometimes I add half the canned juice along with the apricots.

BASAKI

Good drink at brunch the morning after the night before.

Vanilla Ice Cream
1 egg
3 ounces gin (or to taste)
6-8 ounces 7-Up
Dash lemon or lime juice

Fill blender half full with vanilla ice cream. Add remaining ingredients and some cracked ice to fill blender. Mix.
Yield: 6 servings

Nancy Smith Favor (Mrs. William A. Jr.)

SUNSHINE SPECIAL

1 jigger white rum
Dash bitters
Orange juice

In highball glass filled with cubed ice combine rum and bitters and fill glass with orange juice.

William E. Brinkley, Jr.

NANCY'S HOT BUTTERED RUM

Part made ahead

Rum or rum flavoring
1 quart (or more) vanilla ice cream
1 (16-ounce) package light brown sugar
2 cups butter
Cinnamon sticks
Water

Soften and whip butter with sugar; soften and whip ice cream and combine and whip two mixtures together. Return to freezer in freezing container. To serve heat water to boiling. In a mug put 1 tablespoon of butter-ice cream mixture, 1 jigger of rum or rum flavoring to taste, and fill mug with hot water. Use cinnamon sticks as swizzle sticks.

Barbara Straub Stewart

RED DOG'S "PLANE PUNCH"

After two cups of this punch, you'll think you're "flying"—hence the name.

1 fifth of whiskey
1 fifth of brandy
1 fifth of claret
1 fifth of sweet sherry
1 (28-ounce) bottle of soda water
6 lemons, juiced (or equivalent bottled juice)
1 cup sugar

Mix all ingredients together and serve over a block of ice.
Yield: 45 (4-ounce) servings

Curtis D. "Red Dog" Jernigan

MY DADDY'S DANDELION WINE

12 quarts dandelions
12 quarts boiling water
6 oranges
2 lemons
2 pounds black seedless raisins
4 pounds sugar
3 yeast cakes

Combine dandelions and boiling water. Let stand 24 hours. Strain and add the remaining ingredients. Stir morning, noon and night. Let stand cloth covered for 3 weeks. Then strain through cheesecloth. Put in gallon jars and let age for 4 months. I have heard of strawberries being added as one of the fruits, which gives it a pink tint instead of a golden yellow.

Melanie Applegate (Mrs. Earl)

KAHLÚA

Warning! Don't sample too much while bottling!

4 cups water
4 cups sugar
4 tablespoons instant Yuban coffee*
1 quart Smirnoff Vodka (100 proof)*
1½ teaspoons pure vanilla

*Must use brand names
Add water and coffee in a large pan and bring to boil. Add sugar and stir; bring to a boil again and then let simmer for 10 minutes. Then let it cool naturally. When completely cool, add the vodka and vanilla. Cheers! Great over ice cream or as a liqueur.
Yield: 2 quarts

Patricia Byrum McCotter (Mrs. C. Kennedy, Jr.)

Variation:
Using the recipe above use any brand of instant coffee and vodka and substitute 1 vanilla bean, split lengthwise for vanilla extract. Age 5 weeks before serving.

Drusilla White Eckberg (Mrs. David E.)

Variation:
Using the original recipe, substitute any brand coffee; use a vanilla bean instead of extract and substitute a fifth of bourbon for vodka. Better than Mexican Kahlúa.

Elizabeth Scales Marsh (Mrs. Thomas B.)

PERKINS' EGG NOG

Family recipe handed down three generations!

12 eggs
12 tablespoons sugar
12 tablespoons whiskey (or more to taste)
½ pint (or more) whipping cream, whipped—per one dozen eggs

Beat egg yolks and sugar thoroughly until fluffy. Add whiskey. Fold in whipped cream. Fold in well-beaten egg whites.
Yield: 12 servings

Virginia Perkins Sharp (Mrs. C. Edward)

ERIC APPLEQUIST'S SWEDISH GLÖÖG

This will really warm your New Year's Eve!

2 bottles whiskey (Rye or Bourbon)*
3 bottles wine (Port or Sherry)*
1 pint brandy
Handful of cloves
6 sticks cinnamon
2 handfuls of almonds, peeled
2 cups sugar, to taste
1 tablespoon lemon juice
2 handfuls of raisins

*Use bottles of equal size.
Mix well and simmer about 10 minutes. Do NOT let boil. Take off lid and keep on stirring very well so that all ingredients are well-absorbed. Serve hot.
Yield: 1 gallon

Chris Watts Burks (Mrs. Charles L.)

EASY PARTY PUNCH

4-5 (28-ounce) bottles ginger ale
1 fifth Bourbon
1 fifth Cold Duck or Sparkling Burgundy
Ice ring of ginger ale, cherries, and cherry juice

Combine all the ingredients in a large punch bowl and serve. This makes a very festive but light punch, perfect for an afternoon party or luncheon.
Yield: 65 4-ounce cups

Alice Graham Underhill (Mrs. T. Reed)

ORANGE-COCONUT DRINK

5 cups milk
1 (16-ounce) can cream of coconut
1 (12-ounce) can orange juice concentrate, thawed
1 cup vodka (or more to taste)
Shredded coconut, for garnish
Ice cubes
Mint sprigs (optional)

Combine milk, cream of coconut, and orange juice concentrate. When ready to serve, transfer half of mixture to blender and add ½ to 1 cup vodka. Blend until smooth and frothy. Add ice cubes and garnish with coconut or mint. Repeat with the rest of the ingredients.
Yield: Makes 10 (10-ounce) drinks

Carol Coleman Pursell (Mrs. Elliot D.)

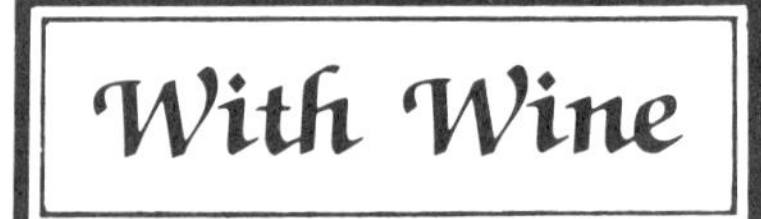

Wine with a special meal can make the meal even more special . . . and people are discovering that wine served with even the simplest meal can make it especially enjoyable.

First, let me say that you shouldn't be intimidated by wines. If you have a favorite wine that you want to serve, by all means—do so. The most important consideration is that wine not have more flavor than the entrée. There is a rule of thumb if you would like a guide, and that is to use white wine with white meats, red wines with red meats, and a rosé is a good compromise. This is not a hard, fast rule but there is reason behind it. If you served a robust red wine with chicken, the red wine would dominate your taste buds and your lovely entrée would be unappreciated. It would be ideal to achieve a good balance so that each complements the other.

Next, all good wines taste better in thin stemmed crystal glasses. My choice is a clear all-purpose eight ounce glass, simple in design that closes slightly at the top. These glasses, of course, are filled no more than one-half to two-thirds full in order for the aroma and bouquet of the wine to be retained above the liquid and savored by the nose. Sparkling wines are commonly served in a shorter, wider six-ounce glass, but there is also a tall, slim nine-ounce glass that is very elegant and retains the bubbles and bouquet of the wine more effectively.

White, rosé and sparkling wines should be served well chilled (50° to 55°) and it is nice to have an ice bucket to keep it in while it is being served. Serve red wines at room temperature (65° to 72°) and if it is a good one, it will benefit the wine to uncork it and let it breathe for an hour or two before serving. Lambrusco is one exception in a red wine that should be served chilled (60°) and another exception is a Beaujolais which should be served slightly cool but not really cold.

The amount of wine served can vary with those you serve, but I usually figure a half bottle per person.

There is nothing wrong with buying a large jug of wine if you are having a good size group and serving it from a carafe. If you are serving from a bottle that has a cork, it is a nice touch to open it at the table. To do this, cut the foil or plastic just below the lip and then wipe the cork clean. Then screw the corkscrew all the way in and slowly draw the cork out and wipe the lip. The host then pours a small amount in his own glass. This is to pour off any bits of cork and also to allow him to taste the wine to be certain it has not spoiled. After this, the ladies are served first and then the gentlemen.

I could at this point suggest a long list of wines. However, I feel that the wine you drink and like is a highly personal matter. For a beginner, I would suggest a Lambrusco or a Beaujolais for a red and a Liebfraumilch for a white. If you are more experienced in wines, try a Cabernet Sauvignon or Zinfandel for your reds and a Chardonnay, dry Chenin Blanc or a premium American Chablis for your whites. Then try different wines and compare them. Keep a list of the ones you like but keep trying new ones as your taste may change. Wines are for enjoyment so make your meals more interesting and fun with this natural beverage.

Barbara Verne Smith of East Carolina Distributing Co., Inc.
Fine Wines and Champagnes,
New Bern, North Carolina

1 jigger = 1½ ounces
1 large jigger = 2 ounces

Most people say jigger when they mean a large jigger.

2 tablespoons = 1 ounce
1 jigger = 3 tablespoons
1 large jigger = 4 tablespoons

½ jigger = 1½ tablespoons
½ large jigger = 2 tablespoons

Hawks House **517 New Street**

The association of this house with the Hawks family lends historical distinction to this architecturally interesting house. Francis Hawks, son of John Hawks who was the architect of Tryon Palace, enlarged the 1760 Georgian house. The Rev. William Hawks who was rector of Christ Church from 1847-1853 lived in this house. The house was moved from Hancock Street in 1975 and restored by former Senior Warden Robert Lee Stallings and his wife, Margaret. The house presently serves as their residence.

MRS. MARIA WHITEHURST'S BEATEN BISCUITS

This is a copy of a handwritten recipe from Miss Sadie Whitehurst's mother's old cookbook. Mrs. Whitehurst's biscuits were famous in New Bern for years.

1 pound (4 cups) flour (Red Band or Roller Champion)
¼ teaspoon soda
1¼ teaspoons salt
¼ pound (½ cup) pure lard
½ cup plus 1 tablespoon cold water

Preheat oven to 450-475 degrees. Sift flour with soda and salt. Rub lard in thoroughly. Add water and mix. Knead thoroughly until it looks smooth and leathery. This is your opportunity to use your antique biscuit machine if you have one. Otherwise, use rolling pin to flatten dough about ¼-inch thick and cut out. Bake 15 minutes on a thin black pan. A tin pan with tin burnt off is preferable or a thin aluminum pan burnt dark.

ANGEL BISCUITS

5 cups self-rising flour
⅓ cup sugar
1 cup Crisco
2 cups buttermilk
3 packages yeast
⅓ cup warm water

Dissolve yeast in ⅓ cup warm water. Mix flour and sugar and cut Crisco into flour mixture. Mix buttermilk with flour mixture and then add yeast mixture. Mix all together and put in refrigerator and chill. Take out as needed. Pat out on floured board or waxed paper and cut out with biscuit cutter or glass. Put in greased pan and let rise in warm place 2-3 hours before baking. Preheat oven to 425 degrees and bake biscuits 12 minutes or until done. Dough will last 10 days refrigerated in Tupperware container.
Yield: 60 biscuits

Sally Harris Pugh, (Mrs. W. Braxton, Jr.)
Mary Ann Psychas Dunn (Mrs. John G., III)

MAYONNAISE BISCUITS

A bit like popovers
Very easy

1 cup self-rising flour
½ cup milk
1 tablespoon mayonnaise
Butter

Preheat oven to 450 degrees. Melt butter in muffin tins, ½ teaspoon per muffin. Mix remaining ingredients and pour into tins. Bake approximately 15 minutes.
Yield: Approximately 12

Margaret Mills Bagg (Mrs. John C., Jr.)

MATTIE'S SWEET POTATO BISCUITS

Part done ahead
Stores well

For a special treat take biscuits hot from oven and fill with butter and a thin slice of sharp Cheddar cheese and/or ham. Keep hot in oven (door ajar and heat off) until cheese is melted. I served these to a hungry crowd after a mixed doubles tennis tournament and they were the hit of the day. The men stood by the kitchen door ready to pounce each time a tray came through.

2 cups sweet potatoes*
⅓ cup butter or margarine
⅓ cup sugar
4 cups self-rising flour
1 cup shortening
1-2 tablespoons water, if needed

*3 medium sweet potatoes or the canned equivalent
Boil peeled and cut sweet potatoes about 20 minutes. Preheat oven to 450 degrees. Drain potatoes, mash and add butter and sugar while still hot. Sift flour into mixture. Cut in shortening. Add water, if needed for right consistency. Roll out and cut to size and thickness you like. Bake about 10 minutes or until lightly browned.
Yield: 4-5 dozen medium-sized biscuits

Dora Winters Taylor (Mrs. John T., Jr.)

BOHEMIAN DUMPLINGS

500 grams flour (2¼ cups)
1 cup milk
2 eggs
2 large rolls
1 tablespoon lard
Salt
Nutmeg

Mix together flour, eggs, spices and milk. Beat until air bubbles form. Dice rolls and brown in lard, add to batter. Bring salted water to boil; add dough by tablespoons. Let simmer for 15-20 minutes.

Gisela N. von zur Muehlen Ives (Mrs. George A., Jr.)

CORN DODGER DUMPLINGS

2 cups white corn meal
1 teaspoon salt
1½ cups boiling water
1 tablespoon bacon fat

Combine the corn meal and salt in a large bowl. Add enough of the boiling water to make a batter that can be shaped with the hands. Stir in the bacon fat and refrigerate for 20 minutes or more. Drop into boiling liquid and cook 20-30 minutes until dumplings are light.
Yield: 16 dodgers

FLOUR DUMPLINGS

1 cup sifted flour
2 teaspoons baking powder
½ teaspoon salt
½ cup milk
2 tablespoons salad oil

Sift dry ingredients together. Combine milk and oil and add to dry ingredients, stirring until mixture is just moistened. Batter will be lumpy. Drop by tablespoonfuls on top bubbling stew. Cover tightly and bring to a boil. Reduce heat and simmer 12-15 minutes *without lifting* the *cover* of the pot!

Soak cotton fabric in mixture of 1 gallon of cold water mixed with 3 tablespoons white vinegar for 10 minutes to check if colorfast. Wash and dry normally.

YORKSHIRE PUDDING

¼ cup roast beef fat drippings
1 cup sifted flour
1 teaspoon salt
2 eggs
1 cup milk

Heat oven to 425 degrees. Coat an 8- or 9-inch square baking pan with fat drippings. Place pan in oven and heat 5 minutes. Meanwhile sift together flour and salt into mixing bowl. In another bowl beat eggs slightly and stir in milk. Stir egg mixture into flour mixture. Beat until smooth using a wire whip. Pour batter into heated pan and bake uncovered for 30 minutes or until puffed and golden brown. Spoon out and serve immediately. Pudding may also be made in individual custard cups or popover pan.
Yield: 6 servings

SALAD CROUTONS

¼ cup vegetable oil
10 slices white bread
½ teaspoon garlic salt
¼ cup Parmesan cheese, grated
Parsley flakes

Preheat oven to 300 degrees. Trim crusts from bread and brush with oil. Mix garlic salt with Parmesan cheese. Cut bread into ½-inch cubes and toss in the mixture. Place on a cookie sheet, sprinkle parsley flakes on top, and bake for 30 minutes, stirring once. Store in plastic bags until ready to use.

Ann Harris Bustard (Mrs. Victor W.)

SOPAPILLAS

Bread to be eaten with Mexican food or used as dessert

2 cups sifted flour
3 teaspoons baking powder
½ teaspoon salt
1 tablespoon sugar
1 cup milk (approximately)

Add milk to all ingredients until firm. Knead until smooth. Let stand in covered bowl for 30 minutes. On floured board roll dough very thin. Cut in 3-inch squares and fry in deep fat for 2 minutes. Serve honey at the table to pour inside the sopapillas.

Nancy Smith Favor (Mrs. William A., Jr.)

SPOON BREAD

2 cups milk, scalded
1 cup white corn meal
4 eggs, separated
¼ cup butter
1 tablespoon sugar
½ teaspoon salt

Preheat oven to 375 degrees. Grease 2-quart baking dish with Pam. Gradually add corn meal to milk. Cook and stir over medium heat until mixture thickens and becomes smooth. Beat egg yolks until thick and lemon colored. Blend corn meal mixture into egg yolks and add butter, salt and sugar. Mix well. Beat egg whites into peaks, stiff but not dry. Fold in with other mixture. Bake in prepared dish for 35-40 minutes. Serve immediately.
Yield: 4-6 servings

Nancy McDaniel Lewis

THE BEST CORN BREAD

This is moist, much like spoon bread
Very good reheated
Very good with maple syrup

2 eggs
1 cup sour cream
½ cup salad oil
1 cup creamed corn *OR* 1 (7-ounce) can
1 cup corn meal
3 teaspoons baking powder
1½ teaspoons salt

Preheat oven to 375 degrees. Beat eggs, sour cream, oil and corn. Blend corn meal, baking powder and salt. Bake for 30-40 minutes in an 8 x 8-inch pan or 9 x 9-inch pan. Shortcut: Use 1 cup Ballard's corn bread mix instead of corn meal, salt and baking powder.

Cathy Gross Hendren (Mrs. Thomas E.)

CORN FRITTERS

¾ cup flour
1 teaspoon baking powder
½ teaspoon salt
1 tablespoon sugar
1 egg, well-beaten
2 tablespoons milk
1 (12-ounce) can whole kernel corn, drained
Hot fat

Sift flour with baking powder, salt and sugar. Mix egg, milk and corn together. Add flour mixture and beat quickly, but thoroughly. Drop batter by tablespoonfuls into deep fat which has reached 360 degrees. Fry a few fritters at a time until golden brown.
Yield: 1 dozen fritters

Ceceila Chrismon Hudson (Mrs. Forrest M.)

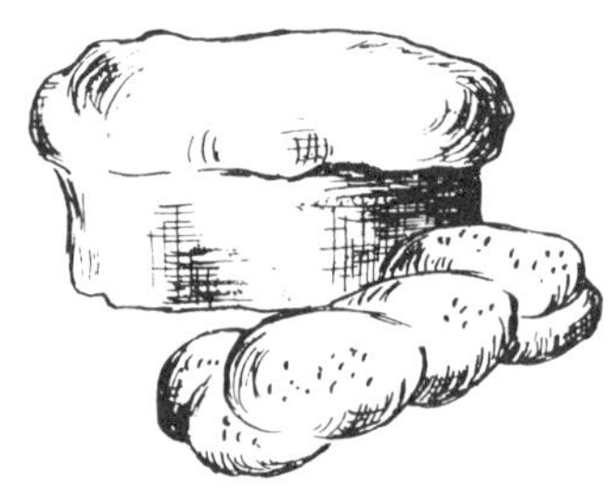

EASTERN NORTH CAROLINA CORN BREAD

Recipe may be halved

1 cup corn meal
½ cup flour
2 teaspoons baking powder
1 teaspoon salt
2 teaspoons sugar
1 cup milk
2 eggs
½ cup shortening

Preheat oven to 400 degrees. Grease baking pan or muffin tins. Sift together corn meal, flour, baking powder, salt and sugar. Stir in milk. Add eggs, one at a time. Add melted shortening. Pour into prepared baking dish and bake 20-25 minutes.
Yield: 8 servings

Myrtle Mason Stephens (Mrs. Ira)

WILLIAMSBURG SALLY LUNN BREAD

Can be frozen

1 yeast cake
1 cup milk, warmed
½ cup butter
⅓ cup sugar
3 eggs, beaten
4 cups flour

Preheat oven to 350 degrees. Put yeast cake in warm milk. Cream together butter and sugar; add eggs and mix well. Sift in flour alternately with the milk-yeast. Let rise in a warm place, then beat well. Pour into one well-buttered Sally Lunn mold or one 3-quart ring mold. Let rise again before baking 45 minutes or until done. Serve hot. Can be frozen and warmed slowly in foil before serving.

Ann Caudle Wells (Mrs. Ronald D.)

Dark breads may be made by substituting white flour in basic white bread recipes. The more dark flour in your recipe, the longer it will take to rise, but they do not double in bulk when they rise. Do not use more than 3 cups of dark flour in the recipe of 6 cups. Add white flour or whole wheat flour during the first, second and sixth additions while other flours should be added the third, fourth and fifth cups added.

ONION CASSEROLE BREAD

1 cup milk
¼ cup sugar
2 teaspoons salt
¼ cup margarine
½ cup lukewarm water
1 egg
4½ cups flour
1 (16-ounce) can French Fried Onion Rings
2 packages or cakes of yeast

Scald milk. Add sugar, salt and margarine. Cool. Dissolve yeast in lukewarm water. Add milk mixture, egg and 3 cups flour to yeast mixture. Beat. Add remaining flour. Cover and let rise 1 hour. Add onion rings and mix well. Put in 2 greased 2½- or 3-quart casseroles. Bake immediately at 350 degrees for 40 minutes. It is done when it "breaks" around the sides. Remove from casseroles and slice.
Yield: 2 loaves

Eleanor Elizabeth Richardson (Mrs. Asa C.)

POP HILLER'S MIXED BREAD

A heavy German bread

2 cups lukewarm water
2 tablespoons Crisco
2 tablespoons sugar
2 teaspoons salt
2 cups cooked grits
1 package dry yeast
6 cups flour (approximately)

In a large bowl, dissolve yeast in water. Add Crisco, sugar, salt and grits. Stir in enough flour to make a stiff batter. Cover with a damp towel and let rise in a warm spot until doubled in bulk. Divide into 2 greased loaf pans. Let double again. Preheat oven to 425 degrees and bake for 50 minutes.
Yield: 2 loaves

Anne Fowler Hiller (Mrs. Carl J.)

Bread dough may be shaped into loaves and wrapped in plastic or foil and frozen. When ready to bake, put frozen dough in greased loaf pan and let thaw and rise in warm place until almost doubled in bulk, about 6 hours, or thaw in refrigerator overnight and let rise 2 hours in warm place before baking.

AUNT ROBERTA'S DILLY BREAD

2½-3 cups flour
2 tablespoons sugar
1 tablespoon instant minced onion
2 teaspoons dill seed
1¼ teaspoons coarse salt
¼ teaspoon baking soda
1 envelope dry yeast
1½ cups creamed cottage cheese
¼ cup water
1 tablespoon butter or margarine
1 egg

In large mixing bowl combine 1½ cups flour, sugar, onion, dill seed, salt, soda, yeast. In saucepan heat cottage cheese, water, and butter until warm. Add egg and warm mixture to dry ingredients in bowl. Blend at lowest speed until moistened. Beat 3 minutes at medium speed. By hand, stir in remaining flour to form stiff dough. Cover and let rise in warm place until doubled in size, about one hour. Stir down batter. Turn into well-greased 8-inch round casserole. Cover and let rise in warm place until light, 35-45 minutes. Bake in preheated 350 degree oven for 35-40 minutes until golden brown. Brush with butter and sprinkle with coarse salt.

Jeanne Upton Freemon (Mrs. Joseph M.)

KNITTING CLASS BEER BREAD

3 cups self-rising flour
3 heaping tablespoons sugar
1 (12-ounce) can beer
Butter

Preheat oven to 350 degrees. Grease and flour baking dish or loaf pan. Combine flour, sugar and beer together. Pour into prepared pan. Bake 60 minutes on middle shelf of oven. Dot top of bread with 6 thin slices of butter placed in a line. Bread slices best using an electric knife.

Ethel Stark's recipe
submitted by Marian Bartlett Stewart (Mrs. Wm. Edward)

FAITH'S PARTY OR LUNCHEON MUFFINS

Tiny muffins cups
1 cup butter, softened
2 cups self-rising flour
1 (8-ounce) carton sour cream

Preheat oven to 350 degrees. Combine all ingredients and bake for 20-25 minutes.
Yield: 3 dozen

Libby Jones Wrenn (Mrs. James H., Jr.)

BEST MUFFINS

2 cups sifted flour
2½ teaspoons baking powder
2 tablespoons sugar
1 teaspoon grated orange peel (optional)
1 cup fresh blueberries (optional)
¾ teaspoon salt
½ cup margarine
1 egg, well-beaten
¾ cup milk

Preheat oven to 400 degrees. Sift together flour, baking powder, sugar and salt in mixing bowl. Cut in shortening until crumbs are size of small peas. Make a hollow in center. Combine egg and milk; add all at once to the hollow in dry ingredients. Stir only until dry ingredients are just moist. Batter will be lumpy. If desired, stir in orange peel and fold in blueberries. Fill greased muffin tins ⅔ full. Cast-iron muffin tins work best. Bake in hot oven about 25 minutes.
Yield: 12 muffins

Lynda Horner

REFRIGERATOR BRAN MUFFINS

Keeps well
Can freeze
Can double

1 cup Bran Buds
1 cup boiling water
¾ cup margarine
1½ cups sugar
2 eggs
2½ cups flour
2½ teaspoons baking soda
Dash salt
2 cups buttermilk
2 cups All-Bran
1½ cups raisins (optional)

Mix Bran Buds and water and set aside to cool. Cream margarine, sugar, and eggs and add to Bran Buds. Add flour, baking soda and salt. Fold in buttermilk and All-Bran. Store in refrigerator and use as needed. Never stir again. Will keep six weeks in refrigerator and longer in freezer. To bake: preheat oven to 400 degrees and spoon batter into lightly greased muffin tins. Bake 15 minutes.

Deborah Cook Tayloe (Mrs. John C.)
Mary Sue Price Pelletier
Elizabeth Allen Brinkley (Mrs. William E., Jr.)

DATE-OATMEAL MUFFINS

1 cup flour
1 cup quick-cooking oats
3 teaspoons baking powder
½ teaspoon salt
⅓ cup brown sugar, firmly packed
¾ cup milk
½ cup applesauce*
¾ cup chopped dates
1 egg, beaten
½ cup margarine, melted

*Applesauce was presweetened with sugar. Cinnamon was added to taste. Preheat oven to 400 degrees. Lightly butter, or spray bottoms of 15 medium cups. Melt margarine. Sift dry ingredients into large bowl. Beat egg in large measuring cup; add milk and applesauce; stir well and add cooled melted margarine. Stir with quick strokes the liquid into the dry ingredients until just combined. Add dates. Spoon into muffin cups. Bake 20-25 minutes.
Yield: 12-15 muffins

Barbara Straub Stewart

COCONUT MUFFINS

2 eggs, separated
2 tablespoons butter, softened
2 tablespoons honey
¼ teaspoon almond extract
⅓ cup boiling water
¾ cup unsweetened coconut
¾ cup unbleached flour

Preheat oven to 350 degrees. Beat egg yolks. Add remaining ingredients except egg whites. Beat whites until stiff and fold in. Pour into greased tins. Bake for 20-25 minutes. If sweetened coconut is used, eliminate the honey.
Yield: 12 muffins

Peggy Witmeyer Bernard

TOP OF THE MORNING MUFFINS

Can freeze
Taste and texture similar to the bakery's best crullers

Muffin batter:
3 tablespoons butter
3 tablespoons vegetable oil
½ cup sugar
1 egg
½ cup milk
2 cups flour
1½ teaspoons baking powder
½ teaspoon salt
¼-½ teaspoon ground nutmeg to taste

Grease 12 muffin cups. Preheat oven to 350 degrees. Beat butter, oil and sugar until creamy. Add egg; beat well; add milk, beat well. Sift dry ingredients together and add to the first mixture. Pour into muffin cups filling ⅔ full. Bake for 25 minutes.

Topping;
3 tablespoons butter, melted
½ cup sugar
1 teaspoon cinnamon

Combine sugar and cinnamon. Set aside. Melt butter. When muffins have finished baking, remove from oven and brush tops with melted butter. Sprinkle with cinnamon-sugar before removing them from tins.
Yield: 12 muffins

Anne Fowler Hiller (Mrs. Carl J.)

GRAHAM CRACKER MUFFINS

2 cups graham cracker crumbs
4 tablespoons sugar
½ teaspoon salt
4 teaspoons baking powder
4 tablespoons shortening, melted
1 cup milk, warmed
2 eggs, slightly beaten
1 cup nuts, chopped
1 cup raisins

Preheat oven to 375 degrees. Add sugar, salt, baking powder to crumbs. Add milk and shortening, beaten eggs, nuts and raisins. Bake 25 minutes.
Yield: 12 muffins

Alice Smith Flood (Mrs. Robert)

ORANGE MUFFINS

Can be frozen

1 cup sugar
2 tablespoons margarine
2 eggs, beaten lightly
⅔ cup orange juice
3 cups flour
1 tablespoon baking powder
½ teaspoon salt
½ cup milk
1 tablespoon orange bits *or* grated orange rind

Grease 18 muffin cups. Preheat oven to 400 degrees.

Cake-like muffins:
Cream butter and sugar; add eggs. Sift dry ingredients together and add ½ dry ingredients to egg mixture. Beat in milk and add the rest of the dry mixture. Add orange bits and orange juice. Fill muffin cups ⅔ full. Bake 20-25 minutes for regular-sized muffin tins and 15-17 minutes for miniature-sized muffin tins.

Muffin-like texture:
Combine sifted dry ingredients including orange bits in a large bowl. Melt margarine; beat eggs; combine milk, orange juice, eggs and cooled melted margarine in a large measuring cup. Pour liquid into dry ingredients stirring with a fork until dry ingredients are just combined and moistened. Batter should NOT be smooth. Fill muffin cups and bake as above.
Yield: 18 medium-sized/36 miniature-sized muffins

Barbara Straub Stewart

VANILLA MUFFINS

2 cups Bisquick baking mix
2 tablespoons sugar
1 egg
⅔ cup milk
1 teaspoon vanilla

Preheat oven to 400 degrees. Grease 12 muffin cups. Mix ingredients together and beat 30 seconds. Fill muffin cups ⅔ full. Bake about 15 minutes or until golden brown.
Yield: 12 muffins

Frances L'Espérance Bollen (Mrs. Russell E.)

MORAVIAN SUGAR CAKE

2 cups milk
1 package yeast
½ cup warm water
1 cup cooled mashed potatoes (best if whipped)
½ teaspoon salt
8½ cups sifted flour
½ cup butter, melted
½ cup Crisco, melted
2 eggs, beaten
1 cup granulated sugar
2 cups light brown sugar
½ cup butter
1½ teaspoons cinnamon
½ teaspoon nutmeg
½ cup pecans, chopped
36 pecan halves

Scald milk, cool to lukewarm. Dissolve yeast in water. In large mixing bowl combine cooled milk, dissolved yeast, mashed potatoes, salt and mix well. Gradually add 4 cups flour and beat well. Cover and let rise in a warm place about 1 hour. Add melted butter, shortening, eggs, granulated sugar and beat well. Gradually add remaining flour. (Cinnamon and nutmeg may be added to flour for a different touch.) Mix the dough well after each addition of flour until a smooth dough is formed. Spread dough in three greased 9 x 2-inch round pans or 3 bread pans or a combination. Cover and let rise in a warm place until doubled in bulk, about 1 hour. Make 12 or more indentations in each cake, fewer for small ones. Using 1 cup brown sugar, ½ cup softened butter, ½ teaspoon cinnamon and chopped pecans, fill each indention. Combine remaining brown sugar and cinnamon and sprinkle proportionately on each cake and top with pecan halves. Bake at 375 degrees for 15-20 minutes. Check doneness with broomstraw.
Yield: 3 (9-inch) round cakes or 3 loaf cakes

Kathleen Harris Ingraham

JEWISH COFFEE CAKE

1 cup sour cream
½ teaspoon baking soda
1 cup margarine
1 cup sugar
2 eggs
1 teaspoon vanilla
1½ cups unsifted flour
1½ teaspoons baking powder

Mix sour cream and soda and let stand 1 hour. Cream margarine and sugar. Add eggs one at a time; add vanilla. Stir in sour cream mixture, flour and baking powder. Set aside.

Topping:
½ cup brown sugar
½ cup nuts, chopped
1 teaspoon cinnamon

Mix topping ingredients together. Pour half the batter into an ungreased 8 x 11-inch pan. Sprinkle half of topping over batter and spread around. Add remaining batter; sprinkle remaining topping over batter. Bake at 325 degrees for 30 minutes. DO NOT OVERBAKE. After baking, this cake will settle as it cools.

Eleanor Elizabeth Richardson (Mrs. Asa C.)

RASPBERRY CREAM CHEESE COFFEE CAKE

1 (3-ounce) package cream cheese, softened
4 tablespoons butter
2 cups Bisquick
⅓ cup milk
½ cup raspberry preserves
1 cup confectioners' sugar, sifted
1 to 2 tablespoons milk
½ teaspoon vanilla or lemon juice

Cut cream cheese and butter into Bisquick mix until crumbly. Blend in ⅓ cup milk. Turn onto a floured surface and knead 8-10 strokes. On waxed paper, roll dough to a 12 x 8-inch rectangle. Turn onto a greased baking sheet and remove paper. Make two ½-inch cuts on both long sides of the rectangle. Spread raspberry jam down the center. Fold cut edges, one overlapping the next and the center giving a braided look. Combine sugar, remaining milk and vanilla and drizzle atop the cake. Bake in preheated 425 degree oven for 12-15 minutes. These freeze well, wrapped in tin foil. Also will make smaller cakes; divide the dough in half. It is good with other fillings such as lemon cream but because the dough is sweet, sour fillings are best.

Jane Ingraham Ashford (Mrs. Charles H., Jr.)

BLUEBERRY COFFEE CAKE

Dough:

4 eggs + 2 yolks at room temperature
1½ cups milk, scalded
½ cup sugar
½ cup butter (half may be margarine)
½ teaspoon salt
2 packages dry yeast
7 cups flour

Allow scalded milk to cool to 110 degrees and add sugar, butter, salt and dry yeast. Let rest 5 minutes. Beat eggs with mixer; add cooled milk-yeast mixture; add flour until dough pulls away from side of bowl. Cover with waxed paper. Allow to double in size, about 1½ hours. Punch down and divide into 6 equal pieces and press into no-stick sprayed pie plates. Cover and let double, about 30 minutes.

Filling:

4 cups blueberries
1 cup blueberries
½ cup water
2 tablespoons cornstarch
¾ cup sugar
1 teaspoon cinnamon
½ teaspoon nutmeg
2 tablespoons lemon juice

Bring 1 cup berries and water to a boil and simmer 2 minutes. Add juice gradually to cornstarch, sugar, cinnamon and nutmeg in another saucepan over medium heat until mixture thickens. Add lemon juice when thick. Pat 4 cups berries divided over six pies. Add syrup and sprinkle on topping. Bake in preheated 350 degree oven 30-35 minutes.

Topping:

1 cup flour
1 cup sugar
½ cup margarine, softened

Mix the above until crumbly.

I like to add confectioners' sugar icing after baking, and before serving. If you plan to freeze, do not add confectioners' sugar icing until after thawed, and reheated.

Yield: 6 coffeecakes

Barbara Straub Stewart

CRUMB-TOPPED COFFEE CAKE

Easy enough for a child to make

1½ cups flour
½ cup sugar
½ cup butter or margarine
½ teaspoon baking soda
¼ teaspoon baking powder
¼ teaspoon salt
1½-2 teaspoons cinnamon
1½ teaspoons unsweetened cocoa
½ teaspoon nutmeg
Dash of cloves
½ cup chopped nuts
½ cup raisins
1 cup buttermilk

Preheat oven to 350 degrees. Grease (not oil) and flour 9-inch square pan. Lightly spoon flour into measuring cup; level off. In large bowl combine flour and sugar. Using pastry blender, cut in butter until particles are size of small peas. Reserve 1 cup crumb mixture; set aside. To remaining crumb mixture, add remaining ingredients except buttermilk; blend well. Make a well in dry ingredients; add buttermilk. By hand, stir just until dry ingredients are moistened. Pour batter into prepared pan; sprinkle with reserved crumbs. Bake 30-35 minutes until toothpick inserted in center comes out clean. Serve warm or cool.
Yield: 10-12 servings

Catherine Scaffide Homendy (Mrs. Edward S.)

MY MOTHER'S DATE NUT BREAD

Stores well
Can be frozen

4 eggs, unbeaten
1 cup sugar
½ cup salad oil
1 teaspoon salt
1 cup flour, sifted
1 pound whole pitted dates
4 cups pecan halves

Grease and flour one 9 x 5-inch pan or two smaller loaf pans, as desired. Combine eggs, sugar and oil. Beat well. Add remaining ingredients and mix well. Place in pan(s) and bake in slow oven (275-300 degrees) which has NOT been preheated. Place pan(s) on a cookie sheet and bake 2 hours for one loaf or 1¼ hours for two smaller loaves. Allow to cool thoroughly before wrapping in plastic wrap or foil. Bread may be kept in refrigerator.

Dora Winters Taylor (Mrs. John T., Jr.)

BANANA NUT BREAD

1 cup butter or margarine
2 cups sugar
4 eggs
¼ teaspoon salt
2 teaspoons soda
4 cups flour
6 large, very ripe bananas, mashed
1 cup pecans, finely chopped
Pecans, for garnish

Preheat oven to 275 degrees. Grease two loaf pans and set aside. Cream together butter and sugar. Add eggs, one at a time, beating well after each addition. Sift dry ingredients together and add to creamed mixture. Add bananas and nuts. Pour into prepared pans and bake for 1½ hours. Additional pecans may be sprinkled on top of loaves prior to baking, if desired.
Yield: 2 loaves

Helen Uzzell Morton (Mrs. John)

Very ripe bananas can be mashed into pulp and frozen for later use in banana bread or daiquiris. Squeeze a small amount of lemon juice on top of the pulp before freezing to prevent browning. However, the thin top brownish layer can be skimmed off, and the banana pulp is ready to use.

CHRISTMAS CRANBERRY BREAD

2 cups flour
1 cup sugar
1½ teaspoons baking powder
½ teaspoon baking soda
1 teaspoon salt
¼ cup shortening
¾ cup orange juice
1 tablespoon orange rind, grated
1 egg, well-beaten
½ cup nuts, chopped
2 cups Ocean Spray cranberries, chopped

Preheat oven to 350 degrees. Sift together flour, sugar, baking powder, soda and salt. Cut in shortening until mixture resembles coarse corn meal. Combine orange juice and grated rind with well-beaten egg. Pour into dry ingredients, mixing just enough to dampen. Fold in nuts and cranberries. Spoon into greased loaf pan. Spread corners and sides slightly higher than the center. Bake for one hour until crust is golden brown and center is done. Remove. Cool and store overnight for easy slicing.
Yield: 1 loaf

Isabelle Schocke Taylor (Mrs. Elijah)

PEANUT BUTTER BREAD

2 cups flour
4 teaspoons baking powder
1 teaspoon salt
1/3 cup sugar
1/2 cup peanut butter
1 1/2 cups milk

Preheat oven to 350 degrees. Grease two small loaf pans. Sift dry ingredients and add peanut butter and mix as for biscuits. Add milk and beat well. Pour into loaf pans and smooth tops. Bake one hour. Cool; remove from pans; wrap and let stand overnight before slicing.
Yield: 2 small loaves

Isabelle Schocke Taylor (Mrs. Elijah)

NANA'S NUT BREAD

4 cups flour
1 1/2 cups sugar
1 cup English walnuts, cut fine
4 teaspoons baking powder
1/2 teaspoon salt
2 cups milk
2 eggs

Preheat oven to 350 degrees. Grease and flour two loaf pans. Mix nuts with flour, sugar, baking powder and salt. Add eggs and milk and mix well. Pour into two bread pans and let set for 20 minutes covered with a dish towel. Bake for 1 hour.
Yield: 2 loaves

Polly Speace Miller (Mrs. Robert F.)

ZUCCHINI BREAD

3 eggs
2 cups sugar
1 cup oil
2 cups unpeeled zucchini, grated
3 cups flour
1 teaspoon salt
1 teaspoon cinnamon
1 teaspoon baking powder
1 teaspoon soda
1 cup nuts, chopped
1 teaspoon vanilla

Mix all ingredients together and pour into greased and floured loaf pans. Bake in preheated 350 degree oven for 1 hour.
Yield: 2 loaves

Nancy Blood Thoman (Mrs. Mark)

STRAWBERRY NUT BREAD

1 cup butter
1½ cups sugar
1 teaspoon vanilla
1 teaspoon salt
½ teaspoon baking soda
¼ teaspoon lemon extract
4 eggs
3 cups sifted flour
1 teaspoon cream of tartar
1 cup strawberry jam or preserves
½ cup sour cream
1 cup walnuts, chopped

Preheat oven to 350 degrees. Grease and flour five 4½ x 2¾ x 2½-inch loaf pans. Cream butter, sugar, vanilla and lemon extract until fluffy. Add eggs, one at a time, beating well after each addition. Sift together flour, salt, cream of tartar and soda. Combine jam and sour cream. Add jam mixture alternately with dry ingredients to creamed mixture, beating until well-combined. Stir in nuts. Divide among 5 small loaf pans. Bake 50 minutes or until done.
Yield: 5 loaves

Ann Harris Bustard (Mrs. Victor W.)

CHRISTMAS STOLLEN

2 cups milk
1 pound shortening (2 cups)
1 cup sugar
2 teaspoons salt
4 eggs, beaten
2 yeast cakes (or dry powdered yeast)
¼ cup water
8 cups flour
1 cup citron
1 cup raisins
2 tablespoons lemon rind, grated
2 tablespoons orange rind, grated
1 teaspoon nutmeg
Butter

Scald milk. Pour over shortening, sugar and salt. Cool to lukewarm. Add eggs; add yeast that has been softened in ¼ cup water. Add 4 cups flour and beat. Add citron, raisins, rinds, nutmeg and remaining flour. Knead and place in covered pan to rise 3-4 hours. Punch down and divide into loaves. Cover and let rise 1½-2 hours. Bake at 325 degrees for 50 minutes. While bread is still hot, spread butter over top of each loaf.
Yield: 2 loaves

Maud Smith Stow

PERK SPEER'S LEMON TEA BREAD

May be doubled
Freezes well

2 cups sugar
¾ cup margarine
4 eggs
1 cup milk
3 cups flour
2 teaspoons baking powder
1 cup nuts, chopped
Grated rind of 2 large lemons
1 teaspoon lemon extract

Preheat oven to 350 degrees. Grease and flour 4 small loaf pans. Cream sugar and margarine. Add remaining ingredients. Divide batter among pans. Bake 45 minutes.

Icing:
Juice of 2 lemons
1½-2 cups super fine sugar

Mix juice and sugar and spoon over bread as soon as it is removed from oven. Leave bread in pans until completely cooled. Use spatula and patience to remove from pans.

Martha Hughes Matthews (Mrs. F. Clayton)

PUMPKIN BREAD

3⅓ cups flour
2 teaspoons baking soda
1½ teaspoons salt
1 teaspoon cinnamon
1 teaspoon nutmeg
4 eggs
⅔ cup water
2 cups pumpkin
1 cup oil
3 cups sugar
1 cup nuts

Preheat oven to 350 degrees. Grease 2 loaf pans and set aside. Mix dry ingredients; add remaining ingredients as listed. Pour into pans about ¾ full. Bake 45 minutes or until toothpick comes out clean.

Shirley Taylor Pridgen (Mrs. Lonnie E., Jr.)

Variation:
Add 1 cup raisins and ¼ cup coconut to above recipe.

Ann Skinner Wade (Mrs. Leon, Jr.)

HEALTH BREAD

1½ cups water
1 cup cottage cheese
½ cup honey
¼ cup margarine
5½-6 cups flour
1 cup whole wheat flour
2 tablespoons sugar
3 teaspoons salt
2 packages yeast
1 egg
¼ cup wheat germ

Heat first 4 ingredients to 120 degrees. Combine warm liquid, 2 cups of the flour and the remaining ingredients in a large mixing bowl. Beat 2 minutes at medium speed. Hand stir remaining flour into mixture to make stiff dough. Knead well on floured surface. Place in greased bowl, cover, and let rise 1 hour. Grease two 9 x 5-inch bread pans. Punch down dough and shape into 2 loaves. Place in pans, cover and let rise for another hour. Bake at 350 degrees for 40-50 minutes. When removed from pan, grease tops of loaves with margarine.
Yield: 2 loaves

Gretchen Deichmann Speer (Mrs. Howard)

NANCY'S BREAD STICKS

3-3½ cups unsifted flour
1 tablespoon sugar
1 teaspoon salt
2 packages dry yeast
¼ cup olive or salad oil
1¼ cups HOT water
1 egg white, beaten with 1 tablespoon water
Coarse salt
Toasted sesame seed
Dill weed
Poppy seed

OIL baking sheets. Put into large mixing bowl, 1 cup flour, sugar, salt and yeast. Stir to blend. Add oil; gradually stir in hot water and beat two minutes. Add ½ cup flour and beat; stir in remaining flour to form soft dough. On floured surface form dough into smooth ball by kneading 5 minutes. Place dough in greased bowl; cover with damp towel and let rise in warm place about 1 hour until double. Punch down and divide into quarters. Roll each into long rope and cut rope into 6-8 sticks. Place parallel on baking sheets about ½-1 inch apart. Brush with egg white and sprinkle with choice of salt, sesame seed, dill weed or poppy seed. Allow to double about 30 minutes then bake in preheated 300 degree oven 25-30 minutes.
Yield: 2-4 dozen (depending on length of stick)

PRETZELS

Do ahead

1 package dry yeast
1½ cups warm water
1 teaspoon salt
1 teaspoon sugar
3½-4 cups flour
1 egg, beaten
Coarse salt

Dissolve yeast in water in large bowl. Stir in salt and sugar plus 2 cups flour. Beat well. Add remaining flour to make dough easy to handle. Knead 5 minutes. Cover and let rise 45-60 minutes. Punch dough down and cut into 16 equal parts. Roll each into a rope of 18 inches and loop to form a pretzel. Brush with beaten egg. Sprinkle with coarse salt. Place on greased cookie sheet and bake 15-20 minutes in preheated 400 degree oven. Slip under broiler for 30 seconds to brown them more.

Diane Roche McQuade (Mrs. John F.)

CRUSTY FRENCH BREAD

May freeze
Prepare ahead

¼ cup warm water*
1 package yeast, dry or compressed
2 cups warm water
2 teaspoons salt
2 tablespoons sugar
6 cups flour, sifted

*105 degrees for dry yeast, 95 degrees for compressed yeast

Add yeast to ¼ cup water with a pinch of the sugar. Let rest 5 minutes. Sift and measure flour. Mix dry ingredients together in mixing bowl with yeast and additional water. Mix until dough leaves the side of the bowl and becomes a ball. Remove from mixing bowl to floured surface and knead in additional flour until dough no longer sticks to the board and is shiny and smooth. Put dough in greased bowl turning to grease top. Cover and set in warm place to rise. Let dough rise until almost doubled, about 1½ hours. Punch down, squeezing out air bubbles and divide in half. Form two elongated loaves, placing on lightly greased cookie sheets. Cover and let rise about 30 minutes. Brush top with water before baking and make diagonal slashes in top with a sharp knife. Bake in preheated 400 degree oven for 45 minutes with a shallow pan of hot water in oven bottom.

Yield: 2 loaves

BLUE RIBBON WHOLE WHEAT BREAD

2 packages yeast
2 cups warm milk
1 egg
½ cup honey
1 tablespoon salt
3½ cups whole wheat flour
1 cup plus 1 tablespoon shortening, melted
3-3½ cups flour

Dissolve yeast in milk. Stir in egg, honey and salt. Mix well. Add whole wheat flour and shortening, mixing well. Gradually add enough flour to form a moderately stiff dough; beating well after each addition. Place dough in slightly greased bowl, turning to grease top. Cover and let rise in a warm place (85 degrees), free from draft, for 1½ hours, or until doubled in bulk. Put into two loaf pans, kneading well to shape of pans. Let rise 1½ hours or until doubled. Bake at 400 degrees for about 25 minutes or until golden brown.
Yield: 2 loaves

Thelma Opphile (Mrs. Marion D.)

SWEDISH RYE BREAD

¼-½ cup lukewarm water
3 yeast cakes or packages
¾ cup honey
1 cup sugar
3 tablespoons salt
6 tablespoons orange rind, grated
3 tablespoons caraway seed
4½ cups water
6 tablespoons butter
7-8 cups rye flour
7-8 cups white flour

Dissolve yeast in ¼-½ cup lukewarm water. Heat water and put in large mixing bowl. Add honey, salt, sugar, grated orange rind, caraway seed and butter. After mixture is lukewarm add yeast that has been softened in water. Add flour and knead. Cover and let rise in warm place for 1½ hours (may take longer). Punch down and let rise again for about 1 hour. Divide and shape. Put in six small greased loaf pans and allow to rise until double in bulk. Put water in cookie sheet. Place loaf pans on cookie sheet and put on bottom of oven during baking. Bake at 350 degrees for 30 minutes. Lay sheet of brown paper over loaves to prevent over-browning and continue to bake an additional 30 minutes. Spread butter over top of each loaf while still hot.
Yield: 6 loaves (1 pound each)

Maud Smith Stow

JHONNIE MOM'S ROLLS

Can freeze
Must do day ahead

¾ cup Crisco
1 teaspoon salt
1 cup boiling water
2 eggs, well-beaten
½ cup sugar
1 cup cold water
2 packages yeast
6 cups flour, white or whole wheat

Put Crisco and salt into boiling water. Let cool. Beat eggs and sugar together. Add cold water. Let stand five minutes. Add the two mixtures together. Reserve half the mixture and add yeast. Mix with reserved mixture. Add sifted flour slowly in large electric mixer. When thoroughly mixed store in refrigerator overnight. The next day, punch down, roll out, cut and let rise on baking sheet until doubled. Bake in preheated 375 degree oven for 20 to 30 minutes. Dough may also be frozen.
Yield: 3 dozen rolls

Elizabeth Hancock (Mrs. Seymour)

MY AUNT'S TURKEY DRESSING

A favorite of ours at Christmas!

Do a day head
Freezes well

1 loaf king-sized thin bread, toasted
1 (8-ounce) bag Pepperidge Farm Seasoned Dressing
1 pound hot sausage
4 onions, chopped
5 stalks celery, chopped fine
4 cups water
1 tablespoon salt
Pepper
2 teaspoons sage

Cook sausage and onion together until done. Crumble sausage. Do not drain. Cook celery until tender in 4 cups salted water. Crumble toast. Mix in Pepperidge Farm dressing. Pour sausage-onion mixture with drippings over the toast. Add seasonings. Add celery and hot celery water to moisten toast mixture. (May add more hot water according to how moist you like the dressing.) Stir well. It is best if made a day ahead. Bake in preheated 350 degree oven until slightly browned and bubbly.

Becky Elmore Clement (Mrs. Joseph M.)

YEAST ROLLS

1 package dry yeast
¼ cup lukewarm water
1 cup milk, scalded
2 tablespoons shortening
2 tablespoons sugar
1 teaspoon salt
1 egg, well-beaten
3½ cups sifted flour

Soften yeast in lukewarm water; set aside. Combine scalded milk with shortening, sugar and salt; cool to lukewarm. Add softened yeast and egg. Gradually stir in flour to form soft dough. Beat well. Cover and let rise in warm place until doubled in bulk, about 2 hours; knead again. Shape as desired and place rolls in greased pans. Cover and leave in warm place until doubled in size. Bake at 400 degrees 20-25 minutes.

Thelma Register Scott (Mrs. George)

For especially tender-crusted rolls, brush tops with melted butter before baking or for crisped crusts, brush with milk or egg beaten with 1 tablespoon milk.

RICH DINNER ROLLS

1 cup milk
¼ cup sugar
1 teaspoon salt
¼ cup Fleischmann's margarine
½ cup warm water
2 packages or cakes yeast
2 eggs, beaten
5¼ cups unsifted flour (approximately)

Scald milk. Stir in sugar, salt and margarine. Cool to lukewarm. Measure warm water into large warm bowl. Sprinkle or crumble in yeast. Stir until dissolved. Add lukewarm milk mixture, eggs and two cups flour. Beat until smooth. Stir in enough remaining flour to make soft dough. Turn out onto lightly floured board. Knead until smooth and elastic; about 8 to 10 minutes. Place in greased bowl turning to grease top. Cover and let rise in warm place, free from draft until doubled in bulk, about 30 minutes. Punch down. Divide dough into three equal pieces. Form each piece into a roll 9 inches long. Cut into 9 equal pieces and form into smooth balls. Place in 3 greased round cake pans. Cover and let rise until doubled in bulk, about 30 minutes. Brush lightly with melted margarine. Bake in preheated 375 degree oven about 15 to 20 minutes.
Yield: 27 rolls

Helen Kulba (Mrs. William)

"NO NEED TO KNEAD" ROLLS

2 cups lukewarm water
2 packages dry yeast
1½ teaspoons salt
1 egg
¼ cup shortening
6½ cups flour

Mix well and shape into rolls. Put rolls into greased round cake pans. Cover and let rise 1½-2 hours. Preheat oven to 400 degrees. Bake rolls 15-20 minutes.

Marguerite Banks Tilghman (Mrs. Donald R.)

SOURDOUGH STARTER AND BREAD

Starter:
2 cups flour
2 cups warm water
1 package yeast

Dissolve yeast in warm water. Add flour and mix well. Use only a glass bowl for mixing. Do not leave metal utensils in starter. Place starter in a warm place or closed cupboard overnight. Next morning, cover container and refrigerate. Use only a glass container to store the starter. Refrigerate starter when not in use, and keep covered.

Every 5 days add and stir into starter:

1 cup milk
¼ cup sugar
1 cup flour, unsifted

Do not use starter on the day it is fed. Always keep at least 2 cups of mixture in the container. Starter can be fed more frequently than every five days.

Sourdough Bread:
2 cups flour, unsifted
1 tablespoon baking powder
1 teaspoon salt
2 tablespoons sugar
1 egg
2 cups starter

Mix dry ingredients together. Add egg and starter. Mix well. Turn into greased loaf pan. Place in warm place and allow to double in bulk. Bake in preheated 350 degree oven for 30-35 minutes.
Yield: 1 loaf

Nancy Blood Thoman (Mrs. Mark C.)

SOURDOUGH COFFEE CAKE AND CINNAMON ROLLS

Coffeecake:

1 cup flour, unsifted
¾ teaspoon baking soda
¼ teaspoon salt
¾ cup sugar
½ teaspoon cinnamon
⅓ cup margarine or butter
1 egg
1 cup sourdough starter

Stir together dry ingredients. Cut in margarine. Add egg and starter. Mix well. Spread into greased 8 x 8-inch pan. Cover with topping.

Topping:

2 tablespoons flour
⅓ cup brown sugar
1 teaspoon margarine
¼ teaspoon cinnamon
¼ cup of nuts or raisins (optional)

Bake in preheated 375 degree oven 20-30 minutes.

Sourdough Cinnamon Rolls:

1 cup flour
1 teaspoon baking powder
¼ teaspoon salt
⅓ cup margarine
1 cup sourdough starter

Filling:

¼ cup sugar
1 teaspoon cinnamon
2 tablespoons margarine

Stir together flour, baking powder and salt. Cut in margarine. Add starter and mix well. On floured surface roll dough into a rectangle, ¼-inch thick. Spread margarine over dough. Sprinkle sugar-cinnamon mixture over area. Roll up. Cut in 1-inch slices. Place in greased 9 x 9-inch baking pan. Bake in preheated 350 degree oven 20 minutes. DO NOT LET DOUGH RISE. Remove from pan and ice while hot.

Icing: Add milk to 1 cup sifted confectioners' sugar for spreading consistency. Add dash of salt and ½ teaspoon vanilla.

Nancy Blood Thoman (Mrs. Mark C.)

A 7-ounce tuna can with ends removed makes a good cutter for English muffins.

SOURDOUGH COOKIES AND BISCUITS

Sourdough Cookies:

½ cup margarine or butter
¼ cup sugar
1 egg
1 teaspoon vanilla
1 cup sourdough starter
1¾ cups plus 2 teaspoons flour
2 teaspoons baking powder
¼ teaspoon salt
½ teaspoon baking soda
¾ cup nuts, chopped

Cream together margarine and sugar. Add egg, vanilla and starter. Mix well and set aside. Sift together flour, baking powder, salt and baking soda. Add dry ingredients to creamed mixture. Add nuts. Drop from teaspoon onto ungreased cookie sheet. Sprinkle with cinnamon and sugar. Bake at 350 degrees for 12 minutes.

Sourdough Biscuits I:

1 cup flour
¼ teaspoon baking soda
¼ teaspoon salt
2 teaspoons baking powder
¼ cup oil
1 cup sourdough starter

Mix all ingredients. On floured surface, knead dough 10 times. Cut into desired shapes and bake on ungreased cookie sheet. Bake at 425 degrees for 10-15 minutes.

Sourdough Biscuits II:

1 cup sourdough starter
1 cup flour
¾ teaspoon baking soda
¼ teaspoon salt
⅓ cup margarine or oil

Mix ingredients together. Drop from teaspoon on greased cookie sheet. Bake at 350 degrees for 10-12 mintues.

Nancy Blood Thoman (Mrs. Mark C.)

If you are going on vacation and don't want to give your sourdough "starter" away, freeze it. Leave at room temperature for 24 hours after thawing before using.

Put 2 cloves of garlic, split, on toothpicks in ⅓ cup softened butter or margarine. Let stand for at least 1 hour; remove and butter bread before baking.

CRESCENT ROLLS

Doubles easily
Freezes well

½ cup warm water
2 packages dry yeast
¾ cup sugar
1 cup Crisco
1½ cups boiling water
1 teaspoon salt
2 eggs
6 cups *sifted* flour

Dissolve yeast in ½ cup warm water with a pinch of sugar and let rest 5 minutes. Put shortening in large mixing bowl; add sugar and pour boiling water over all. Mix at low speed to combine and dissolve sugar and shortening. When mixture has cooled to 150 degrees add salt, eggs and beat. When shortening mixture has cooled to 105-115 degrees, add yeast. Add sifted flour 1 cup at a time, mixing well after each addition. Place in refrigerator until ready to use, about 3 hours at least, or let rise in warm place until double in volume, about 1½ hours. Dough will keep in refrigerator about one week. Keep covered and punch down occasionally.

To bake:
When ready to use, allow refrigerated dough to warm on counter 10 minutes. Divide dough from single recipe into 4 equal parts. Take 1 part at a time and put it on a floured surface. Roll into 14-inch circle; cut into quarters. Divide each quarter into 3 equal-sized pie-shaped pieces. Start at wide end and roll toward point. Curve into crescent shape and lay on well-greased baking sheet and let rise 30 minutes, covered. Preheat oven to 375 degrees and bake until slightly tan if to be frozen (8-10 minutes) or fully browned (12-15 minutes) for immediate use.

Variation:
Roll pinches of dough into marble-sized balls. Roll in your choice of poppy seeds, caraway seeds or sesame seeds and put in well-greased miniature muffin pans. Allow to rise 30 minutes covered and bake in preheated 375 degree oven 10-12 minutes.

To freeze:
Cool baked rolls and wrap in foil or drop into plastic bags. To reheat, thaw rolls and use as brown and serve by placing on baking sheet and baking in preheated 375 degree oven 3-5 minutes. Or, thaw wrapped in foil and bake 10 minutes in preheated oven at 375 degrees, then open foil and allow rolls to "crisp up" a few minutes.
Yield: 5 dozen crescent rolls

Barbara Straub Stewart

Bryan House **605 Pollock Street**

This brick Federal side-hall house features a typical New Bern Portico with open pediment and six-panelled door surmounted by a wooden fanlight transome. Built between 1803-1806, the house is still occupied by descendants of the original owner, James Bryan. It is the residence of Dr. and Mrs. Charles Ashford, Jr.

Eggs and Cheeses

BREAKFAST SOUFFLÉ

Must be done at least 4 hours ahead
May be done day before

1 pound sausage, browned and drained
1 cup Cheddar cheese, grated
2 slices bread, cubed
6 eggs
2 cups milk
1 teaspoon salt
1 teaspoon prepared mustard

Butter, grease or Pam-spray a 9 x 13-inch baking dish. Brown sausage, stirring while cooking to crumble it. Drain on paper towels or brown paper. Beat together eggs, milk, mustard and salt. Scatter bread cubes in baking dish. Sprinkle drained sausage and cheese over bread. Pour egg and milk mixture over all. Cover with plastic wrap and refrigerate at least 4 hours or, preferably, overnight. Bake at 350 degrees for 30-40 minutes.
Yield: 6-8 generous servings

Nancy Robinson Hunt (Mrs. William B., Jr.)

Variation:
4 slices bread
1 cup milk
1 teaspoon dry mustard
Dash of pepper

Prepare as above substituting 4 bread slices for 2; 1 cup milk for 2; dry mustard for prepared and add a dash of pepper. Bake 40-45 minutes rather than 30-40.

Nancy Smith Favor (Mrs. William A., Jr.)

BAKED EGGS HÉLÖISE

Easy
Part done ahead
Can double
Serve immediately

4 slices ham, cooked
3 tablespoons butter
6-8 mushrooms, chopped
Salt
Pepper
4 eggs
8 tablespoons cream
4 tablespoons Parmesan or Cheddar cheese, grated

Sauté ham lightly on both sides in 1 tablespoon butter. Add more butter if necessary. When heated, but not really browned, place each piece in an individual buttered shirred-egg dish. Chop mushrooms and sauté them in 1 tablespoon butter for 3-4 minutes. Spread the mushrooms over the ham and season lightly with salt and pepper. You may cover and refrigerate at this point. At baking time, preheat oven to 350 degrees. Allow dishes to warm to room temperature. Break an egg carefully into each dish. Salt the eggs lightly, pour 2 tablespoons cream over each egg and sprinkle with a little grated cheese, about 1 tablespoon per egg. Bake the eggs for about 10 minutes or until the whites are set but the yolks are still soft and the cheese has melted.
Yield: 4 servings

Carol Webb Pullen (Mrs. John S.)

BASQUE BRUNCH

Can be done night before and cooked following day

12 slices dry bread
12 slices (or 24 if thin slices) Cheddar cheese
4 eggs
¼ teaspoon salt
½ teaspoon dry mustard
1 teaspoon dry onions
2 cups milk
Sliced tomatoes
Limp bacon (partially cooked)

Make 6 sandwiches of cheese with bread. Mix eggs, salt, mustard, onions and milk and pour over sandwiches. Allow to stand at least 3 to 4 hours or overnight. Preheat oven to 350 degrees. Bake 30 minutes then add sliced tomatoes, and limp bacon, return to oven for 10 minutes. Broil until bacon is crisp.

Pat Best Woodward (Mrs. J. Arthur)

CHRISTMAS MORNING BAKED EGG CASSEROLE

Make day ahead

Casserole:

10 eggs, hard-boiled and sliced in half lengthwise
2 (4½-ounce) cans deviled ham
¾ teaspoon dried mustard
1 tablespoon cream
½ teaspoon onion, grated
Salt
Pepper

Remove yolks and mash them with deviled ham, mustard, cream and onion. Salt and pepper to taste. Refill egg whites and put into 7 x 11-inch casserole.

Sauce:

6 tablespoons butter
6 tablespoons flour
3 cups milk
2 cups sharp Cheddar cheese, grated
¼ teaspoon dried mustard
Salt
Pepper

Make cream sauce by melting butter and adding flour. Add milk gradually, stirring constantly until thickened. Add cheese, dried mustard and salt and pepper to taste. Pour sauce over eggs. Cover and refrigerate until baking time.

Topping:

1 cup Corn Flakes, crushed
2 tablespoons butter, melted

Preheat oven to 350 degrees and remove casserole from refrigerator. Toss Corn Flakes with melted butter. Sprinkle over top of casserole and bake 20 minutes or until bubbly.
Yield: 8 servings

Joanne Tedder Spencer (Mrs James T.)

When hard-boiling eggs, pour off hot water at the end of cooking time and fill container with ice cubes. Eggs will peel easily and cool quickly.

Broil bacon on lowest shelf of oven 5-8 minutes per side on Pam-sprayed broiler pan for easy "frying" and easy clean-up.

SAUSAGE SOUFFLÉ

Do a day ahead
This recipe is nice for breakfast, especially when you have company. At my house we have it Christmas morning. While it cooks, we open our Christmas presents. I also have it for brunch along with ham biscuits, fruit (fresh or curried), grits and Butter-Cinnamon Cake.

8 slices white bread, cubed
2 cups sharp Cheddar cheese, shredded
1½ pounds link sausage, cut in thirds
4 eggs
2¼ cups milk
¾ teaspoon dry mustard
1 (10¾-ounce) can cream of mushroom soup
½ cup milk

Grease a 9 x 13-inch baking dish with butter. Place bread cubes in dish and top with cheese. Brown and drain sausage and place on top of cheese. Beat eggs with 2¼ cups milk and mustard, and pour over sausage. Cover and refrigerate overnight. Preheat oven to 300 degrees; dilute soup with ½ cup milk and pour over bread and sausage. Bake 1½ hours until set.
Yield: 12 servings

Bettye Cooke Paramore (Mrs. Walter H., Jr.)

CONFETTI EGG CASSEROLE

Excellent for company breakfast or brunch
Serve immediately

6 slices bacon
⅓ cup onion, chopped
8 eggs, slightly beaten
1 cup milk
2 tablespoons pimiento
1 tablespoon parsley
½ teaspoon salt
1 cup sharp American cheese, shredded
1 cup Swiss cheese, shredded
1 tablespoon flour

Preheat oven to 350 degrees. Fry bacon and drain, reserving 1 tablespoon fat. Cook onion in fat until soft. Crumble bacon; combine onion, bacon, eggs, milk, pimiento, parsley and salt. Toss cheese in flour and add to egg mixture. Pour into 1½-quart casserole and bake for 40 minutes. Serve immediately.
Yield: 6 servings

Genevieve Tolson Dunn (Mrs. Mark S.)

COOK'S NIGHT OFF SCRAMBLED EGGS

This is an old Bartlett family Sunday night supper from the days when 'the cook' went home after the mid-day dinner.

4 eggs, slightly beaten
Salt to taste
Pepper to taste
1/3 cup milk
1½ slices Kraft Deluxe Swiss Cheese, chopped
1 scallion, chopped
1 teaspoon fresh parsley

Mix all ingredients together. Scramble in buttered skillet until fluffy. Serve with buttered "Poppy Seed Twist" toast and hot chocolate.
Yield: 3-4 servings

Marian Bartlett Stewart (Mrs. Wm. Edward)

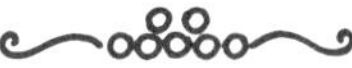

A teaspoon of vinegar added to boiling water can keep the white of a poached egg from separating.

SPINACH MUSHROOM OMELET

Have everything chopped before starting to cook

3 tablespoons butter
3/4 pound mushrooms, chopped
3/4 cup onion, chopped
1 garlic clove, minced
6 eggs
3/4 teaspoon salt
3/4 teaspoon curry powder
1/8 teaspoon pepper
2 teaspoons Worcestershire sauce
10 ounces spinach, steamed
3 tablespoons oil

Heat butter in skillet. Sauté mushrooms, onions, and garlic in butter until golden. Remove from heat. Beat eggs with seasonings. Add mushroom mixture and spinach. Heat oil in skillet. Pour all in. Cook until golden; turn; cook other side. Serve immediately.
Yield: 6-8 servings

Peggy Witmeyer Bernard

FRANCES' FANCY BREAKFAST

3 English muffins, split in half
1/4 cup butter
2 green onions (or 1 small onion), chopped
1 small green pepper, chopped
6-8 large fresh (or canned) mushrooms, sliced
4 eggs, beaten with a small amount of milk
Salt and pepper to taste
6 slices Canadian bacon
1 (10-ounce) can cream of mushroom soup, undiluted
1 cup Cheddar cheese, grated

Lightly butter and toast English muffin halves. Sauté in butter the onions, green peppers and mushrooms until softened. Add the beaten eggs and scramble. Top each muffin half with a slice of Canadian bacon. Mound some of the egg mixture on the bacon and then place a tablespoon of mushroom soup on top. Add grated cheese on top of the soup and heat under the broiler until the cheese is melted and browned. This makes a delightful breakfast or brunch when served with spiced apple rings or fresh fruit.
Yield: 6 servings

Jane Crofton Atkinson (Mrs. C. Lee)

BRUNCH CASSEROLE

Do day head
May freeze

1/2 cup butter
1/2 pound Kraft extra-sharp cheese, grated
1 teaspoon prepared mustard
1 teaspoon salt
1/4 teaspoon red pepper
4 eggs
3 cups milk
12 slices bread, crusts removed

Cream cheese and butter. Cut bread in half. Spread with cheese mixture. Put in buttered 9 x 13-inch casserole, making just one layer. Cover with beaten eggs and milk. Refrigerate overnight. Bake at 325 degrees for 1 hour. Garnish with crumbled bacon, if desired.
Yield: 6-8 servings

Eugenia Hofler Clement (Mrs. Robert L.)

CREOLE JACK RABBIT

4 slices bacon, finely chopped
½ cup onion, minced
½ cup green pepper, minced
¼ cup flour
1 cup milk
2 cups canned tomatoes, drained and chopped
1 cup Monterey Jack cheese, shredded
1 teaspoon Worcestershire sauce
½ teaspoon salt
English muffins *or* toast triangles

Cook bacon until crisp. Add onion and green pepper and sauté until tender. Blend in flour. Stir in milk and tomatoes and cook until thickened. Add cheese, Worcestershire sauce and salt. Stir until cheese melts. Serve over toast or muffins.
Yield: 6 servings

Carol Coleman Pursell (Mrs. Elliot D.)

To hold a poached egg for later serving (up to two days), put poached egg immediately into a bowl or jar of cold water, cover and refrigerate. To reheat, put egg in a generous amount of water just hot to the *touch*. Let egg stand 5-10 minutes in hot bath, adding hot water if necessary to keep the temperature up until serving time. Do NOT cook the egg further.

YORKSHIRE BUCK

1 pound sharp Cheddar cheese, grated
2 tablespoons heavy cream
½-¾ cup stale beer
½ teaspoon salt
½ teaspoon ground nutmeg
1 teaspoon Worcestershire sauce
⅛ teaspoon pepper
2 eggs, lightly beaten
4 poached eggs on toast

Combine cheese, cream and beer in heavy saucepan. Cook over low heat until cheese is melted. Add salt, nutmeg, Worcestershire sauce and pepper. Reduce heat and stir in eggs, whisking constantly with a wire whip. When mixture is thickened and creamy, spoon over poached eggs on toast.
Yield: 4 servings

CHEESE EGG CASSEROLE

9 slices bread, cut into cubes with crusts
½ cup margarine, melted
2 cups milk
12 ounces cheese, grated
3 egg yolks, beaten
½ teaspoon salt
¼ teaspoon red pepper or Tabasco sauce
½ teaspoon dry mustard
3 egg whites, well-beaten

Preheat oven to 350 degrees. Mix ingredients together. Fold in 3 egg whites. Pour into greased 9 x 13-inch pan. Bake 350 degrees for 25 minutes or until set.

Libby Jones Wrenn (Mrs. James H., Jr.)

BOB'S DEVILED EGGS

Easy
Original recipe

4 eggs, hard-boiled
5 level tablespoons mayonnaise
1 teaspoon Worcestershire
6 to 8 drops Tabasco
1 level teaspoon dry mustard
1 light sprinkling Accent
Salt to taste

Boil eggs *only* 15 minutes. Separate yolks from whites. Mix yolks with remaining ingredients and stuff eggs.

Robert D. Darden

SISTER'S CHAFING DISH SUPPER

Easy

1 pound sharp cheese, cut into small pieces
1 green pepper, chopped
1 large onion, chopped
1 (10½-ounce) can tomato soup
Vegetable oil

In saucepan sauté pepper and onion in oil. Add the soup and cheese and cook slowly until cheese is melted. Serve on toast points, rice or saltines. May be served from saucepan or transferred to chafing dish, as desired.
Yield: 4 servings

Kathleen Winslow Budd (Mrs. Bern)

ENGLISH MONKEY

2 cups bread crumbs, crumbled
2 cups milk
2 eggs, beaten
1 cup sharp Cheddar cheese*
Salt
Pepper
English muffins or buttered toast

*Other cheeses may be substituted.
In double boiler, place milk and bread crumbs. When they are *beginning* to heat, add beaten eggs and stir. Add cheese and salt and pepper to taste. Cook until thick and cheese has melted. Serve over buttered toast or English muffins. Accompany with regular or Canadian bacon.

Nancy Scearce Deans

CHEESE FONDUE

Last minute
Do not freeze

4 cups imported Swiss cheese, grated
2 cups dry white wine
2 tablespoons corn flour or potato flour
4 tablespoons Kirsch
Garlic clove
Nutmeg
Pepper
Crusty French bread, cut in cubes

Rub the inside of a chafing dish or skillet with the garlic clove. Heat the wine, add the cheese and stir constantly. As soon as the mixture commences to cook, stir in the Kirsch in which you have dissolved the flour. Season with pepper and nutmeg to taste. Serve and keep the fondue bubbling in chafing dish or on a small spirit-stove. Each guest spears a small piece of bread with his fondue-fork, dips it in the savory fondue, stirs round the pot once or twice, and then pops the delicious morsel into his mouth.
Yield: 4 servings

Kathleen Winslow Budd (Mrs. Bern)

A most important fondue rule is: He who loses a piece of bread in the mixture has to pay for a bottle of wine or the next fondue. Only ladies are free of this venerable law; they forfeit a kiss for every piece of bread they lose.

Willy J. Buholzer
Old Swiss House, Lucerne, Switzerland

QUICHE LORRAINE

Crust:

1 cup flour
½ teaspoon onion salt
⅛ teaspoon basil leaves
2 tablespoons butter
2 tablespoons lard
2-3 tablespoons cold water

In a large bowl sift together the flour and onion salt; mix in basil. Cut in butter and lard until it resembles coarse meal. Gradually add enough water to hold dough together, mixing lightly with a fork. Roll out on lightly floured board; line 9-inch pie plate with dough.

Filling:

1 (8-ounce) package Swiss Emmenthaler Cheese, shredded
6 slices bacon, cooked and crumbled
2 cups light cream or half and half
4 eggs, slightly beaten
1 tablespoon cornstarch
½ teaspoon salt
¼ teaspoon freshly ground nutmeg
Dash cayenne pepper
2 tablespoons butter, melted
2 tablespoons grated Parmesan Cheese

Preheat oven to 375 degrees. Toss together Swiss cheese and bacon; sprinkle over crust. In a mixing bowl combine cream, eggs, cornstarch, salt, nutmeg and cayenne pepper until well-blended. Pour over cheese-bacon mixture. Drizzle on butter and sprinkle with Parmesan cheese. Bake 40 minutes and let stand 10 minutes before cutting. Serve with salad of fresh endive and tomato, thickly sliced.
Yield: 6 servings

Lou H. Proctor (Mrs. Jimmie C.)

Eggs may be frozen: Freeze whole eggs in cubes or in quantities you would usually use. Stir egg with fork just to break yolk and blend with white. Do not incorporate. Add 1 teaspoon salt for eggs that will be used in omelets, scrambled eggs or soufflés. Add 1 tablespoon sugar for eggs to be used in cakes, desserts. Be sure to label. Since eggs are perishable, thaw in closed containers in refrigerator, 6-8 hours. Use immediately. Do not refreeze.

ALPINE ASPARAGUS QUICHE

Easy
Last minute
Serve immediately
This is great for Sunday supper even though the current price of asparagus is astronomical!

1 (9-inch) pie shell
1 (10-ounce) package frozen asparagus
¾ cup milk
¾ cup half and half
½ cup onion, finely chopped
1 teaspoon salt
¼ teaspoon nutmeg
Dash of pepper
3 eggs, slightly beaten
1 cup Swiss cheese, shredded

Preheat oven to 400 degrees. Bake pie shell for 8-10 minutes. Reduce heat to 375 degrees. Prepare asparagus as directed on package, then drain. Sprinkle ⅔ cup cheese over pie crust. Arrange asparagus over cheese. Combine milk, cream, onion, salt, nutmeg, and pepper in saucepan. Bring to a boil then let simmer one minute. Stir this hot mixture into slightly beaten eggs. Pour over asparagus and cheese in pie shell. Sprinkle remaining cheese on top. Bake at 375 degrees for 20-25 minutes, or until a silver knife inserted one inch from center comes out clean.
Yield: 6 servings

Jane Kinnison Millns (Mrs. Dale T.)

SPINACH QUICHE

½ cup margarine
½ cup milk
2 eggs
1 tablespoon cornstarch
1½ cups sharp Cheddar cheese, grated
1 tablespoon onion flakes
2 (9-inch) pie shells
1 (10-ounce) package Stouffer's Spinach Soufflé, thawed

Preheat oven to 350 degrees. Mix all ingredients together well and pour into the two pie crusts. Bake for 30 minutes or until lightly browned.
Yield: 10-12 servings

Jane Pugh Constantine (Mrs. James D.)

QUICHE

1 (9-inch) pie shell, unbaked
½ pound bacon
3 eggs
1½ cups heavy cream
½ teaspoon salt
Pinch of pepper
Pinch of nutmeg
¼ cup Gruyère cheese, grated

Preheat oven to 375 degrees. Cut bacon in 1-inch pieces and cook until crisp. Drain. Spread on bottom of unbaked pie shell. Beat eggs, cream and seasonings enough to blend. Stir in cheese. Pour into pie shell and bake for 35 minutes or until firm.
Yield: 6 servings

Alice Graham Underhill (Mrs. T. Reed)

Cheese may be frozen. Process cheeses will last 4 months frozen and Cheddar or other natural cheese will keep about 6 weeks when properly wrapped. Thaw all cheese overnight in refrigerator and use soon after thawing.

SHIRLEY'S IMPOSSIBLE QUICHE

½ cup butter, melted
1½ cups milk
¼ teaspoon salt
Dash pepper
1 cup Swiss or Cheddar cheese, shredded
½ cup bacon or ham
3 eggs, beaten
½ cup Bisquick

Preheat oven to 350 degrees. Mix all ingredients and pour into greased 9-inch pie plate. Bake for 45 minutes. Let set 10 minutes after removing from oven before slicing.

Variation:
1 (6-ounce) can crab
¼ cup mayonnaise

Use crab and mayonnaise instead of bacon or ham.

Joan Brooks Kunkel (Mrs. Cooper D.)

SARAH RICHARDSON'S PIMIENTO CHEESE

1 pound mild cheese, finely grated*
1 (4-ounce) jar pimiento, chopped, with juice
1¼ cups Duke's mayonnaise

*A Mouli grater works nicely.
Mix ingredients well and refrigerate until ready to use.

Elizabeth Reese Ward (Mrs. David L. Jr.)

Cheese grates more easily if chilled or partially frozen.

INCREDIBLE PIMIENTO CHEESE

Can be frozen

1 pound Velveeta Cheese
1 pound medium Cheddar cheese
1 pound sharp Cheddar cheese
1 pint Miracle Whip Salad Dressing
8 ounces pimiento, drained and chopped
3 tablespoons sugar
Salt to taste
Pepper to taste

Grate cheeses or cut into small pieces. Allow to soften at room temperature. Combine all ingredients and blend using mixer, blender or food processor. It may be necessary to divide ingredients into two batches unless you have an exceptionally large mixing container.
Yield: 2 quarts

Karen Hansen Norman (Mrs. Joseph H., IV)

Leech House **231 Change Street**

Joseph Leech acquired the lot in 1752 and the gambrel roof house was built in the last half of the 18th century. The house is a side hall plan with two rooms on both the first and second floors. It was restored in 1970 by Mr. and Mrs. Robert Lee Stallings.

Cakes, Cupcakes and Icing

MISS SADIE'S BEST FRUIT CAKE

All through Sadie Whitehurst's cookbook are recipes in her own handwriting for fruit cake—each one indicating the year it was made and how well it turned out. This is the one that she noted is the "best I ever made." It was dated Christmas 1929, 1931, and *1934*, the *"best."* We're giving the recipe in her own words.

1 pound cherries, (nearly 2 cups)
1 pound pineapple, (nearly 2 cups)
1½ cups raisins (white in 1934)
½ cup citron
3 cups pecans
½ cup almonds
1½ cups brown sugar
6½-ounces butter or 1 cup Wesson oil (I prefer butter.)
2 teaspoons salt if oil is used, 1 teaspoon if butter is used
2 teaspoons cinnamon
1 teaspoon cloves
1½ teaspoons allspice
1 cup fruit juice (I used orange juice, unsweetened this year—last year I used one cup sherry wine but can't tell the difference)
4 eggs
3 cups Gold Medal flour, sifted before measuring
1 teaspoon baking powder

Mix 2 cups flour in butter, save 1 cup for flouring fruit. Press floured fruit and sugar in cups to measure. Bake in slow oven 275 degrees for about 4 hours. I baked this 4½ hours—just right!

FRESH APPLE CAKE

1½ cups oil
2½ cups sugar
1 teaspoon vanilla
3 eggs
3 cups flour
1 teaspoon baking soda
1 tablespoon cinnamon
3 cups apples, pared, cored and chopped
1 cup nuts, chopped

Preheat oven to 350 degrees. Grease and flour a tube pan and set aside. Cream sugar, oil, and vanilla together. Add eggs. Sift in flour, soda, and cinnamon. Batter will be stiff. Add apples and nuts. Beat thoroughly. Bake for 1½ hours in prepared tube pan.

Mary Moulton Barden (Mrs. Graham A., Jr.)
Genevieve Tolson Dunn (Mrs. Mark S.)
Kathy Turner Anderson (Mrs. William B., V)

HONEY APPLE CAKE

Do early in day

Cake:
1½ cups sugar
½ cup honey
3 eggs, well-beaten
3 cups flour
2 teaspoons soda
2 teaspoons cinnamon
3 cups apples, diced
½ cup nuts, chopped
1 teaspoon vanilla
Dash of salt
1 cup oil

Preheat oven to 325 degress. Combine eggs, honey, sugar, and vanilla. Beat well. Add oil and beat. Add flour, soda, salt, and cinnamon and blend thoroughly. While beating, add apples and nuts. Beat well and pour into 13 x 9-inch greased baking pan. Bake for 35 minutes.

Topping:
½ cup butter, melted
1 cup brown sugar
½ cup milk
1 teaspoon vanilla

Combine ingredients in a pot and bring to a rolling boil until sugar is thoroughly dissolved. Pour over cake.
Yield: 20 servings

Thelma Opphile (Mrs. Marion D.)

BLANCHE'S APPLESAUCE CAKE

Moist and good

2¼ cups sweetened applesauce
½ cup butter, melted
1½ cups sugar
1½ cups nuts
1½ cups raisins
3 cups flour
3 teaspoons soda
¾ teaspoon nutmeg
¾ teaspoon ground cloves
3 eggs
Pinch of salt
¾ teaspoon cinnamon
1 teaspoon vanilla

Preheat oven to 350 degrees. Lightly grease two large loaf pans and set aside. Mix dry ingredients together. Combine applesauce and baking soda. Add applesauce mixture and all the remaining ingredients. Pour into two prepared loaf pans. Bake for one hour. Bake less than one hour if you have hot oven. Yield: 2 loaves

Margaret Manning Preston (Mrs. Ronald A.)

APPLE DAPPLE

3 eggs
2½ cups sugar
1½ cups Wesson oil
3 cups flour
2 teaspoons baking powder
1 cup nuts, chopped
1 teaspoon salt
1 or more teaspoons vanilla
1 teaspoon cinnamon
½ teaspoon ground cloves
½ teaspoon mace
4 cups or more apples, peeled, cored and finely chopped

Grease and flour a 9 x 13-inch pan. Chop apples. (I grate mine. It doesn't matter if they turn brown.) Cream eggs, sugar and oil. Sift dry ingredients together; stir into creamed mixture. Stir in apples, nuts and vanilla. Bake 45-50 mintues at 350 degrees.

Topping:
5 tablespoons butter
¾ cup brown sugar
Scant ¼ cup milk
Pinch of salt
1 teaspoon vanilla

Melt butter in saucepan; add sugar and milk. Cook 4½ minutes. Add vanilla; stir until blended. Pour over still warm cake.

Rena Terrell Knott (Mrs. Edmund T.)

APPLE CHIP CAKE

3 eggs
2 cups sugar
1 cup margarine
½ cup water
2½ cups flour
2 tablespoons cocoa
1 teaspoon soda
1 teaspoon cinnamon
1 teaspoon allspice
1 cup nuts, pecans or walnuts
¾ cup mini-chocolate chips
2 apples, peeled, cored and diced

Grease and flour Bundt pan. Preheat oven to 325 degrees. Beat together until fluffy, eggs, sugar, margarine and water. Sift together and add to first mixture, flour, cocoa, soda, cinnamon and allspice. Beat two minutes. Fold in nuts, chocolate chips and apple pieces. Bake 60-70 minutes. Cool 10 minutes before removing from pan.

Diane Williams Marsh (Mrs. Thomas B., Jr.)

APRICOT NECTAR CAKE

Do day ahead
Stores well
The longer it sits, the better it tastes.

Cake:
1 (18½-ounce) box lemon cake mix
1 cup apricot nectar
4 eggs
¾ cup Wesson oil
½ cup sugar

Combine all ingredients and mix well. Bake in greased and floured tube pan for 1 hour at 350 degrees. Cool 5 minutes, then remove from pan and ice while hot.

Icing:
Juice from 1 lemon
1½ cups confectioners' sugar

Combine ingredients and pour slowly over hot cake so icing seeps into cake. Spread remaining icing on sides of cake.

Melanie Applegate (Mrs. Earl)

EASY CARROT CAKE

Can freeze

4 eggs
2 cups sugar
1⅓ cups oil
2 cups flour
1 teaspoon salt
2 teaspoons baking soda
2 teaspoons baking powder
2 teaspoons cinnamon
3-4 cups carrots, grated
¾ cup nuts, chopped (optional)

Preheat oven to 325 degrees. Combine sugar and eggs, beating well. Sift dry ingredients and add to sugar mixture alternately with oil. Add carrots and then nuts. Bake in three 8-inch layer cake pans which have been greased and floured. Bake for 45 minutes. When cool frost with Cream Cheese Icing.

Becky Melton Kafer (Mrs. C. William)
Margaret Manning Preston (Mrs. Ronald A.)
Myrtle Rodgers West (Mrs. James M.)

Recipes that call for baking pans to be greased and floured may use baking paper or waxed paper on bottom of pan instead. Then grease sides of pan.

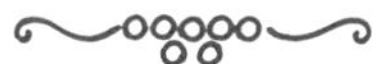

PINEAPPLE CARROT CAKE

2 cups sugar
4 eggs
½ cup cooking oil
2 cups flour
1½ teaspoons baking soda
2 teaspoons baking powder
2 teaspoons cinnamon
1 teaspoon salt
¾ cup pecans
2 cups carrots, grated
1 (8-ounce) can crushed pineapple, drained

Preheat oven to 350 degrees. Beat eggs; add sugar and oil; add sifted dry ingredients. Mix well. Add carrots, pineapple and pecans. Grease and flour three cake layer pans. Bake 40 minutes. Cool and ice with Cream Cheese Icing.

Jane Kinnison Millns (Mrs. Dale T.)

CHESS CAKE

Crust:

1 (18½-ounce) box yellow or chocolate cake mix
½ cup margarine, softened
1 egg

Preheat oven to 350 degrees. Grease a 9 x 13-inch pan. Crumble together cake mix, margarine and egg. Pat into prepared pan.

Filling:

1 (8-ounce) package cream cheese, softened
1 (16-ounce) package confectioners' sugar
2 eggs
3-4 tablespoons lemon juice for yellow cake *OR* coffee for chocolate cake

Mix cream cheese, sugar, eggs and lemon juice or coffee together thoroughly and pour over crust. Bake at 350 degrees 35-40 minutes or until browned.

Becky Breeden Gaeta (Mrs. Anthony, Jr.)

Use cocoa to "flour" cake pans when baking a chocolate cake.

CHOCOLATE CAKE

May be doubled
Do not use an electric beater; mix by hand. Electric beater causes the cake to fall apart.

1 cup sugar
⅓ cup shortening
1 egg
2 squares unsweetened chocolate, melted
1 teaspoon baking soda
1 teaspoon baking powder
1 teaspoon salt
1 cup hot water
1 teaspoon vanilla
1½ cups flour

Preheat oven to 350 degrees. Cream sugar and shortening. Add egg and melted chocolate. Mix well. Add dry ingredients, alternating with hot water and ending with dry ingredients. Add vanilla. Pour into greased 8-inch square pan. Bake for 30 minutes.

Eleanor Elizabeth Richardson (Mrs. Asa C.)

CHOCOLATE PICNIC CAKE

Cake:

2 cups flour
2 cups sugar
1 cup water
½ cup margarine
½ cup shortening
5 tablespoons cocoa
½ cup buttermilk
2 eggs
1 teaspoon baking soda
1 teaspoon vanilla

Preheat oven to 350 degrees. Sift together the flour and sugar. Cook until melted the water, margarine, shortening and cocoa. Cool, then pour over the flour mixture. Mix well. Add buttermilk, eggs, soda and vanilla. Mix well. Pour into greased 13 x 9-inch pan and bake 25-35 minutes.

Frosting:

½ cup margarine
6 tablespoons milk
4 tablespoons cocoa
1 (16-ounce) box powdered sugar
1 teaspoon vanilla
Chopped nuts

Bring margarine, milk and cocoa to a boil. Remove from heat and add sugar, vanilla and nuts. Pour over hot cake and leave cake in pan.
Yield: 12 servings

Susan Henri Johnson
Page Pearson Faulkner (Mrs. A. Gerald)

SOUR CREAM CAKE

1 cup butter or margarine
6 eggs, separated
¼ teaspoon baking soda
3 cups sugar
3 cups sifted flour
½ pint sour cream

Preheat oven to 325 degrees and use a paper-lined or well-greased and floured loaf, tube, or round pan. Cream butter and sugar. Add yolks and beat. Sift flour and soda together and add alternately with sour cream, beginning and ending with flour. Beat egg whites and fold into cake batter. Bake one hour and 20 minutes.

Myrtle Rodgers West (Mrs. James M.)

CHOCOLATE CHIP CAKE

1 cup self-rising flour
1 cup sugar
4 eggs
½ cup margarine
1 teaspoon vanilla
1 (16-ounce) can Hershey's syrup
½ cup semi-sweet chocolate chips

Preheat oven to 350 degrees. Grease and flour Bundt pan. Mix all ingredients together in large mixing bowl and pour into prepared pan. Bake 50 minutes. Let cool and remove from pan.

Frosting:
1 cup sugar
½ cup butter
⅓ cup evaporated milk
½ cup semi-sweet chocolate chips
1 tablespoon peanut butter *OR* ½ cup nuts (optional)

Combine sugar, butter and evaporated milk in saucepan and bring to a boil. Allow mixture to boil 2½ minutes then add peanut butter or nuts and chocolate chips. Beat until glossy. Pour over cake.

Diane Williams Marsh (Mrs. Thomas B., Jr.)

SOUR CREAM CHOCOLATE CHIP CAKE

Easy

1 cup margarine
1¼ cups sugar
3 eggs, lightly beaten
½ pint sour cream
1 teaspoon vanilla
2 cups sifted cake flour
1 teaspoon baking powder
½ teaspoon baking soda
1 (12-ounce) package miniature chocolate chips
1 cup pecans, chopped (optional)

Preheat oven to 350 degrees and use a greased and floured tube pan. Cream margarine and sugar together. Add eggs and sour cream. Sift flour, soda, and baking powder. Add vanilla. Add chips and pecans. Pour into prepared pan. Bake for one hour.

Alma Loveridge (Mrs. Robert)

MISSISSIPPI MUD CAKE

2 cups sugar
⅓ cup cocoa
1½ cups margarine
4 eggs
1 teaspoon vanilla extract
1½ cups flour
1⅓ cups flaked coconut (1 can)
1½ cups pecans, chopped
1 (7-ounce) jar marshmallow cream

Cream sugar, cocoa, and margarine. Add eggs and vanilla. Mix well. Stir in flour, coconut, and pecans. Bake in a 9 x 13-inch pan for 40 minutes at 350 degrees. When done spread marshmallow cream on hot cake. Cool before frosting.

Frosting:
1 (16-ounce) box powdered sugar
½ cup margarine, softened
½ cup evaporated milk
⅓ cup cocoa
1 teaspoon vanilla extract

Sift together sugar and cocoa. Cream margarine with dry ingredients, then stir in milk and vanilla. Spread over cake.

Marjorie Disosway

CRUMB CAKE

Easy and mouth-watering

2 cups brown sugar
2 cups flour
½ cup butter
1 egg
1 (8-ounce) carton sour cream
1 teaspoon baking soda
1 teaspoon salt
1 teaspoon vanilla

Preheat oven to 350 degrees. Sift sugar and flour together and crumble with butter. Set aside 1 cup crumbs. To remainder, add egg, sour cream, soda, salt and vanilla. Pour into 8 x 8-inch greased and floured pan. Sprinkle the "set aside crumbs" on top. Bake for 30 to 45 minutes. Toothpick test for doneness.

Marian Bartlett Stewart (Mrs. Wm. Edward)

FESTIVE CHRISTMAS CAKE

Easy
Do day ahead
Stores well

1 (18-ounce) Duncan Hines Lemon Supreme Cake Mix
1 (12-ounce) package mixed candied fruit, dredged in flour

Follow directions on package for Lemon Supreme Pound Cake and fold in candied fruit to batter before pouring into cake pan. Bake according to package directions. Some fruit may be reserved for decoration.

Icing:
1 cup confectioners' sugar
1/3 stick butter or margarine, softened
1 1/2 tablespoons sherry wine

Cream softened butter and sugar. Add sherry gradually to make icing spreading consistency. Spread on top of cake. Decorate with candied fruit cut to represent poinsettia, if desired.

Bay Dunn McCotter (Mrs. J. Muse)

Cooked frostings do not freeze well.

CHRISTMAS CAKE

1 cup flour
1/2 teaspoon salt
2 teaspoons baking powder
1 pound seeded dates
1 pound English walnut halves
4 egg yolks, beaten
1 cup granulated sugar
4 egg whites, beaten stiff
1 teaspoon vanilla

Preheat oven to 300 degrees. Grease tube pan. Sift together flour, salt and baking powder in a large bowl. Beat egg whites and add vanilla. Add yolks and sugar to flour mixture. Fold in egg whites. Fold in nuts and dates. Pour into tube pan. Bake about 1 hour.

Alma Nelson Hodges (Mrs. F. W.)

FOUR DAY COCONUT CAKE

This is not original; however, several years ago everyone was making it and it *is* good enough to be saved!

1 Duncan Hines white cake mix, baked and split into four layers
2 cups sour cream
2 (12-ounce) packages frozen coconut
2 cups sugar

Mix sour cream, sugar and coconut and refrigerate overnight. Ice cake with this mixture—four layers, top and sides. Loosely cover and refrigerate cake four days.
Yield: 16 servings

Nancy Hagy Chiles (Mrs. Robert M.)
Genevieve Tolson Dunn (Mrs. Mark S.)

Sour cream can be spread more easily if you beat it in the carton with a single beater.

ENGLISH TEA CAKE

This is served at high tea in England—a very highly prized recipe shared with me by a dear friend who brought it back with her in 1936 from Woldingham, England. Very delicious!

1 cup butter, softened
1 cup sugar
2 eggs
2 scant cups flour
½ teaspoon baking powder
¼ teaspoon salt
½ cup white raisins or currants
12 maraschino cherries
1 tablespoon cherry juice
1 teaspoon vanilla

Preheat oven to 250 degrees. Grease and flour small tube pan. Cream butter and sugar together; add eggs, beating thoroughly. Sift dry ingredients together and add to butter mixture gradually. Add vanilla and cherry juice. Fold in cherries and raisins. Pour into prepared pan and bake 1¼ hours or until done by using a wooden toothpick to test.

Polly Speace Miller (Mrs. Robert F.)

HUMMINGBIRD CAKE

Do day ahead
May be frozen

3 cups flour
2 cups sugar
1 teaspoon salt
1 teaspoon cinnamon
1 teaspoon baking soda
3 eggs
1½ cups Crisco oil
3 cups bananas, mashed
3 cups pecans, chopped
1 (8-ounce) can crushed pineapple, undrained

Preheat oven to 325 degrees. Sift together flour, sugar, salt, cinnamon and baking soda. Add eggs and oil, mixing completely with electric mixer. Fold in bananas, nuts and crushed pineapple. Bake in large tube pan for 1 hour 15 minutes. Cool and frost with Cream Cheese Icing. Alternate Method: Bake in three 8 or 9-inch pans at 350 degrees for 25-30 minutes.

Katherine Dodge Beckwith (Mrs. George H.)

To keep the plate or tray clean while frosting the cakes, cover the outer area of plate with strips of waxed paper, extending it beyond the edge of the plate.

HONEY GINGERBREAD

2¾ cups sifted flour
1 teaspoon baking soda
1 teaspoon salt
2 teaspoons baking powder
1 teaspoon ground ginger
1 teaspoon cinnamon
1 egg, beaten
1 cup vegetable oil
¾ cup honey
¾ cup sugar
1 cup buttermilk

Preheat oven to 325 degrees. Grease well and set aside two loaf pans or one 13 x 9-inch pan. Sift flour, soda, salt, baking powder, sugar and spices together. Cream egg and oil together. Add honey in a fine stream, beating constantly. Add sifted flour alternately with buttermilk, beating until smooth after each addition. Pour into two loaf pans or one 13 x 9-inch pan. Bake for 30-50 minutes or until cake tests done. Cool for 5 minutes. Serve with whipped cream.

Thelma Opphile (Mrs. Marion D.)

TOTALLY AMAZING TOMATO-SPICE CAKE

A delicious way to use up your garden's bumper crop! Children ***refuse*** *to* ***believe*** *there are tomatoes in this cake.*

2½ cups tomato purée*
4 cups flour
2½ cups sugar
½ cup shortening
2½ teaspoons baking soda
2½ teaspoons ground cinnamon
2 teaspoons vanilla
1½ teaspoons salt
1 teaspoon ground nutmeg
1 teaspoon ground cloves
½ cup walnuts, chopped

*6 medium tomatoes peeled and seeded and puréed in blender

Preheat oven to 350 degrees. Grease a 9-inch tube pan. Purée tomatoes. In large mixing bowl pour tomatoes and remaining ingredients except walnuts. Beat at low speed just until moistened; increase speed to high and mix 2 minutes, occasionally scraping bowl with spatula. Pour batter into pan; sprinkle with walnuts. Bake 65 minutes or until wooden toothpick comes clean. Serve warm or cold. Especially good warm with whipped cream.

Yield: 12 servings

ITALIAN CREAM CAKE

½ cup butter
½ cup shortening
2 cups sugar
5 egg yolks
2 cups flour (plain or self-rising)
1 teaspoon baking soda
1 teaspoon vanilla
1 cup coconut
1 cup nuts
5 egg whites, beaten
1 cup milk or buttermilk

Preheat oven to 350 degrees. Butter and flour three 8- or 9-inch pans. Cream butter and shortening. Add sugar and egg yolks. Add dry ingredients alternately with milk. Add coconut and nuts, reserving some nuts for top. Fold in beaten egg whites. Bake in 3 layers for approximately 25 minutes. Frost with Cream Cheese Icing when cake has cooled.

Cece Lippit Snow (Mrs. James Byron, III)
Kay Judge Piner (Mrs. William)
Lucille Clark Anderson (Mrs. K. F.)

HAWAIIAN FIESTA CAKE

Cake:

1 Lemon Supreme cake mix
1 (3¾-ounce) package instant vanilla pudding
4 eggs
¾ cup oil
1 (10-ounce) 7-Up

Filling:

1 (20-ounce) can crushed pineapple
2 eggs, slightly beaten
½ cup margarine
3 tablespoons flour
1 can Angel coconut
1½ cups sugar

Grease and flour three 9-inch cake pans. Preheat oven to 350 degrees. Sift cake mix and pudding together. Add eggs one at a time; add oil and then 7-Up. Mix together and pour into pans. Bake 25-30 minutes. Remove from oven and let cool while preparing filling. Mix pineapple, beaten eggs, margarine, flour, coconut and sugar in saucepan. Heat, stirring until smooth. Fill between cake layers and top of cake.

Velma Johnson Edwards (Mrs. Pat)

HONEY FIG CAKE

Easy
Stores Well
Freeze

3 eggs
1 cup sugar
½ cup dark honey
1 cup Mazola oil
½ cup buttermilk
1 teaspoon baking soda
2 cups flour
¼ teaspoon salt
1 teaspoon ground cinnamon
1 teaspoon ground nutmeg
1 teaspoon ground allspice
1 teaspoon vanilla
1 cup fig preserves, cut into small pieces
1 cup nuts

Preheat oven to 350 degrees. Grease and flour a tube pan and set aside. Beat eggs with mixer until lemon colored. Then add sugar and honey. Beat well; add oil. Sift in dry ingredients and add milk. Beat well. Add spices, vanilla and figs. Beat well and add nuts. Bake in tube pan 1-1¼ hours checking after 1 hour.
Yield: Serves 18

Thelma Opphile (Mrs. Marion D.)

ICELANDIC VINARTERTA

Prepare *two weeks* in advance.
This is a five layer Icelandic cake traditionally made during the holidays in our family. The recipe comes from my mother, N. Evelyn Manning and my grandmother, Sigridür Anna Hall.

Cake:

1 cup butter
1½ cups finely granulated sugar
2 large eggs
2 tablespoons whipping cream
4 heaping cups flour
1 teaspoon baking powder
1 tablespoon almond extract
1 teaspoon ground cardamom seed

Preheat oven to 350 degrees. Lightly grease five 9-inch layer cake pans. Cream butter; add sugar gradually. Add eggs and cream. Sift dry ingredients and work into first mixture. Add flavoring. Knead in all the flour mixture and divide into five equal parts. Pat each part into a round cake pan and bake until golden brown, about 20 minutes. Allow cakes to cool *only* 3 minutes and quickly remove them from the pans while *hot* as they become quite hard. Cool and put together with prune filling.

Filling:

1 pound prunes, boiled and pitted and put through a food chopper
1 cup sugar
1 tablespoon cinnamon
½ cup water in which prunes were boiled
1 teaspoon vanilla

Boil prune juice and add vanilla. Add other ingredients and completely cool before using. (I refrigerate mine.) Spread between layers. The traditional recipe calls for an almond paste icing, but I use the following instead:

Icing:

1 (16-ounce) package 10X confectioners' sugar
½ cup butter, softened
Cream
1 teaspoon almond extract

Cream together the butter and sugar; add extract and cream to make icing of spreading consistency. Allow iced cake to "set" in refrigerator *two weeks* before cutting. This time is required for the filling to soften the layers, which are initially very firm. Slice thinly, as it is extremely rich and filling.

Margaret Manning Preston (Mrs. Ronald A.)

LEMON CAKE

Easy
Do early in day
Do not freeze

Cake:

1 (18-ounce) package Duncan Hines yellow cake mix
¾ cup water
4 eggs, stirred in with beater
1 (3-ounce) package lemon Jello
¾ cup cooking oil

Glaze:

2 cups confectioners' sugar
1 teaspoon grated lemon rind
Juice of 2 lemons
1 (7-ounce) package Angel Flake Coconut

Mix cake ingredients in order listed. Beat until fluffy. Add oil, mixing well. Pour into greased and floured 9 x 13-inch pan. Bake 30 to 35 minutes at 350 degrees. Remove cake from oven. Jab with fork at 1-inch intervals to bottom. Spoon the glaze mixture over warm cake. Sprinkle with coconut and serve warm.

Marian Bartlett Stewart (Mrs. Wm. Edward)

"OUT OF THIS WORLD" CAKE

2 cups sugar
1 cup butter or margarine *OR* ½ cup each
5 eggs
1 cup milk
1 (13½-ounce) box graham cracker crumbs (or 3½ cups)
1 tablespoon baking powder
1 (15¼-ounce) can crushed pineapple, drained
1 (6-ounce) package frozen coconut
1½ cups nuts, chopped
1 tablespoon vanilla

Grease and flour tube pan. Mix all ingredients together, using electric mixer. Pour into tube pan. Bake at 350 degrees 1¼-1½ hours. Test at 1¼ hours with straw which will come out clean if done. Set aside to cool before removing from pan.

Edna Avery Cook (Mrs. Sam T.)

PEA PICKING CAKE

Cake layers may be made ahead and frozen.
Cake may be made and assembled the day ahead.

Batter:

1 (18½-ounce) box yellow cake mix
1 (11-ounce) can mandarin oranges, juice reserved
½ cup cooking oil
4 eggs

Preheat oven to 350 degrees. Grease and flour three 8- or 9-inch cake pans. Beat eggs with cake mix; add reserved juice from oranges; stir in oil and fold in oranges using mixer to "break up" oranges. Bake 25 minutes. Cool and remove from pans. Wrap for freezing when cooled.

Icing:

1 (12-ounce) Cool Whip
1 (20-ounce) can crushed pineapple with juice
1 (5¼-ounce) package instant vanilla pudding

Mix ingredients together and ice cooled cake with mixture. Refrigerate cake after icing.
Yield: 12-16 servings

Williver Oglesby Brown (Mrs. Angelo)

MARY'S PECAN CAKE

2 cups flour
1 teaspoon baking soda
½ cup margarine
½ cup Crisco
2 cups sugar
5 egg yolks
5 egg whites, beaten
1 cup buttermilk
1 teaspoon vanilla
1 cup pecans, chopped

Preheat oven to 350 degrees. Grease and flour three 8-inch pans. Sift flour and soda. Cream margarine and Crisco together; add sugar and yolks. Add buttermilk alternately with flour to margarine mixture. Add vanilla and nuts. Fold in beaten egg whites. Pour into cake pans and bake 20-25 minutes. Remove from oven and cool. Ice with Cream Cheese Icing.

Joan Brooks Kunkel (Mrs. Cooper D.)

IDA B'S PECAN CAKE

1 cup butter
2 cups sugar
6 eggs
4 cups flour (reserve part for fruits)
2 teaspoons baking powder
2 teaspoons cinnamon
½ teaspoon allspice
1 teaspoon nutmeg
¾ cup wine, red or rosé
1 pound pecans
2 pounds raisins, cut up

Grease and flour a tube pan. Cream butter and sugar. Add eggs one at a time, beating well after each. Sift flour with baking powder and spices and add alternately with liquid. Add nuts and fruits dredged in part of flour mixture. Start in cold oven. Bake 4 hours at 250 degrees. When my mother makes this cake she leaves out one box of raisins and she says, "Add 1-pound carton mixed fruit, 3 or 4 slices pineapple, and some cherries. You can add figs and dates and extra nuts." With extra fruit do not bake full four hours. Test with wooden toothpick for doneness.

Jeanne Upton Freemon (Mrs. Joseph M.)

PLUM CAKE

Cake:
2 cups self-rising flour
2 cups sugar
1 cup Wesson oil
1 teaspoon cinnamon
1 teaspoon cloves
4 eggs
2 small-size jars Gerber's strained plums*
1 cup nuts, chopped

*Prunes may be substituted for plums.
Preheat oven to 325 degrees. Grease and flour Bundt or tube pan and set aside. Mix oil and sugar. Add eggs one at a time beating well after each addition. Sift dry ingredients together. Add to egg mixture. Add plums and nuts. Pour into prepared pan and bake 55 minutes. Cool 10 minutes and turn onto cake plate.

Glaze:
1 cup confectioners' sugar
2-4 tablespoons dry sherry

Combine sugar and sherry and drizzle over warm cake.

Virginia Perkins Sharp (Mrs. C. Edward)
Mary Stallings Parrish (Mrs. Ben W.)
Carol Coleman Pursell (Mrs. Elliott D.)
Evelyn Bishop Johnson (Mrs. S. H., Jr.)

POPPY SEED CAKE

Freezes well

1 (18-ounce) package yellow cake mix
4 eggs
½ cup salad oil
½ cup cream sherry
1 cup dairy sour cream
⅓ cup poppy seeds
1 (4-ounce) package French vanilla instant pudding
1 (4-ounce) package ground walnuts or pecans

Preheat oven to 350 degrees. Grease and flour tube or Bundt pan. In bowl place all ingredients; with electric mixer beat 5 minutes. Turn into tube or Bundt pan. Bake for 1 hour. If desired, sprinkle confectioners' sugar over top before serving.

Helen Kirk Graham (Mrs. James A.)

POUND CAKE

My great-aunt's recipe. It should be called a ¾ pound cake because the ingredients would weigh out that way.

5 large eggs (or 6 medium)
3 cups flour
3 cups sugar
¾ cup milk
1 scant teaspoon baking powder
1 cup real butter
½ cup Crisco
1 teaspoon vanilla
1 teaspoon mace *or* 1 teaspoon lemon extract
2 tablespoons ice water

Have all ingredients at room temperature. Cream Crisco, butter and sugar well, for at least 5 minutes with an electric mixer. Add eggs, one at a time, beating well after each addition. Dissolve baking powder in milk. Add flour and milk alternately to creamed mixture, beginning and ending with flour. Add vanilla and mace. Add two tablespoons ice water. Line pan with brown paper or grease and flour pan. Use a 10-inch tube pan or 2 loaf pans. Place in a *cold* oven and bake for 1 hour at 300 degrees. Time may vary according to your oven.

Jo Simmons Aiken (Mrs. Hovey E.)

Anna's Dr's wife

EASY POUND CAKE

It's hard to believe something this simple could be so good!

2 cups flour
1 cup butter or margarine, softened
5 eggs
2 cups sugar
½ cup milk
2 teaspoons baking powder
1 teaspoon vanilla

Preheat oven to 350 degrees. Grease tube pan. Combine all ingredients and mix 10 minutes at medium speed. Pour into prepared pan. Bake 50-60 minutes. Cool.

Emily George Zaytoun (Mrs. Kelly)

When frosting a cake from the freezer, thaw it uncovered, then add frosting.

CHOCOLATE POUND CAKE

½ cup butter
½ cup Crisco
3 cups sugar
5 eggs
½ cup cocoa
3 cups flour
1⅛ cups milk
½ teaspoon baking powder
2 teaspoons vanilla

Grease and flour a tube or Bundt pan and set aside. Preheat oven to 325 degrees. Cream together the butter, Crisco, and sugar. Add 5 eggs, cocoa, flour, milk, baking powder, and vanilla and mix well. Pour into prepared pan. Bake for 90 minutes. Cool and ice with chocolate icing.

Chocolate Icing:

1 (16-ounce) box confectioners' sugar
½ cup butter
2 squares chocolate, melted *OR* ¼ cup cocoa
2 teaspoons lemon juice
1 teaspoon vanilla
1 egg
¼ teaspoon salt
1 cup chopped nuts on top of icing for decoration

Mix all ingredients together until smooth and ice cake.

Marie Pethick Hoagland (Mrs. Harrison)

BROWN SUGAR POUND CAKE

1½ cups butter or margarine
1 (16-ounce) box light brown sugar
½ cup granulated sugar
5 eggs, separated
3 cups flour
½ teaspoon baking powder
1 cup milk
½ teaspoon salt
1 teaspoon vanilla
1 cup nuts

Preheat oven to 325 degrees. Cream butter and sugars. Add egg yolks one at a time. Add flour, baking powder and salt alternately with milk. Beat 2 minutes. Beat egg whites until stiff but not dry. Fold whites into cake mixture with vanilla and nuts. Pour into greased and floured 10-cup Bundt pan and bake 1½ hours. Cool 25 minutes. Turn out onto cake plate.

Evelyn Mitchell Farrow

PINEAPPLE POUND CAKE

1 cup butter
½ cup margarine
2¾ cups sugar
6 eggs
3 cups flour
1 teaspoon baking powder
¼ cup milk
1 teaspoon vanilla
¾ cup crushed pineapple *and* its juice

Preheat oven to 300 degrees. Grease and flour a Bundt pan and set aside. Cream butter, margarine and sugar together until light and fluffy. Add eggs, beating well after each addition. Mix in remaining ingredients and pour into prepared Bundt pan. Bake 1½ hours. Cool 10 minutes in pan, then turn out onto serving dish. Drizzle with glaze.

Glaze:
1½ cups confectioners' sugar
4 tablespoons butter
1 cup crushed pineapple, drained

Cream butter and sugar. Add pineapple. Drizzle over slightly cooled cake.

Susan Henri Johnson

COLD OVEN POUND CAKE

Stores well

3 cups sugar
1 cup butter
½ cup Crisco
1 cup milk
5 large eggs
¼ teaspoon salt
3 cups flour
2 teaspoons vanilla
½ teaspoon almond extract (optional)

Have all ingredients at room temperature. Cream shortening and sugar until fluffy. Add eggs, one at a time, mixing after each. Blend in flour and salt alternately with milk (start with about ¼ of the flour mix, blend. Next add ⅓ cup of milk, blend. Repeat twice, ending with flour). Add flavoring. Pour in well-greased tube pan with waxed paper lining the bottom. Bake 1¾ hours. *Start cake in cold oven,* set temperature for 325 degrees.

Rebecca Godley Paramore (Mrs. Walter H., III)
Lucille Clark Anderson (Mrs. K. F.)

BLUE RIBBON POUND CAKE

Easy
Last minute
Freezes well

3 cups cake flour, sifted
3 cups sugar, sifted
1½ cups butter
8 large eggs

Preheat oven to 300 degrees. Grease and flour a 10-inch Bundt pan and set aside. Cream butter and sugar thoroughly. Add eggs, one at a time, beating well after each addition. Add small amounts of flour, beating well after each addition. Pour into Bundt pan and bake 1½ hours or until done. Do not open oven door to test until cake has been cooking 1 hour.

Elizabeth Allen Brinkley (Mrs. William E., Jr.)

BRANDY CAKE

Time consuming
Filling can be made day ahead
Uses 8 whole eggs

Cake:

¾ cup shortening (margarine, butter or Crisco)
2 cups sugar
3 cups flour
1 cup milk
3 level teaspoons baking powder
1 teaspoon almond or vanilla flavoring
5 egg whites

Preheat oven to 350 degrees. Grease and flour three 8- or 9-inch cake pans. Cream shortening or butter with sugar. Add flour and milk alternately to sugar-shortening. Add baking powder and flavoring. Mix well and fold in egg whites which have been beaten until fairly stiff. Bake 20-25 minutes.

Filling:

8 egg yolks
1 cup sugar
4-5 tablespoons brandy or wine
1 cup raisins
1 cup nuts, chopped

Beat egg yolks and add sugar gradually. To this add brandy or wine. Cook in double boiler until thick. When cool add raisins and nuts. Use between layers.

Icing:

2¼ cups sugar
3 tablespoons white Karo syrup
¾ cup water
3 egg whites, well-beaten

Cook sugar, syrup and water until syrup spins a thread or forms a soft ball. Add slowly to egg whites. Spread on top and sides of cake.

Florie Gibbs Dill (Mrs. G. Redmond)

An 8-inch layer cake yields 10-14 servings
A 9-inch layer cake yields 12-16 servings
A 13x9-inch cake yields 15-18 servings.

PRUNE CAKE WITH BUTTERMILK ICING

Men especially like this cake although they turn up their noses at its name. Similar to a super spice cake, this is a very moist cake that will keep covered for several days.

Cake:

3 eggs, well-beaten
1 cup Wesson oil
2 cups sugar
2 cups flour
1 cup walnuts or pecans, chopped (optional)
1 cup prunes*
1 cup buttermilk
1 teaspoon cinnamon
½ teaspoon nutmeg
½ teaspoon allspice
½ teaspoon cloves
1 teaspoon soda
½ teaspoon salt

*1 jar of junior baby food prunes will do nicely.

Preheat oven to 325 degrees. Grease a 9 x 13-inch glass or metal pan and set aside. Sift all dry ingredients together. Add the well-beaten eggs, oil and buttermilk. Mix well. Last add prunes and nuts, if desired. Mix well. Bake 30-35 minutes.

Icing:

1 cup sugar
½ cup buttermilk
½ teaspoon soda
¼ cup butter
1 teaspoon vanilla

Mix all icing ingredients in a saucepan and boil on stove until mixture forms a soft but firm ball. Test for this with a candy thermometer or by putting a spoonful into a glass of cold water; if it forms a soft-firm ball with your fingers, it is ready. Pour icing over partially cooled cake.

Karen Brannock Askew (Mrs. M. H., III)

PAT FANNING'S 7-UP CAKE

Worth the expense

3 cups sugar
1½ cups butter
5 eggs
3 cups flour
2 tablespoons lemon extract
¾ cup 7-Up

Preheat oven to 325 degrees. Cream butter and sugar 20 minutes. Add eggs one at a time. Add flour and extract. Fold in 7-Up. Pour into heavily greased Bundt pan. Bake 1-1¼ hours.

RED VELVET CAKE

Do day ahead
Stores well

½ cup shortening
1½ cups sugar
3 eggs
2 ounces red food coloring
2 tablespoons cocoa
½ teaspoon vanilla
½ teaspoon salt
2¼ cups sifted cake flour
1 cup buttermilk
1 tablespoon baking soda
3 teaspoons vinegar

Preheat oven to 350 degrees. Grease and flour three 9-inch cake pans and set aside. Cream shortening and sugar. Add eggs, food coloring, cocoa and vanilla. Stir until creamed. Add salt to flour. Add flour and buttermilk alternately to creamed mixture and mix well. Sprinkle soda over mixture and then pour vinegar over soda. Blend but do not mix. Pour into pans and bake 20 minutes or until done.

Icing:

1 (8-ounce) package cream cheese
1 (16-ounce) box confectioners' sugar
½ cup butter
1 cup pecans, chopped
1 (12-ounce) package frozen coconut
½ cup milk (more if needed)

Cream butter and cheese. Add remaining ingredients. Spread over cooled cake.

Margaret Heath Cayton (Mrs. A. C., Jr.)

QUEEN ELIZABETH CAKE

Cake:

1 cup boiling water
1 cup chopped dates
1 teaspoon baking soda
¼ cup butter or shortening
1 cup sugar
1 egg
¼ teaspoon salt
1 teaspoon vanilla
½ cup nuts, chopped
1½ cups sifted flour
1 teaspoon baking powder

Add the soda to the dates and pour the boiling water over them. Set aside to cool. Cream shortening. Add sugar and blend well. Beat in the egg and vanilla. Mix and sift the flour, baking powder and salt and add alternately to the creamed ingredients, with the cooled date mixture and nuts. Bake in greased 8 x 12-inch pan at 350 degrees about 30-35 minutes. Prepare icing. When cake is done, remove from oven and spread icing over cake. Return to oven until icing is golden brown.

Icing:

5 tablespoons brown sugar
2 tablespoons cream
3 tablespoons butter
½ cup coconut

Mix in small pan and boil for three minutes. Pour and spread over cake. Return cake to oven for a few minutes.

Margaret L. Scott (Mrs. James H.)

MY GRANDMOTHER'S TIPSY CAKE

Easy
Do day ahead

Custard:

5 eggs
1 quart milk
12 tablespoons granulated sugar (¾ cup)
1 teaspoon vanilla

Heat milk in top of double boiler; beat eggs adding sugar gradually. Pour warm milk into eggs and sugar and put all into double boiler; allow mixture to cook, stirring constantly until thick. Add vanilla to thickened mixture and let cool.

Cake:

2 packages Lady Fingers or sponge cake
6 ounces blanched almonds
1 quart whipping cream
6 teaspoons sherry wine
6 tablespoons brandy or Bourbon
Maraschino cherries (red or green)

Cut Lady fingers or sponge cake in half and line a 2-quart bowl with them. Pour wine over the cake. Dot cake with blanched almonds by sticking almonds into cake. Let this stand covered for awhile. Pour custard over Lady Fingers or sponge cake. Whip cream adding sugar and brandy to taste. Pour this on top of custard. Dot with almonds and cherries.

Virginia Person Hollister (Mrs. J. T., Jr.)

SWEET POTATO CAKE

1½ cups cooking oil
2 cups sugar
4 eggs, separated
4 tablespoons hot water
2½ cups sifted cake flour
3 teaspoons baking powder
¼ teaspoon salt
1 teaspoon ground cinnamon
1 teaspoon ground nutmeg
1½ cups raw sweet potatoes, grated
1 cup nuts, chopped
1 teaspoon vanilla

Preheat oven to 350 degrees. Grease three 8-inch layer pans and set aside. Combine cooking oil and sugar and beat until smooth. Add egg yolks and beat well. Add hot water, then dry ingredients which have been sifted together. Stir in potatoes, nuts and vanilla and beat well. Beat egg whites until stiff and fold into mixture. Pour into prepared cake pans and bake 25-30 minutes. Cool and frost.

Frosting:

1 (13-ounce) can evaporated milk
1 cup sugar
½ cup margarine
3 egg yolks
1 teaspoon vanilla
1⅓ cups flaked coconut

Combine milk, sugar, margarine, egg yolks and vanilla in saucepan. Cook over medium heat about 12 minutes stirring constantly until mixture thickens. Remove from heat and add coconut. Beat until cool and of spreading consistency.

Judith Branch Blythe (Mrs. Charles B.)

VOLCANO CAKE

4 tablespoons butter
1½ cups very fine sugar
4 eggs, separated
½ teaspoon vanilla
1 cup flour
1 teaspoon baking powder
5 tablespoons light cream or milk
⅛ teaspoon salt
2 tablespoons unblanched almonds, flaked
1½ cups heavy cream, whipped
1 quart strawberries *OR* 1 tablespoon strong coffee mixed with ½ tablespoon cocoa, cooled in freezer

Preheat oven to 350 degrees. Cream butter and ½ cup sugar until very light and fluffy. Beat in egg yolks one at a time. Beat in vanilla. Sift flour together with baking powder. Add ½ to creamed mixture along with cream or milk, folding together gently. Add remaining flour gently. Divide into two well-greased round 8-inch layer pans and spread batter evenly. Beat the egg whites together with the salt until stiff, but not dry. Beat in remaining sugar a table-spoon at a time until the meringue is dull and very stiff to the touch. It should not be grainy when rubbed between the fingers. Divide the meringue between the 2 pans and spread carefully over cake batter with a spatula. Leave surface rough and covered with peaks. Sprinkle with almonds over meringue in one pan only. Bake about 45 minutes or until meringue is lightly browned, puffed and crisp. Remove carefully and cool on a rack. Do *not* invert layers. Either of the following should now be done. Slice strawberries reserving 8 whole berries for garnish and sprinkle with sugar to taste. Let stand 15-20 minutes. Fold sweetened, sliced strawberries into whipped cream and use as filling between layers. The almond layer is on top. Garnish top with whole straw-berries. *OR* while whipping cream add mocha paste (coffee and cocoa from freezer) and sugar to taste. Put between layers. Refrigerate finished cake 2-3 hours before serving.
Yield: 10-12 slices

Miriam Schulman Allenson (Mrs. Andrew J.)

Cakes are better frozen before frosting.

Pans for sponge cakes should *not* be greased or floured as that will cause shrinking of cake.

STRAWBERRY CAKE

1 (18-ounce) box white cake mix
3 teaspoons flour
1 (3-ounce) box strawberry Jello
1 (10-ounce) package frozen strawberries, thawed
½ cup water
1 cup corn oil
4 eggs

Preheat oven to 350 degrees. Grease and flour two 8- or 9-inch layer pans or grease and flour sides of pans and cut out a circle of waxed paper to fit on the bottom of the pan. Mix cake mix, flour and Jello together. In a small bowl mix ¾ cup strawberries, water and corn oil. Add this to cake mixture and blend well. Add eggs one at a time and beat 1 minute after adding each egg. Pour into prepared pans and bake 35 minutes.

Icing:
½ cup butter
2½-3 cups confectioners' sugar
2 tablespoons milk
Strawberries

Cream butter and sugar with 2 tablespoons milk. Add small amount of remaining strawberries for color. If icing is too thin add more sugar. Let cake stand in refrigerator several hours or days before serving.

Alice Craig Winters (Mrs. Carmi E.)

APPLESAUCE CUPCAKES

2 cups sugar
2 eggs
3½ cups flour, divided
1 cup butter
1 teaspoon baking soda
1 (16-ounce) can applesauce
1 cup white raisins
1 cup dates, chopped
2 cups nuts, chopped
3 slices candied pineapple
¼ pound candied cherries
1 teaspoon nutmeg
1 teaspoon cinnamon
1 teaspoon allspice
1 teaspoon cloves
1 teaspoon salt

Preheat oven to 325 degrees. Cream butter and add sugar. Add eggs, one at a time. Mix well. Add about 2 cups flour by degrees and mix until blended. Pour applesauce into bowl. Add soda and spices. Add applesauce mixture to cake batter. Use about 1½ cups of the flour to flour your fruit. Pour fruit and any flour that didn't mix with fruit into cake batter and mix thoroughly. Cook in small paper cups (petit-four size) for 25 minutes.

Kitty McCloud Edwards (Mrs. William J.)

BLACK BOTTOM CUPCAKES

Kids and adults love these

3 cups flour
2 cups sugar
½ cup cocoa
2 teaspoons baking soda
1 teaspoon salt
2 cups water
⅔ cup oil
2 tablespoons vinegar
1 teaspoon vanilla

Mix above ingredients together. Fill cupcake papers in tins slightly more than ½ full.

1 (8-ounce) cream cheese, softened
1 unbeaten egg
½ cup sugar
⅛ teaspoon salt
1 cup chocolate chips

Preheat oven to 350 degrees. Mix cheese, egg, sugar, and salt together. Beat well. Add chocolate chips. Put a generous tablespoon of batter on top of each cake. Bake for 25 minutes.
Yield: 3 dozen

Susie Warren Ward (Mrs. John A. J.)

AUNT SUE'S LEMON CUPCAKES

Cake:
3 eggs, beaten
1½ cups self-rising flour
½ teaspoon vanilla
1½ cups sugar
½ cup water
½ cup butter, melted

Preheat oven to 400 degrees. Beat eggs until light. Add sugar. Alternately add flour and water. Add vanilla and 4 tablespoons melted butter. Put ½ teaspoon butter in each muffin tin. Put 1 tablespoon batter in each muffin tin. Bake 12-15 minutes until just barely brown. Ice while hot. These are nice when done in small muffin tins.

Icing:
½ box confectioners' sugar
Juice of 2 lemons and 2 oranges
Grated rind of lemons and oranges

Mix all ingredients and dip cakes while hot.

Lee Thompson McIntyre (Mrs. J. Brooks)

CREAM CHEESE ICING

½ cup margarine, softened
1 (8-ounce) package cream cheese, softened
1 (16-ounce) box confectioners' sugar
1 teaspoon vanilla
1 cup nuts, chopped (optional)

Soften margarine and cream cheese and beat together. Add confectioners' sugar and vanilla. Spread over layers, top and sides of cooled cake.

EASY MOCHA ICING

Can be halved for 9 x 13-inch cake

3 cups confectioners' sugar
6 tablespoons hot coffee
6 tablespoons butter
6 tablespoons cocoa
1 teaspoon vanilla

Pour coffee over butter in large mixing bowl. Add remaining ingredients and beat thoroughly.
Yield: icing for 9-inch layer cake, 30 cupcakes

CHOCOLATE FROSTING

¼ cup shortening (Crisco, butter or margarine), melted
½ cup cocoa
⅓ cup milk
¼ teaspoon salt
1½ teaspoons vanilla
3½ cups confectioners' sugar, sifted if lumpy

Combine melted shortening, cocoa and salt; then add milk and vanilla. Mix in sugar divided into three parts. More sugar may be added to thicken mixture or additional milk may be added to thin frosting.
Yield: Frosting for two (8-9-inch) layers; *OR* one (9 x 13-inch) cake

Hattie Murphy Cobb (Mrs. Charles I.)

Butter-confectioners' sugar icing can be frozen on the cake.

COCONUT PECAN FROSTING

Stores well
Can be doubled or tripled

1 cup light cream *OR* milk
½ cup honey, warmed
3 egg yolks, beaten
½ cup butter
1 teaspoon vanilla extract
1⅓ cups fresh coconut
1 cup pecans, chopped

Combine cream, honey, egg yolks, butter, and vanilla extract in saucepan. Stir over low heat until thickened. Beat until cool. Stir in coconut and chopped pecans. Requires 20 minutes to prepare. Delicious on chocolate or spice cake.
Yield: 2¼ cups

Peggy Witmeyer Bernard

COFFEE ICE CREAM

Do day ahead
Stores well
Freeze

1 cup strong coffee
½ cup sugar
½ teaspoon Knox gelatine
½ pint heavy whipping cream
1 teaspoon vanilla

Heat coffee and sugar. Add gelatine which has been wet with ⅛ cup cold water. Place in refrigerator until cold. Then whip with mixer until light brown. Whip cream and add to light brown mixture. Add vanilla. Place in refrigerator tray and freeze.

Sauce:
1 cup brown sugar
½ cup water
1 cup pecans, chopped

In a saucepan, combine ingredients and cook slowly over low heat until sugar dissolves and just before mixture reaches soft ball stage. Drizzle over ice cream.
Yield: 4 servings

Margaret Hay Stallings (Mrs. Robert L., Jr.)

BUTTERMILK ICE CREAM

1 quart buttermilk
1 pint whipping cream
1 teaspoon vanilla
¼ teaspoon salt
1 cup sugar

Combine ingredients stirring until sugar is dissolved. Pour into ice trays and freeze. When cream is partially frozen, remove from freezer and beat. Return to trays and freeze.
Yield: 2 quarts

Frances Murray Fowler (Mrs. Joseph B.)

CHOCOLATE CHIP ICE CREAM

Milk, as needed
2 cans Eagle Brand condensed milk
1 (13-ounce) can evaporated milk
1 (12-ounce) package chocolate chips, crushed in blender*
2 tablespoons vanilla

*Bananas, strawberries, blueberries or any other fruit or flavor can be substituted for the chocolate chips.
Combine condensed milk, evaporated milk, chocolate chips and vanilla in the container of a home ice cream freezer. Fill remainder with plain milk. Use as much as needed. Freeze according to directions on freezer.

Cherry Sampson Meyers (Mrs. Bruce M.)

FIG ICE CREAM

1 quart half and half
½ pint whipping cream
¾ cup sugar
1 pint figs, peeled and crushed
¼ cup sugar

Combine ¼ cup sugar and figs and set aside. Combine half and half, whipping cream and ¾ cup sugar. Stir until sugar dissolves. Add sweetened figs and stir well. Pour into ice trays and freeze. When partially frozen, remove from freezer and beat. Return to trays and freeze.
Yield: 2 quarts

Frances Murray Fowler (Mrs. Joseph B.)

SNOW CREAM

3 egg yolks
1 cup sugar
1 (5-ounce) can evaporated milk
2 teaspoons vanilla
Snow

Beat egg yolks and sugar until fluffy. Add milk and vanilla. Add snow until of ice cream consistency.

Cecelia Chrismon Hudson (Mrs. Forrest M.)

WATERMELON ICE

⅓ cup orange liqueur
¼ cup sugar
3 tablespoons lemon juice
3 cups watermelon, pared, seeded and cubed

Purée all ingredients together and pour into freezer container. I prefer to purée a second time after freezing as the consistency is better. To serve, let frozen mixture stand at room temperature 5-10 minutes before serving and spoon into dessert dishes.

Phyllis Hurtgen Harke (Mrs. Dennis M.)

AUNT ELVA'S PEACH ICE CREAM

3 eggs, separated
1 can Eagle Brand milk
1 small can Carnation evaporated milk
1 quart fresh milk
1 cup sugar
1 quart fresh peaches puréed with ¾-1 cup sugar *OR* 1 (28-ounce) can peaches in light syrup with no sugar added

Beat egg whites until stiff and set aside. In large bowl beat egg yolks and add sweetened condensed milk, evaporated milk and half of the fresh milk, 1 cup sugar and the peaches. Fold egg whites into mixture and pour into 1 gallon ice cream freezer. Add remaining fresh milk to the mixture stopping before freezer overflows.
Yield: 1 gallon

Lynn Stewart Morris (Mrs. R. L.)

FRUIT ICE CREAM

Easy
Freeze

4 eggs
1 cup sugar
1 tablespoon vanilla
½ pint whipping cream
2 cans Eagle Brand milk
1½ quarts dairy milk
1 quart fruit*

*Your choice. Peaches or strawberries are excellent, mashed or puréed. Combine eggs, cream, sugar, and vanilla in bowl and mix thoroughly with mixer. Pour into can of electric freezer. Add condensed milk and fruit and stir well. Add dairy milk to fill-line on can and stir. Freeze according to directions for electric freezer.
Yield: 4 quarts

Karen Dunn Mason (Mrs. John B.)

HOMEMADE PEACH ICE CREAM

Part may be made ahead

12 peaches, peeled and quartered
4 eggs
3 tablespoons flour
3 cups sugar
5 cups milk
1 pint whipping cream
Juice of half a lemon
Pinch of salt

Put peaches through a meat grinder or blender and add to them 1 cup of sugar and the juice of half a lemon. Put in refrigerator. Beat eggs slightly and add 2 cups sugar, the flour and salt. Put this mixture in top of a double boiler. Scald the milk and slowly add it to the egg mixture. Cook over medium heat in double boiler until thick, stirring frequently. Cool. Put peaches, custard and whipping cream in ice cream freezer can stirring to blend ingredients. Freeze according to manufacturer's directions. Grind peaches and make custard a day or two before you plan to make ice cream.

Alma Hall Johnson (Mrs. Richard S.)

LEMON ICE

Economical
Jiffy
Freeze
Can be doubled

2¼ cups water
1¼ cups sugar
1 cup lemon juice

Bring water and sugar to a boil over moderate heat, stirring until sugar dissolves. Timing from boil, cook 5 minutes. Remove pan from heat, and allow syrup to cool to room temperature. Stir in lemon juice and freeze in ice cube trays. Remove frozen cubes and crush in an ice crusher. Crushed ice refreezes beautifully; or let ice cubes warm up a bit and mash with a fork for a slushy texture.
Yield: 1½ pints

Paulette Cardillo Culpepper (Mrs. George W.)

FRESH STRAWBERRY FROST

3 pints fresh strawberries, hulled
2 cups sugar
1½ cups orange juice
½ cup lemon juice
¼ cup Grand Marnier or Cointreau

In electric blender, put half each of the berries, sugar, orange juice and lemon juice. Cover blender and blend at a high speed for 30 seconds. Turn mixture into 8x12-inch baking dish. Repeat using remaining berries, sugar, orange juice and lemon juice. Pour into baking dish and stir in Grand Marnier. Freeze until partially frozen. Turn mixture into large mixing bowl and beat smooth with electric mixer at medium speed. Put into freezer containers and store in freezer.
Yield: 9 cups

Alice Graham Underhill (Mrs. T. Reed)

NANCY'S PEANUT BRITTLE

2 cups sugar
1 cup white Karo syrup
½ cup water
2 cups raw peanuts
1 teaspoon salt
1 teaspoon vanilla
1 tablespoon baking soda

Combine first five ingredients in heavy saucepan. Boil until candy thermometer reaches 293 degrees. Cool until syrup spins a thread. Add vanilla and beat; sprinkle soda from spoon and quickly beat well; it will foam. Immediately pour onto well-buttered marble slab, large cookie sheet or large aluminum serving tray. When cool, break apart and store.

Leah Jones Ward (Mrs. D. L.)

MAMIE EISENHOWER'S MILLION DOLLAR FUDGE

Can be prepared a week or more ahead

12 ounces semi-sweet chocolate bits
12 ounces German sweet chocolate
2 (7-ounce) jars marshmallow cream*
2 cups nutmeats
4½ cups sugar
Pinch of salt
2 tablespoons butter
1 (13-ounce) can evaporated milk

*Use only one jar marshmallow cream for a more chocolate taste.
Combine chocolate bits, German chocolate, marshmallow cream, and nutmeats in a large bowl. In separate pot, mix sugar, salt, butter, and milk. Boil for 6 minutes. Pour boiling syrup over ingredients in large bowl. Beat until chocolate is melted and pour into pan. Let stand a few hours before cutting. Store in tin box.

Carol Coleman Pursell (Mrs. Elliot D.)
Hilda Willis Warren (Mrs. Webster H.)

SEE'S FUDGE

In Los Angeles, Mother See's candy stores are famous for all kinds of candy. This is the only recipe made public—all other candies are "secret" recipes.

3 (6-ounce) packages chocolate bits
2 cups nuts, any kind
2 teaspoons vanilla
1 cup butter or margarine

Let chocolate bits, nuts, vanilla, and butter in a large bowl stand to room temperature, (overnight is fine).

4 cups granulated sugar
1 (13-ounce) can evaporated milk
20 large marshmallows, cut up

Bring sugar and milk to boil in a large saucepan and keep at rolling boil for 8 minutes. Dump this all at one time over the chocolate mixture, add marshmallows and stir vigorously by hand until chocolate bits and butter are melted and mixture smooth. Pour into buttered pan. (It will do well in a 11x15-inch cake pan, but can be put in more than one smaller pan.) Cool and refrigerate for 24 hours before eating. It will keep well in refrigerator and will last, and last, and last!

Jean Schocke McCotter (Mrs. Clifton L.)

TOFFEE

1 cup butter or margarine
1 cup sugar
1 (6-ounce) package chocolate chips
1 cup pecans, chopped

Line jellyroll pan, cookie sheet or 9x13-inch baking dish with waxed paper. In saucepan combine butter and sugar over medium-high temperature, stirring constantly until mixture reaches a temperature of 300 degrees on a candy thermometer, about 15-20 minutes. While mixture is heating, sprinkle ⅓ of the pecans over the waxed paper and mix remaining pecans with chocolate chips and set aside. Pour butter-sugar mixture over waxed paper and pecans quickly and press remaining pecans and chocolate chips into hot candy with back of wooden spoon. Allow to cool; refrigerate 1-1½ hours to firm up. Break candy into pieces and store in airtight container.

Patricia Byrum McCotter (Mrs. C. Kennedy, Jr.)

REESE CANDY

- 1 (16-ounce) box confectioners' sugar
- 1 cup crunchy peanut butter
- ¾ cup butter or margarine, melted
- 8-ounces Hershey's chocolate bars

Combine sugar and peanut butter, mixing well. Add melted butter, mix well. Spread in 9x13-inch pan. Melt 8-ounces chocolate bar in top of double boiler and spread on top of peanut mixture. Chill until firm enough to cut. Cut into bars.

Betsy Thompson Rose (Mrs. Joe)

friend of Mom's (First Baptist)

CHOCOLATE FUDGE

- 2 squares Baker's unsweetened chocolate
- 2 cups sugar
- 2 tablespoons white corn syrup
- ⅔ cup light cream
- 1½ tablespoons butter
- 1 teaspoon vanilla
- ¼ teaspoon salt

Break chocolate into small pieces and mix with sugar, corn syrup, salt and cream. Cook until soft ball stage about 235 degrees on a candy thermometer. Remove from heat and add butter *without* stirring. Allow to cool until lukewarm; add vanilla and beat until thick.

Bette Ann Divoky

MILLIONAIRES

- ½ cup butter
- 8 (1-ounce) Hershey bars
- 1 (14-ounce) package Kraft caramels
- ¼ bar paraffin, grated
- 2 cups pecans

Melt butter on low heat in top of double boiler. Add caramel; put lid on pot. Stir occasionally. Butter will be hard to get mixed in with caramel, but don't give up! Stir in nuts. Drop by spoonfuls onto well-greased waxed paper. Cool until firm. Melt chocolate and paraffin on very low heat; dip caramel and nuts into chocolate mixture.

Rena Terrell Knott (Mrs. Edmund T.)

SUGARED NUTS

1 cup sugar
¼ cup water
2 tablespoons light Karo syrup
2 cups pecans
Dash salt

Boil sugar, water, and syrup until it spins a thread. When mixture reaches thread stage, add a dash of salt. Add nuts and stir until creamy. Turn out on waxed paper and separate nuts.

Matilda Hancock Turner

PRALINES

1 (16-ounce) box light brown sugar
¾ cup canned milk, unsweetened
1½ cups of pecans, broken or in halves
1½ teaspoons instant coffee *OR* freeze dried coffee

Mix all ingredients thoroughly in medium saucepan and cook slowly over low heat until mixture reaches the soft ball stage stirring *constantly*. Remove from heat and allow to stand five minutes. Beat with a spoon until mixture begins to thicken. Drop by teaspoons onto greased foil. When pralines are cool and hard, peel foil from back and wrap each praline in a square of plastic wrap.

Paulette Cardillo Culpepper (Mrs. George V.)

BAKED CARAMEL CORN

1 cup butter or margarine
2 cups brown sugar, packed
½ cup light or dark corn syrup
1 tablespoon salt
½ teaspoon baking soda
1 tablespoon vanilla
6 quarts popped corn
Peanuts (optional)

Melt butter. Stir in brown sugar, corn syrup and salt. Bring to boil stirring constantly. Boil without stirring for 5 minutes. Remove from heat. Stir in soda and vanilla. Gradually pour over popped corn mixing well. Turn into two large shallow baking pans. Bake in 250 degree oven for 1 hour stirring every 15 minutes. Remove from oven; cool completely. Break apart and store in tightly covered containers.
Yield: 5 quarts

Susanne Darby Thompson (Mrs. Michael B.)

Cookies and Tarts

ORANGE BALLS

Easy
Can keep for 2-3 weeks

1 (12-ounce) box vanilla wafers, crushed
½ cup orange juice concentrate, thawed and undiluted
¾ cup confectioners' sugar, sifted
¾ cup coconut, shredded
½ cup pecans, chopped
Confectioners' sugar (additional)

Combine in bowl and work together to make a smooth mixture all ingredients except additional confectioners' sugar. Shape into balls and store in a covered container. Before serving, roll in additional sugar.
Yield: 42 balls

Lila Dedmon Smallwood (Mrs. E. F.)
Jean Schocke McCotter (Mrs. Clifton L.)

TERRY FAULKNER'S BOURBON BALLS

Keeps well

1 (6-ounce) package chocolate bits
½ cup granulated sugar
3 tablespoons light corn syrup
½ cup bourbon
2½ cups vanilla wafers, finely crushed
1 cup nuts, finely chopped
sifted powdered sugar

Melt chocolate in top of double boiler. Remove from heat and stir in sugar and corn syrup. Add bourbon and blend well. Combine vanilla wafers and nuts in large bowl. Add chocolate mixture and blend well. Form into 1-inch balls and roll in powdered sugar. Put in an airtight can for 3 days.
Yield: 40 balls.

Jean Schocke McCotter (Mrs. Clifton L.)

RUM BALLS

Easy

½ pound vanilla wafers
1 cup confectioners' sugar
2 tablespoons cocoa
1 cup pecans, finely chopped
½ cup light corn syrup
¼ cup rum *OR* bourbon

Roll vanilla wafers with rolling pin until fine. Mix all ingredients and let stand one hour. Coat hands with confectioners' sugar and shape into one-inch balls. Before serving, roll in confectioners' sugar.

Ann Holmes Novak (Mrs. David W.)

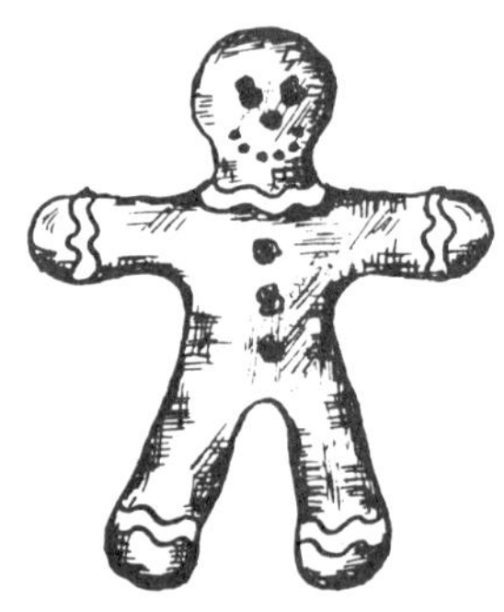

BROWNIES

I use a wooden spoon to beat and mix these brownies.
May be halved

4 ounces Baker's unsweetened chocolate
1 cup butter or margarine
2 cups sugar
4 eggs
1½ teaspoons vanilla
Pinch of salt
1 cup flour
1 cup walnuts, chopped

Preheat oven to 375 degrees. Grease a 9 x 13-inch Pyrex baking dish and set aside. Melt butter and chocolate; put sugar in bowl; add eggs and beat well. Add salt, melted butter and chocolate. Beat well and add vanilla. Beat in flour and fold in nuts. Pour into prepared pan and bake 25-30 minutes, testing after 25 minutes. Brownies should be chewy, so don't overcook.

Henrietta Sherman Mitchell (Mrs. Alexander S., Jr.)
Elizabeth Reese Ward (Mrs. David L., Jr.)
Hilda Willis Warren (Mrs. Webster H.)

CHOCOLATE BROWNIES FOR A CROWD

12 ounces unsweetened chocolate
2 cups butter or margarine
12 eggs
6 cups sugar
4 teaspoons vanilla extract
1 teaspoon salt
3¼ cups flour
5 cups walnuts or pecans, chopped

Grease three 15 x 10 x 1-inch pans. Preheat oven to 325 degrees. Melt chocolate and butter together in heavy saucepan. Beat eggs until thick; gradually beat in sugar, then beat in chocolate mixture. Add vanilla, salt and flour; mix well. Fold in nuts. Spread in the three pans and bake 25-30 minutes. Cool in pans. Cut each pan into 35 pieces.
Yield: 105 brownies

Marguerite Banks Tilghman (Mrs. Donald R.)

SASO'S BLOND BROWNIES

Unbelieveably delicious
Easy
Stores well
May be frozen

1 cup butter
1 (16-ounce) box light brown sugar
2 eggs
2 cups flour
2 teaspoons baking powder
1 teaspoon vanilla extract
Pinch of salt
1 cup pecans, chopped

Preheat oven to 350 degrees. Melt butter in heavy saucepan. Add sugar. Stir in eggs, flour and baking powder. Add vanilla, salt and pecans. Bake in greased 9 x 13-inch pan for 25 minutes.
Yield: 3-4 dozen

Saso Morris Jones (Mrs. Walter C., Jr.)

APRICOT BARS

These bars are a delight to serve at afternoon tea.

1¼ cups flour
¾ cup brown sugar
6 tablespoons margarine
¾ cup apricot preserves

Preheat oven to 350 degrees. Mix flour, brown sugar, and margarine together until well-blended. In square pan, pat firmly one-half of this mixture. Spread on top of mixture the apricot preserves. Sprinkle remaining half of flour mixture on top of preserves and pat lightly. Bake about 30 minutes.

Lynda Horner

COCONUT RAISIN SQUARES

½ cup butter
½ cup brown sugar
1 cup flour
1 cup brown sugar
2 eggs
1 teaspoon vanilla
1 teaspoon baking powder
2 tablespoons flour
½ teaspoon salt
1 cup pecans, chopped
1 cup coconut
1 cup raisins
½ cup candied cherries

Preheat oven to 350 degrees. Cream the butter, ½ cup brown sugar and flour. Pat into an ungreased 9 x 13-inch pan. Bake 10 minutes. Mix together 1 cup brown sugar, eggs, vanilla, baking powder, flour, salt, pecans, coconut and raisins. Spread this over the baked mixture and bake for an additional 25 minutes at 350 degrees. Cool and cut into squares. Place a candied cherry half on each square.
Yield: 2 dozen (2-inch) squares

Page Pearson Faulkner (Mrs. A. Gerald)

CHOCOLATE CARAMEL BARS

Truly unusual and delicious!

1 (14-ounce) bag Kraft light caramels (about 50 pieces)
1 (5-ounce) can Carnation evaporated milk
1 (18½-ounce) German chocolate cake mix*
¾ cup butter or margarine, melted
1 cup nuts, chopped
1 cup chocolate chips

*If using cake mix that has pudding in the mix, bake 18-20 minutes.
Preheat oven to 350 degrees. Spray 9 x 13-inch baking dish with Pam or other non-stick product. Melt caramels and ⅓ cup of the Carnation milk together in the top of a double boiler. Mix together the cake mix, melted butter and remaining ⅓ cup of the milk. Spread *half* of the cake mixture on the bottom of prepared baking dish. Bake for 6 minutes and remove from oven. Sprinkle with nuts and chocolate chips. Spread caramel mixture on top. Spread remainder of cake mixture over all. Bake 15-18 minutes. Remove from oven and let cool before cutting into bars.
Yield: 3-4 dozen

Phyllis Hurtgen Harke (Mrs. Dennis M.)

MISS ELLIOT'S DATE NUT BARS

¾ cup flour
1 cup sugar
½ teaspoon vanilla flavoring
1 teaspoon baking powder
⅛ teaspoon salt
½ cup oil
1 cup dates, chopped
1 cup nuts, chopped
2 eggs

Preheat oven to 325 degrees. Grease 9 x 13-inch baking dish. Baking powder and salt may be omitted if self-rising flour is used. Chocolate chips may be substituted for the dates. Combine all ingredients and bake in prepared pan, for twenty minutes. When cool, cut in squares as desired.

TRIPLE FUDGE BARS

1 (3¾-ounce) package chocolate pudding
1 (18½-ounce) package chocolate fudge cake mix
1 (6-ounce) package chocolate pieces
1 cup coarsely chopped nuts

Preheat oven to 350 degrees. Grease and flour 15½ x 10½-inch jellyroll pan. Cook pudding in a large saucepan as directed on package. Stir cake mix (dry) into hot pudding. Beat two minutes on medium speed. Pour batter into pan, sprinkle with chocolate pieces and nuts. Bake 18-20 minutes. Cut into 2 x 1½-inch bars.
Yield: 50 bars

Phyllis Spada Nashick (Mrs. George H.)

TANGY LEMON SQUARES

Crust:
1 cup butter or margarine, softened
½ cup confectioners' sugar
2 cups flour

Preheat oven to 350 degrees. Grease well a 9 x 13-inch metal baking dish with Crisco. In a large bowl, cream butter and confectioners' sugar until fluffy. Add flour and blend. Spread over bottom of dish; bake 15-20 minutes until lightly browned.

Filling:
4 eggs
2 cups sugar
⅓ cup Minute Maid pure lemon juice
2 tablespoons confectioners' sugar
1 teaspoon baking powder
⅓ cup flour
Additional confectioners' sugar

While crust is baking, beat eggs until foamy. Add sugars gradually. Add lemon juice, baking powder and remaining ⅓ cup of flour. Pour lemon mixture over baked crust and bake 25 to 30 minutes. Sprinkle with additional confectioners' sugar and cool. Cut into bars.
Yield: 2 dozen

Genevieve Tolson Dunn (Mrs. Mark S.)

MARSHMALLOW-CHOCOLATE CHIP BARS

A sticky, quickly devoured delight!

½ cup margarine
½ cup sugar
1 whole egg
2 egg yolks
½ cup flour
1 teaspoon baking powder
¼ teaspoon salt
1 cup pecans
½ cup chocolate chips
1 cup miniature marshmallows
2 egg whites, beaten stiff
1 cup brown sugar, firmly packed

Preheat oven to 350 degrees. Cream together margarine and sugar. Add whole egg and yolks beating well. Add flour, baking powder and salt. Spread dough into greased 9 x 13-inch pan. Sprinkle pecans, chocolate chips and marshmallows over dough. Beat egg whites and add brown sugar a little at a time to make meringue. Spread over marshmallow layer as carefully as possible. Bake 30-40 minutes. Slice into bars when cooled. Store in tightly covered container.
Yield: 24 bars

Susan Omdahl Shaw (Mrs. Phillip A.)

ROCKY ROAD HALLOWEEN SQUARES

Easy
Do day ahead
Stores well
May be frozen

1 (12-ounce) package semi-sweet chocolate morsels
1 (14-ounce) can Eagle Brand Condensed Milk
1 (10½-ounce) package miniature marshmallows
2 cups dry roasted peanuts
2 tablespoons of butter or margarine

In double boiler over boiling water, melt morsels of chocolate, milk, and butter. In separate bowl, mix marshmallows and nuts. Pour chocolate mix over marshmallow mix and blend thoroughly. Pour into waxed paper-lined 13 x 9-inch pan. Chill for 2 hours. Remove waxed paper and cut into squares. Cover and store at room temperature.
Yield: 2 dozen

Caroline Dunn Ashford (Mrs. Charles H.)
Gloria West Wheeler (Mrs. O. Gray, Jr.)

NANAIMO BARS

Bars need to be refrigerated

½ cup butter
5 teaspoons cocoa
2 teaspoons vanilla
1 egg, beaten
¼ cup sugar
2 cups graham cracker crumbs
½ cup nuts, chopped
1 cup coconut

Mix and heat butter, cocoa, vanilla, egg, and sugar until thick. Remove from heat and add graham cracker crumbs, nuts and coconut. Pack into 13 x 9-inch pan which has been sprayed with Pam.

Topping:
¼ cup butter
3 tablespoons milk
2 teaspoons vanilla
2 cups confectioners' sugar
2 teaspoons Jello vanilla pudding powder
2 ounces semi-sweet chocolate
2 teaspoons butter, melted

Mix ¼ cup butter, milk, vanilla, sugar and Jello together and pour over layer already in pan. Melt butter and chocolate together in top of double boiler and cover top of bars. Refrigerate bars.
Yield: 24 bars

Helen Kirk Graham (Mrs. James A.)

PEANUT BUTTER BARS

Can do ahead
Can freeze

1 cup peanut butter (crunchy is best)
1 cup margarine, melted
1½ cups graham cracker crumbs
1 teaspoon vanilla
2 cups confectioners' sugar

Combine all ingredients and pat in a greased 13 x 9-inch Pyrex dish. Chill and cut into bars.

Alice Graham Underhill (Mrs. T. Reed)

HELLO DOLLIES

½ cup margarine
1 cup graham cracker crumbs
1 cup coconut (3½-ounce bag)
1 cup butterscotch chips (6-ounce) bag
1 cup chocolate chips (6-ounce bag)
1 cup pecans
1 (14-ounce) can Eagle Brand milk

Preheat oven to 350 degrees. Melt butter in a 9 x 9-inch pan. Begin with graham cracker crumbs spread evenly in bottom of pan over butter and layer coconut, butterscotch chips, chocolate chips, pecans, then Eagle Brand milk over all. Bake for 30 minutes. Corners will brown. Cool and cut into squares.
Yield: 16 servings

Rosie Zaytoun Smith (Mrs. Carlton)
Uzie Broadstreet Thomas (Mrs. John C.)

MAGIC COOKIE BARS

Easy
Do day ahead
Stores well
Jiffy
Mix in baking pan

1½ cups Kellogg's Corn Flake Crumbs
3 tablespoons sugar
½ cup margarine or butter, melted
1 cup walnuts or pecans, coarsely chopped
1 (6-ounce) package semi-sweet chocolate morsels
1⅓ cups flaked coconut
1 (14-ounce) can Borden Eagle Brand Sweetened Condensed Milk

Preheat oven to 350 degrees. Measure Corn Flake Crumbs, sugar, and margarine into 13 x 9-inch baking pan. Mix thoroughly. With back of tablespoon, press mixture evenly and firmly in bottom of pan to form crust. Sprinkle chocolate morsels, coconut, and nuts evenly over crumb crust. Pour condensed milk evenly over nuts. Bake in oven for 25 minutes or until lightly brown around edges. Cool. Cut into squares.
Yield: 4 dozen

Uzie Broadstreet Thomas (Mrs. John C.)

CHOCOLATE SCOTCHEROOS

Great after school snack

1 cup sugar
1 cup light corn syrup
1 cup peanut butter
6 cups Rice Krispies
1 (6-ounce) package chocolate chips
1 (6-ounce) package butterscotch chips

Cook 1 cup sugar and corn syrup until they begin to boil. Remove from heat and add peanut butter. Stir well. Mix in 6 cups Rice Krispies. Press into 13 x 9-inch Pyrex dish. Melt chocolate and butterscotch chips together. Spread over Rice Krispie mixture. Chill. Cut into squares.

Becky Elmore Clement (Mrs. Joseph M.)

To make cookie tree ornaments; before baking, make a hole near the edge and insert a dry bean. When cookies cool, remove bean carefully. String on bright ribbons.

Baked cookies or dough may be stored frozen 9-12 months.

TOFFEE SQUARES

1 cup butter
1 cup brown sugar
2 cups flour
2 tablespoons margarine
1 egg yolk
1 teaspoon vanilla
1 (8-ounce) Hershey bar
1 cup chopped nuts

Preheat oven to 350 degrees. Cream butter and sugar until light. Add beaten egg yolk, vanilla and sifted flour. Spread thinly on a cookie sheet or jellyroll pan and bake for 15-20 minutes. Cool slightly. Melt chocolate with margarine in a double boiler and spread on cookie surface. Sprinkle with nuts and cut into squares.

Mary Ann Psychas Dunn (Mrs. John G., III)

ALMOND BUTTER STICKS

1 cup butter, softened
1 (8-ounce) package cream cheese
2¼ cups flour
2 teaspoons baking powder
⅛ teaspoon salt
1½ cups sugar
4½ teaspoons almond extract

Preheat oven to 400 degrees. Mix butter, cream cheese, flour, baking powder and salt together. Blend ingredients into dough and knead on a floured surface. Combine sugar and extract. Roll out half of dough to a rectangle about 14 x 8-inches. Place some of the mixed sugar and extract on the center of surface. Fold over ⅓ and layer more of the sugar-extract mixture. Continue to fold the dough down into rectangles until it is about 7 x 3-inches in size. Cut with a sharp knife into 1 x 2-inch slices. Follow same directions for remaining half of dough. Place on ungreased cookie sheet and bake for 8-10 minutes. Remove from cookie sheet immediately.
Yield: 5 dozen sticks

Elizabeth Allen Brinkley (Mrs. William E., Jr.)

NORWEGIAN COOKIES

Crust:
½ cup shortening
½ teaspoon salt
½ cup brown sugar
1 cup flour

Preheat oven to 325 degrees. Mix all ingredients together. Flatten in a greased pan. Bake 15 minutes.

Filling:
1 cup brown sugar
2 tablespoons flour
2 eggs, beaten
1 teaspoon baking powder
1 teaspoon vanilla
1 cup coconut, flaked or shredded
½ cup nuts, chopped

Mix together thoroughly. Pour mixture over crust. Bake 25 minutes at 325 degrees. Cool and cut into squares.

Genevieve Tolson Dunn (Mrs. Mark S.)

CHOCOLATE CRACKLES

Freeze well
Must do ahead

4 ounces unsweetened chocolate, melted
½ cup oil
2 cups sugar
4 eggs
2 teaspoons vanilla
2 cups flour
2 teaspoons baking powder
½ teaspoon salt
½ cup nuts (optional)
Extra powdered sugar for rolling

Blend melted chocolate, oil and sugar. Add eggs; beat well. Add vanilla, then dry ingredients. Add chopped nuts, if desired. Chill 3-4 hours or overnight. When ready to bake, preheat oven to 350 degrees. Shape into balls and roll in powdered sugar. Bake on greased cookie sheet 10-12 minutes.
Yield: 6 dozen

WHOLE WHEAT CHOCOLATE CHIP COOKIES

Delicious
Nutritious

1 cup unsalted butter, softened*
1½ cups light brown sugar, firmly packed
2 large eggs
1 tablespoon unsulfured molasses**
1 teaspoon vanilla
1½ cups whole wheat flour
1 cup unbleached flour
1½ teaspoons baking soda
1 teaspoon salt
1 (12-ounce) package chocolate chips
¾ cup walnuts, chopped
¾ cup raisins (optional)

*If using lightly salted butter, reduce salt to ½ teaspoon.
**Unsulfured molasses can be bought at health food stores.
Preheat oven to 375 degrees. Butter baking sheets. Cream together butter and brown sugar until mixture is fluffy. Add eggs, one at a time, beating well after each addition. Add molasses and vanilla. Combine well. Add whole wheat flour combined with white flour, baking soda, and salt. Mix well. Stir in chocolate chips, walnuts, and raisins. Drop batter by heaping tablespoons 2-inches apart on baking sheets. Bake cookies for 10-12 minutes, or until lightly browned. Let cool on rack.
Yield: 3⅓ dozen

Carolyn Brown Latham (Mrs. Edward B.)

STUFFED DATE DROPS WITH GOLDEN FROSTING

1 pound pitted dates
1 (3-ounce) package pecan halves
1/4 cup shortening
3/4 cup light brown sugar
1 egg
1 1/4 cups sifted flour
1/2 teaspoon baking powder
1/2 teaspoon baking soda
1/4 teaspoon salt
1/2 cup sour cream

Preheat oven to 400 degrees. Grease cookie sheets. Stuff dates with nut halves. Cream shortening and sugar until light; beat in egg. Sift dry ingredients; add alternately with sour cream to creamed sugar mixture. Stir stuffed dates into dough gently. Drop dough with one date per cookie onto cookie sheet. Bake 8-10 minutes and cool.

Golden frosting:
1/2 cup margarine
3 cups confectioners' sugar
3/4 teaspoon vanilla
3 tablespoons water

Lightly brown margarine in saucepan. Gradually beat in confectioners' sugar, vanilla and add water until mixture is of spreading consistency.
Yield: approximately 4 dozen

Sue Omdahl Shaw (Mrs. Phillip A.)

CHRISTMAS COOKIES

1 cup butter, softened
1/4 teaspoon nutmeg
1 1/2 cups sugar
1 teaspoon vanilla
3 eggs
1 teaspoon baking soda
2 1/2 cups flour
1 1/2 cups raisins
1 1/2 cups pecans
2 cups dates
1 cup candied pineapple
1 cup candied cherries

Preheat oven to 350 degrees. Grease baking sheets. Cream butter and sugar. Add nutmeg, vanilla, eggs, soda and flour. Mix well. Mix nuts with fruit; add to batter. Mix with large spoon. Drop by teaspoon onto baking sheet. Bake 12 minutes or until done.

Cecelia Chrismon Hudson (Mrs. Forrest M.)

FRUIT COOKIES

1½ cups sugar
1 cup butter
2 large eggs
2½ cups sifted flour, reserve ½ cup
1 teaspoon cinnamon
1 teaspoon salt
1 teaspoon baking soda
2 pounds dates, cut in small chunks
½ pound candied cherries, chopped
3 slices candied pineapple, chopped
1 pound walnuts
½ pound almonds, sliced
½ pound pecans

Cream sugar and butter; add eggs, one at a time and beat. Add dry ingredients then work in fruits and nuts. Chill for three hours or overnight. Break into chunks, about spoon-sized, and bake on greased cookie sheets at 350 degrees for 15 minutes.

Drusilla White Eckberg (Mrs. David E.)

If sticky fruits remain in your food grinder, dry bread run through the grinder will remove it quickly.

LEMON SUGAR COOKIES

Must do ahead

1 cup butter or margarine
1½ cups sugar
½ cup sour cream
3 cups flour
¼ teaspoon salt
1 teaspoon baking powder
1 teaspoon baking soda
1 teaspoon vanilla
1 tablespoon lemon juice *or* a few drops of lemon extract
Extra sugar

Cream butter and sugar. Add sour cream; blend well. Add vanilla and lemon juice or extract. Add dry ingredients. Chill 3-4 hours. When ready to bake, preheat oven to 350 degrees. Grease cookie sheets. Shape dough into small balls and roll in extra sugar. Flatten balls using the bottom of a glass after arranging on cookie sheets. Bake 10 minutes or until lightly browned.
Yield: 8 dozen

OATMEAL CRISPIES

Easy
May be frozen
May be halved

1 cup margarine
1 cup brown sugar
1 cup granulated sugar
2 eggs, beaten
1 teaspoon vanilla
1½ cups flour
1 teaspoon salt
1 teaspoon baking soda
3 cups quick oats
½ cup nuts
1 teaspoon cinnamon (optional)

Cream margarine and sugars and add eggs and vanilla. Mix well. Sift flour, salt and baking soda together and add to batter. Add cinnamon if desired Add oatmeal and nuts. Shape into rolls and wrap in waxed paper. Chill. Preheat oven to 350 degrees. Line cookie sheets with aluminum foil or grease and set aside. Slice cookies and put on sheets or roll slices into balls and dip in extra granulated sugar for a different touch. Bake 8-12 minutes. Dough may be frozen in rolls and sliced while still frozen.
Yield: 8 dozen

Anne Butler Gooch (Mrs. James C.)
Paulette Cardillo Culpepper (Mrs. George V.)
Julia Woodson Hudson (Mrs. John S.)

POTATO CHIP COOKIES

May be frozen

1 cup butter or margarine
½ cup sugar
1½-2 cups flour
1 teaspoon vanilla
½ cup potato chips, crushed
4X powdered sugar
½ cup pecans, finely chopped (optional)

Preheat oven to 350 degrees. Cream butter, sugar, flour and vanilla well. Add nuts. Add potato chips. Pinch into marble-sized pieces and place on cookie sheet. Press flat with fork. Bake 13 minutes and sprinkle with powdered sugar.
Yield: 5 dozen

Patricia Byrum McCotter (Mrs. C. Kennedy, Jr.)
Carol Coleman Pursell (Mrs. Elliott D.)

PEANUT BUTTER KISS COOKIES

1¾ cups flour
1 teaspoon soda
½ teaspoon salt
½ cup granulated sugar
½ cup brown sugar
½ cup shortening
½ cup peanut butter
1 egg
2 tablespoons milk
1 teaspoon vanilla
48 Hershey's kisses
Extra sugar

Combine flour, soda, salt and both sugars and set aside. Beat shortening and peanut butter together, adding egg, milk and vanilla. Add dry ingredients. Refrigerate until ready to bake. At baking time preheat oven to 375 degrees. Form cookie dough into balls about the size of a walnut. Roll ball in extra sugar and put on greased cookie sheets. Bake 10-12 minutes. Remove from oven and top immediately with unwrapped Hershey's kiss.
Yield: 3-4 dozen

Judith Branch Blythe (Mrs. Charles B.)

A cut piece of apple or orange in a cookie jar keeps cookies moist.

PIE CRUST COOKIES

4 cups flour
2 cups sugar
½ teaspoon salt
1 cup shortening
2 eggs, beaten
1 cup buttermilk
1½ teaspoons baking soda
2 teaspoons vanilla
½ cup sugar
½ teaspoon cinnamon

Preheat oven to 375 degrees. Grease baking sheets. Sift together flour, 2 cups sugar and salt. Cut shortening into dry mixture until fine. Combine beaten eggs and buttermilk. Add soda to egg-buttermilk mixture and stir until foamy. Combine with flour and shortening mixture, and add vanilla. Drop by heaping teaspoons onto baking sheets; flatten a bit; sprinkle mixture of ½ cup sugar and ½ teaspoon cinnamon on top of cookies. Bake about 7 minutes until edges are lightly colored. Store between layers of waxed paper.
Yield: 4 dozen

Eleanor Haley Hickson (Mrs. Robbins G.)

SHORTBREAD COOKIES

Freeze well

1 cup butter, softened
2½ cups flour
½ cup light brown sugar

Cream butter and sugar until light and fluffy. Add flour slowly, mixing well after each addition. Pat out dough lightly to about ⅓-inch thick. Cut in shapes. Bake at 300 degrees for 20-25 minutes on ungreased cookie sheet. Watch in your oven and don't let cookies brown. Cookies may be decorated if desired. Very rich!
Yield: 5-6 dozen small cookies

Martha Hughes Matthews (Mrs. F. Clayton)
Jane Kinnison Millns (Mrs. Dale T.)

SCOTCH SHORTBREAD

1 cup butter (NOT MARGARINE)
½ cup granulated sugar
2½ cups sifted flour (measure after sifting)

Cream butter and sugar until light and fluffy. Stir in flour in small amounts. Form dough into two flattish rectangles. Wrap in waxed paper and chill for about 3 hours. Preheat oven to 300 degrees. Shape dough into 7-inch circles and cut into 16 pie-shaped wedges. *OR* roll dough ¼-½-inch thick and cut into shapes or strips. Bake on ungreased cookie sheet for 20-30 minutes. Check frequently; they are done when the edges are golden. Sprinkle at once with plain sugar or sugar and cinnamon.
Yield: 3 dozen small cookies

Kathleen Harris Ingraham

Variation:
Using same ingredients, cream butter and sugar. Gradually add flour and mix well. Press mixture flat in a 15 x 10-inch baking dish. Prick top with a fork. Bake at 300 degrees 1 hour or until top is lightly browned. Cut into squares.
Yield: 4 dozen (2 x 1½-inch) bars

Susanne Darby Thompson (Mrs. Michael B.)

SHERRY THINS

Keeps well in a covered box
Nutmeg and wine combine for a fine flavor

¾ cup soft butter or margarine
1 cup sugar
1 egg
3 cups sifted flour
2 teaspoons baking powder
½ teaspoon nutmeg
½ teaspoon salt
½ cup cream sherry
Grated almonds or tiny candies

Cream butter and sugar until light. Beat in egg. Add sifted dry ingredients alternately with sherry, beating until smooth. Wrap in foil and chill several hours. Roll thin on floured board or cloth and cut with 2″ round or scalloped cutter. Put on cookie sheets and sprinkle with almonds. Bake in 400 degree oven 8-10 minutes.
Yield: about 9 dozen

Jean Schocke McCotter (Mrs. Clifton L.)

If you dislike greasing a cookie sheet, line it with waxed paper. For the second batch you bake, turn the waxed paper over; for the third batch, start over with a new piece.

PECAN DROPS

Easy

1 cup pecans, chopped
½ cup butter or margarine
½ cup plus 2 tablespoons shortening
1 cup confectioners' sugar
2½ cups sifted cake flour
2 teaspoons vanilla

Preheat oven to 325 degrees. Cream butter and shortening until smooth. Beat in sugar gradually. Stir in flour thoroughly and add vanilla and pecans. Drop by teaspoonfuls onto an ungreased cookie sheet. Bake in oven 15-20 minutes or until a delicate light brown.
Yield: 4 dozen

Grace Dixon Sellers (Mrs. John H.)

PECAN WAFERS

1/3 cup sugar
1/4 cup butter, softened
1 egg, lightly beaten
1/4 cup flour
1/2 cup pecans, finely chopped
36 pecan halves

Preheat oven to 350 degrees. Butter baking sheet. Cream together sugar and butter until mixture is light. Add egg and beat mixture until fluffy. Sift in flour and fold in chopped pecans. Heat the buttered baking sheet in oven for 1 minute. Remove it from oven and with teaspoon, drop the batter in mounds 2-inches apart on heated baking sheet. Spread the batter into rounds with the back of the spoon. Set a pecan half in center of each round and bake for 8-10 minutes, or until golden. Transfer wafers to plate to cool.
Yield: 3 dozen

Deborah Cook Tayloe (Mrs. John C.)

Freshen drop cookies by reheating in a covered casserole in slow oven 300 degrees for 8-10 minutes. To re-crisp cookies, place on an ungreased baking sheet 3-5 minutes at 300 degrees.

SWEET DREAMS

Put these cookies in the oven at bed time, and they are ready at breakfast!

2 egg whites
Pinch of salt
1/4 teaspoon cream of tartar
2/3 cup sugar
1/2 teaspoon vanilla
1 cup chocolate chips
1 cup pecans, chopped (optional)

Preheat oven to 350 degrees. Line cookie sheet with brown paper such as cut from a grocery bag or aluminum foil. Beat egg whites until foamy. Add salt and cream of tartar and beat until stiff. Add sugar a little at a time, beating well after each addition. Add vanilla. Stir in chocolate chips and nuts. Drop by teaspoonfuls onto prepared baking sheets. Turn off oven and put cookies in. Leave door shut! No peeking until oven is cold. Remove in 8 hours!

Wanda Dzula Adsit (Mrs. Spencer M.)
Pat Best Woodward (Mrs. J. Arthur)

ADVENT SPICE COOKIES

Easily doubled

¾ cup soft shortening
1 cup brown sugar
1 egg
¼ cup molasses
2¼ cups sifted flour
2 teaspoons baking soda
¼ teaspoon salt
½ teaspoon ground cloves
1 teaspoon cinnamon
1 teaspoon ginger
Extra sugar

Thoroughly mix shortening, sugar, egg and molasses. Sift together remaining ingredients and stir into first mixture. Chill dough. Shape dough into balls the size of big marbles and roll in granulated sugar. Place balls about 2-inches apart on greased cookie sheet. Bake at 375 degrees 10-12 minutes or until set but not hard. Let cool 2 minutes on cookie sheet before removing.
Yield: 4½-5 dozen

Barbara Straub Stewart

Variation:
By omitting the cloves you will have Old-fashioned Ginger Snaps.

Jane Kinnison Millns (Mrs. Dale T.)

TRYON PALACE GINGER CRINKLE COOKIES

This recipe was provided in answer to many requests by Tryon Palace Restoration Administrator, Donald R. Taylor

⅔ cup Wesson oil
1 cup sugar
1 egg
4 tablespoons molasses
2 cups sifted flour
2 teaspoons baking soda
½ teaspoon salt
1 teaspoon cinnamon
1 teaspoon ginger
¼ cup sugar for dipping

Preheat oven to 350 degrees. Mix oil and sugar thoroughly. Add egg and beat well. Stir in molasses. Sift dry ingredients together and add. Drop by teaspoonfuls into sugar and form into balls coated with sugar. Place on ungreased cookie sheet three inches apart. Bake for 15 minutes. Cookies will flatten and crinkle. Remove to wire rack.
Yield: 5 dozen

Ruth V. Miles (Mrs. Daniel M.)

SNICKERDOODLES

½ cup butter
¾ cup sugar
1 whole egg
1 egg yolk
1⅔ cups flour
½ teaspoon baking soda
½ cup walnut pieces
½ cup raisins
½ teaspoon nutmeg
Sugar and cinnamon to taste

Preheat oven to 375 degrees. Cream butter and sugar. Beat in whole egg and egg yolk. Sift flour and soda with nutmeg. Mix into batter. Fold in nuts and raisins. Drop from a teaspoon 2-inches apart onto a buttered cookie sheet. Sprinkle with sugar and cinnamon. Bake for 10-12 minutes.
Yield: 5 dozen

Jean Schocke McCotter (Mrs. Clifton L.)

WEDDING COOKIES

½ cup butter or margarine
1 cup flour
1¼ teaspoons vanilla
1 tablespoon sugar
½ cup pecans or walnuts, chopped
Confectioners' sugar

Preheat oven to 425 degrees. Lightly grease a baking sheet. Cream butter, vanilla and sugar until soft; add flour and nuts. Roll into small balls. Bake 10-15 minutes. When done, roll balls in confectioners' sugar while still hot.

Alma Nelson Hodges (Mrs. F. W.)

MISS KATE HANES' TEA CAKES

Best rolled cookie recipe I have ever found.
Flavor enhanced by storing a week.

2 cups brown sugar
¾ cup butter
2 eggs
1¾ teaspoons soda
2 tablespoons buttermilk
1½ tablespoons lemon flavoring
5½ cups flour

Cream sugar and butter; add eggs, mixing well. Add soda in buttermilk, lemon flavoring and mix well. Add flour, mixing to form a soft dough. Roll small amount out thinly and cut with favorite cookie cutters. Bake in preheated 350 degree oven until golden.

Judith Branch Blythe (Mrs. Charles B.)

MRS. WOLFSON'S JELLY COOKIES

Guaranteed crowd pleaser
Stores for several weeks

½ cup butter
¼ cup sugar
1 egg yolk
1 cup flour, sifted*
½ teaspoon vanilla
Plum Preserves

*You might need to use a little more flour.

Preheat oven to 350 degrees. Cream butter, sugar, and egg yolk together thoroughly. Add flour and vanilla. Dust hands with flour. Roll dough into balls the size of marbles. Place on ungreased cookie sheet 1½-inches apart. Make hole in middle of cookie with end of wooden spoon handle. Fill with plum preserves. Bake until light brown, about 8 to 10 minutes. Store in tightly covered tin container.
Yield: 4 dozen

Helen S. McCleary

Soft cookies should be stored in an airtight container. Crisp, thin cookies should be covered loosely.

THUMBPRINT COOKIES

The English call these Thimble Cakes and in France, they are Puits d' Amour, which may say something about the French national character.

¾ pound real butter (not margarine)
1½ teaspoon vanilla
1 cup sugar
2 egg yolks, beaten
4 cups flour
Pinch salt
Red currant jam

Preheat oven to 325 degrees. Cream butter, vanilla and sugar. Beat in egg yolks. Add flour, and salt. Pinch off dough, form into balls the size of large marbles. Place on ungreased cookie sheet. Make a well in each with thumb, or a thimble; fill with a bit of jam. Bake ten to fifteen minutes. For variety especially at Christmas time, use green mint jelly, a bit of cherry, or nut, etc.

Jo Simmons Aiken (Mrs. Hovey E.)

POLISH KOLACKY

1½ cups flour
1 cup butter
1 tablespoon milk
1 (8-ounce) package cream cheese
½ teaspoon baking powder
1 tablespoon sugar
1 egg yolk, beaten
Preserves, pineapple or peach
Confectioners' sugar

Preheat oven to 400 degrees. Cream butter with cream cheese, milk and sugar. Add yolk, baking powder and flour. Chill. Cut out with small glass; press indention in center and fill with preserves. Bake for ten minutes. After they have cooled, sprinkle with confectioners' sugar.

Virginia McGehee Borowicz (Mrs. Ronald R.)

MINI-PECAN TARTS

Can freeze

1 cup margarine or butter
2 (3-ounce) packages cream cheese
2 cups flour
½ cup margarine
1 cup sugar
2 eggs, separated
1 teaspoon vanilla
¾ cup dates, chopped
1 cup pecans, chopped
Dash salt

Preheat oven to 350 degrees. Cream 1 cup of margarine and softened cream cheese. Add flour (add more flour if mixture seems sticky). Roll into balls and press into small muffin tins to make a shell. Cream ½ cup margarine, 1 cup sugar. Beat 2 egg yolks and add to the creamed mixture. Add vanilla, salt, nuts, and dates. Fold in 2 beaten egg whites. Put nut mixture into tart shells. Bake approximately 30 minutes.

Becky Elmore Clement (Mrs. Joseph M.)

CHERRY CHEESE TARTS

Do early in day
Can be doubled
Easy

2 (8-ounce) packages cream cheese, softened
¾ cup sugar
2 eggs
1 teaspoon vanilla
½ teaspoon lemon juice
1 can cherry pie filling*
18 vanilla wafers
18 paper muffin cups

*Blueberry pie filling may be substituted.
Preheat oven to 350 degrees. Let cheese soften. Cream cheese and sugar. Beat vanilla into eggs, then add cheese mixture. Stir in lemon juice. Put vanilla wafer into paper muffin cup and add cheese mixture on top. Bake for 20 minutes. Cool and top with cherry pie filling.
Yield: 18 tarts

Sherwood Wright Crawford (Mrs. Thomas R.)

MINIATURE LEMON CHESS TARTS

Pastry for two crust pie

Filling:
2 eggs, slightly beaten
1 cup sugar
¼ teaspoon salt
1 tablespoon lemon rind
1 tablespoon lemon juice
2 tablespoons butter, melted

Preheat oven to 350 degrees. Combine filling ingredients and beat. Cut rounds of pastry with biscuit cutter, fit into miniature muffin tins. Fill with teaspoon of filling. Bake about 15 minutes; remove from pan immediately.
Yield: 30 tarts

Jo Simmons Aiken (Mrs. Hovey E.)

BOILED APPLE DUMPLINGS WITH HARD SAUCE

Several fruits can be used in this recipe: huckleberries, blueberries, peaches, pears. Pears will need to be cooked a longer time and 1 tablespoon lemon juice will need to be added to Hard Sauce.

10-12 medium-sized sour apples
1½ cups milk
½ teaspoon salt
2 teaspoons baking powder
Flour

Peel, core and slice or cut into quarters the apples. Bring to boil 2 quarts water. Mix together milk, salt, baking powder adding enough flour to make a stiff dough. Pinch off medium-sized ball. Roll dough out and place pieces of apple in it. Bring dough edges together on top and pinch together. Dampen dough edges with water to aid bonding. Drop in boiling water. Cook until apples are tender, 30-45 minutes. Test with fork for tenderness of apples. Serve hot with Hard Sauce.

Hard Sauce:
⅓ cup butter or margarine
1 cup brown sugar
½ teaspoon vanilla
⅛ teaspoon salt

Cream butter and sugar together. Add salt and vanilla. Beat until smooth. Serve on hot dumplings.
Yield: ¾ cup

Elizabeth Scales Marsh (Mrs. Thomas B.)

COBBLER

Easy

¾ cup flour
Pinch salt
2 teaspoons baking powder
1 cup sugar
¾ cup milk
½ cup butter
2 cups fresh peaches, sliced OR fresh blueberries
1 cup sugar

Sift flour, salt and baking powder. Mix with 1 cup sugar; slowly stir in milk to make a batter. Melt butter in 8 x 8-inch baking dish. Pour batter over butter. DO NOT STIR. Mix peaches and 1 cup sugar thoroughly and carefully spoon them over the batter. Bake 1 hour at 350 degrees. Serve hot or cold. Yield: 6 servings

Janet Grainger Corcoran (Mrs. James M.)

APPLE KUCHEN

1 cup flour
½ teaspoon baking powder
¼ teaspoon salt
2 tablespoons sugar
2½ tablespoons butter or margarine, softened
2 eggs, beaten
2 tablespoons milk
5 cups apples, sliced (4 large)
½ cup seedless raisins
⅔ cup sugar
1 teaspoon cinnamon
1 tablespoon grated orange rind
Whipped cream

Preheat oven to 425 degrees. Grease 8-inch springform pan. Sift flour, baking powder, salt, and 2 tablespoons sugar together in mixing bowl. Cut in butter until mixture is crumbly. Add eggs and mix well. Slowly add milk, stirring constantly. Spread dough on bottom and partly up sides of prepared pan with spatula. Place apples and raisins in saucepan with water to cover. Cook until apples are tender but not mushy; drain. Combine ⅔ cup sugar, cinnamon, and orange rind. Add to apples and raisins. Stir thoroughly. Spoon fruit mixture on top of pastry in prepared pan. Bake 50 to 60 minutes or until filling is firm and crust is golden brown. Remove cake from pan and cut into individual servings. Serve topped wtih whipped cream.

Eva Bond Littman (Mrs. John E.)

APPLE CRISP

Easy
Stores well
May be frozen

1 (18-ounce) package yellow cake mix
2 cans apple pie filling
1 cup butter, melted*
Lemon juice
Cinnamon
6-8 ounces shelled walnuts

*May use ½ cup of butter and ½ cup of margarine.
Preheat oven to 350 degrees. Grease 9 x 13-inch baking pan. Pour apples into pan. Squeeze small amount of lemon juice over apples. Sprinkle generously with cinnamon. Sprinkle cake mix over apples. Add more cinnamon. Spread walnuts on top. Pour melted butter over all. Bake for one hour. Serve hot, plain or with ice cream or whipped cream.

Kay Best Burrows (Mrs. Charles M.)

PEACH CRISP

Easy
Do early in day

½ cup water
Lemon Juice
Nutmeg
Cinnamon
1½ quarts peaches, peeled and sliced*

*Apples may be substituted. If used, substitute orange juice for water
Arrange peaches in bottom of 2-quart Pyrex dish. Sprinkle lemon juice, nutmeg and cinnamon as desired. Spread topping over peaches and bake at 350 degrees for 30 to 35 minutes until well-browned. Serve plain or with whipped cream or ice cream.

Topping:
½ cup butter, melted
¾ cup self-rising flour
1 cup sugar

Mix all ingredients and spread over peaches.
Yield: 6-8 servings

Ilene Phillips Disosway (Mrs. Donald J.)

BANANA FRITTERS WITH LEMON SAUCE

Fritters:

1½ cups flour
½ teaspoon salt
1 egg
3 teaspoons baking powder
2 tablespoons sugar
¾ cup milk
2 ripe bananas, cut in chunks
Crisco

Combine flour, salt, baking powder, and sugar. Mix thoroughly. Add egg, milk, and bananas. Stir until bananas are small pieces. Heat Crisco in deep saucepan; drop by spoonfuls into pan, (about 3 or 4 at a time). After fritter is cooked and browned, let drain on paper towel. Sprinkle with confectioners' sugar and serve hot with Lemon Sauce.

Lemon Sauce:

¾ cup sugar
¼ cup flour
2 tablespoons butter
Juice of 1 lemon
½ cup water

Mix all ingredients. Heat and let come to a boil. Stir thoroughly. Cook until mix coats spoon. Serve on fritters.

Annie Kinsey Whitford

CHERRY CRUNCH

1 (20-ounce) can crushed pineapple
1 (20-ounce) can cherry pie filling
½ cup pecans, chopped
1 (18-ounce) package Duncan Hines yellow cake mix
1 cup butter

Preheat oven to 350 degrees. Spray a 9x13-inch baking dish with Pam. Combine pie filling and pineapple, juice included, mixing together well. Sprinkle dry cake mix over the mixture in the pan. Melt butter and pour evenly over cake mix. Bake for 30 minutes. Remove from oven and sprinkle pecans over top. Put back in oven for 30 more minutes. Let stand at room temperature for at least 20 minutes before serving.

Microwave adaptation: Completely assemble ingredients and cook on Roast for 17 minutes and on High for 5 minutes.

Anna Gillikin Lamm (Mrs. Ronald B.)

CHARMING CHERRIES

Crust:

½ cup margarine, softened
1 cup flour
¼ cup confectioners' sugar

Preheat oven to 350 degrees. Combine margarine, flour and sugar and press into 8x8-inch pan. Bake 10 minutes. Cool slightly before adding filling.

Filling:

¼ cup flour
½ teaspoon baking powder
¼ teaspoon salt
¾ cup sugar
2 eggs
½ cup nuts
1 cup coconut
½ cup candied cherries

Sift together the flour, baking powder, salt and sugar. Add eggs to sifted dry ingredients. Fold in nuts, coconut and cherries. Spread over crust and bake 30 minutes. Cool. Cut into squares.

Phyllis Spada Nashick (Mrs. George H.)

CHERRY DELIGHT

Do not use metal pans for this unless you line pan completely with foil.

3 cups graham cracker crumbs
½ cup margarine, softened
2 envelopes Dream Whip
1 cup very cold milk
1 (8-ounce) package cream cheese, softened
2 (20-ounce) cans cherry pie filling

Mix graham cracker crumbs with softened margarine. Press into 9x13-inch or two 9x9-inch pans. Blend Dream Whip, milk and cream cheese with mixer until thick and creamy. Spread creamed mixture over graham cracker crumbs. Cover with two cans of cherry pie filling. Chill before serving.
Yield: 12-15 servings

Kathleen Durkin Rice (Mrs. Paul A.)
Margaret Whitehead Wall (Mrs. Lawrence D.)

CASSATA ALLA SICILIANA

Easy
Do early in day

This is frankly an extravaganza, although it is much lighter than you might think from reading the ingredients. Be generous with the measurements here. Anything Sicilian should be done with flourishes, and desserts are no exception.

1½ pounds ricotta or cream-style cottage cheese (about 3 cups)
½ cup sugar
2 teaspoons vanilla extract
1 ounce unsweetened chocolate, grated
½ cup almonds, chopped
6 tablespoons mixed candied fruits, diced
1 (8-inch) sponge or angel food cake
6 tablespoons rum
1½ cups heavy cream, whipped

Combine ricotta, sugar, and vanilla in a large bowl and beat a minute or two until light and fluffy. (If you substitute cottage cheese, it will be easier to get it smooth if you put it through a sieve.) Mix in the chocolate and almonds and 4 tablespoons of the fruit. Cut the sponge cake into three equal layers. Place the bottom layer on a serving plate and sprinkle it with two tablespoons of rum. Spread with one-half the ricotta mixture. Cover with the second cake layer. Sprinkle that with 2 tablespoons of rum and spread it with the rest of the ricotta mixture. Add the third cake layer and sprinkle it with the last 2 tablespoons of rum. Cover completely by wrapping in paper or if you have a covered Tupperware cake top, put it over the cake. Chill at least three hours. About one hour before serving, whip the cream and spread it over the top and sides of the cake. Sprinkle top with remaining 2 tablespoons of fruit. Chill again until ready to serve.
Yield: 8-12 servings

Kathleen Winslow Budd (Mrs. Bern)

PAVLOVA MERINGUE

Easy
This recipe was named for the famous ballerina.

4 egg whites, at room temperature
1 cup very fine sugar
1 tablespoon cornstarch
1 teaspoon vinegar
Fresh or canned fruit
Heavy cream

Preheat oven to 300 degrees. Beat egg whites as stiff as possible, adding sugar slowly until dissolved. Fold in cornstarch and vinegar. Pile on oiled heavy piece of foil the sides of which have been built up to hold heat. (This is better than using a regular cookie sheet.) Bake slowly for one and one-half hours. Turn onto flat platter and decorate with fruit and whipped cream or unwhipped cream.
Yield: 6 servings

Kathleen Winslow Budd (Mrs. Bern)

CHIPS 'N MAC DELIGHT

This recipe has been served to the Tryon Palace Symposium luncheon for two years. The second year it was requested by the group. I have had letters from several members of this group requesting the recipe. It is so easy and economical.

Easy
Do day ahead or longer
Economical
Can double or more

1 (13-ounce) package Jack's Chips 'n Mac cookies
1 (8-ounce) Cool Whip
Milk

Dip each cookie lightly in plain milk and line bottom of 1½-quart Pyrex dish or equivalent size. Cover each layer of cookies with a layer of Cool Whip. Continue until all cookies are used except 2-3 cookies which may be grated on top for decoration. Place in refrigerator overnight or longer. Serve in squares.
Yield: 10-12 servings

Ilene Phillips Disosway (Mrs. Donald J.)

APPLE SISTERS' CHOCOLATE SPECTACULAR

Easy
Do day ahead
Do early in day
Stores well
Can double

Crust:
½ cup margarine, melted
1 cup flour
¾ cup nuts, finely chopped

Preheat oven to 350 degrees. Pam spray a 13x9-inch baking dish. Mix margarine, flour and chopped nuts together. Press into baking dish. Bake 10-15 minutes. Remove from oven to cool.

Filling:
1 cup confectioners' sugar
1 (8-ounce) package cream cheese
1 (12-ounce) container Cool Whip
2 (4½-ounce) packages instant chocolate pudding *OR* 1 (4½-ounce) package instant chocolate *and* 1 (3¾-ounce) package instant vanilla pudding
3 cups milk
¼ cup nuts, chopped

Mix cream cheese, confectioners' sugar and half of the Cool Whip together. Pour over cooled crust. Make up pudding with milk and pour over cream cheese mixture. Put remaining Cool Whip on top of pudding and sprinkle nuts on top over Cool Whip.
Yield: 12-16 servings

Becky Melton Kafer (Mrs. C. William)
Melanie Applegate (Mrs. Earl)

APRICOT DREAM DESSERT

½ pound vanilla wafers
½ cup butter
1 cup confectioners' sugar
½ pint whipping cream, whipped
2 egg yolks
2 egg whites
1 cup apricot pulp

Cook apricots according to directions on bag and put through ricer. Measure one cup. Crush vanilla wafers. Save ½ cup for topping. Line bottom of 8x11-inch or 9x9-inch pan with crumbs. Cream butter and sugar. Add yolks. Beat egg whites stiffly and fold into butter mixture. Spread mixture on top of crumbs; spread pulp over this; spread whipped cream over all. Sprinkle with crumbs. Refrigerate at least 12 hours.
Yield: 9-12 servings

Alyce Faye Tilley Grant (Mrs. David J.)

CHOCOLATE ICE BOX CAKE

For best results, do day ahead
Elegant on a pedestaled cake plate. This is a favorite birthday cake for the men in my family and a tradition at Christmas.

1 dozen eggs, separated
3 packages Lady fingers
4 (4-ounce) packages German sweet chocolate
½ cup water
½ cup sugar
1½ pints whipping cream*

*May substitute Cool Whip. If using whipping cream, include 1 teaspoon of vanilla, and 2 tablespoons of sugar in ingredients.
In top of double boiler melt chocolate with water and sugar. Add egg yolks, one at a time, and beat well after each yolk is added. Cook until thick, usually just a minute or two. Cool. Beat egg whites until dry. Fold into chocolate mixture. Whip ½ pint cream and fold into mixture. Line tube pan with plastic wrap on sides and bottom. Line sides and bottom with Lady fingers. Alternate three layers each of chocolate mixture and Lady fingers until the pan is full. Chill for 12 to 24 hours. Turn out and cover with rest of whipped cream to which sugar and vanilla has been added. For garnish, add chocolate shavings on top.
Yield: 16-20 servings

Dora Winters Taylor (Mrs. John T., Jr.)

NUT ROLL EXTRAORDINAIRE

7 eggs, separated
¾ cup sugar
1½ cups nuts, ground (pecans, walnuts, almonds)
1 teaspoon baking powder
Confectioners' sugar
Cool Whip or Whipped Cream

Preheat oven to 350 degrees. Oil jellyroll pan; line pan with waxed paper and oil again. Beat 7 egg yolks with sugar until light in color and ribbon forms when dropped from spoon. Beat in ground nuts and baking powder. Fold in stiffly beaten egg whites. Spread in prepared pan and bake 15-20 minutes. Cool. Cover with damp towel and chill. Dust the top with confectioners' sugar and turn out onto waxed paper. It is now ready to fill and ice.

Filling #1:
1 (10-ounce) jar apricot preserves
¼ cup Grand Marnier

Blend ingredients in food processor or electric mixer. Spread over roll.

Filling #2:
1 (10-ounce) jar strawberry preserves
¼ cup Cointreau

Blend ingredients in food processor or electric mixer. Spread over roll.

To assemble: After spreading either filling over roll, start at long edge of roll and roll as for jellyroll. Cover with whipped cream or Cool Whip and decorate with Chocolate Leaves or as desired.

CHOCOLATE LEAVES

4 ounces semi-sweet chocolate pieces
Non-poisonous leaves*
½-inch artist brush

*A camelia leaf is a good choice because of its size.
Melt chocolate. Wash leaves. Brush melted chocolate on backs of leaves. Put in freezer for 2-3 minutes or until hard enough to peel leaf from chocolate. Put chocolate leaves into plastic bag which has air in it to cushion the leaves. Keep in refrigerator until needed. To keep leaves for a longer time, use 6 ounces melted semi-sweet chocolate combined with a block of melted paraffin and follow preceeding directions.

Anne Fowler Hiller (Mrs. Carl J.)

DATE ROLL

A delicious dessert!

1 (8-ounce) box chopped dates
2 (10-ounce) bags marshmallows, quartered
1 cup pecans, finely chopped
1 (16-ounce) box graham crackers, rolled
Cream or whiskey
Whipped cream

Mix all ingredients together, adding sufficient cream or whiskey to mold into shape. Work mixture until you can form a roll 3-inches in diameter. Wrap in oiled paper and put in refrigerator for 5 or 6 hours, or overnight. Slice in 1-inch slices and serve with whipped cream.

Naomi Webb Ryder (Mrs. W. W.)

GRAND'S WINE JELLY

8 ounces boiling water
1 (3-ounce) package lemon Jello
Pinch of salt
8 ounces sherry wine
½ pint whipping cream
Sugar to taste

Pour boiling water over Jello. Stir until all Jello is dissolved. Let cool to room temperature. Add sherry and stir well. Cover tightly and refrigerate until completely jelled. Serve with whipping cream which has been whipped and sugared to taste.

Emma Katie Guion Davis (Mrs. Junius)

SLIM STRAWBERRIES ROMANOFF

2 cups fresh strawberries
½ cup orange juice
3 tablespoons sugar*OR* equivalent in sugar substitute*
¼ cup orange liqueur
½ cup prepared low-calorie whipped topping

*With sugar—139 calories, with sugar substitute—104 calores per serving
Wash and hull berries and place in decorative glass serving dish. Stir in orange juice, sugar, liqueur, and chill one hour or more. At dessert time, spoon into footed champagne glasses and top with 2 tablespoons of whipped topping per person.
Yield: 4 servings

Nancy Scearce Deans

COCONUT SNOWBALL

1 large angel food cake, broken in pieces
2 tablespoons Knox gelatine
1 cup hot water
1 cup orange juice
1 cup sugar
Pinch salt
3 (½ pint) cartons whipping cream
Fresh coconut

Dissolve gelatine in 4 tablespoons of cold water, then in cup of hot water. Add juice, sugar and salt. Place in refrigerator until it begins to jell. Whip 1 pint of cream. Mix the jellied juice with the cream and cake pieces. Line bowl with foil or waxed paper and add mixture. Chill 7 or 8 hours. Invert onto serving platter. Peel off foil. Frost with ½ pint whipped cream and cover with coconut.
Yield: 16 servings

Alyce Faye Tilley Grant (Mrs. David J.)

SNOWBALLS

1 (20-ounce) can crushed pineapple
1 cup pecans, chopped
½ cup dates, chopped
½ cup white seedless raisins
½ cup margarine
1 cup sugar
1 box butter cookies*
1 (12-ounce) container Cool Whip
Coconut to garnish
Cherries to garnish

*Nabisco with hole in center are a good choice.

Melt margarine; add sugar, fruit and nuts. Simmer for 10 minutes. Take 3 cookies, one at a time and fill between each with cooked mixture ending with mixture on top. Let set overnight or at least 3 hours. Top with Cool Whip before serving. May garnish with coconut and cherries.
Yield: 15 servings

Mary Poole Predaris (Mrs. Spiro G.)

ORANGE AND LEMON ICE BOX CAKE

Easy
Do night before

1 large orange
1 large lemon
1 cup sugar
2 eggs
⅛ teaspoon salt
½ pint heavy cream
2-layer sponge cake

Cut sponge cake layers in half making four layers. Grate rind of one large orange and squeeze the juice. Grate rind of one large lemon and then squeeze juice. Take juice and rind with one cup sugar and put in top of double boiler. Add two beaten eggs. Cook over hot water until mixture reaches the consistency of custard. Add salt and cool thoroughly. Beat the heavy cream and add all together. Spread this on all layers and top and sides of cake. Put in refrigerator for at least 6 hours or overnight.

Kathleen Winslow Budd (Mrs. Bern)

LEMONADE ICE CREAM CAKE

Easy
Freeze

1 (18-ounce) cake mix
1 quart vanilla ice cream
1 (6-ounce) can frozen pink lemonade concentrate*
1 cup whipping cream

*Instead of lemonade, I have used frozen orange juice and added Cointreau to taste.

Bake cake in two 9-inch pans according to directions. Cool. Soften ice cream and thaw lemonade. Line one of the cake pans with foil. Mix ½ can lemonade with ice cream and fill the foil-lined pan. Freeze 3 hours or overnight.

To assemble cake:
Layer the two cake layers on top and bottom of prepared ice cream layer. Whip cream and add remaining lemonade to it. Ice cake with mixture and freeze. Remove from freezer approximately 20-30 minutes before you plan to serve.

Ann Harris Bustard (Mrs. Victor W.)

BOURBON ON A CLOUD

¾ cup sugar
1 envelope Knox gelatine
3 eggs, separated
¾ cup bourbon
1⅓ cups walnuts, chopped
1 cup heavy cream, whipped
Fresh strawberries (or other fruit for garnish)

Combine 6 tablespoons sugar and gelatine, mix well. Beat egg yolks slightly. Gradually add bourbon, stirring constantly. (Addition of bourbon too quickly tends to "cook" the egg yolks.) Add egg yolk mixture to gelatine. Cook over hot, *not boiling,* water, stirring constantly, until mixture coats metal spoon, about 10 minutes. Beat egg whites until foamy. Gradually add remaining 6 tablespoons sugar and continue beating until stiff and glossy. Fold in yolk mixture. Chill 20 minutes. Fold in walnuts and cream. Turn into 4- or 5-cup mold. Chill until firm. Unmold. Serve garnished with strawberries.
Yield: 6-8 servings

Margaret Whitehead Wall (Mrs. Lawrence D.)

GRAPEFRUIT ALASKA

4 grapefruit
½ cup fine sugar
½ cup rum
4 egg whites
½ cup sugar
Vanilla ice cream

Cut grapefruits in half. Remove pulp leaving membrane. Remove membrane without breaking the skin. Place halves in refrigerator. Place pulp in bowl with sugar and rum. Chill for several hours. At serving time, fill shells with fruit. Top with ice cream. Cover with meringue (add sugar to egg whites while beating) making sure that it touches the edge of shell all around covering ice cream completely. Place in a very hot oven under the broiler for 1 or 2 minutes until brown.
Yield: 8 servings

Ann Harris Bustard (Mrs. Victor W.)

COFFEE MOUSSE

Prepare day before

2 envelopes Knox gelatine
½ cup cold water
1 cup confectioners' sugar
1 cup milk
4 teaspoons instant coffee
1 tablespoon rum
2 egg whites, beaten stiff
2 cups whipping cream, whipped

Sprinkle gelatine over water to soften. Stir sugar, milk, and coffee in top of double boiler. Cook until just hot and add softened gelatine. Set aside to cool to consistency of unbeaten egg whites (about 30 minutes). Add rum and beat until fluffy. Fold in beaten egg whites. Fold in whipped cream. Chill in mold overnight in refrigerator.

Sauce:
2 egg yolks
¾ cup confectioners' sugar
2 tablespoons-⅓ cup rum (as desired)
1 cup whipping cream, whipped
Slivered almonds, toasted

Beat yolks and sugar until creamy and light. Fold in rum with a spoon. Fold in whipped cream. Pour sauce over unmolded mousse and top with slivered almonds.
Yield: 8-10 servings

Bea Lee Newton (Mrs. Eldon S., Jr.)

FROZEN RUM CUSTARD

Prepare in advance

1 cup seedless raisins
1½ cups dark rum
2 cups Cool Whip
1 cup pecans, chopped
1 cup macaroon crumbs*
1½ quarts vanilla ice cream

*I use Jack's Coconut Cookies
Soak raisins in rum for 2 hours. Fold Cool Whip in macaroon crumbs and nuts. Stir mixture into softened ice cream. Place in 12-one cup molds. (I line them with cup cake liners.) Freeze until time to serve.
Yield: 12 servings

Mary Coxe Bullock (Mrs. George P.)

BREAD PUDDING WITH WHISKEY SAUCE

1 loaf French bread
1 quart milk
3 eggs
2 cups sugar
2 tablespoons vanilla
3 tablespoons margarine, melted
1 cup raisins

Preheat oven to 350 degrees. Melt margarine in bottom of 3-quart baking dish. Remove from oven to cool. Soak bread in milk and crush with hands until mixed thoroughly. Add eggs, sugar, vanilla and raisins and stir well. Pour mixture over melted margarine and bake 55-60 minutes or until very firm. Let cool; cube pudding and put into individual dessert dishes. When ready to serve, add Whiskey Sauce.

Whiskey Sauce:
½ cup butter or margarine
1 cup sugar
1 egg, well-beaten
Whiskey to taste

In top of double boiler, heat sugar and butter until very hot and completely dissolved. Add egg, beating quickly so egg doesn't curdle. Let cool and add whiskey to taste.
Yield: 6-8 servings

Elizabeth Allen Brinkley (Mrs. William E., Jr.)

DIETETIC RICE PUDDING

No sugar

2 eggs, well-beaten
2 cups cooked rice
⅓ cup raisins
1 teaspoon vanilla
⅛ teaspoon salt
¼ teaspoon cinnamon
¼ teaspoon nutmeg
1 tablespoon (full) liquid sweetener
2 cups skim milk

Beat eggs well, adding all other ingredients mixing well. Bake in baking dish at 375 degrees until set, approximately 30 minutes.

Ilene Phillips Disosway (Mrs. Donald J.)

ELIZABETH ASHFORD MORRIS'S CHRISTMAS FIG PUDDING

1 pound figs
¾ pound bread crumbs, no crust
4 eggs
½ cup butter or margarine
1½ pounds sugar (6 cups)
1 cup sour milk
½ teaspoon baking soda
Pinch of salt
1 teaspoon cinnamon

Beat eggs thoroughly. Add remaining ingredients. Put in mold and steam 1½ hours. Unmold and serve warm with whipped cream on top and garnished with a cherry and a sprig of holly.

Saso Morris Jones (Mrs. Walter C.)

FUDGE BATTER PUDDING

2 tablespoons butter, melted
1 cup sugar
1 teaspoon vanilla
1 cup sifted flour
8 tablespoons cocoa
1 teaspoon baking powder
¾ teaspoon salt
½ cup milk
1 cup nuts, chopped
1⅔ cups boiling water

Make a batter by mixing butter, ½ cup sugar and vanilla together. Sift flour, 3 tablespoons cocoa, ½ teaspoon salt and baking powder together. Add alternately with milk to first mixture. Mix well. Stir in nuts. Mix together remaining ½ cup sugar, 5 tablespoons cocoa, ¼ teaspoon salt and boiling water. Pour into a 10x6x2-inch baking dish. Drop batter into hot liquid mixture by teaspoonfuls. Bake in 350 degree oven for 40-45 minutes. Serve warm with a scoop of ice cream or Cool Whip.
Yield: 12 servings

Emma Anderson (Mrs. Raymond F.)

PERSIMMON PUDDING

Easy
Do early in day
Stores well
May be frozen

2 cups persimmon, puréed
4 eggs
1⅔ cups sugar
¾ cup self-rising flour
½ cup margarine, melted
1 cup buttermilk
1 teaspoon cinnamon
1 teaspoon vanilla
Dash nutmeg

Grease and flour 9x13-inch baking dish. Preheat oven to 325 degrees. Add above ingredients to persimmon pulp in order given. Beat well after each addition. Bake 1-1¼ hours or until medium brown. Cool completely before cutting.
Yield: 12-16 servings

Nancy Samuel Everhart (Mrs. Charles L.)

REAL ENGLISH PLUM PUDDING

½ pound sultanas (dark)
½ pound seeded raisins
2 pounds currants
½ cup mixed peel, chopped fine
½ pound suet, chopped fine
½ cup almonds, shredded
½ cup bread crumbs
1 cup milk
1 cup brown sugar
Juice and grated rind of lemon
6 eggs, beaten
½ cup wine
2 cups flour
1 teaspoon nutmeg
¼ teaspoon salt

Mix fruit, suet, nuts, crumbs, milk, sugar, lemon juice and rind and let stand overnight. Add beaten eggs, wine, flour sifted with nutmeg and salt. Place in a deep bowl which is in a pan filled with water to one inch of top of bowl. Cover with aluminum wrap and boil five hours. This will keep indefinitely. Boil again for ½ hour before serving.

Natalie Salter Baggett (Mrs. John R., III)

HAZELNUT TORTE

Torte:

5 eggs, separated
3/4 cup sugar
6 tablespoons water
4 ounces hazelnuts, ground
4 ounces almonds, ground
1 1/2 teaspoons baking powder
1 cup flour, sifted

Prepare springform pan with butter and waxed paper. Preheat oven to 350 degrees. Beat egg whites until stiff; set aside. Sift baking powder and sifted flour together; set aside. Beat egg yolks, sugar and water until foamy; add ground hazelnuts and almonds. Add dry ingredients and fold in egg whites. Pour into prepared pan and bake 30-40 minutes. Cool; remove from pan.

Confectioners' Sugar Icing:

1 cup confectioners' sugar, sifted
1/2 teaspoon vanilla
3 tablespoons water
Hazelnuts, to garnish

Mix sugar, vanilla and water together until smooth. Cover cake with icing and garnish with hazelnuts. If more elaborate cake is desired, split baked cake into two or three layers. Prepare either of the following fillings to spread between the layers and top with icing.

Whipped Cream Filling:

Whipping cream
Sugar
Ground hazelnuts

Whip cream and add sugar and hazelnuts to taste. Spread between layers.

Nut Cream Filling:

1 cup hazelnuts, ground
1 cup milk
2 tablespoons cornstarch
4 tablespoons sugar
3 tablespoons butter, softened
1 teaspoon vanilla
2 egg whites, beaten stiffly *OR* 1 cup whipped cream

Mix milk and cornstarch together; add all other ingredients except egg whites or whipped cream. Heat cornstarch mixture, stirring constantly until mixture reaches a boil. Boil 3-4 minutes; remove from heat and let cool, stirring occasionally. When mixture has cooled, add beaten egg whites or whipped cream. Spread between layers and glaze top with confectioners' sugar icing.

Gisela N. von zur Muehlen Ives (Mrs. George A., Jr.)

CHARLOTTE RUSSE

This is an old family recipe, a special favorite at Thanksgiving and Christmas.

1 tablespoon Knox gelatine
½ cup milk, warm
½ pint whipping cream
¼ cup sugar
½ jigger brandy
Lady fingers or pound cake

Dissolve the gelatine in warm milk. Whip cream and add sugar and brandy. Fold whipped cream mixture into gelatine mixture and pour into a dish lined with lady fingers or thinly sliced pound cake. Refrigerate at least 3-4 hours or until well set.

Rosa Hardison Winfree (Mrs. Charles B.)

CHOCOLATE TORTE LILI

1 cup cold strong coffee
1½ tablespoons sugar
2 tablespoons Grand Marnier (or Triple Sec)
1 cup butter
2 large eggs
12 ounces semi-sweet chocolate, melted
40 vanilla wafers
1 cup whipping cream
Cherries, for garnish if desired

Combine coffee with sugar and Grand Marnier. Set aside. Cream butter; beat in eggs and melted chocolate. Line a 2-pound bread pan with foil, allowing enough to hang over edges to cover top. Arrange a layer of wafers on bottom of pan. Sprinkle with coffee mix, then spread with chocolate cream. Continue until both are used, ending with layer of wafers. Fold over foil to cover top. Set an identical pan on top of cake and weight with heavy stone or can. Let season in refrigerator 24 hours. Frost with whipped cream.
Yield: 12 servings

Genevieve Tolson Dunn (Mrs. Mark S.)

GERDA'S TORTE

Easy
Do early in day

2 egg yolks
1 (16-ounce) box confectioners' sugar, sifted
1 cup butter
Blackberry brandy
2 layer cake, vanilla or chocolate (mix or homemade)
6-8 ounces currant jelly
1 cup finely chopped walnuts, pecans or almonds
Garnish of maraschino cherries or candied cherries

Beat egg yolks until thick and sticky, then beat in ½ cup confectioners' sugar. Cream butter until soft. Gradually work in remaining sugar. Combine the two mixtures and flavor with enough brandy for a spreading consistency. Split cake layers, making four layers. Whip jelly until spreadable and spread between first two layers. Spread frosting between second and third layers. Spread jelly between third and fourth layers. Leave top plain. Frost sides and top of cake with butter-cream mixture, saving a little for decorating. Sprinkle nuts over sides and top. Use pastry tube to decorate top of cake with butter-cream. Garnish with well-drained maraschinos or candied cherries.
Yield: 12 servings

Kathleen Winslow Budd (Mrs. Bern)

TYDINGS TORTE

Keeps two weeks

Sara Lee Pound Cake
6 ounces German Sweet Chocolate
1 cup sour cream
1 teaspoon instant coffee

Slice frozen Sara Lee Pound Cake the long way into 7 layers. Put together with the following filling: melt chocolate. Remove from heat and add sour cream and instant coffee. Save enough filling to frost. Will keep in the refrigerator for 2 weeks.
Yield: Servings depend on thickness of slices

Genevieve Tolson Dunn (Mrs. Mark S.)

CHIPMAN INN CHEESECAKE

This dessert, popular at the Chipman Inn in Ripton, Vermont, seems to take forever to set, but it is well worth the wait.
Refrigerated, it will keep 5-6 days.

5 tablespoons margarine
1½ cups graham cracker crumbs
3 teaspoons sugar
⅛ teaspoon cinnamon
4 (8-ounce) packages cream cheese
1½ cups sugar
6 eggs
2 pints sour cream
1 teaspoon vanilla

Grease 10-inch springform pan. Preheat oven to 350 degrees. Mix margarine, crumbs, 3 teaspoons sugar, and cinnamon. Press mixture into bottom of pan. In a large bowl, cut up cream cheese, add sugar and eggs. Blend at low speed with mixer until moistened; then at medium speed until smooth and creamy. Add vanilla and fold in sour cream by hand until well-mixed. Pour this mixture over crust in pan and bake 50-60 minutes. Turn off oven and leave cake in for one hour longer. Remove from oven and let stand at room temperature at least another hour until cool. Remove pan and refrigerate.
Yield: 20 servings

Christine Watts Burks (Mrs. Charles L.)

DOUBLE-CHEESE CHEESECAKE

Easy and quick to fix! Can be topped with fresh or canned fruit or a fruit glaze for variety.

Crust:
2 cups graham cracker crumbs
2 tablespoons sugar
½ cup margarine

Preheat oven to 400 degrees. Melt margarine and combine with sugar and graham cracker crumbs. Reserve ¾ cup of mixture for topping and press the remainder of mixture on bottom and sides of a springform pan. Bake 10 minutes.

Filling:

2 (8-ounce) packages cream cheese, softened
½ pound cottage cheese, drained and sieved
⅔ cup sugar
4 eggs, separated
Vanilla
Juice and rind of 1 lemon
1 cup light cream or half and half
2 tablespoons flour

Reduce oven heat to 325 degrees. Cream together cream cheese, cottage cheese and sugar; add 4 egg yolks, flour, vanilla, lemon juice and rind. Beat until smooth, then stir in light cream or half and half. Beat egg whites until stiff and fold into cheese mixture. Pour into crust-lined pan and sprinkle reserved crumbs on top. Bake at 325 degrees for 1 hour and 20 minutes. At end of baking time, turn off heat, open oven door and allow to cool in oven for 1 hour. Remove rim from pan. Refrigerate if not used the first day. Yield: 16 servings

Jane Kinnison Millns (Mrs. Dale T.)

CHOCOLATE CHEESECAKE

Crust:

⅓ cup butter
2 tablespoons sugar
1 teaspoon almond extract
1 (6-ounce) box zwieback, made into crumbs

Melt butter; stir in sugar and almond extract. Mix with zwieback crumbs. Press into the bottom of a springform pan.

Filling:

2 (8-ounce) packages cream cheese, softened
1¼ cups sugar
⅓ cup cocoa
1 teaspoon vanilla
2 eggs

Mix these ingredients together. Beat until smooth. Pour over crust. Bake at 375 degrees for about 35 to 40 minutes. Cool. Chill in refrigerator until ready to serve.

Birdsall S. Viault

COCOA CRÊPE BATTER

Must refrigerate batter 1 hour
May freeze cooked, unfilled crêpe

3 eggs
1 cup buttermilk
2 tablespoons butter, melted
¾ cup flour
3 tablespoons cocoa
3 tablespoons sugar

In blender container combine all ingredients and blend 1 minute. Scrape down sides and blend until smooth, about 30 additional seconds. Refrigerate batter 1 hour. Heat 8-inch skillet or crêpe pan; grease lightly. Pour batter in skillet, about ⅓ cup per crêpe. Spread batter evenly by tilting pan. Cook for 1-2 minutes over medium heat or until tops are set and undersides are golden. Cool on individual pieces of paper towel. Crêpes may be frozen separated between pieces of waxed paper and wrapped well.
Yield: 2¼ cups or 12 crêpes.

BRANDY ALEXANDER CRÊPES

12 chocolate crêpes
½ cup sugar, divided
1 envelope unflavored gelatine
½ cup water
2 eggs, separated
1 (3-ounce) package cream cheese, softened
3 tablespoons brandy
3 tablespoons Crème de Cacao
¼ teaspoon cream of tartar
1 cup whipping cream, divided
Chocolate curls, garnish

In saucepan combine ¼ cup sugar and gelatine; stir in water. Cook and stir over low heat 3 minutes until gelatine dissolves. Remove from heat. Beat egg yolks until thick and lemon colored, about 5 minutes. Blend a little of the gelatine mixture into yolks. Return yolk mixture to saucepan and blend. Cook over low heat 2-3 minutes. Remove from heat. Stir in cream cheese until blended. Stir in brandy and Crème de Cacao. Cover with plastic wrap. Chill until slightly thickened. Beat egg whites and cream of tartar until soft peaks form. Add remaining sugar, one tablespoon at a time, beating constantly until sugar is dissolved. Whip half of cream until stiff. Gently fold cream cheese mixture and whipped cream into egg whites. Spoon ⅓ cup soufflé mixture down center of each crêpe. Roll up. Cover with plastic wrap. Chill several hours. Whip remaining cream and place dollop on top of crêpes at serving time. Garnish with chocolate curls.
Yield: 6 servings

Cindy Sharpe Burgess (Mrs. Glenn)

CREAM PUFFS

½ cup butter (¼ butter and ¼ Crisco)
1 cup boiling water
1 cup sifted flour
¼ teaspoon salt
4 eggs

Preheat oven to 450 degrees. Melt shortening in boiling water. Add flour and salt all at once. Stir vigorously with a wooden spoon over medium-high heat. Watch for scorching. Cook, stirring until mixture forms a ball that doesn't separate. Remove from heat. Allow to cool slightly. Using metal spoon, add eggs one at a time, beating well after each addition. On greased cookie sheet spoon 2½-inch mounds 2-inches apart. Bake at 450 degrees for 12 minutes then reduce heat to 325 degrees for 20-25 minutes.

Filling:
½ pint heavy cream, whipped
2 teaspoons sugar
1 teaspoon vanilla

Whip cream. Add sugar and vanilla. Beat stiff. Fill puffs.

Custard Filling:
3 tablespoons cornstarch
½ cup sugar
⅛ teaspoon salt
½ cup cold milk
1½ cups milk, scalded
1 teaspoon vanilla
2 egg yolks with 2 tablespoons milk

Mix cornstarch, sugar, salt and cold milk. Gradually add hot milk. Boil, stirring until thick. Don't BURN. Stir some of the hot mixture over the yolks, then add yolks to custard. Stir well. Add vanilla. If desired a tablespoon of butter may be added at this point. Cool slightly and fill cream puffs.

Icing:
2 squares unsweetened chocolate
2-2½ cups confectioners' sugar
1 teaspoon vanilla
2 tablespoons butter

Melt butter and chocolate together. Add sugar and vanilla stirring until smooth. If needed, milk may be added to improve spreading consistency. Drizzle over tops of filled cream puffs.
*Cream puffs may be frozen filled with ice cream or whipped cream for 2 months.
Yield: 9 servings

Diane Roche McQuade (Mrs. John F.)

Pastries and Pies

PIE CRUSTS

Coconut:

3 tablespoons butter or margarine
1½ cups coconut

Melt butter or margarine in skillet. Add coconut and stir over medium heat until golden brown. Press mixture firmly on bottom and sides of 9-inch pie pan. Let stand until cool. Fill with favorite cream or chiffon pie filling.

Nut:

½ cup butter or margarine
¼ cup brown sugar
1 cup flour
½ cup pecans, chopped

Mix all ingredients together with hands. Press mixture in ungreased 9x9-inch pan. Bake about 12 minutes at 350 degrees until light brown. Crumble baked crust with spoon. Cool slightly. Reserve ¼ cup for garnish. Press remainder in pie plate. Good with ice cream or chiffon pies.

Crumb:

Use your choice of zwieback, chocolate wafers, vanilla wafers, coconut, Brazil nuts, or cereals.

1½ cups crumbs (about 24 cookies)
¼ cup sifted confectioners' sugar *or* well-packed brown sugar
1 teaspoon vanilla *or* sesame seed, grated orange rind, cinnamon and nutmeg for chocolate fillings
¼ cup butter, melted

Combine above ingredients. Press into 9-inch pie plate using another pie plate to press down. Trim excess. Bake 3 minutes at 350 degrees.

CHOCOLATE NUT PIE CRUST

1 cup ground nuts*
1 cup ground chocolate wafers
⅓ cup butter, melted

*Pecans, walnuts, almonds, hazelnuts, dried coconut flakes or Brazil nuts are equally fine.

Preheat oven to 375 degrees. In a large bowl combine nuts, wafers and butter mixing thoroughly. Press into 10-inch pie plate and bake 7 minutes.

Yield: 1 (10-inch) crust

DIETER'S PIE CRUST

2 cups unsifted flour
1 teaspoon baking powder
1 teaspoon salt
½ cup diet margarine
1 medium egg
1 tablespoon vinegar
3 tablespoons water

Stir the flour, baking powder, and salt together in a bowl. Blend in the diet margarine with a fork or pastry blender until mixed thoroughly. Beat the egg, vinegar and water together. Add to flour mixture. Blend or knead lightly until pastry leaves the side of the bowl. Separate into four equal-sized balls and flatten. Make four single pie crusts (347 calories each) before trimming. Rolling out this pastry is extra easy. Simply use a well-floured board and rolling pin. Use the pastry to line eight- or nine-inch lightly oiled pie pans.

Yield: 4 single piecrusts

Paulette Cardillo Culpepper (Mrs. George V.)

APRICOT PIE

1 baked pie shell
12-ounces dried apricots, cut up and cooked
1 can Eagle Brand condensed milk
¼ cup lemon juice
Whipped topping

Combine condensed milk and lemon juice. Fold in apricots; pour into baked pie shell. Chill and serve with whipped topping.

Cherry Sampson Myers (Mrs. Bruce M.)

FRESH BLUEBERRY PIE

Delicious warm, served with vanilla ice cream!

1 cup sugar
¼ cup flour
¼ teaspoon salt
½ teaspoon ground cinnamon
½ teaspoon lemon rind, grated
3 cups fresh blueberries, washed and stemmed
1 tablespoon fresh lemon juice
Pastry for 2 crust 9-inch pie, unbaked
2 tablespoons butter

Preheat oven to 425 degrees. Combine first 7 ingredients. Turn into prepared pie shell. Dot with butter. Cover with second crust. Seal, pinching edges together. Decorate top crust with gashes to allow steam to escape. Bake 40 minutes or until crust is browned.
Yield: 6-8 servings

Rena Terrell Knott (Mrs. Edmund T.)

For browning top crust, brush with egg whites, evaporated milk, butter, salad oil or cream. For a sparkling, sugary top, sprinkle with granulated sugar.

HARVEST PIES

Nice addition to a "sweet tray."

Filling may be made ahead

½ cup butter
1 cup sugar
2 eggs
1 cup seedless raisins
1 teaspoon vanilla
1 cup nuts, chopped
1 teaspoon lemon juice
2 dozen small, baked tarts

Cream together butter and sugar. Add eggs and beat well. Add raisins and vanilla. Mix well and bring to a scant boil. Add nuts and lemon juice. If tarts are real small, this should make about two dozen. Filling may be made a day ahead and placed in refrigerator until needed to fill tarts.
Yield: 2 dozen

Margaret Gibbs Dunn (Mrs. John G., Jr.)

GLAZED FRUIT PIE

Easy

4 cups fresh fruit*
1 cup sugar
1 cup water
3½ tablespoons cornstarch
1 baked "deep dish" pie crust
Cool Whip or whipped cream

*Peaches or strawberries are delicious
Crush 1 cup of fruit. In a saucepan mix sugar and cornstarch with crushed fruit and water. Cook until thick. Cool. Place 3 cups of fruit in baked pie shell and pour glaze over fruit. Chill. Top with whipped cream or Cool Whip, if desired.

Genevieve Tolson Dunn (Mrs. Mark S.)

JAPANESE FRUIT PIE

½ cup butter, melted
1 cup sugar
2 eggs
1 tablespoon vinegar
1 teaspoon vanilla
½ cup frozen coconut
½ cup pecans, chopped
½ cup white raisins
Pinch of salt
1 pie shell, unbaked

Preheat oven to 350 degrees. Mix butter and sugar. Add eggs and beat well. Add remaining ingredients and pour into unbaked pie shell. Bake for 30-35 minutes.

Carolyn Brown Latham (Mrs. Edward B.)

HAWAII PIE

Easy

1 (20-ounce) can crushed pineapple, drained
1 can Eagle Brand milk
½ cup lemon juice
1 cup nuts, chopped
1 (12-ounce) container Cool Whip
2 graham cracker crusts

Mix all ingredients together and pour into prepared crusts. Refrigerate at least 2 hours before serving.
Yield: 2 pies; 12 servings

Joyce Currin Stainback (Mrs. Ray)

LEMONADE MERINGUE PIE

Filling:

1 cup sour cream
3 egg yolks, slightly beaten
1 (4½-5-ounce) regular vanilla pudding mix
1¼ cups milk
⅓ cup frozen lemonade concentrate, thawed
1 (9-inch) baked pie shell

Meringue:

3 egg whites
½ teaspoon vanilla
¼ teaspoon cream of tartar
6 tablespoons sugar

Bake pie shell. Reduce oven temperature to 350 degrees. Combine sour cream and egg yolks. Stir in pudding mix, milk and lemonade. Cook in top of double boiler and stir until thickened. Remove from heat and spoon into pie shell. Set aside. Beat egg whites, cream of tartar and vanilla until soft peaks form. Add sugar gradually; spread on pie and bake 12-15 minutes. Cool. Chill.

Dollie Mallard Kellum (Mrs. Norman, Sr.)

LEMON MERINGUE PIE

3 tablespoons cornstarch
1¼ cups sugar
¼ cup lemon juice
1 teaspoon lemon extract
3 eggs, separated
1½ cups boiling water
1 deep dish pie shell, baked
2 tablespoons butter

Combine cornstarch, sugar, and lemon juice. Beat egg yolks and add to cornstarch mixture. Gradually add boiling water. Heat to boiling over direct heat and boil gently for four minutes. Stir constantly. Remove from heat and add lemon extract and butter. Allow the mixture to cool about 10 minutes before putting in pie shell. Cover with Never Fail Meringue.

Jane Pugh Constantine (Mrs. James D.)

ANN LANDERS' LEMON PIE

1 baked pie shell
1½ cups sugar
6 tablespoons cornstarch
2 cups water
⅓ cup lemon juice
3 eggs, separated
3 tablespoons butter
1½ teaspoons lemon extract
2 teaspoons vinegar

Mix sugar and cornstarch in top of double boiler. Add 2 cups water. Combine egg yolks with juice and beat. Add to rest of mixture. Cook until thick over boiling water for 25 minutes to eliminate the starchy taste. Add lemon extract and vinegar and stir thoroughly. Pour into pie shell and let cool. Cover with meringue* and brown in preheated 350 degree oven for 10 minutes.
*See recipe for NEVER-FAIL MERINGUE

Lela Badham Polzin (Mrs. George P.)

NEVER-FAIL MERINGUE

1 tablespoon cornstarch
2 tablespoons cold water
½ cup boiling water
3 egg whites
6 tablespoons sugar
1 teaspoon vanilla
Pinch of salt

Preheat oven to 350 degrees. Blend cornstarch and cold water in saucepan. Add boiling water and cook, stirring until clear and thickened. Let stand until completely cold. With electric beater at high speed, beat egg whites until foamy. Gradually add sugar and beat until stiff but not dry. Turn mixer to low speed, add salt and vanilla. Gradually beat in cold cornstarch mixture. Beat well at high speed. Spread over cooled pie filling and bake 10 minutes.

Jane Pugh Constantine (Mrs. James D.)
Lela Badham Polzin (Mrs. George P.)

GREAT-GRANDMOTHER MANESS' LEMON PIE

Easy
Do early in day

2 cups sugar
2 eggs
Juice of 2 lemons
¼ cup butter, melted
2 tablespoons flour
1 cup milk
1 teaspoon baking powder
Grated rind of 1 lemon
2 (9-inch) pie shells, unbaked

Beat eggs and add sugar. Add remaining ingredients, mixing thoroughly. Bake at 325 to 350 degrees until set, about 30-35 minutes.
Yield: 2 (9-inch) pies

Nancy Samuel Everhart (Mrs. Charles L.)

STRAWBERRY PIE

2 cups strawberries
1 cup sugar
4 tablespoons cornstarch
4 tablespoons strawberry Jello
1 tablespoon lemon juice (optional)
1½ cups water
2 (8- or 9-inch) pie crusts or 1 deep dish crust, baked
Whipped topping

Combine sugar, cornstarch, Jello, lemon juice and water and cook until thickened, stirring occasionally. Cool. Put berries in pie shells and pour thickened mixture on top. Chill at least 3 hours. Serve with whipped topping and garnish with halved or whole berries, if desired. This can also be served as an hors d'oeuvre. Use the smallest tart-sized shells. Chop berries to put in shells and then add thickened mixture.
Yield: 2 (9-inch) pies

Susan Lee Thomas (Mrs. John G.)
Nancy Stilley Turner (Mrs. Charles H., Jr.)

CREAM PUFF PIE

The same grandeur of individual cream puffs without the time

½ cup boiling water
¼ cup shortening
⅛ teaspoon salt
½ cup flour
2 eggs
1 (4-ounce) package instant vanilla pudding
1 cup whipped cream
Strawberries
1 cup whipped cream (optional)

Preheat oven to 400 degrees. Grease a 9-inch pie plate and set aside. Mix boiling water, shortening and salt over heat. Stir in flour all at once. Stir constantly until mixture leaves the sides of pan and forms into a ball. Remove from heat; cool slightly. Beat in eggs, one at a time, beating until smooth and velvety after each addition. Spread in bottom of prepared pan but not onto sides. Bake for 50-60 minutes. Sides will rise up and curl in slightly. Allow to cool slowly away from drafts. Mix up package of vanilla pudding according to directions on box. Fold in 1 cup of whipped cream. Pour cream filling into crust and top with strawberries. Top with additional whipped cream if desired.

Kaye Stewart Smith (Mrs. Richard W.)

KAHLÚA PIE

Try using homemade Kahlúa!

Crust:
36 chocolate wafers
6 tablespoons butter, melted
2 tablespoons sugar

Reserve 12 cookies to stand up around edge of pie plate. Crush 24 cookies and combine with butter and sugar and press into a 10-inch pie plate. Set aside.

Filling:
1 teaspoon instant coffee
½ cup water
1 (10-ounce) package large marshmallows (about 38)
½ cup Kahlúa
1 cup whipping cream, whipped
Unsweetened chocolate

Stir coffee and water together; add marshmallows and cook in saucepan until melted. Put in refrigerator or in sink of ice stirring occasionally until thick and cooled. Stir Kahlúa into marshmallow mixture. Fold in whipped cream. Pile into crust. Refrigerate several hours, overnight or freeze. Will keep in freezer 2 months. Garnish with shaved chocolate before serving.

PINEAPPLE-COCONUT PIE

2 unbaked pie shells
½ cup margarine, melted
2 cups sugar
4 eggs
1 (10-ounce) can coconut (or frozen)
1 (8-ounce) can pineapple, slightly drained

Preheat oven to 350 degrees. Mix together all the ingredients and put the mixture into the 2 unbaked pie shells. Bake approximately 45 minutes to 1 hour, until filling is golden brown and firm.
Yield: 2 pies

Berleen Bryant Burnette (Mrs. Norman)

Green grapes coated with sour cream and brown sugar make a delicious quick summer dessert.

BLACK BOTTOM PIE

1 (9-inch) pie shell, baked
2 tablespoons cornstarch
1¼ cups sugar
3 cups milk
6 egg yolks, well-beaten
1½ teaspoons vanilla
2 squares unsweetened chocolate, melted
1 envelope unflavored gelatine
¼ cup cold water
3 tablespoons rum
4 egg whites

Combine cornstarch with ¾ cup sugar in medium saucepan. Stir in milk slowly. Cook over low heat, stirring constantly until thickened. Blend small amount of the hot mixture into beaten egg yolks; add to hot mixture in saucepan. Cook 2 minutes longer stirring constantly until custard coats spoon. Remove from heat; stir in vanilla. Measure 2 cups of the custard and put into a bowl. Stir in melted chocolate. Cool then pour into pie shell. Chill. Soften gelatine in ¼ cup cold water. Add to remaining hot custard. Stir until dissolved. Stir in rum. Place bowl in a larger bowl partially filled with ice and water to speed setting. Chill, stirring often until slightly thickened. Beat egg whites until foamy white and double in volume. Beat in remaining ½ cup sugar, 1 tablespoon at a time until whites peak. Fold into chilled gelatine mixture. Chill until mixture mounds. Spoon over chocolate layer and chill several hours, preferably overnight. Garnish with whipped cream and chocolate shavings.

Melanie Applegate (Mrs. Earl)

WEIDMANN'S FAMOUS BLACK BOTTOM PIE

Crust:

14 ginger snaps

5 tablespoons butter, melted

Crush ginger snaps, roll out fine, add melted butter, pat into a 9-inch pie pan. Bake in a hot oven for 10 minutes and allow to cool.

Filling:

4 egg yolks, well-beaten
2 cups milk, scalded
½ cup sugar
1½ tablespoons cornstarch
1½ squares unsweetened chocolate
1 teaspoon vanilla

Add eggs slowly to hot milk. Combine and stir in sugar and cornstarch. Cook in a double boiler for 20 minutes, stirring occasionally, until it coats the spoon. Remove from heat and take out one cup. Add the chocolate to the cup you have taken out. Beat well as it cools. Add the vanilla, then pour into pie crust and chill.

Topping:

1 tablespoon unflavored gelatine
2 tablespoons hot water
4 egg whites
½ cup sugar
¼ teaspoon cream of tartar
3 tablespoons whiskey

Dissolve the gelatine in hot water, add the remaining custard, and cool. Beat 4 egg whites until stiff with ½ cup sugar and ¼ teaspoon cream of tartar. Add the whiskey, and then fold into plain custard and pour on top of the chocolate mixture. Chill. Cover top with whipped cream and shavings of chocolate, if desired.
Yield: 8 servings

Betty Bunting Wylie (Mrs. James E.)

ALMOND MOCHA CHIFFON PIE

Worth the effort!
Make day ahead

Crust:

¼ cup butter or margarine
1½ cups chocolate wafers, crushed
¼ cup almonds, finely chopped, NOT blanched
2 tablespoons powdered sugar

Melt butter and mix in rest of ingredients. Pat in 9-inch pie plate and bake 10 minutes at 350 degrees. Cool.

Filling:

1 envelope gelatine
¼ cup cold strong black coffee
1 cup sugar
½ teaspoon salt
1½ ounces semi-sweet chocolate
1¼ cups hot coffee
3 eggs, separated
1 cup heavy cream
1½ teaspoons vanilla
¼ teaspoon cream of tartar
1 tablespoon powdered sugar
¼ cup toasted almonds, chopped or slivered

Soften gelatine in cold coffee. Combine ½ cup sugar, salt, and chocolate in hot coffee. Beat yolks until thick and lemon colored. Add a few tablespoons of hot coffee mix to eggs and cook at low heat until thick. Remove from heat. Add gelatine and stir until dissolved. Cool until almost set; whip until smooth. Mixture should be light and foamy. Whip half of the cream until stiff and add 1 teaspoon vanilla. Fold into chocolate mixture. Whip the egg whites with cream of tartar until they hold soft peaks; gradually beat in the remaining ½ cup sugar. Continue beating until thick and glossy. Fold into the chocolate mixture. Pour into chilled shell and refrigerate several hours. One hour before serving, whip remaining half cream and sweeten with powdered sugar. Add remaining ½ teaspoon vanilla. Spread on top of pie. Sprinkle with toasted almonds. Keep chilled until needed.

Barbara Straub Stewart

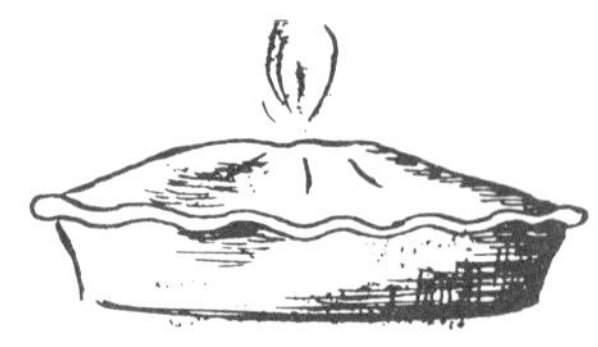

CHOCOLATE PIE

¼ cup butter or margarine
¾ cup sugar
¼ teaspoon salt
3 tablespoons flour
3 egg yolks, beaten
1 (13-ounce) can evaporated milk
5½ ounces Hershey's Chocolate syrup
1 tablespoon vanilla
1 (9-inch) pie shell, baked
Whipped cream or Cool Whip

Mix sugar and flour together in saucepan. Add butter or margarine, salt, beaten egg yolks, evaporated milk, chocolate syrup and vanilla. Stir until all ingredients are moistened. Bring to boil over medium heat and cook 8-10 minutes stirring constantly. Cool, stirring several times and pour into prepared pie shell. Top with whipped cream or Cool Whip. Decorate with shaved chocolate, if desired.

Anne Knott Branch (Mrs. S. P.)
Nedgelina Speight Jennings (Mrs. George M.)

CHOCOLATE LAYER PIE

2 eggs, separated
2 cups milk
½ cup sugar
⅓ cup self-rising flour
¼ teaspoon salt
2 tablespoons margarine
¾ teaspoon vanilla
1 (8-inch) pie shell, baked
½ cup semi-sweet chocolate morsels
½ cup pecans, broken

In top of double boiler mix the egg yolks with ¼ cup milk. Add sugar, flour and salt, mix thoroughly. Add remaining milk. Cook over boiling water, stirring constantly until thickened—about 6-7 minutes. Cover and cook 15 minutes longer, stirring occasionally. Remove from boiling water and stir in margarine and vanilla. Pour into pie shell and sprinkle chocolate morsels and pecans over filling.

Meringue:
2 egg whites
¼ cup sugar

Preheat oven to 425 degrees. Beat egg whites until foamy. Add sugar until meringue forms stiff peaks. Spread over pie and bake until delicately browned. To keep crust crisp, do not refrigerate unless necessary.

Cindy Cratch Hart (Mrs. S. Tyler)

CHOCOLATE ANGEL PIE

Can be made 1-2 days ahead

2 egg whites
1/8 teaspoon cream of tartar
1/8 teaspoon salt
1/2 cup sugar, sifted
1/2 cup walnuts or pecans, finely chopped
1/2 teaspoon vanilla
1 (4-ounce) package Baker's German Sweet Chocolate
3 tablespoons water
1 teaspoon vanilla
1/2 pint cream, whipped

Beat egg whites with salt and cream of tartar until foamy. Add sugar gradually, beating until very stiff peak holds. Fold in nuts and 1/2 teaspoon vanilla. Spread in greased 8- or 9-inch pie plate.* Build up sides to 1/2-inch above pan. Bake at 300 degrees for 50-55 minutes. Cool. Melt chocolate and water in double boiler over low heat, stirring constantly. Cool until thickened. Add vanilla, then fold into whipped cream. Pile into meringue shell. Chill at least 2 hours before serving.
Yield: *Meringue may be divided into 8 individual pie shells, and baked according to directions.

Margaret Ayres Midyette (Mrs. Charles T.)

FRENCH CHOCOLATE PIE

1/2 cup butter or margarine
3/4 cup sugar
2 squares Baker's unsweetened chocolate, melted and cooled
2 eggs
1 (4-ounce) container Bird's Eye Cool Whip
1 (9-inch) pie shell, baked and cooled
Pecans (optional)

Cream butter and blend in sugar beating until light and fluffy. Stir in cooled chocolate. Add eggs, one at a time, beating at high speed for 5 minutes for each addition. Fold in whipped topping. Spoon into pie shell. Chill until firm, about 2 hours or freeze until firm, about 4 hours. Garnish with additional whipped topping if desired. Delicious with about a half cup of pecans. Also for company, use the small individual pie crust. They come ten in a package.
Yield: 1 (9-inch) pie or 10 individual pies

Bay Dunn McCotter (Mrs. J. Muse)

CHOCOLATE CHESS PIE

1 (8- or 9-inch) pie crust, unbaked
½ cup butter
1 square unsweetened chocolate
1 cup sugar
2 eggs
Dash salt
1 teaspoon vanilla
Whipped cream (garnish)
½ cup nuts (optional)

Preheat oven to 450 degrees. If desired, crust may be baked about 5 minutes. Remove crust from oven and *reduce heat to 350 degrees.* Melt butter and chocolate in top of double boiler. Blend remaining ingredients, except whipped cream and nuts, and thoroughly combine with melted butter and chocolate. Pour into pie shell and bake 25-30 minutes. Top with whipped cream and nuts.

Jane Pugh Constantine (Mrs. James D.)
Cecelia Chrismon Hudson (Mrs. Forrest M.)

For an easy and quick dessert, partially thaw peaches and add slices along with several teaspoons of peach juice to a champagne glass. Pour champagne over fruit. After peaches have been eaten, drink the juice!

GERMAN CHOCOLATE PIE

Easy
Do ahead
May be frozen

2 unbaked pie shells
3 cups granulated sugar
Pinch of salt
7 tablespoons cocoa
1 teaspoon vanilla
4 eggs
1 (13-ounce) can evaporated milk
½ cup butter or margarine
2 cups flaked coconut
1 cup nuts, chopped (optional)

Preheat oven to 350 degrees. Mix sugar, salt and cocoa together. Add eggs and mix well. Stir in vanilla and milk. Add melted butter or margarine, then coconut. Pour into 2 unbaked pie shells. Bake for 40 minutes or until firm. Yield: 2 pies

Sharon Nichols Hobson (Mrs. Steve R.)

LAST MINUTE BROWNIE PIE

Forget to make dessert? Try this.

2 ounces unsweetened chocolate
½ cup margarine
2 eggs
½ cup flour
1 teaspoon vanilla
1 cup sugar

Preheat oven to 350 degrees. Grease a 9-inch pie pan. In top of double boiler melt margarine and chocolate. When melted, let cool and beat in eggs, flour, vanilla and sugar. Pour into pie pan and bake 20-25 minutes. Top with ice cream and fudge sauce or whipped cream or serve plain.
Yield: 6-8 servings

Mary Hammond Gordon (Mrs. Paul)

BROWNIE PIE

A special treat!

1 cup sugar
½ cup flour
2 eggs, beaten slightly
½ cup butter, melted
1 cup pecans, chopped
1 cup chocolate chips
1 teaspoon vanilla
Cool Whip
1 (9-inch) pie shell, unbaked

Preheat oven to 350 degrees. Mix sugar and flour. Add eggs which have been slightly beaten. Add cooled, melted butter. Mix well. Add pecans, chocolate chips and vanilla and pour into unbaked pie shell. Bake 45 minutes and top with Cool Whip.

Sarah Jones Strange (Mrs. Curtis)

COLD OVEN PECAN PIE

½ cup margarine
3 tablespoons flour
1 (16-ounce) box light brown sugar
3 eggs
6 tablespoons milk
2 teaspoons vinegar
1½ teaspoons vanilla
2 pie shells, uncooked
2 cups pecans, broken

Melt margarine, set aside to cool. Mix flour and sugar together, add milk and eggs. Beat well. Stir in vinegar and vanilla. Add margarine and nuts. Pour into 2 pie crusts and place in *COLD* oven. Bake at 300 degrees for 1 hour. Yield: 2 pies

Mary Sutherland Hasell (Mrs. Thomas M., Jr.)

PECAN CHIFFON PIE

Serve same day
Do not freeze
Do not double or half

1 cup pecans, toasted and coarsely chopped
1 cup dark or light brown sugar
1⅓ cups plus 2 tablespoons water
4 tablespoons cornstarch
¼ cup water
⅔ cup egg whites (at room temperature)
¼ cup sugar
2 (8- or 9-inch) baked pie shells
½ pint whipping cream

Spread pecans on a baking sheet and bake at 250 to 275 degrees for 10 to 15 minutes or until nuts barely begin to brown. Watch carefully so the nuts will not burn. Combine brown sugar and 1⅓ cups plus 2 tablespoons water. Bring to a boil. Mix together cornstarch and ¼ cup water and stir, with a whisk into boiling sugar mixture. Stir constantly and cook until mixture becomes clear and is the consistency of a thick pudding. Remove mixture from heat. Whip egg whites at high speed with mixer until peaks form. Slowly add ¼ cup sugar and beat until peaks are stiff. Reduce mixer speed to low and gently add the hot brown sugar mixture and nuts. As soon as everything is blended turn off mixer. Do not over mix. Pile filling lightly into baked pie shells. Chill. Whip cream until stiff. Divide and spread over both pies. Sprinkle a few additional finely chopped pecans over top for garnish. Best when served the same day but it can also be kept overnight in the refrigerator.

Paulette Cardillo Culpepper (Mrs. George V.)

COMPANY PUMPKIN PIE

1 (8-ounce) package cream cheese, softened
¼ cup sugar
½ teaspoon vanilla
1 egg
1 (9-inch) pie shell, unbaked
1¼ cups of 16-ounce can pumpkin
½ cup sugar
1 teaspoon cinnamon
¼ teaspoon ginger
¼ teaspoon nutmeg
Dash of salt
1 cup of a 13-ounce can evaporated milk
2 eggs, beaten slightly

Preheat oven to 350 degrees. Mix cream cheese, sugar, and vanilla together until blended. Add egg and mix well. Spread on bottom of pie shell. In a bowl combine remaining ingredients and pour over cream cheese mixture. Bake 65 minutes.
Yield: 1 (9-inch) pie

Nancy Blood Thoman (Mrs. Mark)

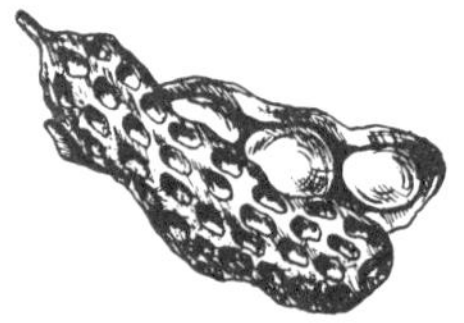

PEANUT PIE

Must make ahead and freeze

1 (3-ounce) package cream cheese*
½ cup smooth peanut butter*
1 cup confectioners' sugar
½ cup milk
1 (8-ounce) container Cool Whip
¼ cup peanuts, finely chopped
1 deep dish graham cracker crust *OR* 2 shallow graham cracker crusts
Chopped peanuts for garnish

*Cream cheese may be increased to 4 ounces and peanut butter decreased to ⅓ cup.
Blend cream cheese, peanut butter, confectioners' sugar and milk until smooth. Fold in Cool Whip. Pour into crust and top pie with peanuts. Freeze. Do NOT thaw before cutting and serving pie.

Elizabeth Allen Brinkley (Mrs. William E., Jr.)
Betty Simon (Mrs. Donn L.)

PEACH PARFAIT PIE

3½ cups sliced peaches, (sweetened with ½-¾ cup of sugar) OR 1 (29-ounce) can sliced peaches*
1 (3-ounce) package lemon Jello
½ cup cold water
1 pint vanilla ice cream
1 (9-inch) graham cracker crust
Cool Whip

*If using fresh peaches, let stand 15 minutes after mixing with sugar.
Drain peaches, fresh or canned, and reserve syrup. Add water to syrup to make 1 cup. Heat to boiling. Add Jello and stir until dissolved. Add cold water. Spoon ice cream into mixture and stir until melted. Chill until mixture mounds slightly when dropped from spoon. Fold in peaches. Turn into cooled pie crust and chill until firm. Top with Cool Whip and additional peaches if desired.
Yield: 1 (9-inch) pie

Susan Lee Thomas (Mrs. John G.)

MACAROON CRUNCH PIE

Stores well
May be frozen

1 (9-inch) baked shell
½ cup toasted coconut*
3 cups sherbet, softened
1½ cups whipping cream
⅓ cup confectioners' sugar
1 cup crisp macaroon cookies, crushed
½ cup chopped pecans
2 tablespoons coconut (not toasted)

*Toast in shallow pan at 325 degrees. Stir often.
Sprinkle toasted coconut on baked shell. Cover with sherbet. Place in freezer. Beat cream and sugar together until thickened. Reserve one cup for topping. Fold crushed cookies and nuts into remaining cream. Spoon over sherbet. Top with whipping cream and two tablespoons of coconut. Freeze for 6 hours.

Nancy Stilley Turner (Mrs. Charles H., Jr.)

PHYLLIS'S ICE CREAM PIE

Must freeze

½ cup brown sugar, packed
¼ cup margarine, melted
½ cup Special K cereal
½ cup nuts
½ cup flaky coconut
1 quart ice cream

In a bowl, mix all ingredients together except ice cream. Save several tablespoons of crust mixture to sprinkle on top of pie. Press mixture into 10-inch pie plate. Chill 10-15 minutes. While crust is chilling, remove ice cream from freezer to soften slightly. Add ice cream to crust; sprinkle with reserved topping; return to freezer and cover with aluminum foil when hardened. May be kept 1-2 weeks in freezer if well-covered. Breyer's French Vanilla is a tasty ice cream choice; however, any good quality ice cream is delicious.

HEATH BAR ICE CREAM PIE

Prepare day ahead

1¼ cups chocolate wafer crumbs
¼ cup butter or margarine, melted
12 (about 12 ounces) Heath bars, refrigerate to harden
½ gallon vanilla ice cream, softened

Mix chocolate wafer crumbs with ¼ cup butter, melted. Line 9x13-inch pan with crumb mixture. Pat down and refrigerate until firm. Crush hardened Heath bars by placing unwrapped candy in plastic bag and hitting with rolling pin. Mix with softened ice cream. Put in crust and freeze overnight. Serve with warmed sauce.

Sauce:
¼ cup butter
1 (6-ounce) package chocolate chips
1 cup confectioners' sugar
6½ ounces evaporated milk
1 teaspoon vanilla

Melt butter with chocolate chips in top of double boiler. Add confectioners' sugar and evaporated milk. Cook 8 minutes or until thickened. Add vanilla. Serve sauce warm over pie.
Yield: 12 servings.

Mary Stallings Parrish (Mrs. Ben W.)

SINFUL SUNDAE PIE

Must do ahead and freeze

1 cup evaporated milk
1 (6-ounce) package semi-sweet chocolate pieces
¼ teaspoon salt
1 cup miniature marshmallows
1 quart vanilla ice cream
Walnut or almond slivers
9-inch pie plate, buttered and lined with whole vanilla wafers
***OR* vanilla wafer crumb crust**

Combine milk, chocolate and salt in saucepan. Stir over low heat until melted and thick. Remove from heat and add marshmallows, stirring until melted and smooth. Cool to room temperature. Spoon half the ice cream into crust. Cover with half the chocolate mixture. Repeat With remaining ingredients. Decorate with nuts and freeze until firm - at least 5 hours.

Vanilla Wafer Crumb Crust:
1½ cups vanilla wafer crumbs
¼ cup butter or margarine, melted

Preheat oven to 350 degrees. Mix ingredients together and bake for 10 minutes. Cool.

Janet Creager Furman (Mrs. John E.)
Becky Elmore Clement (Mrs. Joseph C.)

1 ounce square of unsweetened chocolate = 3 tablespoons unsweetened cocoa + 1 tablespoon shortening.

2 ounces unsweetened chocolate + 7 tablespoons sugar and 2 tablespoons shortening = 6 ounces semisweet morsels.

When melted, semisweet squares and morsels are interchangeable.

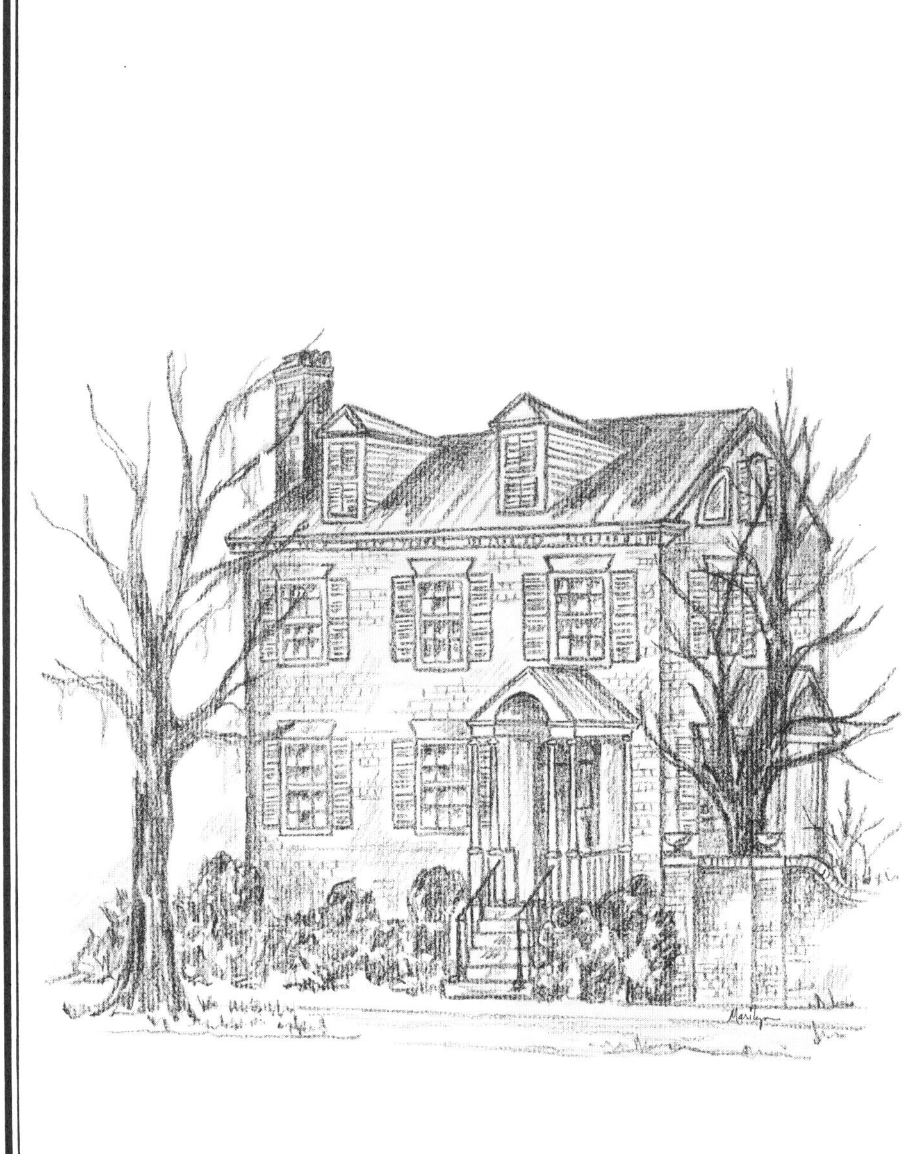

Eli Smallwood House **524 East Front Street**

Cited by architectural historians as one of the most beautiful in North Carolina, this handsome three story brick home, built in 1810 is a perfect example of the New Bern side hall plan, Federal town house. Its restoration and preservation were carried out over a period of years, first by John Haywood Jones and later by David L. Ward, both of whom served Christ Church as wardens and vestrymen.

Main Dishes

RARE ROAST BEEF

This is a basic and infallible recipe for obtaining a rare roast.
Hint: Quality of roast after cooking will equal the quality of meat you started with.

Preheat oven to 500 degrees. Place thawed roast (preferably a rib eye) in preheated oven; *no seasoning necessary.* Cook at 500 degrees 5 minutes for each pound. Example: a 4 pound roast should be cooked 4 pounds x 5 minutes = 20 minutes total baking time. Cut oven off and let roast remain inside 2 hours. *Do not open oven door.*
Yield: Depends on size of roast

Deborah Cook Tayloe (Mrs. John C.)

SIRLOIN TIP ROAST "CUT THE OTHER WAY"

Ask butcher to cut a sirloin tip "the other way". (It's split in the middle)

Roast
1 teaspoon seasoning salt
¼ teaspoon pepper
½ teaspoon paprika
½-1 package onion soup mix, to taste
1 cup beef broth
Dash oregano
Worcestershire sauce, to taste

Preheat oven to 350 degrees. Mix salt, pepper, and paprika, and rub on roast, fat side up. Combine soup mix, broth, oregano, and Worcestershire in pan and place roast on top. Bake uncovered 15 minutes per pound for rosy pink. Baste frequently after first fifteen minutes.

Rena Terrell Knott (Mrs. Edmund T.)

MARINATED FAMILY ROAST

Must do ahead

1 4-pound Family Roast (or chuck roast, flat cut, bone-in)

Marinade:
¾ cup red wine
¼ cup soy sauce
¼ cup lemon juice
¼ cup Worcestershire sauce
Tenderizer
Sprinkling of garlic powder

NOTE: If possible, let the meat age several days in the refrigerator uncovered, but turn several times a day to make meat more tender.
Place meat into large pan. First apply lemon juice directly to meat. Pierce with table fork or two-tined long fork. Next pour on soy sauce and Worcestershire, piercing again. Add the wine. Now sprinkle on garlic powder and tenderizer. Pierce. Let marinate for one hour. Turn meat and marinate reverse side in like fashion. Leave meat in marinade 6 to 8 hours at room temperature, turning occasionally and applying tenderizer and continued piercing. Place roast on grill, searing initial side with some 8 minutes of heat. Turn and leave other side on approximately 12 minutes. Rotate to the initial side and turn over every ten minutes. For rare doneness, cook 30-35 minutes.

Alice Graham Underhill (Mrs. T. Reed)

FILET MIGNON OR CHOPPED STEAK IMPERIAL

4 (7-ounce) filets
***OR* chopped sirloin patties**
Salt and pepper to taste
¼ cup butter
½ cup onion, chopped
¼ cup chicken livers, chopped
¼ cup mushrooms, sliced
½ cup dry red wine
Toasted almonds
4 (8x8-inch) pieces aluminum foil

Lightly season filets or patties with salt and pepper. Sauté onions in butter until just soft; add mushrooms and chicken livers. Stir in wine. Simmer until reduced by one quarter. Broil meat to desired doneness. Have 4 pieces of aluminum foil (8x8-inches) spread out. Put 2 tablespoons sauce in center of each. Place meat on top and divide rest of sauce evenly. Sprinkle toasted almonds on top. Wrap tightly. Put into hot oven 5 minutes to heat through.
Yield: 4 servings

Evelyn Ipock Dill (Mrs. William L.)

MARINATED STEAK

Do ahead
Stores well
May be doubled or tripled
May be used for chicken
Marinade may be stored 10-12 days and reused

2½-3 pounds London broil or flank steak, trimmed
2 tablespoons onion, minced
1 teaspoon dry mustard
1 teaspoon salt
¼ teaspoon black coarse pepper
1 teaspoon sugar
⅓ cup soy sauce
⅓ cup Wesson oil
3 tablespoons red wine vinegar
2 tablespoons chopped chutney
1 clove garlic, minced

Prick meat on both sides several times with fork. Place in 9x13-inch pan. Combine remaining ingredients to make marinade and pour over meat. Cover pan with foil; refrigerate 24 hours turning meat often. Grill, as desired.
Yield: 4-6 main dish servings, 20-30 hors d'oeuvre servings.

Beverly Moore Perdue (Mrs. Gary R.)

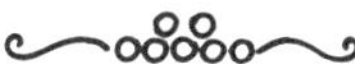

Dry onion soup sprinkled over a roast which is to be sealed in foil will make a delicious gravy while the roast is cooking.

DRIP BEEF

3 (5-pound chuck roasts), trim fat, or use rump or sirloin tip
2 cloves garlic, minced
1½ teaspoons oregano
¾ teaspoon rosemary
2¼ teaspoons Lawry's seasoned salt
3 cubes beef bouillon

Combine all ingredients in a large roaster, almost covering beef with water. Bake at 300 degrees for 5 hours. Cool, tear apart with fork until literally shredded. Serve on plate with a heated hard roll and a small bowl of the broth for each person. Instruct guests to break bite-sizes pieces of bread on plate with fork. Or, place shredded beef on/in the roll for each person and instruct them to dip bread into broth. It is served this way at the Driftwood in Pensacola, Florida.

BEEF KABOBS

Beef*, cut into 1½-inch cubes
1 cup water
¼ cup brown sugar
2 teaspoons Worcestershire
1 (5-ounce) bottle soy sauce
2 teaspoons lemon juice

*Sirloin steak or roast is delicious.
Marinate meat in a mixture of brown sugar, Worcestershire sauce, water, soy sauce and lemon juice in the refrigerator all day.

1 large onion, cut into quarters
1 large Bell pepper, cut into quarters
12 cherry tomatoes
12 mushroom caps
Hot, cooked rice

Build and light charcoal fire. On 4 long skewers, alternate meat, tomatoes, meat, onion, meat, pepper, meat and mushrooms. Grill over fire until meat is cooked to taste. Serve on a bed of fluffy rice, along with green salad and garlic bread.
Yield: 4 servings

Rick Askew (M. H., III)

SUKIYAKI

1½ pounds round steak, sliced across the grain in ¼-inch strips
3 tablespoons vegetable oil
½ pound mushrooms, sliced
1 green pepper, sliced
1 large onion, sliced
3 stalks celery, bias cut in slices
1 (5-ounce) can bamboo shoots, drained and diced
1 (6-ounce) can water chestnuts, drained and sliced
⅓ cup soy sauce
1 beef bouillon cube, dissolved in
½ cup boiling water
2 cups hot cooked rice

In skillet over medium-high heat, or electric skillet set at 400 degrees, brown meat in oil. Add 3 tablespoons of water and all ingredients except rice. Cover lower heat to low or 275 degrees in electric frying pan. Cook about 10 minutes. Vegetables should be crisp and retain their color. Serve with rice.
Yield: 4-6 servings

Sally Gray White (Mrs. George

STEAK TARTARE

You will never know this is raw meat when served. It is genuinely delicious!

Easy
Do early in day
Stores well

Filling:

1 pound lean raw beef (filet, sirloin or round)
2 raw eggs
¼ cup chives, finely chopped
1 tablespoon onion, finely chopped
1 teaspoon ground paprika
½ teaspoon dry mustard
1 teaspoon Worcestershire sauce
1 tablespoon Cognac Brandy
⅛ teaspoon cayenne pepper
⅛ teaspoon salt
⅛ teaspoon black pepper
Rye bread
Anchovy filets
Capers
Lemon wedges
Parsley sprigs

Grind meat twice in chopper with medium blade. Mix all ingredients except bread, anchovies, capers, lemon and parsley. Chill about one hour in refrigerator. Form patties and place on slices of good rye bread. Garnish with anchovies, capers, parsley and lemon wedges. Serve immediately.
Yield: 4-6 servings

Kathleen Winslow Budd (Mrs. Bern)

ASPARAGUS AND DRIED BEEF

1 (15-ounce) can asparagus spears
1 (3-ounce) jar dried beef
Butter
Toast
Mustard
3 tablespoons butter
3 tablespoons flour
½ teaspoon salt
Pepper
1 cup milk
½-1 cup grated American cheese

Roll asparagus in dried beef and put on pieces of toast which have been buttered and spread with a little mustard. Place in 9x13-inch casserole which has been sprayed with Pam. Make a cheese sauce of the last six ingredients and pour over casserole ingredients. Bake at 350 degrees until light brown.
Yield: 8-10 servings

Caroline Ashford Smith

SAVORY PEPPER STEAK

Easy

1½ pounds round steak cut ½-inch thick
¼ cup flour
½ teaspoon salt
⅛ teaspoon black pepper
¼ cup cooking oil
1¾ cup water
½ cup onion, chopped
1 small clove garlic, minced
1 tablespoon beef-flavor gravy base *OR* dissolve 2 beef bouillon cubes in the above 1¾ cup water
1½ teaspoons Worcestershire sauce
2 large green peppers, cut in strips
1 (8-ounce) can tomatoes, drained
Hot cooked rice

Combine flour, salt and black pepper and coat steak. In large skillet cook meat in hot oil browned on both sides. Reserving tomatoes, drain juice and add it to the skillet, with water, onion, garlic and gravy base. Cover and let simmer 1¼ hours until meat is tender. Uncover, stir in Worcestershire. Add green peppers and cover, simmering 5 minutes more. If necessary, thicken gravy with a small mixture of flour and cold water. Add drained, canned tomatoes. Cook 5 minutes longer. Serve over hot rice.
Yield: 6 servings

Diane Gough Fowler (Mrs. Phillip L.)

BEEF STROGANOFF

1 pound round steak
¼ cup flour
⅛ teaspoon nutmeg
2 cups hot water
2 beef bouillon cubes
1 envelope dry onion soup
½-¾ cup sour cream
1 (8-ounce) package of noodles

Combine flour and nutmeg. Cut steak in small cubes, dust with flour. Brown in small amount of oil. Add the water, bouillon cubes and onion soup. Cook for 1½-2 hours over low heat. Stir from time to time. Cook noodles according to directions; drain. Combine noodles, sour cream and meat mixture.
Yield: 6 servings

Fay Huff Willingham (Mrs. Obie

BEEF STEAK STROGANOFF

2 pounds sirloin steak, cut 1-inch thick
2 tablespoons oil
1½ teaspoons salt
⅛ teaspoon pepper
2 onions, sliced
1 (3-ounce) can sliced mushrooms
2 tablespoons flour
¼ teaspoon paprika
1 (12-ounce) can beer
1 teaspoon Worcestershire sauce
1 cup sour cream
Noodles

Slice steak in ½-inch strips. Brown in oil, remove from pan and keep warm. Cook onions and undrained mushrooms covered for 3-4 minutes; push aside and blend flour and paprika into pan drippings. Add beer and Worcestershire, and cook until thickened. Add beef and heat. Stir in sour cream until blended but *do not* boil. Serve over noodles.
Yield: 5-6 servings

Elizabeth Reese Ward (Mrs. David L., Jr.)

EASY CHOP SUEY

Stores well
Freeze

1 pound veal or beef, chopped
½ pound pork, chopped
2 cups celery, chopped
1 cup onion, chopped
1 (10-ounce) can chicken-rice soup
1 (10-ounce) can cream of mushroom soup
2 cups water
½ cup dry rice*
4-6 tablespoons soy sauce
1 (5-ounce) can Chinese noodles

*You may omit the rice, reducing water to 1 cup, then chop suey may be served over freshly-cooked rice.
Brown meat. Drain. Place in 2-quart casserole. Sauté celery and onions. Mix with remaining ingredients and pour over browned meat in casserole dish. Bake 1½ hours at 350 degrees, stirring occasionally. Serve over Chinese noodles.
Yield: 8-10 servings

Gabrielle Paluzsay Lippitt (Mrs. Devereux H.)

BAKED STEAK CASSEROLE

1 (2-pound) round steak
Salt
Pepper
1 (10½-ounce) can cream of mushroom soup
1 envelope Lipton Onion Soup Mix

In a medium-sized casserole place round steak which has been seasoned to taste with salt and pepper. Pour mushroom soup over steak. Sprinkle with onion soup. Cover tightly and bake at 350 degrees for two hours.
Yield: 6-8 servings

Eleanor Jones Carr (Mrs. W. E.)

EGGPLANT PARMIGIANA BARBARA

This recipe may be altered for a meatless meal by eliminating ground beef and doubling or tripling the amount of Mozzarella.

2 tablespoons butter or margarine
½ cup onion, chopped
1 clove garlic, minced
1 pound ground beef
1 (16-ounce) can tomatoes
1 (6-ounce) can tomato paste
½ cup water
2 teaspoons dried oregano
1 teaspoon basil
1½ teaspoons salt
¼ teaspoon pepper
1 tablespoon brown sugar
1 large eggplant
2 eggs, beaten slightly
1¼ cups Parmesan cheese
½ cup dry bread crumbs
¼ cup salad oil
6-8 ounces Mozzarella, shredded

In large skillet sauté onion, garlic and ground beef in butter until meat is no longer red. Add tomatoes, tomato paste, oregano, basil, salt and pepper. Stir well. Add ½ cup water and brown sugar. Bring all ingredients in skillet to a boil. Simmer uncovered 20 minutes. Heat oven to 350 degrees. Spray baking dish with non-stick product. Peel eggplant and cut into ½-inch slices. Combine eggs and 1 tablespoon water; mix well. Dip eggplant in egg; coat well. Dip in crumb mixture and coat well. Sauté eggplant in oil until brown and arrange in bottom of baking dish; sprinkle with half Parmesan; top with half of Mozzarella cheese and cover with half of tomato sauce. Repeat. Bake uncovered 20 minutes. Arrange Mozzarella cheese over top and bake 20 minutes longer or until Mozzarella is melted and slightly brown.
Yield: 6 servings

MARY ANN'S BEEF PIQUANT

Easy and economical when you've forgotten to thaw something for dinner!

1 pound ground beef
1 large onion, sliced
3 tablespoons butter or margarine
2 tablespoons Worcestershire sauce
1 tablespoon vinegar
2 tablespoons sugar
2 (8-ounce) cans tomato sauce
Hot cooked rice

In skillet, brown ground beef and season to taste. In a separate skillet sauté onion in butter until transparent. Add drained cooked ground beef to onion and remaining ingredients except rice. Bring to a boil. Simmer 15 minutes. Serve over cooked rice.
Yield: 4 servings

DE LORENZO'S ZUCCHINI-BEEF BAKE

4 small zucchini (about 1½ pounds)
1 pound ground beef
½ cup onion, chopped
1½ cups soft bread crumbs (2 slices)
¾ teaspoon salt
½ teaspoon dried crushed thyme
½ teaspoon pepper
4 tablespoons butter or margarine
½ cup flour
½ teaspoon salt
2 cups milk
1 (5-ounce) jar processed cheese spread
1 tablespoon butter or margarine, melted

Wash and remove ends of zucchini and cut into ½-inch slices. Cook in boiling salted water for 5 minutes or until tender but not soft. Drain. In skillet cook ground beef with onions until browned; drain off oil. Stir in half of the bread crumbs, ¾ teaspoon salt, the thyme and pepper. Remove from heat. In saucepan melt 4 tablespoons butter; blend in flour and the remaining ½ teaspoon salt. Add the milk all at once. Cook and stir until mixture thickens and bubbles. Add cheese, stirring until melted. Combine with the meat mixture. Alternate layers of meat mixture and zucchini in a greased 7x11-inch casserole. Refrigerate or freeze until ready to use. Combine remaining bread crumbs with 1 tablespoon melted butter. Sprinkle on top of casserole just before baking. Bake in 350 degree oven for 35 minutes for thawed casserole or until heated thoroughly.
Yield: 6 servings

STUFFED ZUCCHINI

Easy
Can do ahead

2 pounds zucchini
½ pound ground beef
¼ cup mayonnaise
2 teaspoons dehydrated onion flakes
2 teaspoons parsley flakes
1 teaspoon oregano leaves
1 teaspoon salt
1 teaspoon lemon juice
¼ teaspoon pepper
⅔ cup spaghetti sauce*

*I use Ragu Sauce with Mushrooms.
Half zucchini lengthwise; scoop out centers leaving ¼-inch shell. Place shells in shallow baking dish. Coarsely chop zucchini centers; mix with next eight ingredients and spoon into shells. Top with sauce. Bake 45 minutes at 350 degrees. This can be served as a main dish or an accompaniment.
Yield: 4 servings

Eugenia Hofler Clement (Mrs. Robert L.)

SUPER HAMBURGER SOUR CREAM CASSEROLE

Can be doubled
Can freeze

4 ounces egg noodles
1 (8-ounce) can tomato sauce
1 tablespoon flour
1 cup cottage cheese
½ cup sour cream
1 teaspoon salt
1 pound ground beef

Preheat oven to 350 degrees. Cook noodles according to package directions. Brown meat; drain grease; add tomato sauce and flour. Simmer until thickened. Combine sour cream, cottage cheese and salt. Place cooked noodles in bottom of quart casserole. Layer with the sour cream mixture, and top with the hamburger mixture. Cover, bake 30 minutes.
Yield: 4-6 servings

Rebecca Godley Paramore (Mrs. Walter H., III)

MORE

Freezes well
Can double

This is good with a green salad and French bread.
When this recipe was first made, it was to be a masterpiece. Its author kept saying it needs "more" of this or "more" of that. Hence the name. The name could have as easily originated by the popularity of the dish.

12 ounces uncooked spaghetti
1 medium onion
1 pound sausage or ground pork
1 pound ground round steak or chuck, or hamburger
1 (16-ounce) can whole kernel corn
1 (16-ounce) can tomatoes
1 (4-ounce) jar pimientos, sliced
1 jar stuffed olives, sliced
1 cup Cheddar or American cheese, grated

Cook spaghetti in salted, boiling water while you cut the onion in thin slices. In a skillet, cook the onion, pork and beef until the meat is brown. Combine the cooked, drained spaghetti and the meat mixture in a large pot. Add corn (with juice), tomatoes (with juice), pimiento (*without* juice), olives (*without* juice), and ½ cup cheese. Mix well. Taste, and salt if needed. Pour into 9x13-inch pan, and sprinkle the other ½ cup of cheese on top. Bake 1 hour in slow oven (300-325 degrees).
Yield: 8 servings

Catherine Gross Hendren (Mrs. Thomas E.)

If you hate to fry things or to brown them in oil, place in large shallow pan and brown on both sides under the broiler. Spray the casserole first to cut down on clean-up. This method eliminates a grease-spattered stove top and cuts down on calories and cholesterol, too.

To keep a casserole hot for hours, double-wrap in foil and again in newspaper.

TOMATO-MUSHROOM MEAT LOAF

3 pounds ground beef
1 envelope dry Lipton Onion Soup
1 (6-ounce) can tomato paste
***OR* (8-ounce) can tomato sauce with mushrooms**
2 slices bread, crumbled
2 eggs, beaten
1 (10½-ounce) can cream of tomato soup
1 (10½-ounce) can mushroom soup

Mix beef, onion soup and tomato paste or sauce. Work in bread crumbs and eggs. Form into 2 loaves. Bake 30 minutes at 325 or 350 degrees. Then, mix tomato soup and mushroom soup. Pour over loaves and return to oven and bake about 30 additional minutes at the same temperature.
Yield: 8 generous servings

Elizabeth Cross Parker (Mrs. Charles E.)

SWEET AND SOUR MEAT LOAF

1 (15-ounce) can tomato sauce
½ cup light brown sugar
¼ cup vinegar
1 teaspoon dry mustard
2 pounds lean ground beef
½ pound ground pork
2 eggs, lightly beaten
½ cup onion, minced
½ cup fine soft bread crumbs
1 tablespoon salt
½ teaspoon pepper

Mix together tomato sauce, sugar, vinegar, and mustard. In a separate bowl mix beef, pork, eggs, onion, bread crumbs, salt and pepper. Stir in up to 1 cup of sauce mixture to moisten. Pack into a 1½-quart casserole. Pour ¼ cup sauce over top. Reserve remaining sauce to heat and serve with meat loaf. Bake at 350 degrees for 1 hour.
Yield: 6-8 servings

Susanne Darby Thompson (Mrs. Michael B.)

MIRACLE MEATLOAF

Make early in day or day before

1½ pounds ground beef
¼ cup dry bread crumbs
1 egg
½ teaspoon salt
2 cups mashed potatoes
2 hard-boiled eggs, chopped
⅓ cup Miracle Whip Salad Dressing
⅓ cup Kraft Grated Parmesan Cheese
¼ cup celery, finely chopped
2 tablespoons green onion, sliced
Salt
Pepper

Combine meat, bread crumbs, egg and salt; mix well. Pat meat mixture into 14x8-inch rectangle on foil or waxed paper. Combine potatoes, eggs, salad dressing, cheese, celery and onion; mix lightly. Season to taste. Spread potato mixture over meat. Roll up jellyroll fashion, beginning at narrow end. Chill several hours or overnight. Slice meat roll into 6 servings. Bake on rack of broiler pan sprayed with Pam at 350 degrees for 25-30 minutes.

Barbara Straub Stewart

MEAT LOAF WITH PIQUANT SAUCE

¾ cup dry bread crumbs or Corn Flake crumbs
1 cup milk
1½ pounds ground chuck
2 eggs, slightly beaten
¼ cup onion, grated or finely chopped
1 teaspoon salt
⅛ teaspoon pepper
½ teaspoon sage
¼ cup catsup
3 tablespoons brown sugar
¼ teaspoon nutmeg
1 teaspoon dry mustard

Soak crumbs in milk, add meat, eggs, onion, salt, pepper, sage and mix well. Shape in 2 loaves or 1 large loaf. Place in greased pan. Prepare piquant sauce by mixing together catsup, brown sugar, nutmeg and dry mustard. Pour mixture over meat loaves. Bake at 350 degrees for 45 minutes, or 1 hour if large loaf.

Stephanie Noonan (Mrs. Karl P.)

BEEF ROLL MOZZARELLA

A very fancy meat roll

Assemble early in day
Part done ahead

1½ pounds lean ground beef
1 teaspoon salt
¼ teaspoon pepper
1 teaspoon dehydrated onion flakes
1 egg, lightly beaten
½ cup dry bread crumbs
1 (4-ounce) can mushroom stems and pieces
6 ounces Mozzarella, shredded
1 (15-ounce) can tomato sauce
2 tablespoons dry vermouth

Combine meat, salt, pepper, onion, egg and bread crumbs in a large bowl. Drain mushrooms *reserving liquid.* To mushroom liquid add enough water to make ½ cup and add to meat mixture. Mix lightly, just until well-combined. Press mixture into a 14x10-inch rectangle on a piece of waxed paper. Sprinkle surface with Mozzarella, leaving a ½-inch border. Roll up, jellyroll fashion starting with one of the short sides. Place, seam side down in a 13x9-inch baking dish which has been lightly greased. Cover and refrigerate until ready to bake. Remove from refrigerator and preheat oven to 375 degrees. Combine tomato sauce and vermouth. Spread half the sauce over the roll. Bake 45 minutes. Combine remaining sauce with mushrooms; spread over roll; bake 10 minutes longer. Lift onto heated platter using two wide spatulas.
Yield: 6 servings

RUSSIAN CABBAGE PIE

My children adore this!

1 two-crust pie shell
1 small cabbage, shredded
1 onion, chopped
1 (4-ounce) can sliced mushrooms
½ pound ground beef
1 (3-ounce) package cream cheese
3 tablespoons butter

Preheat oven to 375 degrees. Bake one pie shell, remove from oven and spread cream cheese on this shell. Sauté cabbage, onion and mushrooms until cabbage is done. Brown beef, add to cabbage and toss. Put mixture in pie shell on top of cream cheese. Put other pie shell on top of pie. Slice four air vents and bake until top pie shell is brown—20 to 30 minutes.
Yield: 6 servings

Jane Moore Stubbs (Mrs. Trawick H., Jr.)

BIFTEK VIENNESE

Easy
Part done ahead
Serve immediately

1 pound minced steak (twice ground round will suffice)
1½ teaspoons celery salt
½ teaspoon paprika
2 teaspoons lemon juice
1 small onion, minced
1 egg, well-beaten
2 tablespoons butter
¾ cup yogurt
Black pepper
Pinch nutmeg
Noodles or potatoes

Mix by hand the meat, celery, salt, egg, paprika, lemon juice, onion and nutmeg. Fork into eight patties about ½-inch thick. Can keep in refrigerator until cooking time. Melt butter in large pan and fry patties until just done. Remove and place in shallow serving dish. Keep warm in oven. Add yogurt to frying pan and heat without boiling. Pour over patties and serve immediately. This is good with noodles and also with potatoes.
Yield: 4 servings

Carol Webb Pullen (Mrs. John S.)

GOLDEN DOME PIE

Economical
Can freeze baked or unbaked

1 pound ground beef
½ cup evaporated milk
½ cup catsup
⅓ cup fine bread crumbs
¼ cup onion, chopped
½ teaspoon oregano
½ cup green pepper, chopped
¼ cup Parmesan cheese, grated
1 cup Cheddar cheese, shredded
1 tablespoon Worcestershire sauce
1 unbaked pastry shell

Preheat oven to 350 degrees. Mix beef, milk, catsup, crumbs, onion, green pepper and oregano. Press into unbaked pastry shell. Bake 35-40 minutes. Toss shredded cheese and Worcestershire sauce. Sprinkle cheese mixture and Parmesan cheese on top of pie. Bake 10 minutes more. Remove from oven and let stand 10 minutes before serving.
Yield: 6 servings

JOHNNY MAZETTI

May do ahead
Can freeze

2 pounds ground round
1 pound green peppers, chopped
1 pound onions, chopped
1 stalk celery, finely chopped
1 (8-ounce) can sliced mushrooms with juice
1 (10-ounce) can tomato soup
2 (8-ounce) cans tomato sauce
1 (8-ounce) jar stuffed olives, halved
1 (12-ounce) package of medium wide noodles
1 pound sharp Cheddar cheese, grated

Cook noodles according to package directions. Fry ground round, green peppers, onions, and celery separately in very little oil. Do not over cook. Mix these with mushrooms, soup, tomato sauce, olives, and cheese. Fold in noodles gently. Pour into 3-quart casserole. Bake at 350 degrees until thoroughly heated, 15 to 20 minutes at room temperature or 30-45 minutes if refrigerated.
Yield: 12 servings

Jean Schocke McCotter (Mrs. Clifton L.)

AFRICAN CHOW MEIN

Freezes well

Butter
1 pound hamburger
3 small onions, chopped
1 cup celery, diced
¾ cup uncooked rice
2 cups boiling water
1 (10-ounce) can cream mushroom soup or golden mushroom soup
⅓ cup soy sauce

Note: Variations are: 1 can drained mushroom, toasted slivered almonds or ½ can water chestnuts sliced thinly.
Preheat oven to 350 degrees. Brown together in a little butter using a large frying pan the hamburger, onions and celery. Add rice, water, soup and soy sauce and pour into large buttered casserole and bake covered for ½ hour. Stir and bake uncovered for additional ½ hour.

Betty Simon (Mrs. Donn L.)

CHEROKEE CASSEROLE

Quick and easy

1 pound ground beef
3/4 cup onion, chopped
1 1/2 teaspoons salt
1/8 teaspoon garlic powder
1/8 teaspoon ground thyme
1/8 teaspoon oregano
1 (16-ounce) can tomatoes
1 (10-ounce) can cream of mushroom soup
1 cup Minute Rice, uncooked
2-3 slices American cheese (in strips)
Dash pepper
1/2 small bay leaf

Brown meat and onion; cook until onion is tender. Stir in seasonings, tomatoes, soup, rice. Simmer 5 minutes, stirring occasionally. Spoon into baking dish. Top with cheese strips. Broil until cheese is melted.
Yield: 6 servings

Janet Johnson Peregoy (Mrs. Kip)

BEEF PARMIGIANA

1 pound round steak
1/2 cup Parmesan cheese
1/2 cup bread crumbs
Oil
Garlic (optional)
1 onion, chopped
1 teaspoon salt
1/4 teaspoon pepper
1/2 teaspoon sugar
1/2 teaspoon marjoram
1 teaspoon oregano
1 (16-ounce) can tomato sauce
1/2 cup water
6-8 ounces Mozzarella cheese

Preheat oven to 350 degrees. Pound meat and cut into serving pieces. Dip meat in mixture of Parmesan cheese and crumbs, coating well. Brown in oil. Add garlic, if desired. Remove to baking dish. Brown onion and put on top of meat with seasonings. Pour over tomato sauce and 1/2 cup water. Bake 1 hour. Top with Mozzarella cheese just before done, to melt.
Yield: 4-6 servings

Genevieve Tolson Dunn (Mrs. Mark S.)

CAVATINI

1 cup shell macaroni
1 cup twist macaroni
1 cup Rigatoni
2 pounds hamburger
1 green pepper, chopped
2 onions, chopped
2 (4-ounce) cans mushrooms, drained
½ package sliced pepperoni
2 packages Sauer's Spaghetti Sauce Mix
Italian Seasoning to taste
2 (6-ounce) cans tomato paste
6 tomato paste cans of water
Mozzarella cheese

Brown hamburger, add pepper and onion; cook until soft. Add mushrooms, pepperoni and Italian seasoning. Add spaghetti sauce mix, water and tomato paste. Cook until blended together. Cook pasta as directed on boxes and add to sauce. Place in casserole dish and top with cheese. Heat until cheese is melted at 350 degrees, 15-20 minutes.
Yield: 8 servings

Sally Gray White (Mrs. George)

DOT-LEE'S "CRAVEN OLÉ"

This recipe can easily be doubled, and is good for an informal gathering.

1 pound ground beef
⅔ cup evaporated milk, undiluted
1 medium onion, chopped
1 (4-ounce) can green chile peppers, chopped
1 (15-ounce) can chili beans
1 teaspoon salt
¼ teaspoon pepper
1 tablespoon chili powder
2 tablespoons flour
1 (8-ounce) jar mild taco sauce
2 cups regular corn chips
Monterey Jack cheese

Preheat oven to 350 degrees. Combine ground beef, evaporated milk, onion, green chiles, salt, pepper and chili powder in skillet. Cook over medium heat until browned, stirring occasionally. Add flour, stir well. Add taco sauce and chili beans, mix well. Cover bottom of 1½-quart casserole with 1 cup corn chips. Pour in meat mixture. Top with remaining corn chips. Spread evenly over the top with grated Monterey Jack cheese, using any amount you desire. Bake at least 30 minutes. With this dish, serve a guacamole salad and beer for the beverage, instead of wine. Follow the meal with either a caramel or chocolate dessert. These are favorites with Spanish-speaking people.
Yield: 6-8 servings

Dorothy Lee Taylor Jernigan (Mrs. Curtis D.)

UPPER PENNINSULA PASTIES (TURNOVERS)

Pasties:

8 cups flour
2 teaspoons salt
2 cups Crisco or lard
2½ cups ice cold water

Sift flour and salt into a large mixing bowl. Cut in Crisco or lard with pastry blender. Add ice water to make a soft dough. On a floured board, roll out dough into 12 circles about the size of dinner plates.

Filling:

1 pound lean beef, cut in small pieces
¾ pound lean pork, cut in small pieces
8 medium potatoes
1 small rutabaga
4 small onions
6 carrots
Salt and pepper to taste

Dice all vegetables. They may be placed in separate containers or mixed together. Layer meats and vegetables on pasties. Salt and pepper to taste and fold top over filling. Crimp edges together with wet tines of fork. Cut small slits in the top of pasties to release steam. Bake on a lightly greased baking sheet, leaving a little room between pasties for oven browning. Bake in a preheated 425 degree oven for 45 minutes. Remove from oven and place a tea towel over pasties and let set for about ten minutes before serving. Leftover pasties may be frozen in foil and reheated later. Some folks like to open pasties and add catsup.
Yield: 12 servings

Gail Council Moore

PIZZA

Part made ahead

Dough:

1 package dry yeast
1 cup warm water
1 teaspoon sugar
1 teaspoon salt
3 cups flour

Combine yeast, water and sugar in mixing bowl and let rest 5 minutes. Add flour and salt with yeast mixture and beat until mixture balls. Turn dough into greased bowl and allow to rise in warm place 1 hour. Turn onto floured surface and roll into desired shape and size. Use either greased pans or corn meal on pans before placing dough. Bake dough at 450 degrees for 5 minutes. Remove from oven and add sauce and toppings. Return to oven for 10 additional minutes at the same temperature.
Yield: 2 (14-inch) round crusts.

Sauce:

1 pound ground beef, browned and drained
1 (16-ounce) can tomato sauce
2 teaspoons oregano
1 teaspoon basil
1 teaspoon onion salt
1 teaspoon garlic salt

Brown beef, breaking up into small pieces; drain. Mix remaining ingredients in large 4-cup measuring cup, add beef and pour on partially cooked pizza dough. Add toppings and return to oven 10 minutes.

Toppings:

1 (8-ounce) package Mozzarella, shredded
Ripe olives
Minced onion
Pepperoni
Sausage, cooked and drained
Green peppers
Anchovies
Parmesan cheese

Crusts may be made, covered and refrigerated until baking time. Sauce may be prepared, covered and refrigerated and toppings readied for baking time in advance.

Remove candle wax from a tablecloth by scraping as much wax as possible from cloth with a dull knife. Pour boiling water through remaining wax. Treat then as any other stain. Boiling water may need to be applied more than once.

FLORENCE'S ITALIAN SPAGHETTI

Let this sauce simmer all afternoon or morning; it is even better the next day. Also, a great sauce for lasagne.

1 (28-ounce) can tomatoes, drained
1 (6-ounce) can tomato paste
1 (6-ounce) can water
1 (14-ounce) bottle catsup
1 (14-ounce) bottle water
2 tablespoons leaf oregano
½ teaspoon celery salt
½ teaspoon seasoned salt
½ teaspoon garlic powder
4 tablespoons grated Kraft Parmesan cheese
1½ pounds hamburger
½ pound sausage
Spaghetti

Scramble hamburger and sausage until browned in fry pan. Drain. In large saucepan combine the rest of the ingredients. Add meat mixture; bring to boil, then simmer for 3 or 4 hours. Serve that day or next with spaghetti, cooked according to package directions.

Diane Gough Fowler (Mrs. Phillip L.)

ITALIAN GOULASH

1½ pounds ground round steak
3 strips bacon
4 medium onions, chopped
1 green pepper, chopped
4 stalks celery, chopped
1 (16-ounce) can Chinese vegetables, drained
1 tablespoon Worcestershire sauce
1 tablespoon parsley
1 (10-ounce) can tomato soup
1 (16-ounce) can spaghetti
1 (16-ounce) can spaghetti sauce with mushrooms
1 (8-ounce) can water chestnuts, sliced thin
1 (5-ounce) can Chinese noodles (more if desired)
Grated cheese

Fry bacon and save for garnish. Add onions and beef to bacon grease and brown. Add tomato soup and sauce with mushrooms. Add green pepper and celery and cook until slightly tender. Add spaghetti, Chinese vegetables, water chestnuts and season with Worcestershire sauce and parsley. Salt to taste. Serve on Chinese noodles and top with grated cheese and bacon.
Yield: 8 servings

Eugenia Hofler Clement (Mrs. Robert L.)

GROUND BEEF CHAIN COOKING

Can freeze

Meat Sauce:

½ cup oil
8 garlic cloves, crushed
2 cups onion, chopped
4 pounds ground beef
4 (28-ounce) cans tomatoes
4 tablespoons salt
4 bay leaves
8 (6-ounce) cans tomato paste

Heat oil in saucepan. Add garlic, onion and beef and brown lightly. Add tomatoes, salt, bay leaves, and tomato paste. Simmer, covered 2½-3 hours until thickened and reduced. This can be cooked in the oven in a large roasting pan at a low temperature.
Yield: 16 cups *

*4 cups are used to make one lasagne. Recommend freezing in 4 cup units.

Ann Harris Bustard (Mrs. Victor W.)

ANN'S LASAGNE

1 (4 cup) container meat sauce*
1 garlic clove, minced
1½ teaspoons oregano
1 (16-ounce) box lasagne noodles
2 pounds ricotta cheese *OR* large curd cottage cheese, drained if too creamy
1 cup Parmesan cheese, grated
8 ounces Mozzarella cheese, thinly sliced

*Meat sauce is from GROUND BEEF CHAIN COOKING
Thaw meat sauce, if frozen. Add garlic and oregano. Cook lasagne noodles according to directions on package. Drain and separate noodles on paper towel. Cover bottom of 9x13-inch casserole dish with several spoonfuls of meat sauce. Top with criss-cross layer of noodles, then ricotta, Mozzarella, sauce and Parmesan. Repeat layering, ending with sauce and topping with Mozzarella. If meat sauce has *not* been frozen, entire lasagne may be frozen at this point. To serve, thaw and bake at 350 degrees for 50 minutes.
Yield: 6-8 servings

Ann Harris Bustard (Mrs. Victor W.)

LASAGNE

Can be frozen
Can be made ahead

Sauce:

2 (29-ounce) cans Italian-style tomatoes
4 (8-ounce) cans tomato sauce
3 teaspoons dried oregano
¼ teaspoon pepper
2 teaspoons onion salt
2 cups onion, minced
2 cloves garlic, minced
⅓ cup salad oil
2 pounds ground beef
2 teaspoons MSG
2 teaspoons salt

Sauté onion and garlic in salad oil until barely tender. Add salt and MSG. Add ground beef and sauté until beef is browned and in small pieces. Drain if necessary. Combine tomatoes, tomato sauce, oregano, pepper and salt in Dutch oven. Add cooked beef and simmer 2½ hours.

1 pound lasagne noodles
1½ pounds ricotta cheese or cottage cheese
1 pound Mozzarella
1 cup Parmesan

Cook noodles according to manufacturer's directions. Rinse in cool water for easier handling. Divide ingredients between two 8x12-inch pans. Place several spoonfuls of sauce on the bottom. Top with noodles laid lengthwise then crosswise in dish. Cover with ½ ricotta, ⅓ Mozzarella, and ½ Parmesan. Spoon sauce over. Repeat noodles and cheeses ending with sauce. Top with remaining Mozzarella. Cover and refrigerate until baking time. Bake at 350 degrees 30-50 minutes. If frozen, leave aluminum foil on and bake 2-2½ hours. Let sit 15 minutes before serving.
Yield: 12 servings

Dr. Ray Houghton

SPAGHETTI SAUCE WITH MEATBALLS

Diet-low calorie
Crockpot
Meatballs may be made in advance

Sauce:

3 cups tomato juice
1 tablespoon Worcestershire sauce
2 tablespoons wine vinegar
1 onion, chopped
½ teaspoon basil
½ teaspoon oregano
½ teaspoon Italian Seasoning
Garlic powder to taste
1 teaspoon salt

Meatballs:

1 pound ground beef
¼ cup dry instant milk
1 teaspoon dry mustard
½ teaspoon Tabasco

Mix all ingredients for *sauce* and cook on low in crockpot all day or on top of stove 2 hours on low heat. Mix all ingredients for *meatballs* and shape into balls. Balls may be frozen or refrigerated until ready to use. Broil meatballs until done. Drain well. Add to sauce and simmer until ready to serve. Serve over cooked spaghetti.
Yield: 6-8 servings

Anna Cartner Kafer (Mrs. Oscar A., III)

ITALIAN MEATBALLS AND SAUCE

A very different spaghetti!

Part made ahead and frozen

Meatballs:

1 clove garlic
2 teaspoons salt
2 pounds ground beef
2 eggs
¼ cup bread crumbs
¼ teaspoon cayenne

Crush garlic in salt. Mix all ingredients together thoroughly and shape int balls. Place balls on cookie sheet and put into freezer until fairly firm. Transf balls to plastic bag suitable for freezer. Remove from freezer as desired f use.

Sauce:

1½ cups onions, sliced
⅓ cup salad oil
3 tablespoons flour
1 bouillon cube
1 cup boiling water
¼ cup wine vinegar
1 (16-ounce) can tomatoes
½ teaspoon oregano
½ teaspoon salt
2 medium green peppers, sliced
8 ounces thin spaghetti
¼ cup parsley
½ cup Parmesan cheese

Cook onions in ¼ cup of the salad oil saving the remainder of oil. When onions are tender remove from pan and add meatballs browning balls on all sides. Remove balls from pan. Stir in flour into pan drippings. Dissolve bouillon cube in boiling water; add to pan. Add vinegar, tomatoes, oregano, salt and onions; stir to mix well. Cook UNCOVERED 15 minutes. Return balls to pan; add green pepper; cook 5-10 minutes. Cook spaghetti according to manufacturer's instructions. When al dente, drain spaghetti and toss with remaining salad oil, Parmesan cheese and parsley in a bowl. Serve with meatballs and sauce on top.
Yield: 8 servings

ITALIAN SHELLS

1 (12-ounce) package jumbo shell pasta
1 (24-ounce) container cottage cheese
1 (12-ounce) package Mozzarella, shredded
¾ cup Parmesan cheese
3 eggs, slightly beaten
1 (10-ounce) package frozen spinach, thawed and drained
1½ teaspoons salt
2 teaspoons parsley, chopped
¾ teaspoon oregano
¼ teaspoon pepper
4 cups Italian sauce*

*Sauce may be homemade or bought and may be meat, meatless or mushroom.

Cook shells as directed on package; drain. While shells are cooking combine cheeses with eggs, salt, parsley, oregano, pepper and spinach. Some Mozzarella may be reserved to sprinkle on completed dish. Grease 9x13-inch baking dish and spread several tablespoons of sauce on the bottom. Stuff drained shells with two tablespoons cheese mixture and arrange in prepared pan. Pour sauce over top and sprinkle with reserved Mozzarella. Cover and refrigerate until baking time. Allow shells to approach room temperature before baking. Preheat oven to 350 degrees and bake shells 35 minutes or until thoroughly warmed.
Yield: 10 servings

SWEDISH MEATBALLS WITH RICE

2 (10-ounce) cans cream of celery soup
1 pound ground beef
⅔ cup fine dry bread crumbs
1 egg, slightly beaten
2 tablespoons onion, minced
1 tablespoon parsley, chopped (optional)
1 teaspoon salt
Rice

Blend soup with 1 can water. Measure out ¼ cup mixture and combine with remaining ingredients. Shape into 1-inch balls. Brown in large skillet in 1 tablespoon shortening. Add remaining soup mixture. Cover and cook over low heat for about 20 minutes. Stir occasionally. Serve over hot cooked rice.

Susan Lee Thomas (Mrs. John G.)

SPAGHETTI CASSEROLE

Original recipe by my Mother, Anne Bratton Allen

Do ahead
Can be frozen

1 large onion, minced
1 tablespoon butter or margarine
1 pound hamburger
1 (10-ounce) can tomato soup
1 soup can water
1 cup catsup
1 tablespoon brown sugar
2½ teaspoons chili powder
Garlic salt, salt and pepper to taste
Mushrooms, (optional)
8 ounces egg noodles, cooked and drained
½ cup Cheddar, grated
⅓ cup cracker crumbs

Brown onion in butter. Brown hamburger, drain off fat and add to browned onion. Add remaining ingredients, stirring carefully to mix sauce and noodles. Pour into 3-quart casserole sprayed with Pam; top with crumbs and cheese. Bake at 400 degrees until heated thoroughly and cheese has melted. The time will vary if the dish is frozen. Casserole may be thawed and baked covered 30-45 minutes or bake frozen covered 1 hour to 1½ hours. If casserole is put together just before serving, baking time may be reduced to 25 minutes as all ingredients are still warm.
Yield: 6 servings

Elizabeth Allen Brinkley (Mrs. William E., Jr.)

LA STRATA

1 pound ground beef
½ cup onion, minced
1 (8-ounce) can tomato sauce
1 teaspoon basil
1 teaspoon parsley, chopped
¼ teaspoon oregano
Dash garlic salt
Dash pepper
1 (4-ounce) can mushrooms, drained
1 (10-ounce) package frozen chopped spinach, cooked and well-drained
1 (8-ounce) container cottage cheese
4 ounces Mozzarella cheese, shredded

Preheat oven to 375 degrees. Cook spinach as directed on package. In medium skillet, sauté ground meat and onion until onion is tender and meat is browned. Add tomato sauce, basil, parsley, oregano, garlic salt, pepper and mushrooms. Combine spinach and cottage cheese. In 8-inch square casserole arrange in layers the spinach mixture, meat mixture, then Mozzarella cheese. Repeat layering ending with cheese. Bake 15-20 minutes or until hot and bubbly.
Yield: 4 servings

Polly Speace Miller (Mrs. Robert F.)

HARD TIMES TAMALE PIE

Economical. This was our Depression entertaining stand-by . . . it always drew raves!

1 large onion, sliced
1 green pepper, chopped
1 clove garlic, minced
1½ pounds ground beef
1 (28-ounce) can tomatoes
1 (16-ounce) can creamed corn
⅔ cup yellow corn meal (granulated)
1 tablespoon salt
Pepper to taste
Paprika for color
½ teaspoon chili powder
1 (6-ounce) can pitted ripe olives, drained and sliced
Parmesan cheese

Sauté onion, green pepper and garlic. Add ground beef and when brown, add tomatoes, corn and corn meal; simmer on top of stove about 10 minutes. Mixture will thicken. Add salt, pepper, paprika, chili powder and olives. Put in 4-quart casserole and sprinkle generously with Parmesan cheese. Bake 30-40 minutes at 375 degrees. Serve with crusty French bread.
Yield: 8 servings

Marian Bartlett Stewart (Mrs. Wm. Edward)

HOLUPCHI

Stuffed Cabbage

Time consuming
Do early in day

2 pounds ground beef
1 cup rice, parboiled
2 onions, chopped and sautéed
1 large cabbage, or 2 small cabbages
Salt to taste
Pepper to taste
2 tablespoons butter or margarine
1 (10-ounce) can tomato soup
1 soup can water
1 (8-ounce) can tomato sauce

Core whole cabbage head and steam in large kettle of boiling salted water, separating leaves until just wilting. Remove a few leaves at a time and trim off thick ridge on back of leaves to make it easier for rolling. Wash rice after partially cooking and strain. Sauté onions in butter. Combine with meat, rice, salt and pepper. Spread 1 heaping tablespoon of meat mixture on thick end of each cabbage leaf and roll up. Tuck in ends, or roll leaf tight and fold over. Place rolls in casserole lined with discarded leaves. Mix water, soup and tomato sauce and pour over Holupchi. The liquid should cover the top layer. Protect top by covering with a few cabbage leaves. Bake covered in 350 degree oven for 2 hours.
Yield: 18-20 rolls depending on size

Helen Kulba (Mrs. William)

STUFFED LAMB SLICES

Easy

6-8 slices cooked leftover lamb
4 ounces Pepperidge Farm Bread Stuffing
Celery
Onion
Poultry seasoning
½ cup hot bouillon
2 tablespoons grape jelly
2 tablespoons butter

Preheat oven to 350 degrees. Prepare stuffing according to package directions and add celery, onion and poultry seasoning to taste. Put lamb slices together with stuffing in the middle, like a sandwich. Mix butter and jelly in hot bouillon and pour over stuffed slices. Bake for about 20 minutes, basting several times.
Yield: 3-4 servings

Robertha Kafer Coleman (Mrs. Thomas B.)

MOUSSAKA

Time consuming
Stores well
Do day ahead
This is better when made a day ahead and left in refrigerator overnight.

4 medium eggplants
2 pounds ground lean lamb
3 onions, chopped
1 cup butter
2 tablespoons tomato paste
¼ cup dry red wine
¼ cup extra strong black coffee
¼ cup parsley, chopped
2 teaspoons salt
¼ teaspoon freshly ground pepper
⅛ teaspoon ground cinnamon
2 eggs, slightly beaten
1 cup grated Parmesan cheese
1 cup freshly ground bread crumbs
Enough vegetable oil for browning
4 medium fresh tomatoes, sliced

Sauce:
6 tablespoons flour
3 cups hot milk
⅛ teaspoon nutmeg
4 egg yolks, slightly beaten
2 cups ricotta cheese

Peel eggplant, slice ¼-inch thick. Sprinkle with salt and let stand 5 minutes. Brown lamb; sauté onions in 2 tablespoons butter. Add tomato paste, wine, coffee, parsley, salt, pepper, cinnamon. Simmer until liquid is absorbed. Stir in the eggs, ⅓ cup of Parmesan cheese and ¼ cup bread crumbs. Wipe off excess moisture from eggplant. Brown lightly in oil. In large heavy casserole, at least 3-quart size, alternate layers of the remaining bread crumbs, Parmesan cheese, the eggplant, lamb mixture and tomato slices ending with eggplant. Melt the remaining butter, blend in flour; gradually stir the hot milk into this and bring to a boil, stirring constantly. Add nutmeg. Pour this mixture over the egg yolks, cook two minutes and cool slightly. Add the ricotta cheese. Pour over the casserole slowly for absorption. Bake in oven one hour at 350 degrees.
Yield: 12 servings

Kathleen Winslow Budd (Mrs. Bern)

LAMB AND SPINACH CASSEROLE

Easy
Do day ahead
Freeze
Can double
This is a special recipe of Father Robert Farrar Capon, an Episcopal Priest and a mighty fine cook.

1 pound (or more) cooked lamb, cut into bite-sized pieces
2 pounds fresh spinach *OR* 3 or 4 (10-ounce) packages frozen spinach, cooked and chopped
¼ cup butter
4 tablespoons mayonnaise
4 tablespoons Parmesan or Cheddar cheese, grated
A few drops of sherry
Salt and freshly ground pepper to taste

Preheat oven to 350 degrees. Add all ingredients to the hot, drained spinach; season to taste with salt and pepper; place in 1½-quart casserole; cover and heat thoroughly in oven for 25-30 minutes, (longer if casserole is cold when put into oven).
Yield: 4-6 servings

Carol Webb Pullen (Mrs. John S.)

HUNGARIAN PÖRKELT

2 pounds veal, diced in 1-inch pieces
1 tablespoon lard
2 large onions, diced
Salt
Pepper
Paprika
1 teaspoon caraway seeds
1 cup water or chicken broth

Brown meat and onions in lard adding spices. Add water *or* broth. Cover and simmer until onions have become transparent. Serve on boiled potatoes or noodles.
Yield: 4-5 servings

Gisela N. von zur Muehlen Ives (Mrs. George A., Jr.)

VEAL PARMESAN

2 pounds thin veal steak
Salt and pepper
1 egg
⅓ cup grated Parmesan cheese
⅓ cup Italian bread crumbs
¼ cup salad or olive oil
2 tablespoons butter
1 onion, finely chopped
1 (6-ounce) can tomato paste
1 (28-ounce) can tomatoes
1 teaspoon salt
½ teaspoon marjoram
½ pound Mozzarella

Preheat oven to 350 degrees. Cut veal in pieces; salt and pepper; beat egg with 2 teaspoons water. Dip veal in egg then roll in mixture of cheese and crumbs. Fry in oil until brown. Put into baking dish. In same skillet cook onions in butter until soft; add paste, tomatoes, salt and marjoram. Boil a few minutes, scrapping up browned bits around bottom. Pour most of sauce over veal. Top with sliced Mozzarella and pour remaining sauce over all. Bake for 30 minutes.
Yield: 6 servings

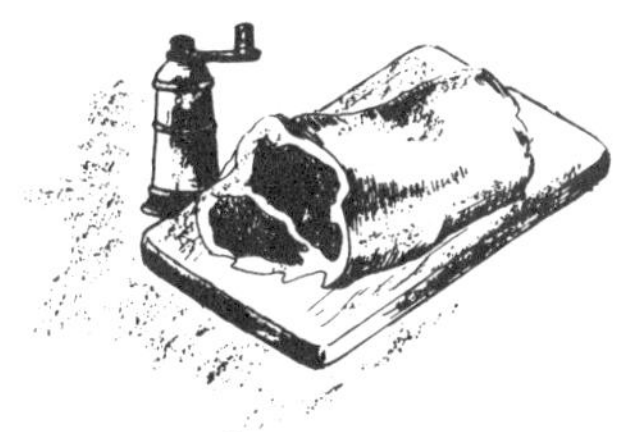

VEAL GOULASH

1-1½ pounds veal, diced
3 tablespoons butter
2 onions, diced finely
1-2 tomatoes, skinned and sliced
Salt
Pepper
Paprika
1 cup water
3 tablespoons flour

Cook onions in butter until golden; add veal and tomatoes and brown gently; add seasonings and water. Simmer covered until almost done, about 45 minutes. Meat will be very tender. Remove lid and let liquid boil down a little. Dust flour over meat mixture; stir. If sauce appears too thick, water may be added to give desired thickness. Serve over noodles, potatoes or Bohemian dumplings.
Yield: 4 servings

Gisela N. von zur Muehlen Ives (Mrs. George A., Jr.)

Brinson House **213 Johnson Street**

The earliest part of the house dates from 1755. Additions were made between 1755 and 1800 which made the main part of the present house. With these additions the house developed into a Federal side hall plan by 1800. The house was restored in 1980 by Dr. Dale Millns, a former vestryman and Senior Warden, and Mrs. Millns, also a former vestry member.

POLYNESIAN PORK

1 (1-pound) pork steak, 2-inches thick
1 teaspoon paprika
2 tablespoons hot shortening
3 tablespoons brown sugar
¼ cup instant dry milk
2 tablespoons cornstarch
½ teaspoon salt
1 (15-ounce) can pineapple tidbits, well-drained (reserve syrup)
⅓ cup vinegar
1 tablespoon soy sauce
1 teaspoon Worcestershire sauce
⅓ cup water
1 green pepper, cut into 2x⅛-inch strips
1 small onion, thinly sliced
Rice

With sharp knife cut meat into 2x½-inch strips. Sprinkle pork with paprika. Brown well in hot shortening in a 10-inch skillet over medium heat. Cover and cook about 3-5 minutes or until tender, stirring occasionally. Drain off drippings. Push meat to one side of skillet. Combine brown sugar, dry milk, cornstarch, and salt in a 1½-quart bowl. If necessary, add water to reserved pineapple syrup to make ⅔ cup. Gradually add syrup, vinegar, soy sauce, Worcestershire sauce and water to dry ingredients and stir until smooth. Pour into skillet. Cook over low heat until thick and smooth, stirring constantly. Stir in green pepper, onion and pineapple. Cover and simmer over very low heat 8-10 minutes or until vegetables are tender but crisp. Serve over hot rice.
Yield: 4-6 servings

Eva Bond Littman (Mrs. John E.)

BARBECUED PORK CHOPS

6 pork chops
1 tablespoon chili powder
1 teaspoon salt
1 teaspoon paprika
¼ cup brown sugar
½ cup vinegar
1 (10½-ounce) can tomato soup

Place chops in bottom of baking dish. Combine remaining ingredients and pour over chops. Bake at 350 degrees for 1½ hours.
Yield: 4-6 servings

Patricia Byrum McCotter (Mrs. C. Kennedy, Jr.)

PORK CHOPS IN GINGER ALE

2 large onions, sliced
¼ cup butter, divided
6 (¾-to 1-inch thick) pork chops
2 tablespoons firmly packed brown sugar
1 tablespoon tomato purée or chili sauce
1 tablespoon flour
1 cup ginger ale
Salt and pepper to taste

Preheat oven to 350 degrees. In a skillet sauté onions in ⅛ cup butter over medium heat until golden brown. Remove onions and place in a 2-quart oblong baking dish. In the same skillet brown the pork chops in remaining ⅛ cup of butter over medium heat. Remove and place on top of onions. Sprinkle with brown sugar. Blend tomato purée and flour together in a small bowl; add ginger ale and pour over chops. Sprinkle generously with salt and pepper and bake for 1 hour or until chops are tender.
Yield: 6 servings

Isabelle Schocke Taylor (Mrs. Elijah)

HERBED BAKED PORK CHOPS

4-6 pork chops
1 egg, beaten
2 tablespoons milk
1 cup Pepperide Farm Stuffing, crushed
1 (10-ounce) can cream of mushroom soup
½ cup sherry
½ teaspoon dry mustard
Salt and pepper to taste

Dip pork chops in egg with 2 tablespoons of milk. Coat with crushed stuffing. Brown. Put in greased casserole and pour over the chops the mushroom soup mixed with the sherry and dry mustard. Cover and bake 325 degrees about 1 hour.
Yield: 4-6 servings

Caroline Dunn Ashford (Mrs. Charles H.)

A wire whisk is super for blending canned soups and water.

Use margarine rather than butter to save calories.

SPANISH PORK CHOPS

8 pork chops, salted and peppered to taste
¼ cup margarine
1 cup uncooked long-cooking rice
½ cup onion, chopped
½ cup green pepper, chopped or in strips
1 teaspoon paprika
1 (15-ounce) can tomatoes, puréed
1 (29-ounce) can tomatoes, puréed
1 teaspoon salt

In large skillet brown pork chops in margarine. Add remaining ingredients in order listed. Cover and simmer 1 hour or until rice is done. Add water if necessary to keep from sticking.
Yield: 4 servings

Cindy Cratch Hart (Mrs. S. Tyler)

PORK CHOP CASSEROLE

Part done ahead

¾ cup rice, uncooked
6 pork chops, floured
1 large onion, chopped
1 medium bell pepper, cut in rings
2 tablespoons cooking oil
1 (16-ounce) can tomatoes
¼ teaspoon thyme
¼ teaspoon marjoram
1 teaspoon salt
1 (10-ounce) can beef bouillon

Put rice in bottom of 2-quart shallow casserole. Brown floured chops in oil and place on top of rice. Brown onion and bell pepper in remaining oil and pour over pork chops. Mix tomatoes, thyme, marjoram, salt. Pour over pork chops. Pour beef bouillon over all. Cover and bake at 350 degrees for 1 hour.
Yield: 6 servings

Anna Cartner Kafer (Mrs. Oscar A., III)

SAVORY PORK CASSEROLE

6 pork chops
4 tablespoons vegetable oil, divided
Salt to taste
Pepper to taste
1 (6-ounce) package yellow saffron rice
½ cup onion, chopped
¼ cup celery, chopped
2½ cups boiling water
6 apple rings
Margarine or butter, melted
¼ teaspoon cinnamon
6 cherries

Trim excess fat from chops. Brown slowly in 2 tablespoons oil; season with salt and pepper; set aside. Sauté rice, onion and celery for 5 minutes in remaining 2 tablespoons oil. Add boiling water and stir. Turn into oblong casserole. Top rice with chops; cover tightly. Bake at 350 degrees for 40-45 minutes. Top pork chops with apple rings, melted butter and sprinkle with cinnamon. Cover and bake 15 additional minutes. If desired, run under broiler to brown apple rings. Garnish apple rings with a cherry.
Yield: 4-6 servings

Nedgelena Speight Jennings (Mrs. George M.)

PORK BACKBONE

Economical

4 pounds of pork backbone*
3 tablespoons chili sauce
½ cup cooking sherry
Salt and pepper to taste
½ cup water
½ teaspoon Crisco

*Careful selection of meat, sometimes called backrib, will insure its success on your menu.

Preheat oven to 300 degrees. Slice backbone into individual serving pieces. Salt and pepper to taste. Lightly grease bottom of small roasting pan with Crisco; place meat in roaster; pour sherry over backbone and then spoon on chili sauce. Cover. Place in oven for 30 minutes. Remove from oven, turn meat over and add ½ cup water. Replace cover and cook for another 30 minutes.

Yield: 4-5 servings

Marjorie Morey Latham (Mrs. J. R.)

TAIWAN STUFFED SPARERIBS

2 pounds lean spareribs
3 tablespoons oil
15 pieces of scallion, each 3-inches long
2 pieces of scallion, 6-inches long
3 slices ginger
5 tablespoons soy sauce
1 tablespoon white wine
2 tablespoons sugar
1 tablespoon vinegar
3 cups boiling water
1 teaspoon sesame oil

Cut each piece of rib into 1½-inch pieces. Heat 3 tablespoons oil. Stir fry ribs in wok. Add two longer pieces of scallion, ginger and cook 1 minute. Splash in wine, soy sauce, sugar and water. Cover pan tightly and stew over low heat for ½ hour. Sauce should be about 1 cup. Splash in vinegar and cook 1 more minute. Remove ribs; pull bone out of each piece; place a 3-inch piece of scallion in the place of the bone. Put stuffed ribs in pan; cook with sauce 1 additional minute. Splash in sesame oil. This may be served on a bed of rice.

Yield: 4 servings

Donna Volney

PERFECT HAM

Prepare day ahead

1 country ham
1 cup molasses
1 cup vinegar

In a large pot or ham boiler completely cover the ham with water. Soak ham for 12 hours; wash and clean before cooking. In ham boiler cover the ham with water; add 1 cup molasses and 1 cup vinegar. Bring to a boil, turn heat down to simmer. Cook 20 minutes to the pound. Another indication that it is done is when the bone in the butt end begins to separate from the ham. Let cool in water. This method is suitable for a half or a whole country ham.

Helen Cannon Mewborn

To calculate how large a ham you will need, allow ¼-⅓ pound per serving of boneless ham and ⅓-½ pound bone-in ham per person.

CAROLINA COUNTRY HAM

Part done ahead

1 smoked ham
1 apple
1 onion
1 cup molasses
1 teaspoon mixed pickling spices
½ cup brown sugar
1 teaspoon Worcestershire sauce
1 (20-ounce) can pineapple, slices
Cloves

Soak ham overnight. Clean thoroughly. Place ham in a large container and cover with cold water. Put in an apple and an onion—-big if the ham is big, small if small. Pour in molasses and pickling spices. Simmer very slowly. Allow 20 minutes per pound. Remove from heat just before the meat leaves the bone. Let the ham remain in the water until it has cooled. Remove it later, skin and cut off the fat. Place the trimmed ham in a baking dish. Mix brown sugar and Worcestershire . Drain pineapple and cut into halves forming crescents. Spread the brown sugar over the ham. Place pineapple halves in rows over brown sugar piercing each slice with cloves. Bake at 275 degrees 20 minutes or until sugar glaze browns.

Miss Gertrude S. Carraway

HAM LOAF WITH MUSTARD SAUCE

Loaf:

1½ pounds ground ham
1½ pounds ground pork
1 egg, beaten
½ (10¾-ounce) can tomato soup
½ cup milk
1 cup bread crumbs
½ teaspoon paprika
¼ teaspoon salt
½ onion, sliced
4 tablespoons water

Sauce:

½ can tomato soup
½ cup prepared mustard
½ cup vinegar
3 egg yolks, beaten
½ cup sugar
½ cup margarine

Preheat oven to 300 degrees. Mix all ingredients for loaf except onion and water. Shape into loaf. Put in bottom of roaster pan. Add water to pan and slice half onion over loaf. Bake *covered* for 1½ hours. Remove to serving platter. Mix all ingredients for sauce in top of double boiler. Cook, stirring until thickened. Spoon over baked ham loaf.
Yield: 8 servings

Julia Woodson Hudson (Mrs. John S., Jr.)

HAM AND NOODLE CASSEROLE

Easy and economical

¾ cup milk
½ pound sharp cheese, cubed
2 cups ham, diced or ground
½ cup onion, diced
3 cups noodles, cooked
¾ cup sour cream
¼ cup parsley, chopped
Salt and pepper to taste
Bread crumbs (optional)

Preheat oven to 350 degrees. Grease a 2-quart casserole dish. Combine milk and cheese in saucepan; heat until cheese melts. Stir in remaining ingredients. Spoon into casserole. Top with crumbs, if desired. Bake at 350 degrees for 30 minutes or until bubbly.
Yield: 4-6 servings

Grace Dixon Sellers (Mrs. John H.)

HAM BALLS Á L'ORANGE

Great way to use the last of the ham!

3 cups ground ham
1 slice bread, crumbled
1 teaspoon orange bits
2 eggs, well-beaten
1 medium onion, chopped
2 tablespoons cooking oil
1 tablespoon apple jelly or orange marmalade
3 tablespoons wine vinegar
½ teaspoon Worcestershire sauce
¼ teaspoon dry mustard
½ cup orange juice

Blend ham, bread crumbs, orange bits, eggs and onion together; form into balls and brown in oil. Mix remaining ingredients to make sauce. Pour over browned balls; simmer 15-20 minutes. Serve with rice.
Yield: 4-6 servings

Barbara Straub Stewart

Use CocaCola to baste a ham.

HAM AND CHEESE SOUFFLÉ

1-1½ cups leftover baked ham
2 tablespoons butter or margarine
2 slices soft white bread
¼ pound sharp Cheddar cheese, grated or slivered
2 eggs, separated
¼ teaspoon paprika
½ teaspoon salt
1⅓ cups hot milk
1 tablespoon butter (extra)
1 tablespoon parsley, minced

Cut ham in slivers and lay on bottom of greased 1½-quart baking dish. Crumble bread into small pieces. Grate cheese coarsely or sliver. Combine bread, cheese, beaten egg yolks and heated milk. Add extra tablespoon butter, salt and paprika. Let stand 20 minutes or until ready to bake. When ready to bake, preheat oven to 325 degrees. Add parsley to bread-egg mixture. Fold in stiffly beaten egg whites. Pour into baking dish over ham. Bake 45 minutes or until silver knife comes out clean when inserted in center of soufflé.
Yield: 6 servings

SAVORY SAUSAGE CASSEROLE

1 pound pork sausage
1 (16-ounce) can red kidney beans, drained
1 cup apple, chopped or diced, peeled or unpeeled
1 onion, chopped or sliced
2 to 4 tablespoons brown sugar
½ cup tomato juice
***OR* V-8 juice**
⅛ teaspoon pepper
1-2 teaspoons chili powder

Cook sausage lightly in skillet until "crumbly" and no longer pink; pour off fat. Mix sausage and all other ingredients and pour into 1½-quart casserole. Cover and bake at 350 degrees about 1 hour and 15 minutes.
Yield: 4 servings

Nancy Robinson Hunt (Mrs. William B., Jr.)

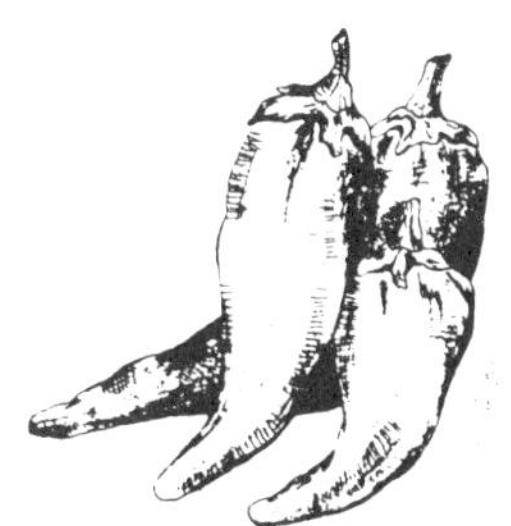

GREEN CHILI

6 pork steaks
2 teaspoons salt
2 (4-ounce) cans green chiles, diced
1 (16-ounce) can tomatoes, cut up
⅓ cup onion, diced
6 garlic cloves, diced
3 cups water
1 jalapẽno pepper, diced
2 tablespoons flour
1½ cups water

Trim fat from pork steaks, dice meat and brown slowly until very brown. When meat is tender, add salt. In a large pot on medium heat, put green chiles, tomatoes, onion, garlic and 3 cups of water. Add 1 hot jalapẽno pepper to make it hotter. Add browned meat to chile mixture, saving drippings from meat. To the drippings add flour and brown until *almost* burned. Gradually add 1½ cups water to the flour mixture to make a gravy. Add gravy to the chili and meat and simmer 2-3 hours. Serve with burritos filled with refried beans and cheese.
Yield: 6 servings

Terry Trippe Brubaker (Mrs. William J.)

CHEESE AND GREEN CHILE PIE

2 (4-ounce) cans green chiles, rinsed and seeded
12 ounces Cheddar cheese, grated
3 eggs, well-beaten
½ teaspoon Worcestershire sauce
¼ teaspoon dry mustard
¼ teaspoon salt
⅛ teaspoon pepper
Paprika

Butter bottom of 8 x 8-inch baking dish. Place chiles on the bottom of the dish. Mix eggs, Worcestershire sauce, dry mustard, salt and pepper together. Add cheese and pour over chiles. Sprinkle with paprika. Bake at 350 degrees for 40-50 minutes.
Yield: 6 servings

Terry Trippe Brubaker (Mrs. William J.)

Dried out cheese can be grated and stored in covered container for later use in cooking.

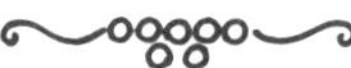

CHEESY-SOUR CREAM ENCHILADAS

2 (10-ounce) cans cream of mushroom soup
1 (8-ounce) container sour cream
1 (4-ounce) can green chiles, chopped
¼ teaspoon salt
¼ teaspoon pepper
½ teaspoon garlic powder
2 cups Cheddar cheese, shredded
1 cup onion, chopped
1 dozen corn tortillas

Combine soup, sour cream, and seasonings in a medium saucepan and mix well. Cook over medium heat until hot. Combine cheese and onion mixing well. Heat or cook tortillas in oil; drain. Spoon 1½ tablespoons cheese and onion and 2 tablespoons soup mixture onto each tortilla. Roll up and place seam side down in greased 13 x 9-inch baking dish. Spoon remaining soup mixture over top of enchiladas and sprinkle with remaining cheese. Bake at 350 degrees for 20-30 minutes.
Yield: 4-5 servings

Terry Trippe Brubaker (Mrs. William J.)

CHILES RELLENOS

1 (7-ounce) can green chiles, rinsed and seeded
6-8 ounces Cheddar, cut in fingers
2 eggs, separated
Flour
Salt
Hot oil

Heat oil. Insert cheese "fingers" into cavity of rinsed and seeded chiles. Beat egg whites stiff and fold into beaten yolks. Roll stuffed peppers in flour mixed with salt. Dip in egg combination and slide each pepper into hot oil. Cook until golden brown, about 3-4 minutes per side. Drain on paper towels.
Yield: 4-6 servings

Terry Trippe Brubaker (Mrs. William J.)

Sifting ¼ cup flour into grease will stop hot grease from sputtering.

MEXICAN BURRITOS

12 flour tortillas
1 (16-ounce) can refried beans
1 (16-ounce) can Stokes Green Chili With Pork*
1 medium onion, chopped (optional)
Grated Cheddar cheese

*or try homemade Green Chili

Warm refried beans. Put one spoonful of beans and chili and grated cheese and onions in each tortilla. Fold and roll. Place in casserole dish. Pour remaining green chili and cheese over casserole. Heat 20 minutes at 350 degrees.
Yield: 12 burritos, 4-6 servings

Terry Trippe Brubaker (Mrs. William J.)

Mayhew-Hendren House **217 Change Street**

This early 19th century townhouse was moved in February, 1974, from its original site adjoining Centenary Methodist Church on Middle Street to a new location on Change Street by the Historic New Bern Foundation, Inc. The first library in New Bern was organized by Miss Mayhew with the aid of a literary society and the volumes were kept on the second floor of this house and could be borrowed by any applicant. The house was restored by Mr. Ben Parrish, a former vestryman, and Mrs. Parrish in 1975.

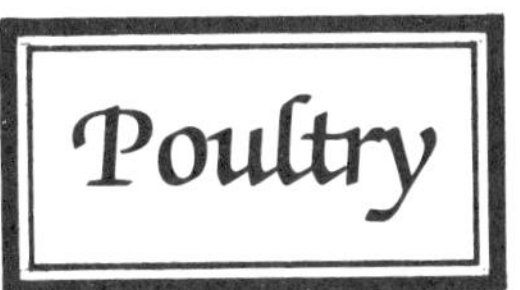

INGLIS FLETCHER'S CHICKEN COUNTRY CAPTAIN

Before the main house at Bandon burned, Mrs. Fletcher often featured this at her Sunday night buffet suppers. We "younguns" often escaped from the large, diverse crowd, taking our plates to the old school house in the yard. This retreat, however, was urged by the authoress.

8 chicken breasts (preferably boned)
¼ cup flour
½ teaspoon pepper
3 tablespoons salad oil or cooking oil
2 medium green peppers, chopped
¾ cup onion, chopped
1 clove garlic, crushed or ¼ teaspoon garlic powder
⅓ cup parsley, chopped
1 tablespoon curry powder
½ cup currants
¼ pound blanched almonds
1 teaspoon salt
½ teaspoon mace
½ teaspoon thyme (optional)
Hot cooked rice
1 (20-ounce) can tomatoes

Combine flour, ½ teaspoon salt and pepper and dredge chicken in the mixture or shake in brown paper bag. Fry in hot oil until brown. Remove chicken and set aside. Sauté onion, peppers, garlic, parsley and curry powder in the pan drippings until tender, about 10-15 minutes. Add tomatoes, remainder of salt, the mace and the currants and simmer for another 5 minutes. Transfer sauce to a large casserole and lay the chicken in the sauce. Cover and cook in 275 degree oven 1-1½ hours or until chicken is tender. Toast the almonds in a slow oven and sprinkle on the chicken in the casserole before serving over hot rice, ladling some of the sauce over the rice and the chicken. (NOTE: sauce can be thinned and stretched with chicken broth. If doubled, cook in a roasting pan. Can be kept in warm oven if done early in day.)
Yield: 8 servings

Junius W. "Sonny" Davis, Jr.

CHICKEN CRÊPES

Can freeze
Make day ahead
Can double

Crêpes:

1 cup milk
2 tablespoons butter
2 eggs, beaten
½ cup sifted flour
1 teaspoon baking powder
½ teaspoon salt
1 cup sour cream
2 whole chicken breasts, cooked and cut into strips
½ pound ham, cooked and cut into strips
¼ cup sweet chile peppers, cut into strips

Heat milk and butter in saucepan until butter is melted; cool. Beat in egg, then flour, baking powder and salt sifted together; beat until smooth and well-blended. Lightly grease 4- or 5-inch skillet; heat and pour in 3 tablespoons batter for each crêpe; tilt skillet to cover evenly. Cook about 1 minute to brown; flip and brown other side. Spread one side of all crêpes with sour cream; place several pieces of chicken, ham and chili peppers on crêpes; roll and place in 7x11-inch baking dish. Crêpes may be frozen at this point or refrigerated for 24 hours then baked and served. Crêpes may be baked before freezing if desired. To freeze, wrap, seal, date and label baking dish. Do NOT leave in freezer over one month. To serve, let thaw in refrigerator.

Topping:

⅓ cup milk
1 cup sour cream or half and half
½ cup Gruyère cheese, grated

Preheat oven to 350 degrees. Mix milk and sour cream and pour over crêpes. Sprinkle with cheese. Bake, uncovered, 20 minutes just to melt cheese and warm crêpes.
Yield: 10 crêpes

Mary Wolcott Taft (Mrs. Howland G.)

If legs and thighs cost up to ⅓ more per pound than whole chickens, the legs and thighs are a better buy.

CRÊPES SUPREME

All parts may be made the day before serving and combined just before cooking.

Crêpes:

2 eggs, beaten
⅔ teaspoon salt
2 tablespoons butter, melted
⅔ cup flour
1⅓ cups milk
½ teaspoon vegetable oil

Combine eggs, salt, and melted butter. Alternately add flour and milk to the egg mixture. Beat until smooth. Oil 6-inch skillet. Pour ¼ cup of batter on at a time, covering bottom. Cook on one side until completely firm and brown around the edges.
Yield: 12 to 14 crêpes

Filling:

5 ounces Italian sausage
1 clove garlic, crushed
1½ (10-ounce) packages frozen spinach or 1 pound fresh spinach
1 cup chicken, cooked and chopped
¾ cup Parmesan cheese

Sauté sausage until golden. Drain. Add garlic to sausage. Cook spinach until limp. Drain. Add to sausage. Add chicken and cheese to sausage mixture, cool and divide among crêpes.

Cheese Sauce:

6 tablespoons butter
6 tablespoons flour
3 cups light cream
2 cups Parmesan cheese
1 tablespoon onion, minced
¼ teaspoon curry powder

Melt butter. Blend in flour until smooth. Stir in cream and cook over low heat until thickened, stirring constantly. Add cheese, onion and curry powder and stir until cheese is melted. Fill each crepe with sausage filling. Place seam-side down in a 8x8-inch baking dish. Preheat oven to 300 degrees. Cover all with cheese sauce and bake about 30 minutes.
Yield: 6 servings

Peggy Witmeyer Bernard

To make a smoother cream sauce, warm the milk before adding into the flour-butter roux.

CHICKEN ÉLÉGANT

This is rich, but worth the calories!

3 tablespoons butter
3 tablespoons flour
1¾ cups milk
½ cup sharp process American Cheese, shredded
½ cup Swiss cheese, shredded
½ teaspoon Worcestershire sauce
1 cup chicken or turkey, cooked and diced
1 cup ham, cooked and diced
1 (3-ounce) can mushrooms, drained and sliced
2 tablespoons pimiento, chopped
Toast points

Melt butter in saucepan; blend in flour. Add milk all at once; cook and stir until sauce thickens and bubbles. Remove from heat and add cheeses, stir until melted. Stir in Worcestershire sauce, chicken or turkey, ham, sliced mushrooms and pimiento. Heat thoroughly. Serve over toast points.
Yield: 4-5 servings.

Lee Thompson McIntyre (Mrs. J. Brooks)

A boned chicken breast will cook in 8-12 minutes.

BREAST OF CHICKEN CHEROKEE

Must do ahead

6 chicken breasts
1 quart half and half cream
1 pound flour (4 cups)
1 teaspoon salt
1 teaspoon black pepper
1 cup cooking oil
1 cup margarine
½ cup flour
½ cup almonds, chopped, toasted

Marinate chicken in cream 24 hours in refrigerator. Drain, reserving cream. Roll chicken in flour mixed with salt and pepper. Pan-fry in oil and butter combination until golden brown. Remove. Mix flour into chicken drippings. Stir in cream left from marinating chicken. Cook until mixture has thickened. Mix in chopped almonds. Serve on rice.
Yield: 6 servings

Mary Sutherland Hassell (Mrs. Thomas M., Jr.)

GINNY'S CHICKEN BOOBIES

4 whole chicken breasts, boned
1 (10-ounce) can cream of chicken soup
1 (10-ounce) can cream of celery soup
1 (10-ounce) can cream of mushroom soup
½ cup butter or margarine
¼ cup sherry
3 ounces Parmesan cheese, grated
¼ cup almonds, slivered
1¼ cups Uncle Ben's Long-grain and Wild Rice

Mix soups and heat. Add butter and sherry. Mix half soup mixture with rice and put in bottom of a 13x9-inch casserole. Top with chicken breasts and cover with rest of soup mixture. Sprinkle with Parmesan cheese and almonds. Bake uncovered 2½ hours at 275 degrees.
Yield: 4-6 servings

Alyce Faye Tilley Grant (Mrs. David)

If chicken breasts cost less than 50% more per pound than whole chickens then the breasts are a better buy.

GOURMET CHICKEN

This dish is very colorful and should be served with rice.

Easy
Quick

4 chicken breasts, boned
1 large onion, chopped
1 large green pepper, roughly chopped
1 large tomato, quartered
¼ cup capers
¼ cup butter
1 (6-ounce) package Mozzarella slices
Salt and pepper to taste

Brown both sides of chicken breasts in butter. Set aside. In same skillet, sauté onions and green peppers which have been cut up in large chunks; add cut tomato and sauté for about 1 to 2 minutes. Put chicken back in pan and place a slice of cheese on each chicken breast. Spoon vegetables over chicken and sprinkle ¼ cup capers over entire mixture. Put lid on and simmer for ½ hour.

Nancy Springett Wetherington (Mrs. John S.)

TARRAGON CHICKEN TRIESTE

½ pound fresh mushrooms
¼ cup butter
6 large chicken breasts
2 teaspoons Beau Monde Seasoned Salt
½ teaspoon tarragon
1 cup dry white dinner wine
1 cup dairy sour cream
½ cup green onions, chopped

Slice mushrooms; sauté in 2 tablespoons butter until golden. Remove mushrooms. Add remaining butter to pan; brown chicken well. Sprinkle with seasoned salt during browning. Add mushrooms, sprinkle with tarragon. Pour wine over chicken. Cover and simmer 45 minutes until tender. Spoon sour cream into pan juices; sprinkle with green onions to serve.
Yield: 6 servings

Anne Haughton Hansen (Mrs. Raymond S.)

CHICKEN WITH COUNTRY HAM

Can be doubled
Can be frozen
Part can be prepared in advance

1 (2½-3½ pound) fryer, cut up
1 (12-16 ounce) package thin sliced country ham, trimmed and cut into 2-or 3-inch pieces
Vegetable oil
1 cup flour
½ teaspoon salt
½ teaspoon pepper
1 (10-ounce) can beef bouillon

Mix flour, salt and pepper. Coat chicken pieces. Fry at 375 degrees in 1-inch of oil until brown, about 8 minutes per side. Drain; place in 2-quart casserole, one layer deep and top with pieces of ham. May be refrigerated at this point up to one day ahead. Pour undiluted bouillon over top and bake covered at 350 degrees for 45 minutes.
Yield: 4-6 servings

Pauline Morris Blair (Mrs. Robert G., Jr.)

CHICKEN - SAUSAGE MARENGO

Do day ahead
Do early in day
Stores well
Can double

1 pound sweet Italian sausage (optional)
2 tablespoons butter or margarine
2 tablespoons salad or olive oil
2 fryer chickens, cut into pieces
1 (28-ounce) can tomato purée or tomato sauce
1 (6-ounce) can sliced mushrooms, reserve ½ cup drained liquid
1 (8-ounce) can ripe or green olives, sliced, reserve juice
¼ cup sweet pepper flakes
2 teaspoons celery flakes or chopped celery and leaves
1½ teaspoons Italian seasoning or oregano
½ teaspoon salt
¼ teaspoon ground pepper
¼ teaspoon garlic powder
¼ cup drained liquid from olives
1 bay leaf
1 tablespoon parsley flakes
1 teaspoon onion, minced

Prick sausage and place in Dutch oven to brown. Remove. Add butter and oil with chicken. Sauté until brown. Remove chicken. Add tomato purée to drippings; add remaining ingredients. Return chicken and sausage to pan. Cover and simmer over low heat for 30-40 minutes, or until meats are tender. Serve with rice.
Yield: 6 servings

Anne Haughton Hansen (Mrs. Raymond S.)

JANET'S CRUNCHY CHICKEN OR PORK CHOPS

Better and less expensive than using Shake and Bake

Marinate or coat chicken or pork chops in Italian Dressing. Coat both sides of meat in crushed Corn Flakes. Bake on broiler pan 45 minutes at 375 degrees.

AUNT MILLIE'S CHICKEN

3 whole chicken breasts, split and deboned
1 clove garlic
½ cup oil
1 cup fine bread crumbs
½ cup Cheddar cheese, finely grated
¼ cup Parmesan cheese, grated
1 teaspoon salt
⅛ teaspoon pepper
1 teaspoon monosodium glutamate (MSG)

Preheat oven to 350 degrees. Cut garlic clove and add to oil, letting it stand for 20 minutes. Remove garlic from oil. Mix bread crumbs, cheeses and seasonings. Dip breasts in oil, then in crumb mixture. Place in 2-quart shallow baking pan brushed with oil. Do not let chicken pieces touch. Pour remaining oil seasoned with garlic over chicken. Bake uncovered for about 40-45 minutes. Baste occasionally with pan juices.
Yield: 6 servings

Rena Terrell Knott (Mrs. Edmund T.)

CHICKEN SUPREME

Do early in day
Can freeze

6-8 chicken breasts
¾ cup butter or margarine
½ cup flour
1 teaspoon salt
¼ teaspoon pepper
2 (10¾-ounce) cans cream of chicken soup
1 teaspoon paprika
½ cup cooking sherry

Preheat oven to 400 degrees. Salt, pepper and flour chicken. Melt butter in 3-quart baking dish. Lay chicken, skin-side down, in dish of melted butter. Bake 30 minutes or until brown. Turn chicken; add soup, sherry and paprika. It makes a smoother gravy if this has been heated in a saucepan. Cover with foil. Reduce heat to 350 degrees and bake one hour more. If gravy is too thick, add a little water. Serve with rice and a fruit salad.
Yield: 4-6 servings

Diane Hall Willis

COMPANY CHICKEN

Do day ahead
Stores well
Freezes

12 whole chicken breasts, skinned, boned and cut in half
2 envelopes Lawry's Italian salad dressing mix
1 pound fresh mushrooms, sliced
2 (3-ounce) containers Kraft cream cheese with chives
2 (10-ounce) cans cream of mushroom soup
1¼ cups dry white wine
½ pound cooked shrimp (optional)
Rice

Dip breasts in Lawry's Italian salad dressing mix. Sauté in oil or butter. Brown lightly on each side. Set chicken on paper towels to get rid of excess fat. In same pan sauté mushrooms. Set aside. In double boiler mix together cream cheese with chives, cream of mushroom soup, undiluted, and the dry white wine. Heat until blended. You may need a whisk to blend. Layer chicken, mushrooms, sauce in large casserole or 2 small ones. Pour remaining sauce over all. Cook uncovered at 350 degrees for 1-1½ hours. If desired may sprinkle shrimp over top during last 10 minutes of cooking. Serve with rice and salad.
Yield: 12 generous servings

Ann Harris Bustard (Mrs. Victor W .)

CHICKEN VERMOUTH

8 chicken breasts, boned and rolled
¾ cup dry vermouth
¼ cup oil
¼ cup soy sauce
2 tablespoons water
1 teaspoon ginger
¼ teaspoon oregano
1 tablespoon brown sugar

Preheat oven to 375 degrees. Arrange the chicken breasts in a shallow Pyrex dish. Mix the rest of the ingredients together and pour over the chicken. Bake for 1½ hours, covered. Allow 1 whole chicken breast (2 halves) per person.

Nancy Philibosian Hollows (Mrs. William H.)

CHICKEN BREASTS SUPREME

3 chicken breasts, split
½ teaspoon salt
⅛ teaspoon pepper
¼ cup butter or margarine
1 (10-ounce) can condensed cream of chicken soup
¾ cup Sauterne or chicken broth
1 (8½-ounce) can water chestnuts, drained and sliced
1 (4-ounce) can sliced mushrooms, drained
2 tablespoons green peppers, chopped
¼ teaspoon thyme leaves, crushed

Brown chicken breasts in butter on all sides. Arrange chicken in ungreased 13x9-inch pan. Sprinkle with salt and pepper. Stir soup into butter in fry pan; slowly stir in Sauterne or broth. Add remaining ingredients and heat to boiling. Pour soup mixture over chicken. Cover and bake at 350 degrees for 45 minutes. Remove cover; bake 15 minutes longer.
Yield: 6 servings

Catherine Scaffide Homendy (Mrs. Edward S.)

Bone chicken breasts with kitchen shears for a neater job.

CHICKEN BREASTS LOMBARDY

6 whole chicken breasts, boned, skinned and quartered
Flour
1 cup plus 2 tablespoons butter, melted, (or less to taste)
Salt and pepper
1½ cups mushrooms, sliced
¾ cup *Marsala* wine
½ cup chicken stock
1½ tablespoons butter
½ cup Fontina or Mozzarella
½ cup Parmesan

Dredge chicken lightly with flour; cook over low heat in a little butter 3-4 minutes on each side. (I cook longer). Place chicken in greased 13x9x2-inch pan. Sprinkle with salt and pepper. Reserve butter drippings. Sauté mushrooms in ¼ cup butter. Sprinkle evenly over chicken. Stir wine and chicken stock into drippings. Simmer 10 minutes stirring occasionally. Stir in ½ teaspoon salt, ⅛ teaspoon pepper, and 1½ tablespoons butter. Combine cheeses; sprinkle over chicken. Bake at 450 degrees 10-12 minutes.
Yield: 8 servings

Phyllis Hurtgen Harke (Mrs. Dennis M.)

CHICKEN KIEV

Can freeze
Part done ahead

Herb Butter:

1 cup butter or margarine, softened
2 tablespoons chopped parsley
1½ teaspoons dried tarragon leaves
1 clove garlic, crushed
¾ teaspoon salt
⅛ teaspoon pepper

In small bowl thoroughly mix soft butter, parsley, tarragon, garlic, salt and pepper. Shape into 6-inch square on foil and freeze until firm.

6 chicken breasts, boned, skinned and split
¾ cup unsifted flour
3 eggs, well-beaten
1½ cups packaged dry bread crumbs
Salad oil or shortening for deep-frying

To flatten chicken, place each half, smooth-side down, on sheet of waxed paper; cover with second sheet. Using a mallet, pound chicken to about ¼-inch thickness. Cut frozen butter in 12 pats; place a pat of butter in center of each piece of chicken. Bring long sides of chicken over butter; fold ends over, making sure that no butter is showing; fasten with toothpick. Roll each piece of chicken in flour, then dip in eggs, then roll in crumbs. Shape each piece with hands to form triangles. Refrigerate, covered until chilled, about 1 hour. In Dutch oven or large, heavy saucepan, slowly heat oil (3-inches deep) to 360 degrees. Add chicken pieces, 3 at a time. Fry, turning with tongs until browned, about 5 minutes. Drain. Do NOT pierce coating. Keep warm in 200 degree oven 15 minutes (no more) in large pan lined with paper towels. Chicken Kiev can be cooked ahead and frozen: Cool, wrap in freezer wrap and freeze. To serve, unwrap but do not defrost. Bake uncovered, 35 minutes in 350 degree oven.
Yield: 6 servings; 12 pieces

Pat Farrell Thompson (Mrs. T. R.)

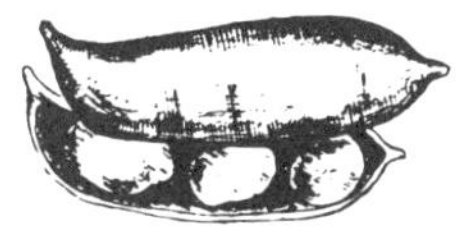

CHICKEN SCARBOROUGH FAIR

Make early in day and refrigerate or prepare 1 hour prior to serving

3 boned chicken breasts, skinned and halved
½ cup butter
Salt to taste
Pepper to taste
6 slices Mozzarella cheese
Flour
1 egg, beaten
Dry bread crumbs (I use Progresso Italian)
2 tablespoons chopped parsley
¼ teaspoon sage
¼ teaspoon rosemary
¼ teaspoon thyme
½ cup dry white wine

Preheat oven to 350 degrees. Flatten chicken between sheets of waxed paper; spread flattened breasts with half the butter. Season with salt and pepper and place one slice of cheese on each piece of chicken. Roll chicken tucking in ends. Coat lightly with flour; dip in egg; roll in bread crumbs. Arrange chicken rolls seam-side down in baking dish. Refrigerate at this point. When ready to bake remove from refrigerator and melt remaining butter adding parsley, sage, rosemary and thyme. Bake chicken 30 minutes basting with butter mixture. Pour wine over chicken and bake 20 additional minutes basting with pan liquid.
Yield: 6 servings

Barbara Straub Stewart

Flatten boned breasts or any other meat between two sheets of waxed paper using the flat side of a wooden mallet or the bottom of your heaviest skillet.

NAMELESS SWEET-SOUR CHICKEN

2 chickens, split; or 6 chicken breasts or equivalent parts
1 (10-ounce) jar apricot jam
1 (8-ounce) bottle red Russian dressing
1 envelope Lipton Onion Soup Mix

Put chicken in baking dish. Mix ingredients and pour over chicken coating all pieces. Bake at 350 degrees for 1-1½ hours, basting occasionally. Serve with rice or noodles, string beans and garlic bread.
Yield: 4 servings

Kathy Turner Anderson (Mrs. William, V)
Florence Woods Christie (Mrs. Charles W.)

ROAST CHICKEN

Easy

1 (3½ to 4-pound) whole broiling chicken
1 whole onion
1 celery stalk
Pure vegetable oil
Paprika

Clean chicken. Cut celery in half and with onion, insert into chicken cavity. Tie legs and rub chicken with oil. Sprinkle with paprika. Roast in open pan 35 minutes per pound at 325 degrees. Baste every 40 minutes. To serve, remove onion and celery which may be reused for soup or stew. Chicken will be extra juicy and moist with no onion flavor.
Yield: 4 servings

Frances L'Espérance Bollen (Mrs. Russell E.)

Allow about 1 cup stuffing per pound of bird. Since most birds don't hold enough, this allows for some to be baked separately. Almost any stuffing can be made to serve separately. It can be baked in a covered casserole in a preheated 350 degree oven for 30 minutes. Extra moistness may be obtained by adding a little butter and broth or water before baking.

HONEY CHICKEN

Quick, easy and always a hit, especially with children!

Freezes well

3 pounds chicken pieces
4 tablespoons butter or margarine
½ cup honey
¼ cup prepared mustard
1 teaspoon salt
1 teaspoon curry powder

Preheat oven to 375 degrees. Wash, dry and skin chicken. Melt butter and add remaining ingredients. Roll chicken pieces in mixture to coat both sides. Arrange meaty side up in a single layer; pour sauce over it. Bake for 1 hour or until chicken is tender and glazed. The sauce makes a delicious marinade. Serve over hot cooked rice, with peas, and a green salad with mandarin oranges for a delicious family meal.
Yield: 6 servings

Laura Helen Underhill

CHICKEN ROSEMARY

1 (2½ to 3-pound) chicken
¼ cup white wine
¼ cup margarine, melted
½ teaspoon rosemary
Salt to taste

Preheat oven at 350 degrees. Combine wine, rosemary, salt and margarine and pour over chicken. Bake 1 hour in covered casserole.

Libby Jones Wrenn (Mrs. James H., Jr.)

FLORENCE BENNETT'S ARROZ CON POLLO

Chicken with Rice

1 fryer chicken, cut up in quarters
½ cup Crisco oil
Salt
Pepper
Onion powder
Garlic powder
1½ cups Carolina Rice
1 cup celery, cut up
1 green pepper, cut up
1 large onion, cut up
Saffron
1 fresh tomato, cut up
1 (10-ounce) can Swanson's chicken broth
1 (4-ounce) jar Green Giant sliced mushrooms
1 (2-ounce) jar pimiento, cut up
1 (4-ounce) jar stuffed olives
½ (10-ounce) package frozen peas

Fry chicken pieces in Crisco oil. Season with salt, pepper, onion and garlic powders. Fry until golden brown on both sides. Remove from frying pan to platter. In drippings, add rice, chopped celery, peppers, onion, mushrooms, tomato, and saffron. Add chicken broth; add about 6-8 strings of saffron. Watch cooking at this point that mixture does not dry up. If so, add small amount of water. Cook on low heat until rice, and vegetables are tender and rice is yellow colored. If it is not, add more saffron. Mix well. Grease or oil roasting tin, and place rice mixture in it. Arrange chicken pieces on top. Add pimiento, and stuffed olives. Bake about ½ hour at 350 degrees or until chicken is done. Meanwhile, cook peas, and then arrange on top of chicken dish. Serve immediately.
Yield: 4 servings

Melanie Applegate (Mrs. Earl)

ARROZ CON POLLO

Chicken and Rice Puerto Rican Style

1 large onion, chopped
Several buds garlic (optional)
½ cup celery, chopped
¼ cup green pepper, chopped
1 (8-ounce) can tomato sauce
1 (2½-3 pounds) frying chicken, cut in pieces
Salt
Pepper
¼ cup sherry
5 cups hot water
¼ teaspoon oregano
2 cups regular long-grain rice
Strips of pimiento, garnish
Cooked green peas, garnish

In Dutch oven or large heavy skillet on medium high temperature, sear onion, garlic, celery and green pepper in ⅓ cup oil until tender. Add and stir tomato sauce. Add salted and peppered chicken. Cook about 5 minutes, turning on all sides. Add sherry, hot water and oregano to above mixture and cook until chicken is nearly done, about 1 hour. Add 2 cups rice, bring to boil for several minutes, then lower heat and cook until rice is done, about 20 minutes. Garnish rice with pimiento and peas. Place garnished rice on serving platter. Surround with chicken.
Yield: 4-6 servings

Mary Moulton Barden (Mrs. Graham A., Jr.)

MARINATED CHICKEN

Do ahead

1 or 2 small fryers, halved
½ cup lemon juice
½ cup dry white wine
1-2 tablespoons fresh ginger, finely chopped
½ teaspoon dill weed

Mix lemon juice, wine, ginger and dill in shallow non-metalic dish or large "zip-lock" bag. Place chicken halves in marinade. Let stand at room temperature 2-3 hours, basting often. Place chicken in baking dish and pour the marinade over it. Bake at 325 degrees for 1½-2 hours, basting often.
Yield: 4-6 servings

Sarah "Johnny" Greene

JIM'S SECRET CHICKEN

This recipe was given to me as a parting gift by our California neighbor who did all of the photography for "The Old Man and the Sea".

2 teaspoons sugar
1 teaspoon salt
½ teaspoon Accent
1 tablespoon butter
1 tablespoon Gebhardt's chili powder
2 cloves garlic
1 onion, grated
2 jiggers gin
10 ounces soy sauce
3 tablespoons catsup
3 tablespoons Wesson oil
Ginger
2 chickens halved or quartered

Combine all ingredients except ginger and chicken. Put in a small pan, simmer for 10 minutes. Pour over chicken which has been placed in a 13x9-inch baking dish. Marinate at least 12 hours turning chicken 3 or 4 times. Sprinkle with ginger each time chicken is turned. Place on grill turning frequently. Baste often with pastry brush. Watch closely or chicken will burn.
Yield: 2-4 servings

Margaret Shields Volney (Mrs. Frank, Jr.)

BAKED ITALIAN CHICKEN

Economical
Easy
Do ahead

½ cup water
½ cup chili sauce
½ teaspoon salt
½ teaspoon oregano
¼ teaspoon celery seed
⅛ teaspoon pepper
½ cup bread crumbs
4 tablespoons margarine
1 fryer, cut up

Preheat oven to 375 degrees. Combine water, chili sauce, salt, oregano, celery seed and pepper. Dip chicken in sauce mixture and coat skin side with crumbs. Melt margarine in 13x9-inch baking dish. Place chicken, crumb-side up in baking dish and pour remaining sauce over chicken. Bake 1 hour. Chicken may be skinned and placed in melted margarine in baking dish with sauce and crumbs poured over top, if desired.
Yield: 4 servings

Betty Simon (Mrs. Donn L.)

OVEN PAELLA

Can do ahead
Can do early in day
Can double

1 chicken, cut-up *OR* 6 pieces of breast *OR* 8 thighs
1 green pepper*, seeded and chopped
1 medium onion, chopped
¼ cup margarine *OR* corn oil *OR* olive oil
1 cup long-cooking rice, uncooked
½ pound fresh or frozen shrimp, peeled and deveined
1 (8-ounce) can artichoke hearts, drained and sliced
2½ cups (29-ounce) can tomatoes, broken up
2 cups chicken broth *OR* 3 chicken bouillon cubes dissolved in 2 cups hot water
Salt and pepper
⅛ teaspoon minced or granulated garlic

*If family hates green pepper, then increase onions and omit peppers

Brown chicken under hot broiler or in margarine in skillet; arrange in 3-quart deep casserole. Sauté green pepper, onion and rice in margarine until vegetables are softened and rice golden. Add to casserole, pouring over chicken. Scatter artichoke hearts and shrimp into casserole and sprinkle salt, pepper and garlic over all. Pour canned tomatoes and juice and chicken broth over all. Cover and bake at 350 degrees for 1 hour.
Yield: 4-6 servings

Nancy Robinson Hunt (Mrs. William B., Jr.)

BARBECUED CHICKEN

1 cup butter
½ cup catsup
1 cup vinegar
½ teaspoon Tabasco
1 tablespoon lemon juice
½ tablespoon mustard
½ teaspoon salt
2 tablespoons brown sugar

Skin chicken and put into long shallow glass casserole. Combine ingredients for sauce and pour over chicken. Bake at 350 degrees for 45 minutes to 1 hour. Baste occasionally.

Susan Jones Collins

CHICKEN TARRAGON

6 pieces chicken, lightly salted, peppered and floured
1 onion, minced
1 teaspoon tarragon, or to taste
2 teaspoons lemon juice
1 cup canned chicken broth
1 cup fresh mushrooms, sliced
2-3 cucumbers

Peel cucumbers; slice in half lengthwise. Remove seeds and pulp with tip of teaspoon. Slice. Brown chicken. Turn and add other ingredients, except cucumber. Cook, covered,on top of stove for 25 minutes. Add cucumbers last two minutes of cooking. This is nice served over rice and one of our favorite dishes.
Yield: 4-6 servings

Sheila Nelson Darden (Mrs. Robert)

CHICKEN MARENGO

1 cup fresh mushrooms, sliced
2 tablespoons margarine
1 (3-pound) chicken (save the backs to make stock for something else)
3 tablespoons olive oil
4 green onions, sliced
1 clove garlic, minced
½ cup white wine or consommé
2 tomatoes, seeded and cut in wedges or canned tomatoes
¼ teaspoon thyme
1 tablespoon parsley sprigs, minced
Salt and pepper to taste

Sauté mushrooms in margarine for 2 minutes and set aside. Sauté chicken, which you have cut up, in the olive oil with a bit of salt and pepper. Remove chicken from skillet. Sauté the onion and garlic in the drippings from the chicken until the onion is soft. Stir in wine, tomatoes, thyme and scrape the bottom of the skillet to get all the oil flavor. Add chicken to skillet; cover and simmer for 30 minutes or until chicken is done. Add the mushrooms and sprinkle with parsley. Serve with a sprig of parsley for garnish.
Yield: 6 servings

Jean Schocke McCotter (Mrs. Clifton L.)

CANTONESE SHOYU CHICKEN

¾ cup soy sauce
2 tablespoons honey
½ cup brown sugar
2 tablespoons fresh ginger, chopped
1½ cups water
3 cloves garlic, grated
1 seed star anise
¼ cup green onions, cut in ½-inch lengths
1 (3-pound) fryer
2 tablespoons cornstarch
4 tablespoons water

Bring soy sauce, honey, brown sugar, water, ginger, anise, garlic, and green onion to a boil. Lower heat and let simmer for 2 minutes. Add chicken; cover and simmer for 40 minutes. Arrange chicken on a platter. Mix cornstarch with water; add to sauce to thicken. Pour sauce over chicken and serve.
Yield: 4-6 servings

Margaret Manning Preston (Mrs. Ronald A.)

Cornstarch used to thicken sauces makes a clear, shiny appetizing sauce. Add cornstarch to cold water before adding to sauce. Use twice as much water as cornstarch for mixing.

GEN'S CHICKEN CHOW MEIN

2 cups chicken, cooked and chopped
2 tablespoons margarine, melted
2 cups celery, sliced
1½ cups onion, sliced
Pepper to taste
1 teaspoon salt
2 cups chicken broth or beef broth
1 (16-ounce) can Chinese vegetables, drained
1 (4-ounce) can sliced mushrooms, drained
2 tablespoons cornstarch
3 tablespoons soy sauce
Hot cooked rice

Lightly brown chicken chunks in butter or margarine. Add celery, onion, pepper, salt and broth. Cook, covered, 5-10 minutes or until celery is tender-crisp. Add Chinese vegetables and mushrooms; simmer 1-2 minutes. Dissolve cornstarch in soy sauce and add to chicken mixture. Cook, stirring until slightly thickened. Serve over rice.
Yield: 6 servings

Genevieve Tolson Dunn (Mrs. Mark S.)

CHICKEN CURRY

Parts may be done ahead

1 (5-pound) stewing hen
1 teaspoon salt
Celery leaves
1 onion, peeled and sliced
1 teaspoon parsley

Stew hen in enough water to cover adding salt, celery leaves, onion and parsley. When tender (about 1 hour) lift out of stock and cool. Strain stock and save for sauce. When hen has cooled, remove skin and cut chicken up. Put bones back in strained stock. Add 1 cup more water and simmer slowly 45 minutes. Strain again and save.

1 tart apple, cored, peeled, chopped
4 onions, peeled, chopped
5 tablespoons margarine
4 tablespoons flour
1 quart strained stock
1 cup seedless raisins
½ lemon, juiced
Strip of lemon peel ½x1½-inch
1 cup light cream
2 teaspoons salt
2-5 tablespoons curry
Rice

Sauté apple and onions slowly in margarine stirring often. Do not use high heat; no browning here. Push to one side of pan and stir in flour until flour turns light brown. Remove from heat and add chicken stock. If there is not enough to make 1 quart of stock, add chicken broth. Stir over low heat until sauce is smooth and has become thick. If mixture should become too thick add broth or stock. Add raisins, lemon juice and lemon peel and simmer 5 minutes. Add light cream and season with salt. Mix curry powder with a little cold water and stir into sauce. When sauce is well-seasoned remove lemon peel and add cut up chicken. Simmer until heated thoroughly. Sauce should be consistency of heavy cream or soft custard. Serve over rice with condiments.

Condiments:
Chutney
Chopped nuts
Coconut
Chopped eggs
Chopped bacon
Chopped onions

Yield: 12 servings

Barbara Straub Stewart

LAKE CHAMPLAIN CHICKEN CASSEROLE

2 large onions, diced
2-3 cups celery, diced
2-3 green peppers, diced
1 pound mushrooms, sliced
1 (2-ounce) jar pimientos
2 cups long-cooking rice
8 cups water
2 (28-ounce) cans tomatoes
4-5 pound stewed hen, meat removed*
1 cup butter

*12 chicken breasts may be substituted

Sauté onions, when soft add mushrooms and pimientos. Boil celery 20 minutes; add green pepper for the last 5 minutes. Boil rice 20 minutes in 8 cups of water until water has boiled dry. Whirl the tomatoes in a blender. Cut cooked chicken into bite-sized chunks. Mix all these ingredients together in a 4-quart covered casserole dish, or divide into smaller casseroles. Top with butter and bake 1 hour at 350 degrees. The secret of this dish is in the mixing of the ingredients. Mix very well!

Yield: 12 servings

Dorothy Marshall Johnson (Mrs. Nelson F.)

CHICKEN CACCIATORE

Easy and almost dietetic. Only 250 calories per serving!

2 (1½-pound) broiler-fryers
2 cups water
1 (15-ounce) can tomato sauce
1 tablespoon oregano
½ cup dry white wine
1 medium onion, chopped
1 large green pepper, sliced thin
1 clove garlic, minced
½ teaspoon salt
¼ teaspoon pepper

Bring chicken to a boil in a pot of water. Simmer chicken for 30 minutes. Remove from heat and cool. Pour stock into measuring cup to make 2 cups and refrigerate. Skim any fat from top of reserved stock when cooled. Debone the chicken. Discard bones and skin. Cut chicken into chunks. Place all ingredients in a pot and cover. Bring to boil, turning heat down immediately. Simmer 30 minutes uncovered, or until sauce has thickened. Serve on a bed of rice.

Yield: 6 servings

Miriam Schulman Allenson (Mrs. Andrew J.)

TAKE IT EASY CHICKEN

1⅓ cups instant rice, uncooked
1 (10½-ounce) can cream of chicken soup
1 (10½-ounce) can cream of celery soup
½ cup warm water
1 package dried onion soup
1 fryer, cut up

Mix rice with soups and water in a 9x13-inch baking dish. Sprinkle ½ of the onion soup on top. Cover mixture with pieces of chicken. Top with remaining onion soup. Cover pan tightly with aluminum foil. Bake at 250 degrees for 2½ hours.
Yield: 6-8 servings

Susanne Darby Thompson (Mrs. Michael B.)
Caroline Ashford Smith

CHICKEN SOUFFLÉ

Do a day ahead

6 slices white bread, crusts trimmed, left whole
2 cups chicken, cooked and diced
½ cup onion, chopped
½ cup green pepper, chopped
½ cup celery, chopped
¼ cup pimiento, chopped
¾ teaspoon salt
Pepper to taste
6 slices white bread, crusts trimmed, cubed
2 eggs, beaten
1½ cups milk
1 (10-ounce) can cream of mushroom soup
½ cup sharp cheese, grated

Cover the bottom of a greased 9x13-inch casserole with 6 slices of trimmed bread. Mix the chicken, onion, green pepper, celery, pimiento, salt, and pepper together and spoon over bread layer. Cover with bread cubes. Beat eggs and milk together and pour over all. Cover and chill thoroughly overnight. Just before baking, preheat oven to 325 degrees. Spoon mushroom soup over the top and bake for 1 hour. During the last 15 minutes of baking time spread grated cheese on top.
Yield: 6-8 servings

Lawton Lumsden Parker (Mrs. John H.)

ITHACA CHICKEN

Easy
Do day ahead
Stores well

I have used the boneless frozen turkey after roasting but the fresh cooked chicken or turkey breasts are best. This is a good dish for a large number of guests when at a buffet and have to balance food on their laps. The wife of the President of Ithaca College in New York often had Sunday night get-togethers and served this meal.

22 slices white bread, crusts removed
8 cups cooked chicken breasts (8 double), or leftover chicken or turkey
1 pound mushrooms *OR* 2 (8-ounce) cans
¼ cup butter
2 (8-ounce) cans water chestnuts, drained, sliced thin
1 cup mayonnaise, (preferably Hellman's)
20 or 22 slices sharp cheese, Old English or other
8 eggs, well-beaten
4 cups milk
2 teaspoons salt, less if chicken is salted
2 (10¾-ounce) cans cream of mushroom soup
2 (10¾-ounce) cans cream of celery soup
2 (2-ounce) jars pimiento, chopped
4 cups Pepperidge Farm Dressing
Butter

Line a deep buttered pan with bread (pan should be at least 11x17-inches or make in two smaller pans). Spread the chicken, in good-sized pieces, over the bread, then the chestnuts and then the mushrooms. Dot with mayonnaise. Combine soups and pour over. Spread pimiento and top with cheese. Mix eggs, milk and salt. Pour over mixture. You will think you have too much liquid but try to use it all. It takes a little time for it to soak around the cheese and bread. Place in refrigerator at least 4 hours, but it is better left overnight. Bake covered at 350 degrees for 1 hour. Sauté Pepperidge Farm Dressing in butter. Sprinkle over casserole and bake uncovered an additional ½ hour. Total baking time is 1½ hours.
Yield: 24-25 servings

Kathleen Winslow Budd (Mrs. Bern)

HERBED CHICKEN CASSEROLE

1 unsalted chicken, boiled, meat removed, save broth
1 (10¾-ounce) can cream of mushroom soup
1 (10¾-ounce) can cream of chicken soup
½ cup margarine
1 (8-ounce) package Pepperidge Farm Herb Dressing
1¾ cups reserved broth

Melt margarine and mix with dressing mix. Put half of mixture on bottom of 9x13-inch baking dish. Spread cream of mushroom soup over dressing and arrange chicken on top. Put a fourth of the dressing mix on top of the chicken and spread cream of chicken soup over dressing. Put remainder of dressing mix over the top of soup. Pour chicken broth over all. Bake at 350 degrees for 30 minutes or until bubbly.
Yield: 6-8 servings

Rebecca Godley Paramore (Mrs. Walter H., III)
Sharon Nichols Hobson (Mrs. Steve R.)
Stevie Kennedy Zaytoun (Mrs. George)

CHICKEN DI VIOLI

Serve with Salad Celestine

1 (5-pound) hen, stewed and boned
1½ pounds lean pork, boiled
1 medium onion
1 cup bread crumbs, toasted
1 pint chicken butter or salad oil
4 eggs, hard-boiled
2 tablespoons salt
White pepper to taste
Cayenne to taste
Parsley to taste

Grind chicken and pork with onion and eggs. Mix with chicken butter, crumbs, seasonings and parsley. Put in double boiler and steam for three hours. Serve with a heavy cream sauce with mushrooms.
Yield: 14 servings

Miss Rose B. Carraway

CHICKEN DIVAN

2 (10-ounce) packages frozen broccoli or fresh equivalent
6-8 chicken breasts, cooked, boned and sliced (about 2 cups) *OR* turkey may be substituted
2 (10½-ounce) cans cream of chicken soup
1 cup mayonnaise
1 teaspoon lemon juice
½ teaspoon curry powder or Worcestershire sauce
1½ cups sharp cheese, shredded
½ cup soft bread crumbs
1 teaspoon butter, melted

Cook broccoli until tender, drain. Arrange stalks in a greased 9x13-inch baking dish. Place chicken on top. Combine mayonnaise, soup, lemon juice, curry and ¾ cup of cheese. Pour over chicken. Combine bread crumbs and butter. Sprinkle on top. Sprinkle remaining cheese on top. Bake at 350 degrees for 25-35 minutes. Thaw, if frozen, before baking or cover and extend baking time.
Yield: 8-10 servings

Susanne Darby Thompson (Mrs. Michael B.)
Kathy Turner Anderson (Mrs. William, V)
Mary Sue Price Pelletier
Lindy Allmond Emory (Mrs. Robert R., Jr.)

TOOTSIE'S CHICKEN SPECTACULAR

2 cups chicken, diced and cooked
1 (16-ounce) can green beans, drained
1 cup cooked white rice
1 (10½-ounce) can cream of celery, chicken or mushroom soup
½ cup salad dressing or mayonnaise
½ cup water chestnuts, sliced
2 tablespoons pimiento, chopped
2 tablespoons onion, chopped
¼ teaspoon salt
Dash pepper

Preheat oven to 350 degrees. Combine ingredients; mix well. Place in a 1½-quart casserole. Bake 25-30 minutes.
Yield: 6-8 servings

Greta Black Mitchell (Mrs. Thomas J., IV)

PARROTT ACADEMY CHICKEN DIVAN WITH RICE

2 (10-ounce) cans cream of celery soup
½ cup milk
1 (13-ounce) can evaporated milk
1 cup mayonnaise
2 teaspoons Worcestershire sauce
2 (10-ounce) packages frozen broccoli
3 cups chunked chicken (3½ pound chicken)
1 cup Parmesan cheese, grated
3 cups cooked rice (1½ cups uncooked)*

NOTE: Cook rice in 3½ cups strained chicken stock. Bring stock to boil. Stir in rice. Cover and reduce heat to low. Cook 20 minutes.
Mix soup and ½ cup milk and heat on low. Combine evaporated milk, mayonnaise, and Worcestershire sauce in a bowl and stir in soup mixture. Cook broccoli according to package and drain. Place cooked rice in bottom of buttered Pyrex dish. Spoon ½ cup soup mixture over rice. Place broccoli over rice in single layer. Spoon ½ cup soup mixture over broccoli and cover with chicken. Add remaining soup mixture and sprinkle with cheese. Bake at 350 degrees for 20 minutes or until bubbly.
Yield: 12 servings

Eugenia Hofler Clement (Mrs. Robert L.)
Ann Harris Bustard (Mrs. Victor W.)

CRANBERRY GLAZED CORNISH GAME HENS

6 Cornish hens
Salt and pepper
1 (16-ounce) can whole cranberry sauce
¼ cup butter
¼ cup frozen orange juice concentrate
2 teaspoons grated orange rind
Pinch of poultry seasoning
½ tablespoon brown sugar

Allow hens to defrost, wash under cold water and wipe dry, seasoning inside and out. Place in shallow pan without rack and put into hot oven at 450 degrees. Bake for 35 minutes. Heat together cranberry sauce, butter, orange juice, rind and poultry seasoning and pour over hens. Lower heat to 350 degrees and continue roasting, basting often with cranberry sauce until well-browned, about ½ hour longer. If desired sprinkle brown sugar lightly over the birds and slip under broiler to glaze further.
Yield: 6 servings

Ann Harris Bustard (Mrs. Victor W.)

COQ-A-NOODLE-DOO

Can be frozen

2 cups chicken, cooked and cubed*
1 cup celery, sliced
¼ green pepper and/or onion, diced
2 tablespoons butter or margarine
1 (10¾-ounce) can cream of chicken soup
⅔ cup milk
1½ cups Cheddar cheese, grated
½ cup slivered almonds, toasted
¼ cup pimiento, diced (optional)
4 ounces medium noodles
1 cup bread crumbs, buttered

*3 chicken breasts will yield about 2 cups chicken, cooked and cut up; a 3½ pound whole chicken will yield about 3 cups.
Preheat oven to 350 degrees. Butter 1½-quart casserole. Sauté celery, green pepper and/or onion in butter until tender. Stir in soup and milk and heat, stirring constantly; stir in cheese until melted. Add chicken, almonds and pimiento. Cook noodles in boiling salted water until just tender, drain and combine with chicken mixture. Put mixture into casserole and cover with bread crumbs and dot with butter. Bake uncovered for 30-35 minutes.
Yield: 6 servings

Nancy Robinson Hunt (Mrs. William B., Jr.)

AUNTIE'S CORNISH HENS

Cornish hens or small broilers
Flour
Salt
Pepper
Butter
¼ cup sherry
1 tablespoon tarragon vinegar
2 bay leaves
1 teaspoon parsley, chopped
½ teaspoon garlic powder

Preheat oven to 325 degrees. Cut up birds and dip them in flour, salt and pepper to your taste or as you would for fried chicken. Brown pieces in butter in skillet. Put pieces in a casserole dish. To the butter left in the frying pan add sherry, vinegar, bay leaves, parsley and garlic powder. Stir well and pour over birds. Cover. Cook for 1 hour.
Yield: Depends on number of birds used

Betsy Dunn (Mrs. Frank H.)

FAMILY SECRET TETRAZZINI

Can prepare ahead and refrigerate
Can be frozen

¼ teaspoon garlic powder
¼ teaspoon pepper
½ teaspoon basil
½ teaspoon parsley
½ teaspoon salt
¼ cup butter or margarine
½ cup flour
1 pint milk
1 (4-ounce) can mushrooms
1 (10½-ounce) can cream of mushroom soup
1 (2-ounce) jar pimientos
1 (4-pound) stewing hen, cooked and meat diced
2 cups chicken stock
2 (8-ounce) packages medium egg noodles
¼ pound Cheddar or American cheese, grated
Paprika

In a saucepan over medium heat melt butter; add flour and seasonings; add milk slowly stirring constantly until thickened. Add chicken stock, mushrooms, mushroom soup, pimientos and diced chicken. Cook noodles according to package directions, salting to taste. Drain. Mix noodles with sauce stirring gently. Pour mixture into 9x13-inch Pyrex dish. Sprinkle with cheese and paprika. Cover and refrigerate until baking time. Preheat oven to 350 degrees and bake 20-30 minutes until thoroughly heated.
Yield: 10-12 servings

Dorothy Oglesby Stewart (Mrs. A. L.)

TURKEY CROQUETTES

Very easy
Freezes well after they have been cooked

1½ cups turkey, chopped
1 (10-ounce) can cream of chicken soup
1 cup Pepperidge Farm Herb Dressing
2 eggs
1 tablespoon onion, minced
Flour
Oil

Mix and chill for several hours. Shape in patties or rolls. Roll in flour and fry in deep fat until brown.
Yield: 4-6 servings

Helen Cannon Mewborn

BRUCE'S SMOKED TURKEY

Sauce for basting:

½ cup butter
1 lemon, juiced
⅛ teaspoon garlic powder
Soy sauce, few dashes
3-4 stalks celery
1 (8-12-pound) turkey

This recipe must be cooked in a closed grill. Prepare the fire for indirect heat. Additional charcoal must be added during cooking. Baste the bird with sauce. Place a few sprigs of celery in the cavity. Place breast side up in a shallow pan lined with foil. Cook about 4 hours with lid of cooker closed. Check for doneness, as heat in the cooker may vary. While cooking add hickory chips, as desired, for smoked flavor. Baste often with sauce. This is a good meat to serve sliced cold in a warm weather buffet.

Bruce Meyers

SMOKED TURKEY

This may sound incredible, but it works!

1 aluminum foil disposable roasting pan
1 butter-basted turkey
2 or 3 strips uncooked bacon
1 onion, peeled and halved
2 or 3 small strips celery
Poultry seasoning, salt and pepper

Start coals and get them "good and hot". Buy a turkey of such size that will fit on your covered grill. May add soaked hickory chips to coals. Put washed and dried turkey in disposable aluminum foil roasting pan. Insert onion and celery in cavity of turkey. Put poultry seasoning, salt and pepper on turkey inside and out. Lay strips of bacon across top of turkey. Pour a little water in pan to prevent sticking. Place on grill. Cover with grill cover. Cook at 11 minutes per pound. (Shortly before bird is done, you may want to cover legs with foil to keep from getting too brown). Baste occasionally during cooking time. This cooking method produces a beautifully browned turkey. The meat will look slightly pink due to the smoking procedure, but it is done! The pan drippings left in the roaster are ready for gravy making! By using this procedure, Thanksgiving cooking is so much easier because your oven is free for other dishes—and—just throw away the messy pan when you are finished! (The real trick is to teach your husband to smoke the turkey! Thanksgiving is much more enjoyable with a "little help in the kitchen"!)

Martha Hughes Matthews (Mrs. F. Clayton)

CHICKEN LIVER SAUTÉ

Although directions are given for an electric frying pan, this may be made in a conventional frying pan on top of the stove. Our family prefers this made with sweet sherry.

½ cup butter or margarine
1 pound fresh or defrosted chicken livers, halved
1 medium onion, sliced
¼ pound fresh mushrooms, sliced
3 tablespoons flour
1 teaspoon salt
Dash of pepper
½ teaspoon ginger
1 (10½-ounce) can beef bouillon or consommé
½ cup dry or sweet sherry

Melt butter in electric frying pan. Sauté chicken livers over low heat (340 degrees) for eight minutes. Remove from pan to a platter and keep warm in oven. Sauté onion and mushrooms in the fat remaining in the frying pan for five minutes. Stir in flour, salt, pepper and ginger. Gradually stir in consommé. Cook over low heat, stirring constantly, until thickened and smooth. Stir in sherry and livers. Simmer two minutes. Serve over rice if desired.
Yield: 4-6 servings

Henrietta Sherman Mitchell (Mrs. Alexander S., Jr.)

SOUTHERN STUFFED PEPPERS

6 large green peppers
½ pound chicken livers, chopped
6 slices bacon, diced
1 cup onion, chopped
1 cup celery, sliced
1 clove garlic, crushed
½ cup canned sliced mushrooms
2 cups cooked rice
1 teaspoon salt
¼ teaspoon pepper
Dash of cayenne pepper

Wash peppers, cut slice from stem end and remove seeds. Cook peppers about 5 minutes in a small amount of boiling salted water. Remove from water and drain. Cook chicken livers, bacon, onion, celery and garlic until vegetables are tender. Add mushrooms, rice and seasonings. Stuff peppers with this mixture. Arrange in baking pan; seal and freeze. To serve, thaw and add ½-inch water to pan; cover and bake in a preheated 375 degree oven 20-25 minutes.
Yield: 6 servings

Verona Jackson Zeigler

HEAVENLY DOVE

6 doves, cleaned and dressed*
Flour
2 tablespoons butter or margarine
1/8 teaspoon thyme
1/8 teaspoon rosemary
1 teaspoon parsley, finely chopped
1 (4-ounce) can mushrooms, undrained
1 cup Sauterne
1 teaspoon salt
1 medium onion, finely chopped

*Quail or squab may be substituted for doves.
Cut doves along backbone; butterfly by removing the large bones of the lower back and legs. Press flat; roll in flour, brown lightly in butter; sprinkle with herbs and parsley. Cover and cook slowly for 15 minutes. Add onions, mushrooms with liquid and Sauterne. Cover and simmer for 1 hour or until tender. Add salt 5 minutes before removing from heat. Serve with wild rice or hot buttered rice.
Yield: 2 servings

Anne Fowler Hiller (Mrs. Carl J.)

ORIGINAL QUAIL

I brown the quail in the morning and bake late in the afternoon if they are to be used for dinner that night. Keep warm until time to serve.

Quail
Scallion (1 per every 2 birds)
Butter
Mushrooms, finely minced
Sherry (2 tablespoons for each bird)

Flour quail and sauté in skillet 30 to 40 minutes until well-browned. Prepare sauce of chopped scallions sautéed in butter, finely minced mushrooms, and sherry. Place browned quail in flat casserole, add sauce, cover, and place in 350 degree oven for 45 minutes until tender.

Anne Bratton Allen (Mrs. H. Eldrige)

ROAST WILD GOOSE WITH BAKED APPLE

1 large wild goose
Goose giblets
2 cups bread crumbs
1 onion, chopped
2 tablespoons fat (butter or bacon drippings)
¼ teaspoon sage
1 teaspoon salt
Pinch of pepper
6 to 8 apples
¼ cup brown sugar
3 sweet potatoes, cooked and mashed

Cook goose giblets until tender; chop and add to stuffing made by mixing bread crumbs, onion, fat, sage, salt and pepper. After blending and washing the goose thoroughly, stuff; sew the neck and back closed. Roast for 15 minutes at 500 degrees; reduce the heat to 350 degrees; cook about 1½ hours. Wash and core apples; sprinkle with brown sugar. Stuff with seasoned sweet potatoes; bake until tender; serve hot with goose.
Yield: 4 servings

Anne Fowler Hiller (Mrs. Carl J.)

Mix 1 quart water, 1 teaspoon white vinegar and 1 teaspoon detergent together for a good spot remover. Apply with toothbrush.

STEWED GOOSE
(or other wild ducks)

1 goose, cleaned, cut-up and parboiled
2 quarts water
Salt and pepper to taste
Flour dumplings*
Corn dumplings*
2 tablespoons vegetable oil

*Recipes in bread section
Place prepared fowl in large, heavy pot; cover with water and oil and bring to boil; reduce heat and simmer until tender, 2 hours or more. Then turn heat up and bring to boil again placing dumplings in pot. Allow to boil 10 minutes; reduce heat and simmer 1 hour, stirring occasionally to prevent burning.
Yield: 10 servings

Joseph D. McClees

DUCK A L'ORANGE

2 (4-pound) ducks, quartered
2-3 teaspoons salt
2 tablespoons butter
2 tablespons flour
2 cups chicken broth
1 cup dry white wine

Preheat oven to 450 degrees. Rub each duck with about 1 teaspoon salt; prick well with fork. Place on rack in open roasting pan; roast for 20 minutes, turning and pricking often. Remove duck from pan; drain off all but 1 tablespoon of fat. Melt butter in roasting pan; stir in flour. Add chicken broth and white wine; cook and stir until slightly thickened. Return duck to pan without rack; cook 1 to 1½ hours at 350 degrees.

Orange Sauce:
½ cup sugar
½ cup water
Orange rind, slivered
1 cup orange juice
1 cup lemon juice
¼ cup brandy
Salt and pepper

Caramelize sugar and water in saucepan; add orange rind, orange juice, lemon juice and brandy. Strain sauce from roasting pan; add to caramel mixture. Salt and pepper to taste. Strain over duck or pass in sauce-boat.
Yield: 8 servings

Anne Fowler Hiller (Mrs. Carl J.)

Allow ½-1 duck per person.

Mock Sour Cream with a mere 176 calories per cup may be made in your blender using ¼ cup buttermilk to 1 cup low-fat creamed cottage cheese. Blend at high speed, scraping sides of container often. This sour cream is interchangeable with real sour cream EXCEPT in recipes which must be heated. This sour cream can not take the heat!

BROILED VENISON LOIN CHOPS

1 or 2 chops per person (only the loin or rib chops can be used)
Thin sliced onions (use 2 whole onions, sliced, for 6 or 8 chops
Butter or margarine
Salt and pepper

Heat griddle or frying pan to very hot, 375 to 400 degrees. Salt and pepper chops liberally. Put butter into hot pan. It will be really sizzling. Quickly add chops, sprinkling the thin onion slices over them. Cook about 3 minutes on each side. While the chops are cooking, lightly stir onions about pan to cook. It is important to serve these hot, so take from pan and place on warmed platter.

Anne Fowler Hiller (Mrs. Carl J.)

ROAST VENISON

4 pounds venison roast
1 package dry onion soup mix
¼ cup vinegar
1 tablespoon soy sauce
1 tablespoon Worcestershire sauce
1 large onion, sliced
1 piece suet

Wash and trim meat. Soak overnight in salted water to cover. Drain off water and re-soak in salted water. Trim off shreds of whitish substance, if any. Into bottom of a deep baking pan, sprinkle dry onion soup mix. Set roast into mix-sprinkled pan. Combine vinegar, soy sauce and Worcestershire sauce and spoon over meat. Place onion slices on top of meat. Cut strips of suet and secure to meat with toothpicks. Cover pan with heavy aluminum foil; seal edges of foil around lip of pan. Cover loosely to allow space for steam. Bake 4 hours at 325 degrees.
Yield: 8 servings

Anne Fowler Hiller (Mrs. Carl J.)

DOVE WITH GRAVY

6-16 dove breasts
¾ cup butter, melted
1 tablespoon Worcestershire sauce
1 teaspoon garlic salt
⅓ cup sherry or brandy
1 cup chopped mushrooms with liquid
½ teaspoon nutmeg
Salt
Pepper
⅓ cup flour
Grapes
Cooked rice

Brown doves in melted butter. Remove from frying pan. Add remaining ingredients except flour, grapes and rice to butter, stirring well. Return doves to pan; cover and simmer 15-20 minutes. Remove doves and add flour to thicken gravy. Garnish with grapes and serve with rice.

ROAST QUAIL

6 quail
8 tablespoons butter
Seasoned flour
1 onion, sliced paper thin
1 bay leaf
4 mushrooms, sliced (optional)
1 cup sherry

Dust quail in flour, brown in melted butter. Transfer to baking dish. Cook onion until transparent; add bay leaf and mushrooms; cook 1-2 minutes. Remove bay leaf, add wine; stir sauce and pour over the quail in the baking dish. Bake covered on top shelf of oven 45 minutes at 375 degrees.

Oliver House **512 East Front Street**

This charming, gambrel-roofed cottage was moved in 1958 from its original location on Pollock Street by Dr. Charles H. Ashford, who served as Senior Warden of Christ Church, and Mrs. Ashford, who was one of the first women to be elected to the Vestry. The federal details and interior woodwork would date this house to the early 19th century.

SAUSALITO SCAMPI

3 whole chicken breasts, cut in 1-inch pieces
1 pound shrimp, shelled and deveined
⅓ cup butter
⅓ cup olive oil
2 cloves garlic, minced
1 teaspoon salt
Juice of one lemon
Parsley
Ground pepper

Melt butter and oil in a large skillet. Sauté garlic for two minutes; add chicken, cook, until brown, stirring constantly; push to one side. Add shrimp and cook, stirring constantly, until pink. Season with salt, pepper, lemon juice and parsley and cook one more minute. This is good on rice served with a dry red wine.
Yield: 6 servings

Jane Ingraham Ashford (Mrs. Charles H., Jr.)

QUICK SHRIMP DINNER

½ cup water
1 medium onion
1 egg
1 pound shrimp, cooked, cleaned and deveined
1 cup Minute Rice, cooked
Parsley (garnish)

Boil water in medium-sized saucepan. Add chopped onion, cook for 1 minute. Add beaten egg. Cook 2 minutes. Add cooked shrimp. Heat until shrimp are hot, about 1 minute. Pour over cooked rice. Serve with peas or any green vegetable. Sprinkle parsley on top.
Yield: 2-3 servings

Florence Bennett (Mrs. Harry)

MARINATED SHRIMP

Can be used as a main dish, salad or hors d'oeuvre.

3 pounds shrimp, cooked and cleaned
2 (8-ounce) cans button mushrooms, drained
3 medium onions, sliced in rings
Bay leaves

French dressing:
¾-1¼ cups oil
6 tablespoons vinegar
2 teaspoons salt
⅛ teaspoon pepper
¼ teaspoon paprika
1 tablespoon lemon juice
1½ teaspoons Worcestershire sauce
Hot pepper sauce to taste

Mix all sauce ingredients well and add shrimp, mushrooms, onion rings and bay leaves. Marinate in refrigerator overnight. Serve over hot, cooked rice for a light, summer supper.

Phyllis Spada Nashick (Mrs. George H.)

EXQUISITE SHRIMP

Easy
Last minute

2 pounds raw shrimp
6 peppercorns
1 bay leaf
½ teaspoon salt
6-7 tablespoons butter
3 tablespoons flour
2 cups liquid*
Exquisite Rice

*Use half water and half wine or half chicken stock in place of wine.
Remove shells and clean shrimp. Put shells in pan with liquid. Add peppercorns, bay leaf and salt. Bring to boil, lower heat to simmer and cook for 15 minutes. Strain through sieve and set aside. Over medium heat in a large saucepan, melt 3 tablespoons butter. Blend in flour and add 1½ cups liquid that shells were cooked in, stirring constantly until sauce thickens. Heat 3-4 tablespoons butter in another skillet. Add shrimp; cook 4-5 minutes or until they turn pink. Add to the sauce. Serve over Exquisite Rice.
Yield: 6 servings

Nancy Springett Wetherington (Mrs. John S.)

CRABMEAT AND SHRIMP CASSEROLE

May be prepared in advance and refrigerated until baking time.

1 pound crab
½ pound cooked shrimp
6 tablespoons butter
3 heaping tablespoons flour
1 teaspoon salt
Red pepper
¼ cup sherry
1 pint half and half
Shredded cheese

Melt butter and add spices and flour. Gradually blend in half and half. Stir, cooking over medium heat until mixture thickens. Add sherry; fold in seafood and pour into buttered casserole. Top with cheese. Put in cold oven; heat to 325 degrees and bake 30 minutes.
Yield: 4-6 servings

Carole Beasley McKnight (Mrs. Thomas J.)

CURRIED SHRIMP

¼ cup butter or margarine
¼ cup flour
½ teaspoon salt
Dash paprika
Dash cayenne pepper
1 teaspoon curry powder
1½ cups milk
3 teaspoons catsup
¼ cup cooking sherry
2 cups whole shrimp, deveined and cooked
2 cups cooked rice
Parsley (optional)

Condiments:
Toasted coconut
Peanuts
Hard-boiled eggs, diced
Raisins
Chutney

Make a sauce over medium heat using butter, flour and milk. Stir in seasonings and continue to cook, stirring constantly until mixture is thick and smooth. Add catsup, sherry and shrimp and continue to cook until shrimp is heated through. Serve sauce on mounds of rice and sprinkle with parsley, if desired. This is delicious plain, but any or all of the condiments may be sprinkled on top of curry.
Yield: 4 servings

Lila Dedmon Smallwood

SECOND GENERATION SHRIMP CREOLE

2 tablespoons butter
1 tablespoon onion, chopped
12 stuffed olives, sliced
1½ cups Del Monte stewed tomatoes
½ small green pepper, chopped
1 teaspoon capers
1 teaspoon sugar
¾ cup chili sauce
¼ cup cooking wine (optional)
1 pound shrimp, cooked and cleaned
Cooked rice

Sauté onion, olives and green pepper in butter; add stewed tomatoes and remaining ingredients, except shrimp. Simmer over low heat 15 minutes. Add shrimp and heat thoroughly. Serve immediately over rice.
Yield: 4 servings

Betty Smith Constant (Mrs. Howard B.)

SPLENDID SHRIMP

Part done ahead
Can freeze
Can double

¼ cup onion, chopped
2 tablespoons butter or margarine
2 tablespoons flour
½ teaspoon salt
Dash pepper
1 cup light cream
½ teaspoon Worcestershire sauce
1 (3-ounce) can mushrooms, drained and sliced
2 cups cleaned shrimp, fresh or frozen
Sherry to taste
½ cup sharp processed cheese, shredded
½ cup buttered cracker crumbs
2 cups hot cooked rice

Preheat oven to 350 degrees. Grease 1½-quart casserole dish. Sauté onion in butter until tender, but not brown. Blend in flour, salt and pepper. Gradually stir in cream and Worcestershire sauce. Cook and stir until thick. Add mushrooms, sherry and shrimp. Place rice in casserole dish; add shrimp mixture. Top with cheese, border with cracker crumbs. Bake for 20 minutes or until bubbly.
Yield: 4 servings

Becky Melton Kafer (Mrs. C. William)

NEW ORLEANS SHRIMP AND SPAGHETTI

Use electric skillet

½ cup salad oil
½ cup scallions, chopped
2 pounds shrimp, cooked
2 teaspoons lemon peel, grated
Salt and pepper
1 tablespoon lemon juice
½ cup ripe olives, sliced
½ pound thin spaghetti, cooked and drained

Using electric skillet sauté scallions 5 minutes in heated salad oil on medium setting. Add shrimp, lemon peel, salt, pepper. Cook until heated through. Stir in lemon juice. Add olives and spaghetti, mix well. Set heat at serving temperature.
NOTE: A big electric skillet will hold 1½ times this recipe.
Yield: 6-8 servings

Anne Haughton Hansen (Mrs. Raymond S.)

ASPARAGUS-SHRIMP CASSEROLE

2 (16-ounce) cans green asparagus spears
1½ pounds shrimp, boiled, chopped coarsely
4 eggs, hard-boiled and sliced
½ pound cheese, grated
¼ cup butter or margarine
1 tablespoon onion juice
1 (10¾-ounce) can mushroom soup
¾ cup milk
24 saltines, coarsely rolled

Preheat oven to 325 degrees. Grease 8x12-inch casserole with butter and put half of the cracker crumbs on the bottom. Place in layers the asparagus, eggs and shrimp. Lightly salt and pepper each layer as you build casserole. Mix soup with the milk and onion juice and pour over casserole mixture. Top with cheese and remaining crumbs. Dot with remaining butter and bake in oven for about 20 minutes before serving.
Yield: 8 servings

Leah Jones Ward (Mrs. D. L.)
Gloria West Wheeler (Mrs. O. Gray, Jr.)

SHRIMP MOUSSE

Easy
Do day ahead
Stores well in refrigerator
Use as appetizer, salad or main dish

1 (10¾-ounce) can Heinz condensed tomato soup, undiluted
1½ tablespoons unflavored gelatine
½ cup cold water
2 (3-ounce) packages cream cheese, softened
1 cup mayonnaise or salad dressing
1 tablespoon prepared horseradish
1 tablespoon Worcestershire sauce
½ teaspoon salt
4 cups shrimp, cooked and finely chopped*
1 cup celery, finely chopped
⅓ fresh or frozen onions, chopped

*This is about 2 pounds of shrimp.
Heat soup, just to boiling. Soften gelatine in cold water in large bowl. Pour hot soup over gelatine. Stir until dissolved. Beat in cream cheese and next four ingredients. Stir in shrimp, celery, and onions. Pour mixture into 1½-quart mold. Chill until firm. Can be refrigerated overnight or 24 hours. Unmold on platter. This can be used as a spread for crackers for hors d'oeuvres or molded in a square Pyrex casserole and cut out in separate servings as an entrée for luncheon or dinner. Serve on lettuce leaf with a green vegetable and lemon tart.
Yield: 8 servings as an entrée

Isabelle Schocke Taylor (Mrs. Elijah)

Save calories by using yogurt rather than sour cream.

SALMON MOUSSE

Serve with Dill Sauce

Do early in day
Stores well

1 envelope unflavored gelatine
¼ cup cold water
½ cup boiling water
½ cup mayonnaise
1 tablespoon lemon juice
1 tablespoon onion, grated
½ teaspoon Tabasco sauce
¼ teaspoon paprika
1 teaspoon salt
2 cups canned salmon
1 tablespoon capers, chopped
½ cup heavy cream
3 cups cottage cheese

Soften gelatine in cold water; add boiling water and stir until dissolved. Cool. Add mayonnaise, lemon juice and onion; mix well. Add paprika, Tabasco, salt and mix well. Chill until mixture reaches the consistency of unbeaten egg white. Add salmon and capers. Beat well. Whip cream and fold into salmon mixture. Turn into 2-quart oiled mold. Cover top with cottage cheese. Chill until firm, at least 2 hours. To serve: unmold on serving plate and garnish as desired with watercress, lemon slices, or salmon roe. Serve with Dill Sauce.
Yield: 12 servings

Kathleen Winslow Budd (Mrs. Bern)

DILL SAUCE

Serve with Salmon Mousse

1 egg
1 teaspoon salt
⅛ teaspoon pepper
⅛ teaspoon sugar
4 teaspoons lemon juice
1 teaspoon onion, grated
2 tablespoons finely cut dill, fresh or dried
1½ cups sour cream

Beat egg until fluffy and lemon colored. Add salt, pepper, sugar, lemon juice, onion and dill. Mix well. Stir in sour cream until blended. Chill until serving time.
Yield: 12 servings

Kathleen Winslow Budd (Mrs. Bern)

SALMON CROQUETTES

1 (16-ounce) can salmon with juice
¾ cup cracker meal
2 eggs, hard-boiled and chopped
1 tablespoon lemon juice or vinegar
½ cup Worcestershire sauce
2 tablespoons butter, melted
½ teaspoon salt
1 teaspoon prepared mustard
Cayenne pepper to taste
1 egg, beaten with a little water

Remove backbone from salmon. Mix all ingredients together. Shape into family-sized or tiny cocktail croquettes; roll in beaten egg and fry in deep fat. Yield: Number varies with size of croquettes

Leah Jones Ward (Mrs. D. L.)

A thin cream sauce is for cream soups; medium for soufflés; thick for croquettes. It acts like paste, holding meat together.

SALMON PATTIES

1 (16-ounce) can salmon, flaked
¼ teaspoon pepper
1 tablespoon mustard
2 eggs, beaten
½ cup milk
1 tablespoon flour
Soda cracker crumbs (about 4 crackers)
Corn oil
Lemon wedges

Mix salmon, pepper and mustard together. Mix eggs, milk and flour in heavy pan and cook slowly, stirring constantly, until quite thick. Add salmon mixture and cracker crumbs. Let cool; make into patties. Heat corn oil in skillet. Fry patties, brown on both sides. Serve with lemon wedges.

Lucille Clark Anderson (Mrs. K. F.)

SCALLOPED OYSTERS

Terrific and guaranteed not to be runny. This is used for "State" occasions at our home.

1 cup bread crumbs (4-5 slices)
2 cups cracker crumbs
¾ cup butter, melted*
3 pints oysters
1½ teaspoons salt
White pepper to taste
Worcestershire to taste
½ cup heavy cream

*Real butter should be used for the best flavor, but half butter and half margarine will do.
Melt butter and mix half with bread crumbs. In a separate bowl mix remaining half of melted butter with cracker crumbs. Mix cream with salt, pepper and Worcestershire. In a buttered casserole layer ingredients beginning with oysters and ending with a layer of bread crumbs. Bake 30 minutes at 400 degrees. If you prefer your oysters well-done, bake longer.

Jane Kinnison Millns (Mrs. Dale T.)

OYSTERS AND EGGPLANT IN A DISH

1 quart fresh oysters
12 or more slices of eggplant (fairly thick)
15-20 saltines, enough to layer on bottom and top of recipe-amount depends on size and shape of baking dish
Butter
½ pint heavy cream (whipping cream)
1 medium onion, chopped
2-3 stalks celery, chopped
Salt and pepper to taste
Worcestershire sauce to taste

Cook slices of eggplant in small amount of water for 3-4 minutes. Set aside to drain. Slice onion and celery and sauté. Grease well with butter a baking dish large enough to arrange eggplant so layer will be no more than 2 slices deep. Spread broken saltines in bottom of this dish. Arrange eggplant over saltines. Sprinkle a little salt and pepper over eggplant. Add a few pats of butter. Pour in oysters and their liquor and distribute evenly. Sprinkle salt and pepper, Worcestershire sauce. (Not too much salt as some is provided by saltines). Over the oysters spread sautéed onion and celery. Pour desired amount of cream over all. Cover with pats of butter and thick layer of crumbled saltines. Bake 325 degrees for 35 to 45 minutes.

Jeanne Upton Freemon (Mrs. Joseph M.)

TRENT SHORES PANNED OYSTERS

Easy
Jiffy
Serve immediately

1 pint oysters, drained
¼ cup butter
2 tablespoons dry white wine
1 tablespoon lemon juice
1 teaspoon Worcestershire sauce
½ teaspoon salt
Toast points, *OR* rounds of Holland Rusk
Lemon wedges

Sauté oysters gently in butter for 8-10 minutes. Remove oysters; add wine and seasonings; heat to a boil. Pour over oysters. Serve on toast with lemon wedges. Great!
Yield: 6 servings

Junius W. "Sonny" Davis, Jr.

CAD LUMSDEN'S ORIGINAL CRABMEAT CASSEROLE

Can freeze

6 pounds crabmeat
2 cups butter
2 cups flour
4 quarts milk
¾ (1 pound) box saltine crackers, crushed
5 tablespoons prepared mustard
5 tablespoons Worcestershire sauce
3 teaspoons celery salt
3 teaspoons parsley
Hot sauce to taste
Salt to taste
Mayonnaise
Paprika

Make a cream sauce using the butter, flour and milk and let it cool. Combine the crabmeat and cream sauce with the rest of the ingredients except the mayonnaise and paprika. Freeze in pint freezer bags. When ready to serve, thaw for several hours and empty contents into a baking dish and smooth mayonnaise over the top and sprinkle with paprika. Bake at 350 degrees for about 30 minutes or until browned.
Yield: 6 pint freezer bags, each containing 4 to 6 servings

Lawton Lumsden Parker (Mrs. John H.)

CRAB AU GRATIN

May be made ahead

1 pound crabmeat
4 tablespoons butter
4 tablespoons flour
1 teaspoon salt
1¾ cups milk
½ cup thin cream
1 teaspoon Worcestershire sauce
1 tablespoon lemon juice
2 tablespoons butter, melted
1 cup soft bread crumbs
1½ cups sharp cheese, grated

Melt 4 tablespoons butter in heavy saucepan; stir in flour and salt. Add milk and cream; stir constantly until sauce thickens and boils. Stir in cheese, Worcestershire, lemon juice and crabmeat. Pour into buttered 1½-quart shallow baking dish. Sprinkle with buttered crumbs. If cooking at once, bake 15 minutes at 425 degrees. This may also be made ahead and heated at 350 degrees about 30 minutes or until bubbly. May serve with rice.
Yield: with rice 6 servings
without rice 4 servings

Nancy Hagy Chiles (Mrs. Robert M.)

EDNA'S CRABMEAT CASSEROLE

Easy

1 pound crabmeat
3 of 4 eggs, hard-boiled and chopped
1½ cups bread crumbs
½ cup celery, chopped
½ cup green pepper, chopped
¼ cup onion, chopped
1 cup mayonnaise
1 tablespoon dry mustard
1 tablespoon vinegar
1 tablespoon lemon juice
1 tablespoon dry horseradish
½ cup white wine
½ cup bread crumbs, buttered
Paprika

Butter 1½-quart casserole. Preheat oven to 350 degrees. Sauté celery, green pepper and onion until tender, not brown. Combine all ingredients in casserole and top with buttered bread crumbs. Sprinkle with paprika. Bake 20 minutes or until heated through.
Yield: 4-6 servings

Harriet Divoky (Mrs. Robert J.)

JO'S CRAB CAKES

1 pound crab
¾ cup Waverly cracker crumbs
1 large egg, lightly beaten
2 tablespoons onion, minced
2 tablespoons mayonnaise
1 tablespoon Worcestershire sauce
1 tablespoon mustard
¾-1½ teaspoons Tabasco
1 teaspoon salt
½ teaspoon freshly ground pepper

Mix all ingredients together except cracker crumbs. Shape crab into six patties and roll in cracker crumbs. Fry approximately 3 minutes on each side. Drain.
Yield: 6 patties

Joan Brooks Kunkel (Mrs. Cooper D.)

SEAFOOD SCALLOP

This is an easy dish and very good to use for company and as an accompaniment to ham.

2½ cups cooked seafood, lobster, crab, shrimp, or scallops
¼ cup butter
3 tablespoons flour
½ teaspoon paprika
Dash of red pepper
1 teaspoon salt
⅛ teaspoon onion seasoning
1¼ cups milk
½ cup mushrooms, chopped or eggs, hard-boiled and chopped
½ cup bread crumbs, buttered

Preheat oven to 375 degrees. In saucepan, make a smooth white sauce from milk, flour, butter and seasonings. Add mushrooms, or eggs and seafood; blend. Fill scallop shells or put in a 1½-or 2-quart casserole dish. Top with crumbs. Bake for 20 minutes or until crumbs are lightly browned. Serve in scallop shells or over fluffy white rice.
Yield: 6 servings

Karen Brannock Askew (Mrs. M. H., III)

SEAFOOD BAKE

2 cups shrimp or crab, (or 1 cup of each)
1 cup celery, finely chopped
1 cup green pepper, chopped
1 tablespoon Worcestershire sauce
⅔ cup mayonnaise
⅓ cup chili sauce
Onion juice
Salt to taste
Pepper to taste

Topping:
1 cup Corn Flakes, crushed
Paprika
1-2 tablespoons butter or margarine

Preheat oven to 350 degrees. Butter 1½-quart casserole. Mix ingredients together in casserole dish. Dot with butter; sprinkle with paprika and crushed Corn Flakes. Bake 30 minutes.
Yield: 4-6 servings

Robertha Kafer Coleman (Mrs. Thomas B.)

CRAB IMPERIAL

Bake before freezing

1 tablespoon pimiento, minced
1 tablespoon green pepper, minced
2 heaping tablespoons mayonnaise
1 teaspoon prepared mustard
½ teaspoon Worcestershire sauce
½ teaspoon Accent
1 whole egg
6 saltines, crumbled
1 pound *backfin* crabmeat
2 egg yolks
½ cup mayonnaise

Preheat oven to 425 degrees. Mix together pimiento, green pepper, mayonnaise, mustard, Worcestershire, Accent, egg and saltines. Gently fold in crabmeat and pile high in 4 or 5 shells. Beat 2 egg yolks in ½ cup mayonnaise. Cover crab with this mixture and bake until golden brown, about 20 minutes. If this is frozen it must be completely cooked before freezing. When used it should be completely thawed before reheating.
Yield: 4-5 servings

Robertha Kafer Coleman (Mrs. Thomas B.)

KING CRAB CASSEROLE

Can do ahead

1 (10-ounce) package frozen broccoli spears or asparagus
½ cup sharp Cheddar cheese, grated
2 tablespoons onion, minced
¼ cup butter
2 tablespoons flour
¼ teaspoon curry powder
½ teaspoon salt
1 cup milk
1 tablespoon lemon juice
1 (6-ounce) package frozen King crab, thawed and drained
2 tablespoons butter
2 slices bread

Preheat oven to 350 degrees. Cook broccoli or asparagus according to package directions; drain. Arrange broccoli in a greased 8x8-inch baking dish. Sprinkle cheese over broccoli. Melt ¼ cup butter in a saucepan; add onions and sauté until soft. Add flour, seasonings and milk. Stir constantly until thick and smooth over low heat. Stir in lemon juice; add crab. Pour mixture over broccoli. Spread 2 tablespoons butter over soft bread and cut into cubes. Sprinkle over crab mixture. Bake 30 minutes.
Yield: 4 servings

Barbara Straub Stewart

TINA'S CRAB CASSEROLE

2 pounds crab
2 cups mayonnaise
2 cups half and half
2 tablespoons onion, chopped
2 tablespoons parsley
1 pound fresh mushrooms
4 hard-boiled eggs, diced
1 (8-ounce) package Pepperidge Farm Herb Stuffing

Slice and sauté mushrooms. Mix all ingredients together saving some stuffing for topping. Bake in 13x9-inch pan sprayed with Pam at 350 degrees for 40 minutes.
Yield: 8 servings

Joan Brooks Kunkel (Mrs. Cooper D.)

SAVANNAH-STYLE DEVILED CRABS

Delicious for brunch, lunch or supper.

Can be made in advance and refrigerated until baking time.

½ pound backfin or claw crabmeat
1 hard-boiled egg, diced
½ cup cracker crumbs
1½ tablespoons butter, melted
1 tablespoon Worcestershire sauce
2 tablespoons dry sherry *OR* any dry white wine
¼ teaspoon Tabasco
¼ teaspoon salt
3½ tablespoons *Hellman's* mayonnaise
1 tablespoon Dijon mustard
¼ teaspoon paprika
¼ teaspoon nutmeg
4 clean crab shells

Carefully pick over crabmeat for bits of shell. Toss crumbs in butter. Add all other ingredients except ½ tablespoon mayonnaise and the paprika. Mix well and then pile into crab shells. "Ice" top of each mound with remaining mayonnaise and dust with the paprika. Bake 15 minutes at 350 degrees and then place under broiler 1-2 minutes until mayonnaise topping puffs somewhat and browns slightly.
Yield: 4 servings

Junius W. "Sonny" Davis, Jr.

Remove a wine stain from a tablecloth by pouring a mound of ordinary table salt on the stain while still wet. Brush salt away when dry.

CRABMEAT OVER RICE

3 pounds Alaskan King Crab
3 (8-ounce) containers sour cream
½ cup butter
3 tablespoons white wine
Rice

Sauté crab in butter. Add sour cream and wine. Serve over cooked rice.
Yield: 14 servings

Margaret Ayres Midyette (Mrs. Charles T.)

ELEGANT LUNCHEON CRAB QUICHE

Easy

1 (6½-ounce) can crabmeat
1 cup Swiss cheese, grated
5 eggs
1¼ cups milk or half and half
½ teaspoon salt
⅛ teaspoon black pepper
½ cup mushrooms, sliced
1 (9-inch) unbaked pie shell

Preheat oven to 375 degrees. Sprinkle cheese into pie shell. Beat eggs. Mix with milk and seasoning. Pour over cheese. Sprinkle crab meat over pie. Bake 35 to 55 minutes until firm, when knife inserted comes out clean.
Yield: 6 servings

Margaret Mills Bagg (Mrs. John C., Jr.)

DAUGHTER-IN-LAW'S CRABMEAT PIE

Easy

1 (9-inch) pie shell, unbaked
6 ounces Swiss cheese, grated
6-8 ounces crabmeat*
2 teaspoons seasoned salt
1 cup light cream
2 eggs
2 tablespoons flour

*Shrimp or ham may be substituted for crab.
Sprinkle cheese and crabmeat in the bottom of the pie shell. Mix and pour remaining ingredients over crab mixture. Bake for 45 minutes in 400 degree oven.
Yield: 6 servings

Bettye Cooke Paramore (Mrs. Walter H., Jr.)

CRABMEAT QUICHE

3 eggs
3/4 teaspoon salt
1/2 pound fresh crabmeat, (carefully picked over for shell)
1 cup light cream
1 1/4 cup Gruyère cheese, grated
1 (8-inch) unbaked pie shell

Preheat oven to 375 degrees. Beat eggs, cream and salt together. Combine cheese and crabmeat and spread evenly on bottom of crust. Pour in cream mixture. Reduce oven heat to 350 degrees. Bake on lowest rack 35-40 minutes or until puffed and lightly browned.
Yield: 4-6 servings

Martha Hughes Matthews (Mrs. F. Clayton)
Bay Dunn McCotter (Mrs. J. Muse)

"Butter" casseroles with vegetable oil or spray with a non-stick product for easier clean-up.

BAKED CRABMEAT SANDWICH

Super luncheon recipe! Delicious with Molded Asparagus Salad.

Do ahead

12 slices thin bread, trimmed and buttered
1 cup (7 1/2-ounces) crabmeat
4 eggs, beaten
1/2 teaspoon salt
1/2 pound cheese, grated
3 cups milk
1/2 teaspoon curry

Place six slices bread, butter-side up in casserole. Spread crabmeat over; add 6 more slices bread, butter-side up. Sprinkle with grated cheese. Mix eggs, seasonings and milk together and pour carefully over bread. Cover and place in refrigerator several hours or overnight. Bake 45 minutes at 325 degrees.
Yield: 8-10 servings

Linda Rice Morris (Mrs. Kenneth)

TUNA CASSEROLE

Do early in day
Can freeze
Can double

½ cup onion, chopped
1 (10¾-ounce) can cream of mushroom soup
⅔ cup evaporated milk or light cream
⅓ cup grated Parmesan cheese
1 (9¼-ounce) can tuna, drained
1 (3-ounce) can mushrooms, drained
½ cup ripe olives, chopped (optional)
2 tablespoons minced parsley
2 teaspoons lemon juice
3 cups (6-ounces) cooked noodles
Parmesan cheese, paprika and parsley (garnish)

Butter a 2-quart casserole. Preheat oven to 375 degrees. Sauté onions until tender. Add soup, milk and cheese; heat and stir. Break tuna in chunks; add with the remaining ingredients. Pour into casserole. Sprinkle with additional Parmesan cheese and paprika. Bake for 20 to 25 minutes. Top with additional parsley.
Yield: 6 servings

Lee Thompson McIntyre (Mrs. J. Brooks)

CHOPSTICK TUNA

1 (10-ounce) can cream of mushroom soup
¼ cup water
1 cup chow mein noodles (½ 3-ounce can)
1 (6½-ounce) can tuna, drained
1 cup celery, sliced
½ cup salted cashews
¼ cup onion, chopped
Dash pepper

Combine soup and water; add ½ noodles, tuna, celery, cashews, onion and pepper. Toss lightly. Place in greased 10x6-inch baking dish. Sprinkle other half of noodles over top. Bake in preheated 375 degree oven 15 minutes or until heated through.
Yield: 4-6 servings

Eleanor Elizabeth Richardson (Mrs. Asa C.)

MICKIE'S LOBSTER DIP

1 cup mayonnaise
1 tablespoon anchovy paste
½ teaspoon Tabasco
½ teaspoon dry mustard
¼ teaspoon garlic powder
2 tablespoons tarragon vinegar
3 hard-boiled eggs, finely chopped
3 tablespoons stuffed olives, finely chopped
3 tablespoons gherkins, finely chopped
1 tablespoon chopped parsley
1 teaspoon onion, finely chopped
2 (12-ounce) South African Rock Lobsters

Boil lobster tails and cut meat into small chunks. Save shells. Blend mayonnaise, anchovy paste, Tabasco, dry mustard and garlic powder. Stir in vinegar, eggs, olives, gherkins, parsley and onion and mix well. Add lobster to sauce and serve in shells.
Yield: 2 cups sauce without meat

Leah Jones Ward (Mrs. D. L.)

BAKED ROCKFISH OR FLOUNDER

2 to 3 pounds fish, dressed whole
3 or more strips bacon
4 medium-sized potatoes
2 or more onions
1 lemon cut in wedges
1 (8-ounce) can tomato sauce
Parsley
Pepper

Put fish in greased Pyrex baking dish after salting fish inside and out and cutting slits on top side. With knife blade, press strips of bacon in slits. Bake in hot oven until fish browns. Take dish out of oven and arrange over fish ring of potatoes and onions which have been steamed until tender. Pour over this the tomato sauce and enough water to keep the fish moist, using water in which the onions and potatoes were cooked. (Make sure water is warm—never add cold water to anything you cook). Place dish in oven and cook until done, perhaps 20 minutes, basting once. Before serving, place lemon wedges and parsley around the fish on the platter or as desired.

Margaret Whitehead Wall (Mrs. Lawrence D.)

CRISP OVEN-FRIED FISH

2 pounds fish filet
¼ cup milk
1 egg, beaten
1 cup Corn Flake crumbs
¼ teaspoon thyme
¼ cup Parmesan cheese
⅓ cup butter, melted
Parsley
Lemon

Preheat oven to 500 degrees. Mix egg and milk in a shallow pan. Mix crumbs, thyme and cheese together in another shallow pan. Dip filet in egg-milk mixture; roll in crumb mixture and lay filets side-by-side in greased baking dish. Drizzle with melted butter. Remainder of crumbs may be poured on top. Bake 12-15 minutes. Serve with parsley and lemon.
Yield: 4-6 servings

Proper care for your catch:
Put 4-inches crushed ice in insulated chest; leave drain open. Make a salt-ice mixture: 1 pound coarse salt per 20 pounds crushed ice. Arrange fish in layers in chest covering each layer with salt-ice mixture. Secure lid. Drain off excess liquid and replenish salt-ice daily.

BROWNED BUTTER FISH

The browned butter gives this dish its extra flavor.

1 (2 pound) fish filet
½ cup butter
Lemon juice
Marjoram
Salt to taste
Paprika to taste
Pepper to taste

Preheat oven to 450 degrees. Put butter in shallow baking dish in hot oven until butter is melted and browned. Place filets in hot butter and cook 10-15 minutes at 400 degrees. Turn and baste with pan juices. Sprinkle fish with lemon juice, marjoram, salt, paprika and pepper. Bake about 5 more minutes. Serve with pan juices.

Cherry Sampson Meyers (Mrs. Bruce M.)

TOPPING FOR BROILED FISH

2 tablespoons sour cream
1 tablespoon mayonnaise
Pinch of curry, dill, snipped parsley, minced onion

Combine ingredients. About 3 minutes before fish is done, spread sauce liberally over fish. Return to broiler and continue cooking until done. Serve immediately with lemon wedges.

Allow 1 pound of fish per person if fish includes skin, bones, head and tail. Allow ½ pound per person if fish is cleaned and scaled.

SHRIMP ROLLED FILET

Part done ahead

¼ cup butter
1 clove garlic, crushed
1 small onion, minced
¼ cup green pepper, chopped
12 cooked shrimp
¼ cup bread crumbs
1 tablespoon parsley, chopped
½ teaspoon salt
⅛ teaspoon pepper
4 filets of sole or flounder

Melt butter, garlic, onion and green pepper. Sauté until golden. Dice 8 shrimp and add to skillet with bread crumbs, parsley, salt and pepper. Mix. Remove from heat. Put 2 tablespoons of mixture on each filet. Roll and chill. Can be refrigerated at this point and brought out 30 minutes before serving time. When ready to bake, preheat oven to 350 degrees. Arrange rolls in greased 10x6-inch pan. Melt remaining butter and brush over filets. Bake 25-30 minutes.

Sauce:
½ cup butter
3 egg yolks
2 tablespoons lemon juice
⅛ teaspoon cayenne pepper
¼ teaspoon salt

While filets are baking, mix sauce ingredients. Heat over low heat. Pour over filets before serving.
Yield: 4 servings

Peggy Witmeyer Bernard

FISH MORNAY

Delicious for family or company!

Easily doubled
Part done ahead
Use waxed paper for easy clean up

1 large bunch fresh broccoli, washed and separated
2 (16-ounce) packages frozen fish* filets, thawed
Milk
2 tablespoons butter or margarine, melted

*Our family prefers flounder filets.

Heat water in large kettle to rolling boil. Add salt. Remove tough outer leaves and ends of broccoli and slice lengthwise so that flowerets are about 2 inches wide. Drop trimmed broccoli into boiling water and simmer three minutes. Drain broccoli in colander and dip colander in cold water to stop the cooking process. Broccoli may be refrigerated at this point. Preheat oven to 325 degrees. Spray 13x9-inch baking dish with Pam. Rinse thawed fish under running water checking for bones. Place fish in platter of milk. After dipping in milk; place filet on waxed paper: lay 2-3 pieces of broccoli over each filet with flowerets alternating across the shorter side of filet. Roll fish around broccoli and secure with toothpick. Place roll in baking dish with the seam-side down. Brush tops of filets with melted butter. Bake 20-25 minutes.

Sauce:

3 tablespoons butter or margarine
3 tablespoons flour
1 cup milk
½ cup Miracle Whip Salad Dressing
¼ cup Kraft Grated Parmesan Cheese
Salt
Pepper

While fish is baking, melt butter in saucepan; add flour, salt and pepper to taste and gradually add milk. Stir constantly until smooth. Add cheese and stir in salad dressing. Keep warm over simmering water in double boiler. When fish is done, pour sauce over fish and place under broiler until sauce begins to brown.

Yield: 6-8 servings; 2 cups sauce

Barbara Straub Stewart

STUFFED FLOUNDER WITH CRAB OR CLAMS

Part done ahead

8 flounder filets
¼ cup onion, chopped
½ cup margarine
1 (3-ounce) can mushrooms, chopped, reserve liquid
1 (6½-ounce) can crabmeat or clams, minced
½ cup coarse saltine cracker crumbs *OR* 1 cup Pepperidge Farm Stuffing
2 tablespoons parsley (or less)
½ teaspoon salt

Cook onion in butter until tender, not brown. Add all other ingredients and mix. Spread mixture over flounder filets. Roll and place seam-side down in baking dish. Cover and refrigerate until ready to bake.

Sauce:
3 tablespoons butter
3 tablespoons flour
¼ teaspoon salt
⅓ cup dry white wine
Milk added to reserved mushroom liquid
1 cup Cheddar cheese, shredded
Paprika

Preheat oven to 400 degrees. Remove baking dish from refrigerator. Add enough milk to reserved mushroom liquid to make 1½ cups. Set aside. In a saucepan melt butter; blend in flour and salt. Gradually add milk mixture to flour, stirring until well-blended. Add wine. Cook and stir until mixture thickens and bubbles. Pour over filets. Bake 25 minutes. Sprinkle cheese and paprika over fish and bake 10 additional minutes.

Robertha Kafer Coleman (Mrs. Thomas B.)
Ann Holmes Novak (Mrs. David W.)

Glazing fish:
Measure 2 ounces lemon juice into a pint container: fill the rest of the container with water. Dissolve packet of unflavored gelatine in 4 ounces of mixture. Heat remaining liquid to boiling. Stir dissolved gelatine into boiling liquid. Cool to room temperature. Dip fish in mixture. Drain. Wrap properly and freeze immediately.

Marine Resource Center
Pine Knoll Shores, N. C.

Slover House **201 Johnson Street**

New Bern has several examples of the Italian Renaissance style; this is perhaps the finest. Built in 1848 for George Slover, a wealthy merchant, it came through the War Between the States and the Federal occupation with its marble mantles, silver fittings, original hardware and gaslight chandeliers intact—perhaps because it served as headquarters for Union General Ambrose Burnside. In 1908 C. B. Bradham, the New Bern druggist who invented Pepsi Cola, bought the house from the Slover heirs. Today it is the residence of Mr. and Mrs. L. A. Stith.

Salads, Dressings and Sauces

HIDDEN TREASURE SALAD

1 (3-ounce) package lemon Jello
½ cup sherry wine
1 (16-ounce) can pitted Bing cherries, juice reserved
1½ cups liquid, (cherry juice plus water), boiled
⅓ cup pecan halves

Dissolve Jello in cherry juice and water. Add sherry. Stuff cherries with nuts. Chill Jello until partially thickened. Push stuffed cherries into Jello. Serve topped with dressing.

Dressing:
1 (3-ounce) package cream cheese, softened
¼ cup sour cream
2-3 tablespoons currant jelly
1-2 teaspoons lemon juice to taste

Mix all ingredients until smooth. Top salad with dressing.

Carol Coleman Pursell (Mrs. Elliott D.)

SHERRIED CRANBERRY SALAD

2 (6-ounce) packages raspberry Jello
1 (16-ounce) can whole cranberry sauce
Pecans and celery, chopped (amount as desired)
1 cup sherry

Heat cranberry sauce; mix in Jello, pecans and celery. Stir in sherry. Congeal.

Margaret Whitehead Wall (Mrs. Lawrence D.)

APRICOT SALAD

Can do ahead
Easy and good
Will refrigerate several days

1 (3-ounce) package apricot Jello
1 (3-ounce) package orange Jello
1 envelope Knox gelatine
2 (16-ounce) cans apricots, drain and reserve syrup
1 (20-ounce) can crushed pineapple, drain and reserve syrup
1 pint sour cream
1 cup nuts, chopped

Soften Knox gelatine in 1/4 cup cold water. Add water to syrups from fruit to make 2 cups. Heat. Dissolve Jello in syrup. Add dissolved Knox gelatine Mash apricots and mix in pineapple and sour cream. Add nuts. Pour into mold. Refrigerate until congealed.
Yield: 8 servings

Frances Mason Clement (Mrs. Donald H.)

CURRIED BANANA PINEAPPLE SALAD

2 (3-ounce) packages lemon Jello
1 teaspoon curry powder
1 (8½-ounce) can crushed pineapple, drained (save juice)
2 tablespoons lemon juice
3 ripe bananas
1 cup celery, sliced
Small amount Knox gelatine

Mix Jello and curry and add 2 cups boiling water. (I always add a small amount of Knox gelatine to any Jello recipe). Add pineapple syrup, lemon juice and enough cold water to make 2 cups. Stir into Jello mixture and pour a thin layer into mold. Chill until firm. Slice 1 banana lengthwise into thirds. Make design in mold. Bind with another thin layer of Jello. Chill remaining Jello mixture until thick. Slice remaining bananas and add to thickened Jello with pineapple and celery. Spoon into mold and chill.

Genevieve Tolson Dunn (Mrs. Mark S.

BLUEBERRY DELIGHT

2 (3-ounce) packages black raspberry Jello
1 (15-ounce) can crushed pineapple, drained and syrup reserved
2 cups blueberries, fresh or canned, drained
1 cup sour cream
1 cup Cool Whip

Dissolve Jello in 2 cups boiling water. Add enough water to drained pineapple liquid to make 1 cup. Stir that into dissolved Jello. Add pineapple and blueberries. Pour into 2-quart mold or Pyrex dish. Refrigerate to congeal. Combine sour cream and Cool Whip. When ready to serve, cover Jello with sour cream mixture.

Susan Stuart Weatherly (Mrs. Jerry)

DREAMY BLUEBERRY SALAD

2 (3-ounce) packages blackberry Jello
1 (8-ounce) can crushed pineapple, juice reserved
1 (16-ounce) can blueberries, drained

To pineapple juice add enough water to make 3 cups. Put in a saucepan and bring to a boil. Pour hot liquid over Jello and dissolve. Chill until mixture is consistency of egg whites. Mix berries and pineapple into Jello and refrigerate.

Topping:
1 (8-ounce) package cream cheese
1 (8-ounce) container sour cream
½ cup sugar
Chopped pecans

Blend together cream cheese, sour cream, sugar and nuts and spread over congealed salad.

Ann Holmes Novak (Mrs. David W.)

CHERRY BLOSSOM MOLD

2 cups pitted dark sweet cherries, drained *OR* 1 (16-ounce) can dark sweet cherries, drained
2 cups boiling liquid (water plus cherry juice)
1 (6-ounce) package cherry gelatin
2 cups sour cream
⅓ cup slivered blanched almonds
Additional cherries, to garnish (optional)

Add water to cherry juice to make 2 cups. Bring to boil and pour over gelatin. Mix until dissolved. Cool. Add sour cream and beat until smooth. Chill until slightly thickened. Stir in cherries and almonds. Pour into 6-cup mold; chill until firm. If desired, garnish with additional cherries.

Virginia McGehee Borowitz (Mrs. Ronald R.)

SOUR CHERRY MOLD

Mold in square or oblong pan
Makes very lovely individual molds, having a festive red color
Make day ahead

1 pint frozen sour red cherries
1 cup pecans or walnuts, chopped
¼-½ cup sugar
Juice of 2 lemons
1 cup orange juice
2 (3-ounce) boxes cherry Jello
1 (16-ounce) can crushed pineapple

Combine cherry, lemon, orange juices and water to make 2 cups of liquid. Add sugar and bring to a boil. Dissolve Jello in hot juices. Add 1 cup cold water. Add undrained pineapple. Let partially congeal. Add cherries and nuts and congeal.
Yield: 8 servings

Nancy Samuel Everhart (Mrs. Charles L.)

RALEIGH CRANBERRY FOAM SALAD

Delicious!!

1 (3-ounce) package strawberry Jello
1 cup hot water
½ cup mayonnaise
½ cup pecans, broken
½ cup crushed pineapple, drained
1 (16-ounce) can whole cranberry sauce, drained

Dissolve Jello in hot water. Chill. Blend mayonnaise into Jello with beater. Add pineapple, cranberry sauce, and pecans. Stir well. Pour into molds.
Yield: 8 servings

Martha Hughes Matthews (Mrs. F. Clayton)

Variation:
Use 1 (3-ounce) lemon Jello instead of strawberry and omit the mayonnaise. Remaining ingredients and instructions are the same.

Patty Starr Willis (Mrs. A. Rexford, Jr.)

THANKSGIVING SALAD

A grand accompaniment to turkey or with turkey or chicken salad!

1 (6-ounce) package Jello (raspberry, cherry or strawberry)
2 cups water (1 boiling, 1 cold)
1 (15-ounce) can crushed pineapple, juice *included*
1 (14-ounce) jar Ocean Spray cranberry-orange relish
1 cup pecans, chopped
1 envelope Knox gelatine
¼ cup cold water

Dissolve Knox gelatine in ¼ cup water. Dissolve Jello in 1 cup boiling water. Mix all ingredients together and pour into 13x9-inch pan or other 2-quart mold. Chill until set.
Yield: 10-12 servings

Barbara Straub Stewart

FROZEN CRANBERRY FRUIT SALAD

1 (8-ounce) package cream cheese, softened
½ cup confectioners' sugar
1 tablespoon lemon juice
½ cup mayonnaise
1 (16-ounce) can whole cranberry sauce
1 cup Cool Whip

Blend cream cheese, confectioners' sugar, lemon juice and mayonnaise well. Add cranberry sauce and Cool Whip to first mixture and turn into 8x8-inch pan. Freeze. To serve, cut into squares.
Yield: 8-9 servings

Matilda Hancock Turner

LIME CHRISTMAS SALAD

First Layer:
1 (3-ounce) package lime Jello
1¾ cups boiling water
1-2 drops green food coloring

Pour boiling water over Jello to dissolve. Add food coloring and blend thoroughly. Pour into 2-quart mold or pan. Refrigerate until congealed.

Second layer:
1 (8-ounce) can crushed pineapple, drain and reserve syrup
1 (3-ounce) package lime Jello
Water
1 tablespoon lemon juice
1 cup evaporated milk
½ cup celery, chopped
½ cup pecans, chopped

Add enough water to pineapple syrup to equal 1 cup. Pour into a saucepan and heat to boiling. Pour over Jello to dissolve. Add lemon juice and evaporated milk. Fold in celery and pecans. Pour over congealed first layer and return to refrigerator to congeal second layer. Cut into squares or remove from decorative mold to serve.

Margaret Manning Preston (Mrs. Ronald A.)
Deborah Brown Bonner (Mrs. John H.)
Muriel Meier Coombs (Mrs. Bruce)
Susan Lee Thomas (Mrs. John G.)

ORANGE SURPRISE SALAD

1 (3-ounce) package orange Jello
2 tablespoons Tang
1¾ cups boiling water
1 (8-ounce) container Cool Whip, thawed
1 (8-ounce) can crushed pineapple, drained
1 cup Cheddar cheese, shredded

Dissolve Jello and Tang in boiling water; chill until slightly thickened. Fold in remaining ingredients. Pour into lightly oiled 5-cup mold and chill until firm.
Yield: 6 servings

Sandra Durham Madren (Mrs. S. Thomas)

PINEAPPLE-GINGER SALAD

1 (15¼-ounce) can pineapple chunks, dràin and reserve
1 (6-ounce) package lime Jello
1½ cups boiling water
1 cup ginger ale
¼ teaspoon ground ginger

Dissolve Jello in boiling water. Add ginger ale, ginger and pineapple juice to Jello mixture. Chill until slightly thickened. Fold in pineapple chunks and spoon into 8x4-inch loaf pan or into individual serving dishes.
Yield: 5 cups or 10 (4-ounce) servings

Susan Lee Thomas (Mrs. John G.)

STRAWBERRY MOLD

2 (3-ounce) packages strawberry Jello
1 (20-ounce) can crushed pineapple, drained (reserve juice)
2 tart apples, chopped
Pinch of salt
½ pint cream, whipped
¼ cup sugar
1 envelope Knox gelatine

Dissolve Jello and gelatine in 2 cups boiling water. Add 2 cups liquid (pineapple juice plus water to make 2 cups). Chill until syrupy. Mix in fruit and fold in whipped cream. Chill until firm.

Rena Terrell Knott (Mrs. Edmund T.)

LOW-CALORIE LOVELY AND LUSCIOUS STRAWBERRY SALAD

1 (20-ounce) can crushed pineapple, packed in its own juice
1 (1⅝-ounce) box Dezerta Wild Strawberry gelatin
1 (8-ounce) carton low-calorie cottage cheese
1 (8-ounce) carton Cool Whip

Heat pineapple and juice to boiling. Add Dezerta and cool. Add cottage cheese and Cool Whip. Chill until firm.
Yield: 8 generous servings

Anna Cartner Kafer (Mrs. Oscar A. Kafer, III)

STRAWBERRY SALAD

2 (3-ounce) packages strawberry Jello
1⅔ cup boiling water
2 (10-ounce) packages frozen strawberries
1 cup crushed pineapple, not drained
1 cup chopped walnuts*
1 pint sour cream

*or substitute pecans and add 2 ripe bananas, finely diced.
Dissolve Jello in boiling water. Add frozen strawberries and remove from heat, stirring occasionally until strawberries melt. Add crushed pineapple, nuts and bananas, if desired. Pour half of the mixture into 8x8-inch or 13x9-inch pan and refrigerate until firm, about 1½ hours. Spread sour cream over firm mixture and pour remaining mixture over top. Refrigerate until set.
Yield: 8-10 servings

Nancy Smith Favor (Mrs. William A., Jr.)
Lindy Allmond Emory (Mrs. Robert R., Jr.)
Helen Kulba (Mrs. William)
Chris Dixon (Mrs. Roy)

MANDARIN SHERBET SALAD

1½ cups boiling water
1 (3-ounce) package orange Jello
1 (3-ounce) package lemon Jello
1 (11-ounce) can mandarin orange sections, reserve juice
1 pint orange sherbet

Add enough water to reserved syrup to make 1 cup. Set aside. Heat 1½ cups water to boiling and pour over Jello to dissolve. Add reserved syrup water. Add sherbet and stir until well-mixed. Add orange sections and pour into mold. Refrigerate until congealed.

Lee Thompson McIntyre (Mrs. J. Brooks)

MARSHMALLOW SALAD

Easy
Stores well
Can be done ahead
Can be doubled

1 (10½-ounce) bag miniature marshmallows
1 (15-ounce) can crushed pineapple, *un*drained
1 (12-ounce) container Cool Whip
½ cup pecans, chopped
2 tablespoons maraschino cherries, chopped and drained

Pour pineapple into bowl. Mix in marshmallows. Let stand about one hour, until soft. Stir occasionally. Mix in pecans and cherries. Fold in Cool Whip and mix well. Chill until firm—about 4 hours. Should be chilled in serving bowl. Cover and refrigerate any leftovers.
Yield: 8 servings

Beverly Moore Perdue (Mrs. Gary R.)

MANDARIN ORANGE SALAD

1 (3-ounce) package orange Jello
1 cup boiling water
1 cup juiced drained from mandarin oranges
1 can mandarin oranges
1 banana, cut up
1 cup cottage cheese

Boil water and add orange Jello. Dissolve. Add cup of cold juice. Refrigerate until it begins to thicken. Then add oranges, bananas and cottage cheese.
Yield: 6 molds

Eugenia Hofler Clement (Mrs. Robert L.)

WILLIAMSBURG SALAD

2 envelopes Knox gelatine
½ cup water, to soften gelatine
1 cup boiling water
½ cup cold water
½ cup vinegar
½ teaspoon salt
1 cup sugar
1 cup pecans, chopped
1 cup sweet pickle relish, chopped
1 cup crushed pineapple, drain and reserve ½ cup juice
1 cup stuffed olives, sliced

Soften gelatine in ½ cup water. Dissolve gelatine in boiling water; add cold water, vinegar, salt, sugar, pecans, pickle relish, pineapple and ½ cup of pineapple juice and olives Chill and pour into molds.
Yield: 9 individual molds

Frances Mason Clement (Mrs. Donald H.)

FROZEN PISTACHIO SALAD

1 (4-ounce) package instant pistachio pudding
1 (15½-ounce) can crushed pineapple
1 (8-ounce) container Cool Whip

Stir instant pudding and pineapple together and fold in Cool Whip. Pour into shallow pan and freeze. To serve, cut into squares.

Fannie Daniels (Mrs. T. F.)

ANNETTE LEE'S FROZEN FRUIT SALAD

2 (3-ounce) packages cream cheese
1 cup mayonnaise
1 cup heavy cream, whipped
½ cup diced red cherries
1 (20-ounce) can crushed pineapple, drained
2½ cups miniature marshmallows

Combine cream cheese and mayonnaise. Blend until smooth. Fold in whipped cream, fruit and marshmallows. Freeze in flat 2-quart casserole. Take out of freezer, cut into squares and put in refrigerator 3 hours before serving.
Yield: 12 servings

Anne Bratton Allen (Mrs. H. Eldridge)

MINIATURE FROZEN FRUIT SALAD

Keeps well
Men love this salad

2½ cups sour cream
2½ tablespoons lemon juice
1 cup sugar
⅛ teaspoon salt
1 cup drained, crushed pineapple
½ cup nut meats
¼ cup maraschino cherries, halved
1 large, firm banana, sliced

Mix all ingredients. Pour into paper cupcake liners in 2¼-inch muffin tins. Freeze and store in a plastic bag after individual servings are frozen, or, pour into 8x8-inch pan. Freeze. Cut in squares to serve.

Cathy Gross Hendren (Mrs. Thomas L.)
Patty Starr Willis (Mrs. A. Rexford, Jr.)
Linda Allmond Emory (Mrs. Robert R.)

SALAD CELESTINE

Serve with Chicken di Violi

1 (20-ounce) can pineapple
½ pound marshmallows, quartered
½ pound almonds, slivered
½ pint cream

Combine pineapple, marshmallows and almonds and refrigerate overnight. Fold in cream and add following dressing:

Dressing:
4 egg yolks
4 tablespoons sugar
2 tablespoons vinegar

Mix in double boiler until thick. Add dressing to salad mixture and color with green food coloring, if desired. Mold and freeze. Unmold and top with following sauce.

Sauce:
1 tablespoon butter
½ cup sugar
Juice of 2 oranges
Juice of 1 lemon
2 egg yolks, lightly beaten

Melt butter. Dissolve sugar in orange-lemon juices. Add beaten yolks and cook until thick. Serve as a sauce for the salad.

Miss Rose B. Carraway

DRIFTWOOD SALAD

1 (3-ounce) package lime Jello
1 (3-ounce) package lemon Jello
2 cups boiling water
1 (8-ounce) can crushed pineapple, undrained
1 (3-ounce) package cream cheese
1 (12-ounce) package cottage cheese
1 (5-ounce) can evaporated milk
1 cup mayonnaise
3 tablespoons lemon juice
1 cup nuts, chopped
2 tablespoons horseradish

Dissolve together both packages Jello in boiling water. Chill until partially set. Blend in remaining ingredients, including pineapple juice. Chill until firm in a 6-cup mold sprayed with a non-stick product. Unmold on bed of lettuce. Yield: 12 servings

FROZEN SLAW

This is a good way to keep cabbage from the garden.

2 medium heads cabbage, chopped
6 green peppers, chopped
8 onions, chopped
1 quart white vinegar
⅓ cup (or less) salt
4 cups sugar
1 tablespoon celery seed or mustard seed, as desired

Mix chopped cabbage, green pepper and onion together in a large bowl. Put vinegar, salt, sugar and celery or mustard seed in a saucepan and bring to a boil. Pour over chopped vegetables and mix well. Pack in freezer containers, being sure vegetables are covered with liquid. Keeps about 2 months. Thaw and drain to serve.

Cherry Sampson Meyers (Mrs. Bruce M.)

MOLDED ASPARAGUS SALAD

Great for luncheon served with Baked Crabmeat Sandwich!

1 (6-ounce) package lime gelatin
½ teaspoon salt
1½ cups boiling water
2 (15-ounce) cans cut asparagus
1 cup mayonnaise
1 cup milk
2 tablespoons tarragon vinegar
1 cup Cheddar cheese, shredded
2 tablespoons onion, grated
Hot sauce to taste

Dissolve gelatin and salt in boiling water; chill until slightly thick. Drain asparagus, reserving ¾ cup liquid. Combine asparagus liquid, mayonnaise, milk, vinegar and gelatin; beat until smooth. Stir in cheese, onion, hot sauce and asparagus. Pour into a six-cup mold and chill until firm.
Yield: 10-12 servings

Linda Rice Morris (Mrs. Kenneth)

AVOCADO MOUSSE

2 tablespoons Knox gelatine
½ cup cold water
½ cup boiling water
½ cup whipped cream
2 cups mashed avocado
1 teaspoon onion juice
½ cup mayonnaise
½ teaspoon salt

Sprinkle gelatine over cold water and let stand 5 minutes; then dissolve in hot water. Cool, then stir in cream with mayonnaise. Add avocado, salt and onion juice and pour into a wet 1-quart ring mold. Let set. Unmold and garnish with sliced, peeled tomato wedges and French dressing. This is good on spinach leaves with peeled cherry tomatoes that have been marinated in dressing filling the center.

Jane Ingraham Ashford (Mrs. Charles H., Jr.)

To unmold congealed salads, loosen edges of mold with a knife which has been dipped into warm water. Dip mold to rim in warm water for 10 seconds. Shake slightly. Place a chilled, moistened plate over mold and invert.

CARROT SALAD

2 (3-ounce) packages lemon Jello
2 cups boiling water
1 (20-ounce) can crushed pineapple, reserve juice
1 cup carrots, grated
1 cup sharp Cheddar cheese, grated
¾ cup pecans, chopped
1 tablespoon vinegar or lemon juice
½ teaspoon salt

Dissolve Jello in boiling water. Add vinegar and salt. Drain pineapple and add enough water to equal 2 cups. Add to Jello mixture. Chill. When thickened, fold in cheese, carrot, pineapple and pecans. Pour into mold that has been rinsed in cold water. Chill until firm. Unmold on a platter and serve plain or make a dressing of mayonnaise and sour cream (⅔ to ⅓).

Marian Bartlett Stewart (Mrs. Wm. Edward)

CONGEALED CUCUMBER-ASPARAGUS SALAD

1 (3-ounce) package lime Jello
½ cup boiling water
1 (10-ounce) can cream of asparagus soup
½ cup mayonnaise
1 tablespoon vinegar
1 teaspoon onion, grated
Dash pepper
½ cup unpeeled cucumber, minced
¼ cup celery, diced

Dissolve Jello in hot water. Cool, then add soup, mayonnaise, vinegar, onion and pepper. Allow to partially set before adding cucumber and celery.
Yield: 6-8 servings

Ann Harris Bustard (Mrs. Victor W.)

OLD DOMINION CUCUMBER MOLD

1 (3-ounce) package lime Jello
1 cup boiling water
2 teaspoons vinegar
¼ teaspoon salt
2 large cucumbers, grated
1 small white onion, grated
1 cup sour cream
½ cup mayonnaise

Pour boiling water over Jello and dissolve. Add remaining ingredients and stir well. Pour into 6-cup mold. Refrigerate.
Yield: 8 servings

Helen Cannon Mewborn

SPINACH SALAD MOLD

1 (10-ounce) package frozen chopped spinach, thawed
1 (3-ounce) package lemon or lime gelatin
¾ cup boiling water
1 cup mayonnaise
1 cup cottage cheese
⅓ cup celery, diced
⅓ cup onion, diced

Squeeze liquid from thawed spinach. Set aside. Do not cook. Dissolve gelatin in boiling water. Cool. Add spinach and all other ingredients. Mix well. Pour into ring mold. Refrigerate until firm. Unmold and garnish as desired to serve.

Eleanor Haley Hickson (Mrs. Robbins G.)

SNAPPY TOM ASPIC

3 cans Snappy Tom mix
1½ packages Knox gelatine
2 teaspoons onion, grated
1 tablespoon lemon juice
¼ cup ice water
¼ small cabbage, shredded
1 cucumber, seeded and chopped
½ green pepper, chopped
1 carrot, shredded
½ cup celery, chopped
Salt, pepper, Worcestershire sauce, and Tabasco to taste

Heat Snappy Tom to a slow boil; add onion and lemon juice. Dissolve gelatine in ice water. Add to heated mixture and stir until dissolved. Cool. Combine all ingredients and pour in a lightly oiled mold pan or loaf. Chill at least 8 hours.

Nancy G. Taylor (Mrs. Harry C.)

Mayonnaise may be used to "butter" a gelatin mold.

TERRIFIC TOMATO ASPIC

3 (3-ounce) packages lemon Jello
6 cups V-8 juice
1 envelope gelatine
¼ cup cold water

Sprinkle gelatine over ¼ cup cold water to soften. Heat 2½ cups V-8 juice in saucepan. Stir in lemon Jello until dissolved. Add gelatine and stir well. Add remaining juice and mix thoroughly. This will fit into a 13x9-inch pan. Refrigerate until set and keep refrigerated until ready to serve.

Ann Harris Bustard (Mrs. Victor W.)

Variations:
Add a chopped green pepper, grated onion, grated carrots, chopped olives, chopped celery, dash Tabasco.

Grace Green Burnette (Mrs. A. W., Jr.)
Jane Moore Stubbs (Mrs. Trawick H., Jr.)
Karen Hansen Norman (Mrs. Joseph H., Jr.)

PICKLED BEANS AND ONIONS

Prepare day ahead

2 (16-ounce) cans Blue Lake Whole Long String Beans
3 medium onions, sliced and separated into rings
1⅔ cups vinegar
⅔ cup water
1½ cups sugar
1 tablespoon oil
Salt to taste
Pepper to taste

Drain beans and layer with onions in a bowl. In a saucepan combine vinegar, water, sugar, oil, salt and pepper; bring to a rolling boil, stirring to keep sugar from burning. Pour hot liquid over beans and onions. Cool. Cover and refrigerate overnight to marinate.

Susie L. Scales (Mrs. Gilbert W., Jr.)

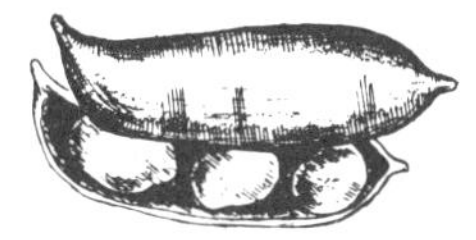

COPPER PENNIES

Must do ahead

18 carrots, sliced
1 teaspoon sugar
2 green peppers, sliced
1 large onion, sliced
1 (10½-ounce) can tomato soup
½ cup salad oil
¾ cup vinegar
½ cup granulated sugar
½ cup brown sugar
1 teaspoon prepared mustard
1 teaspoon Worcestershire sauce
Salt to taste
Pepper to taste

Boil carrots 3 minutes with 1 teaspoon sugar. Drain and cool. Alternate layers of carrots, green peppers and onions. Blend remaining ingredients and cook in saucepan until heated. Pour over vegetables. Refrigerate at least 24 hours.

Chris Watts Burks (Mrs. Charles L.)
Jeanne Upton Freemon (Mrs. Joseph M.)

MARINATED BROCCOLI BUDS

Do day ahead

3 bunches broccoli
1 cup cider vinegar
1 tablespoon sugar
1 tablespoon dill
1 tablespoon Accent
1 teaspoon salt
1 teaspoon freshly ground pepper
1 teaspoon garlic salt
1½ cups vegetable oil

Break off tops of broccoli. Do NOT use stems. Combine other ingredients and pour over broccoli. Refrigerate for 24 hours. Drain before serving.
Yield: 20 servings

Janet Grainger Corcoran (Mrs. James M.)

MARINATED BROCCOLI SALAD

Prepare ahead

1 bunch fresh broccoli
1 head cauliflower
1 (4-ounce) can sliced mushrooms
2 stalks celery, chopped
1 medium red onion, sliced thin
2 carrots, sliced thin *OR* 1 cucumber, peeled and sliced
½ cup oil
¼ cup vinegar
1 lemon
Morton's Seasoning Salt
Pepper

Wash broccoli and trim off leaves. Remove stalks and cut florets into bite-sized pieces. Do the same with cauliflower. Combine all vegetables in large bowl and squeeze the juice of one lemon over all. Gently toss adding oil and vinegar to taste. Add Morton's Seasoning, salt and pepper. The dressing should be light so the vegetables will not "swim" in liquid. Marinate at least two hours.

Anne Norman Tayloe

ORIGINAL HUNGARIAN CUCUMBER SALAD

Easy to prepare
Stores well
Can double

4 large cucumbers, sliced thin
2 teaspoons salt
Paprika
¼ cup vinegar
¼ cup sour cream
1 medium to large onion

Peel cucumbers and slice thin. Sprinkle with salt. Let stand 30 minutes to 2 hours. Peel onion and cut into very thin slices. Pour vinegar over onion slices. Drain water from cucumbers. With both hands squeeze remaining moisture out. This makes them crisp. Mix with sour cream and vinegar and onion mixture. Sprinkle with paprika.
Yield: 6 servings

Gabrielle Paluzsay Lippitt (Mrs. Devereux H.)

PINEAPPLE COLESLAW

Easy
Stores well

2 cups cabbage, shredded
1 cup red cabbage, shredded
3 heaping tablespoons Hellman's Mayonnaise
Milk, enough to cream mayonnaise
½ teaspoon paprika
1 (20-ounce) can pineapple chunks, drained
Salt to taste

Toss cabbages together with pineapple. Add creamed mayonnaise, paprika and salt. Toss and chill.
Yield: 6 servings

Frances L'Espérance Bollen (Mrs. Russell E.)

CABBAGE SLAW

Do day ahead

1 medium head cabbage, shredded
1 green pepper, chopped
1 small onion, chopped
1 cup cider vinegar
1 cup sugar
¾ cup Wesson oil
1 teaspoon salt
1 teaspoon celery seed
1 teaspoon dry mustard

Bring vinegar, sugar, oil, salt, celery seed and mustard to a boil and pour over vegetables while hot. Will keep several weeks in refrigerator.

Patricia Byrum McCotter (Mrs. C. Kennedy, Jr.)

COLESLAW FOR A CROWD

Must do ahead

15 pounds cabbage
2-3 carrots
2½ pounds sugar (5 cups)
¼ cup salt
1 quart vinegar
1 cup mayonnaise

Shred cabbage and carrots. Dissolve sugar and salt in 1 quart of vinegar. Mix and pour over cabbage and carrots. Marinate in the refrigerator from 3 hours to overnight. Drain *well*. Add one cup mayonnaise and mix.
Yield: 30-40 servings

Nancy Stilley Turner (Mrs. Charles H., Jr.)

CORN RELISH SALAD

3 (16-ounce) cans shoepeg corn, drained
1 green pepper, chopped
3 bunches small green onions, tips and all, chopped
1 (6-ounce) bottle salad olives with juice
1 (8-ounce) bottle Wishbone Italian Dressing

Cover in refrigerator for 24 hours. Will keep 3 weeks. Good with Drip Beef.

CAULIFLOWER AND MUSHROOM SALAD

Must do ahead

1 head cauliflower, broken
⅔ cup oil
¼ cup lemon juice
Mushrooms, fresh or 1 (4-ounce) can, drained
1 small onion, chopped
1 (16-ounce) can green peas, drained
Bacon bits

Mix all ingredients, except bacon bits, and marinate overnight. Add bacon just before serving.
Yield: 8 servings

Genevieve Tolson Dunn (Mrs. Mark S.)

MEXICAN CAULIFLOWER SALAD

A real winner!

Must do ahead

4 cups raw cauliflower, thinly sliced
1 cup ripe olives, pitted and chopped
1 cup green pepper, finely chopped
½ cup pimiento, chopped
⅓ cup onion, chopped

Combine 5 salad ingredients in a large bowl.

Dressing:
½ cup salad oil
3 tablespoons lemon juice
3 tablespoons wine vinegar
2 teaspoons salt
½ teaspoon sugar

Mix dressing ingredients with beater until well-blended. Pour over the cauliflower mixture, cover and chill at least 3 hours.
Yield: 6-8 servings

Alice Graham Underhill (Mrs. T. Reed)

MEDITERRANEAN SALAD

2 (10-ounce) packages frozen mixed vegetables, cooked, drained and chilled
½ cup olives, sliced
½ cup spring onions, sliced

Mix vegetables, olives and onions together in large bowl and set aside.

Dressing:
⅓ cup olive oil
3 tablespoons wine vinegar
1 tablespoon capers
1 clove garlic, crushed
1½ teaspoons salt
⅛ teaspoon pepper

Mix ingredients for dressing together and pour over vegetables. Chill several hours.

Elizabeth Reese Ward (Mrs. David L., Jr.)

MARINATED GREEN PEA SALAD

Must do ahead

3 (10-ounce) packages green peas with pearl onions
1 pound cocktail tomatoes
1 pound fresh mushrooms
1 cup Simple French Dressing

Cook peas 2 minutes and drain. Cool 5 minutes. Slice mushrooms and tomatoes; mix with peas. Add Simple French Dressing and let stand 3 hours or overnight. Serve in lettuce-lined bowl for buffet or in lettuce cups for individual servings.
Yield: 12 servings

Simple French Dressing:
⅓ cup vinegar
⅔ cup oil
2 teaspoons salt
Dash of pepper
¼ teaspoon dry mustard

Mix ingredients together for dressing and pour over salad.
Yield: 1 cup

Carol Webb Pullen (Mrs. John S.)

PERFECT POTATO SALAD

3 medium potatoes
1 teaspoon sugar
1 teaspoon vinegar
½ cup celery, sliced
⅓ cup onion, finely chopped
¼ cup sweet pickle, chopped
1 teaspoon salt
1 teaspoon celery seed
¾ cup mayonnaise or salad dressing
2 hard-boiled eggs, sliced

In covered pan cook whole potatoes in boiling salted water to cover for 25 minutes or until almost tender. Drain well and peel. Cut potatoes into quarters and slice ¼-inch thick. Add remaining ingredients except mayonnaise and eggs. Stir mixture to combine. Fold in mayonnaise then carefully fold in egg slices. Cover and chill thoroughly.
Yield: 4 servings

Alice Graham Underhill (Mrs. T. Reed)

MOTHER'S GERMAN POTATO SALAD

½ dozen medium or 1 dozen small potatoes
4 strips bacon
2 rounded tablespoons flour
¼ cup vinegar
¼ cup water
¼ cup sugar
2-3 stalks celery
2 eggs, hard-boiled and sliced
Chopped onion
Salt to taste
Pepper to taste

Fry bacon. When nearly brown pour off part of grease. Take bacon out and brown onion. Add flour to browned bacon and onion; then vinegar and water. Finally add sugar and more water if necessary. Boil potatoes with skins in salted water until fork-tender. Pour off water; cool; peel and slice potatoes. Add celery and eggs. Pour sauce on top and mix gently. Add salt if necessary. I double the amount of sauce.

Phyllis Hurtgen Harke (Mrs. Dennis M.)

RICE SALAD

Early in day

2 packages chicken Rice-a-Roni
¾ cup green pepper, chopped (optional)
8 green onions, chopped
16 stuffed or ripe olives, sliced
2 (6-ounce) jars marinated artichoke hearts, cut
½-⅔ cup mayonnaise
1 teaspoon curry powder (optional)
1 cup boiled shrimp (optional)

Cook rice according to directions on package, omitting margarine. Cool. Add pepper, olives, onions, and drained artichokes. Save marinade and mix with mayonnaise and curry powder. Add this to rice mixture with shrimp. Press into mold and chill.

Penny Johnson McCaughan (Mrs. Mark R.)

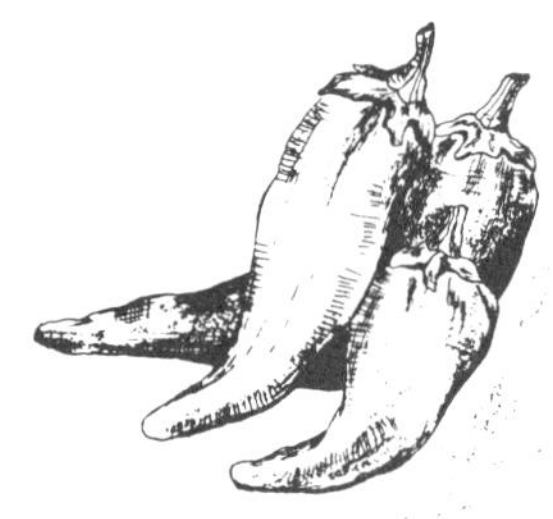

TACO SALAD

1 head lettuce, torn into small pieces
1 pound Cheddar cheese, grated
1 (16-ounce) can Mexican beans, drained
Tomatoes, chopped (amount as desired)
Onions, chopped (amount as desired)
1 (8-ounce) bottle Catalina dressing
1 (7-ounce) package cheese-flavored Doritos

Combine all ingredients and serve immediately. If desired, salad may be prepared in advance and refrigerated with Doritos and dressing added just before serving.

Katherine Dodge Beckwith (Mrs. George H.)

JIFFY VEGETABLE SALAD

Stores well

1 green pepper, chopped
1 cup celery, chopped
1 cup onion, chopped
1 (16-ounce) can French-style green beans, drained and cut in half
1 (7-ounce) can Le Sueur peas, drained
1 (7-ounce) can LeSueur corn, drained
1 (2-ounce) jar pimientos, chopped
½ cup vinegar
½ cup vegetable oil
½ cup sugar
1 teaspoon salt
1 teaspoon pepper
1 carrot, shredded
1 (2-ounce) can sliced mushrooms
1 tablespoon dry parsley

Mix all ingredients together in large bowl. Cover and refrigerate several hours.

Yield: 12 servings or more

Karen Brannock Askew (Mrs. M. H., III)

CHICKEN GARDEN SALAD

3 cups chicken, cooked and cubed
1 (10-ounce) package raw spinach
¾ cups walnuts, chopped
2 apples, chopped
½ cup corn or safflower oil
¼ cup red wine vinegar
⅛ teaspoon garlic powder
3 teaspoons chives, chopped
½ teaspoon salt
⅛ teaspoon pepper
1 teaspoon sugar

Combine oil, vinegar and seasonings. Chill. Wash spinach; drain and discard stems. Tear into bite-sized pieces. Add chicken, walnuts and apples. Pour on dressing and toss lightly.
Yield: 6-8 servings

Sandra Durham Madren (Mrs. S. Thomas)

MARINATED VEGETABLE-BACON BOWL

1 (16-ounce) can English peas, drained
1 pound fresh mushrooms, sliced
1 medium onion, sliced
⅔ cup vegetable oil
¼ cup lemon juice
1¼ teaspoon salt
½ teaspoon dry mustard
¼ cup bacon, crumbled

Combine vegetables, tossing lightly. Combine remaining ingredients except bacon, mixing well. Pour over vegetables and toss lightly. Cover and chill at least 3 hours, stirring occasionally. Sprinkle bacon over salad before serving.

Carol Coleman Pursell (Mrs. Elliott D.)

Low-calorie whipped butter (50 calories per tablespoon) may be made by softening ½ cup butter in mixing bowl. Whip with electric mixer until fluffy. Add pinch of salt. Continue to mix at high speed. Gradually add ½ cup cold water.

EASY MARINATED SALAD

1 (16-ounce) can asparagus, drained
1 (16-ounce) can English peas, drained
1 (2-ounce) can mushrooms, drained
1 (5-ounce) can water chestnuts, drained and sliced
Italian salad dressing to cover vegetables

Combine first four ingredients and marinate in Italian Dressing overnight in refrigerator. Serve on bed of lettuce.

Sandra Phillips Moore (Mrs. William M., Jr.)

CHICKEN SALAD HABAÑERA

Easy, everything is done ahead except the mixing.

2 cups chicken, cooked and diced
½ cup green pepper, cut in 1x¼-inch strips
¼ cup onion, chopped
¼ cup ripe olives, sliced
1 avocado, cut in crescents
Lettuce leaves
3 medium tomatoes, cut in wedges
4 slices bacon, cooked crisp and crumbled

Dressing:
⅓ cup salad oil
¼ cup red wine vinegar
1 tablespoon lemon juice
2 teaspoons sugar
1 teaspoon salt
½ teaspoon dry mustard
¼ teaspoon pepper
⅛ teaspoon garlic powder

Mix together, chicken, green pepper, onion and olives. Cover and chill. Combine dressing ingredients in jar and shake well. Refrigerate. Just before serving add avocado to salad ingredients. Shake dressing and pour over salad; toss lightly. Serve on bed of lettuce. Place tomato wedges around salad. Sprinkle with crumbled bacon.
Yield: 4 servings

Sandra Durham Madren (Mrs. S. Thomas)

CHICKEN SALAD

4 cups chicken, diced and cooked
1 (4½-ounce) jar whole mushrooms, drained
½ cup pecan halves, toasted*
4 slices fried bacon, crumbled
1 cup mayonnaise
1 cup sour cream
1½ teaspoons salt
2 tablespoons lemon juice

*Toast pecans in shallow baking pan at 350 degrees for 15 minutes
Combine chicken, mushrooms, pecans and bacon in a large bowl. Blend together mayonnaise, sour cream, salt and lemon juice. Add to chicken mixture and toss lightly to mix. Chill thoroughly.
Yield: 6-8 servings

Wanda Dzula Adsit (Mrs. Spencer M.)

MOTHER-IN-LAW'S CHICKEN SALAD

1 large roasted chicken, skinned, boned and chunked
½ pound fresh mushrooms, sliced
1 (17-ounce) can LeSueur Early Peas
3 ripe tomatoes, chunked
1 teaspoon onion, minced
Lemon-pepper to taste
Dill weed to taste
1 (8-ounce) bottle Italian or Herb-spice Dressing

Combine all ingredients and refrigerate.
Yield: 5-6 servings

Miriam Schulman Allenson (Mrs. Andrew J.)

MOLDED CHICKEN SALAD

Do a day ahead
Stores well in refrigerator

2 envelopes Knox gelatine
1 cup cold water
1 (10¾-ounce) can cream of celery soup, undiluted
½ teaspoon salt
2 tablespoons lemon juice
1 teaspoon instant minced onion
1 cup salad dressing or mayonnaise
2 tablespoons pimiento, diced
1 cup celery, diced
2 cups cooked chicken, diced
Salad greens for garnish, optional

Soften gelatine in water in large saucepan. Cook over medium heat, stirring constantly, until dissolved (about 3 minutes). Add soup, salt, lemon juice, onion and salad dressing, stirring well. Chill mixture until slightly thickened, then stir in pimiento, celery and chicken. Spoon into a six-cup mold, rinsed with cold water before filling.
Yield: 6 main dish servings

Miss Janet Latham

CHICKEN SALAD SUPRISE

Delicious with sliced fresh fruit such as apples and bananas or natural Cheddar cheese or Havarti.

2½ cups chicken, cooked and diced
½ cup celery, diced
½ cup apple, unpeeled and diced
½ cup blanched almonds, slivered and toasted
1 small onion, minced
⅓ cup mayonnaise
1 teaspoon lemon juice
½ teaspoon salt
⅛ teaspoon pepper
2 teaspoons curry powder

Mix the chicken, celery, apple, almonds and onion in a bowl. Combine mayonnaise with lemon, pepper, salt and curry. Stir into chicken mixture. Serve on crisp leaf lettuce or on toast points of whole wheat or as a sandwich.

Lou H. Proctor (Mrs. Jimmie C.)

CONGEALED CHICKEN SALAD

This is a great luncheon dish with asparagus and baby beets or pickled peach. Can be made several days ahead.

½ cup water
1 cup celery, diced fine
1 small onion, diced fine
1 small can baby green peas
½ cup nuts, chopped
3 (or more) cups chicken, diced
4 hard-boiled eggs, chopped
3 tablespoons sweet pickle, chopped
2-ounces pimiento, chopped
1 cup mayonnaise
3 tablespoons (2 envelopes) Knox gelatine
1½ cups chicken broth

Dissolve gelatine in ½ cup cold water, then in 1½ cups hot chicken broth. Combine all other ingredients. Put in flat casserole or in 16 individual molds. Chill.
Yield: 16 servings

Mary Moulton Barden (Mrs. Graham A., Jr.)

HOT CHICKEN SALAD

Must do ahead

4 cups cold chicken, cooked and chunked
2 cups celery, chopped
4 hard-boiled eggs, diced
2 tablespoons onion, finely minced
1 teaspoon salt
½ teaspoon Accent (MSG)
2 tablespoons lemon juice
¾ cup mayonnaise
¾ cup condensed cream of chicken soup
1 cup cheese, grated
1½ cups potato chips, crushed
⅔ cup toasted almonds, finely chopped

Combine chicken, celery, eggs, onion, salt, Accent, lemon juice, mayonnaise and soup together mixing well. Spread in 9x13-inch baking dish. Combine cheese, potato chips and almonds and spread over top. Cover and refrigerate overnight. When ready to bake, remove casserole from refrigerator; preheat oven to 400 degrees and bake 20-25 minutes.
Yield: 8 servings

Susanne Darby Thompson (Mrs. Michael B.)

AS YOU LIKE IT SALAD

Salad:
2 cups macaroni (twists, elbow or shells)
2 cups cooked, turkey, chicken or ham, diced
4 ounces Cheddar cheese, diced
1 or 2 ribs celery, diced
¼ cup olives (green or ripe)

Cook and drain macaroni. Add remaining ingredients. You may also add: green pepper, onion, peanuts, sunflower seeds, etc. Serve with dressing.

Dressing:
2-3 tablespoons mayonnaise
1-2 tablespoons sour cream or yogurt
1 teaspoon mustard
Paprika

Mix all ingredients except paprika. Sprinkle with paprika.

Karen Daniels Burks (Mrs. William L.)

SHRIMP SALAD MOLD

2 envelopes Knox gelatine
¼ cup cold water
1 (10-ounce) can tomato soup, heated
¼ cup onion, chopped
¼ cup green pepper, chopped
1 tablespoon lemon juice
¼ teaspoon salt
1 (8-ounce) package cream cheese, softened
1 cup mayonnaise
1 cup celery, chopped
2 cups shrimp, cooked, shelled, deveined and cut into bite-sized pieces

Dissolve gelatine in cold water; add to heated soup. In blender pureé green pepper, onion, lemon juice, salt and add to soup mixture. Mix mayonnaise and cream cheese until smooth. Add this mix to soup mixture. Stir in celery and shrimp. Pour into a 9-inch mold. Chill.
Yield: 10-12 servings

Janet Grainger Corcoran (Mrs. James M.)

To keep a casserole cold for hours, double-wrap in foil, then wet newspapers, and again in foil to insulate the cold.

SHRIMP SALAD

2 (5-ounce) cans *OR* 1 pound shrimp, cooked, shelled and deveined
1 cup celery, coarsely chopped
2 eggs, hard-boiled and coarsely chopped
3 tablespoons dill pickle, diced
1 tablespoon lemon juice
½ cup mayonnaise
1 tablespoon catsup
½ teaspoon Worcestershire sauce
¾ teaspoon salt
¼ teaspoon pepper
Lettuce

Chill shrimp. Reserve a few nice shrimp and toss the remainder with celery, eggs and pickle. Combine lemon juice, mayonnaise, catsup, Worcestershire sauce, salt and pepper and toss with shrimp mixture. Serve on lettuce and garnish with reserved shrimp and additional egg, if desired.
Yield: 4 servings

Shirley Taylor Pridgen (Mrs. Lonnie E., Jr.)

CURRIED SHRIMP SALAD

Can double

1 (6-ounce) package curried rice mix
2 cups shrimp, cleaned, cooked, halved lengthwise
1 cup celery, diced
½ cup green pepper, diced
4 slices bacon, crisp cooked and crumbled
½ cup whipping cream
½ cup mayonnaise
1 teaspoon curry powder
Lettuce
Shredded coconut
Cashews
Chutney

Cook rice mix according to directions; cool. Reserve 6 shrimp halves for garnish. Combine remaining shrimp, the cooked rice, celery, green pepper and bacon. Whip cream to soft peaks. Combine with mayonnaise and curry. Stir into rice mixture. Cover and chill at least 1½ hours. To serve, turn salad into lettuce lined bowl or in individual lettuce cups. Top with reserved shrimp. Pass coconut, cashews and chutney.
Yield: 6 servings

Carol Webb Pullen (Mrs. John S.)

SHRIMP MACARONI SALAD

¾ pound shrimp, cooked, shelled and deveined
2 cups cooked macaroni
1 cup cauliflower, chopped
1 cup celery, diced
¼ cup parsley, chopped
¼ cup sweet pickle, chopped
½ cup mayonnaise or salad dressing
3 tablespoons garlic French dressing
1 tablespoon lemon juice
1 teaspoon grated onion, or onion juice
1 teaspoon celery seed
1 teaspoon salt
¼ teaspoon pepper

Peel and devein shrimp. Combine with macaroni, cauliflower, celery, parsley and pickle. Mix mayonnaise, French dressing, lemon juice, onion, celery seed, salt and pepper. Add to macaroni mixture; toss and refrigerate. Serve on lettuce.
Yield: 6 servings

Evelyn Ipock Dill (Mrs. William L.)

SHRIMP AND RICE SALAD

2 cups shrimp, boiled, shelled and deveined
1 cup celery, chopped
3 scallions or green onions, chopped
1 bunch chopped chives, *or* 1 tablespoon dried chives
2 tablespoons chopped sweet pickle
2 eggs, hard-boiled and chopped
1 cup mayonnaise
½ teaspoon celery salt
½ teaspoon dried dill weed
1 cup rice, cooked and cooled
Salt and pepper to taste
Lemon juice to taste, start with 2 tablespoons
Toasted sesame seed, optional

Mix all ingredients, except shrimp. Do the "good-cook" tasting and add anything your taste fancies; this is the beauty of this recipe. After all tasting is done fold in the shrimp. Serve on lettuce and garnish with parsley.

Variations:
Elbow macaroni instead of rice, add cooked, frozen peas
Yield: 6-8 servings

Jean Schocke McCotter (Mrs. Clifton L.)

TABULI (LEBANESE SALAD)

2 cups cracked wheat*
4 tomatoes, cut in wedges
4 regular-sized bunches of parsley
1 teaspoon salt
1 teaspoon pepper
½ cup lemon juice
1 cup Mazola corn oil
1 tablespoon dried mint *OR* fresh, if available

*Available in the gourmet section of most supermarkets, called bulgur.
Soak cracked wheat in cold water for 1 hour. While the wheat is soaking, clean and finely chop parsley. Squeeze wheat in handfuls and add to parsley with remaining ingredients. Serve in lettuce cups with any meal.
Yield: 6 servings

Aggie Shapou Derda (Mrs. Cletus F.)

SHIPBOARD SALAD

Do a day ahead

1 large head of lettuce, cut in chunks and well-drained
1 cucumber, medium to large, shredded
2 celery stalks, medium to large, shredded
1 can water chestnuts, thinly sliced
1 package uncooked frozen peas, thawed and well-drained
1 large onion, thinly sliced
Mayonnaise
⅓ cup Parmesan cheese
6-8 slices bacon, fried and crumbled
Cherry tomatoes

Layer in order listed. Spread mayonnaise over top of salad, covering completely. Sprinkle Parmesan cheese over top, cover and refrigerate. Before serving, sprinkle on crumbled bacon, halve the cherry tomatoes and arrange around edge of salad. Your food processor can be helpful in making this recipe.

Nancy G. Taylor (Mrs. Harry C.)

SPINACH SALAD AND DRESSING

Make day ahead or early in day

Salad:
1 pound spinach
7 strips bacon, fried and crumbled
2 eggs, hard-boiled and crumbled
1 (4-ounce) can water chestnuts (optional)

Wash spinach thoroughly and tear into bite-sized pieces. Wrap drained spinach in clean tea towel and refrigerate until needed. Crumble the eggs and bacon and refrigerate in separate covered containers. Slice water chestnuts and refrigerate in covered container. At serving time combine salad ingredients in large salad bowl.

Dressing:

3 tablespoons catsup
½ cup corn oil
2 teaspoons Worcestershire sauce
2 tablespoons sugar
½ onion, chopped fine
2 tablespoons vinegar
Salt to taste

Combine dressing ingredients in a jar and shake well. Refrigerate until needed. At serving time pour dressing over salad and toss lightly.
Yield: 6-8 servings

Bea Lee Newton (Mrs. Eldon S., Jr.)

GRAPEFRUIT SALAD AND CHILI DRESSING

Part prepared ahead

Dressing:

1 (12-ounce) bottle chili sauce
1 large onion, quartered
1 scant cup salad oil
2 teaspoons sugar
1 cup vinegar (more or less)

Dissolve sugar in vinegar. In a quart jar combine the chili sauce, onion and oil. Add enough vinegar to fill the jar. Refrigerate until serving time.

Salad:

1 head lettuce
Canned or fresh grapefruit slices
Bermuda onion, thinly sliced
Mandarin orange slices (optional)

In a large salad bowl or on individual salad plates, combine cleaned and drained lettuce which has been torn into bite-sized pieces, onion slices and grapefruit slices in desired quantity. Mandarin orange slices are also a nice addition to the grapefruit. Toss salad with chili dressing.
Yield: 6-8 servings

Barbara Straub Stewart

LAYER SALAD

Do day ahead

2 packages fresh spinach, torn in pieces
1 pound bacon, cooked and crumbled
10 hard-boiled eggs, sliced
1 cup (or less) green onions, sliced
1 head iceburg lettuce, torn in pieces
1 (8-ounce) package frozen green peas, defrosted
2½ cups Duke's mayonnaise
2½ cups sour cream
Worcestershire to taste
Tabasco to taste
Salt to taste
Pepper to taste
Lemon juice to taste
1½ cups Swiss cheese, grated

Mix the mayonnaise, sour cream, Worcestershire, Tabasco, salt, pepper and lemon juice together. Wash and prepare salad greens, vegetables and bacon. Layer ingredients in 13x9-inch casserole in order listed above. Spread sour cream mixture evenly over top of salad. Sprinkle Swiss cheese over top. Cover and refrigerate for at least 24 hours.
Yield: 10-12 servings

Janet Grainger Corcoran (Mrs. James M.)

OVERNIGHT SALAD

Prepare day ahead
Stores well

1 head lettuce
½ cup celery, chopped
½ cup green pepper, chopped *OR* water chestnuts, chopped
½ cup purple onion rings
1 (16-ounce) can LeSueur peas, drained
¼ cup Parmesan cheese
8 strips bacon, fried and crumbled
Dressing

Shred lettuce. Place in salad bowl. Add in layers remaining ingredients. You may have one layer of each or divide ingredients so that there are two layers of each. Spread dressing evenly over top. Sprinkle with cheese. Add bacon bits. Cover tightly and refrigerate overnight or 8-12 hours.

Dressing:

1-2 cups Miracle Whip Salad Dressing

2-5 teaspoons Italian dressing

Mix ingredients and blend until smooth.
Yield: 8-12 servings

Becky Melton Kafer (Mrs. C. William)
Grace Dixon Sellers (Mrs. John H.)

MAGNIFICENT CAESAR SALAD

Part done ahead

1 clove garlic, chopped
¼ cup salad oil
2½ cups (¼-inch) bread cubes, toasted
2 quarts crisp chilled salad*
½ cup salad oil
1 teaspoon Worcestershire sauce
Black pepper, freshly ground
Salt to taste
1 raw or coddled egg**
¼ cup lemon juice
1 (3-ounce) wedge Blue or Roquefort cheese, crumbled

*Salad may be head lettuce, watercress, Bibb lettuce, endive or romaine.
**To coddle an egg, place cold egg in warm water. Heat to boiling in enough water to completely cover egg. Transfer egg from warm water to boiling water using a spoon. Remove pan from heat. Cover and let stand 30 seconds. Immediately cool egg in cold water.
Add garlic to ¼ cup salad oil; let stand several hours in a jar; remove the garlic and pour oil over the toasted bread cubes. Toss well. Tear salad greens into bite-sized pieces. Place them in a large bowl with ½ cup salad oil and the seasonings. Drop raw or coddled egg into greens; sprinkle with lemon juice; add cheese; toss salad until all greens are coated with the oil dressing. When ready to serve, toss the croutons into the salad, mixing lightly. Serve immediately.
Yield: 6 servings

Jane Johnson Straub (Mrs. Robert L.)

BLUE CHEESE DRESSING

Better than any store-bought dressing!

½ pint cider vinegar
2 beef bouillon cubes
1 pint Wesson oil
2 tablespoons sugar
20 stuffed olives, sliced
2 teaspoons capers
¼ pound blue cheese, mashed
1 clove garlic, minced
½ pint tomato catsup
1 teaspoon paprika
1 teaspoon salt
2 teaspoons Worcestershire

Heat vinegar and bouillon cubes over medium heat until cubes are completely dissolved. Add remaining ingredients. Store in the refrigerator.
Yield: More than 1 quart

Julia Woodson Hudson (Mrs. John S., Jr.)

ROQUEFORT DRESSING

May be made ahead
Keeps several weeks in refrigerator

1 pint mayonnaise
1 pint sour cream
½ pound Roquefort or 2 (3-ounce) packages, grated
Juice of ½ lemon
1 teaspoon vinegar
1 small onion, grated
Salt
Pepper

Mix all ingredients together until blended using salt and pepper to taste.

SOUR CREAM DRESSING

1½ cups sour cream
¼ teaspoon salt
½ teaspoon curry powder
¼ teaspoon sugar
1 teaspoon prepared mustard
½ teaspoon Worcestershire sauce
1 teaspoon lemon juice
¼ teaspoon garlic salt

Combine all ingredients; mix thoroughly. Serve on salad greens, vegetable salad or cole slaw.
Yield: 1½ cups

Ruth V. Miles (Mrs. Daniel M.)

JANE'S FRENCH DRESSING

1 cup Heinz hot catsup
1 tablespoon to 1 cup sugar or artificial sweetener
1 cup oil
1 cup vinegar
¼ teaspoon salt
¼ teaspoon pepper
½ teaspoon oregano
2 cloves garlic, minced

Combine all ingredients in blender. Refrigerate. Can be stored in 32-ounce catsup bottle.

Deborah Cook Tayloe (Mrs. John C.)

FRENCH DRESSING

½ cup oil
¼ cup sugar
¼ cup vinegar
¾ cup catsup
1 teaspoon salt
¼ teaspoon paprika
1 small onion, chopped or quartered

Place in blender and mix well.
Yield: 2 cups

Katherine Dodge Beckwith (Mrs. George H.)

MASON JAR DRESSING

1 can tomato soup
¾ cup salad vinegar
1 teaspoon salt
½ teaspoon paprika
½ teaspoon pepper
1 teaspoon onion juice
1 tablespoon Worcestershire sauce
1 tablespoon dry mustard
1½ cups oil
½ cup sugar (or less, according to taste)

Put all ingredients in quart jar and shake well. A clove of garlic kept in jar adds to the flavor. Refrigerate.

Kay Best Burrows (Mrs. Charles M.)

COOKED SALAD DRESSING

Do day ahead
Stores well - can keep for weeks
Can double
Very good with slaw and potato salad

4 tablespoons butter
2 tablespoons flour
1 cup milk
3 eggs
1 tablespoon dry mustard
1 teaspoon salt
1/8 teaspoon cayenne pepper
1/4 teaspoon paprika
1 1/2 tablespoons sugar
1/2 cup cider vinegar

Melt butter. Add flour; then half the milk. Place in double boiler. Beat eggs; add all seasonings and vinegar. Stir this into mixture in double boiler. Add remaining milk and cook, stirring constantly until custard consistency. Pour into a jar and keep covered in refrigerator.
Yield: about 2 cups

Carol Webb Pullen (Mrs. John S.)

RUSSIAN DRESSING

3/4 cup mayonnaise
1/2 cup tomato catsup
1 green pepper, chopped
1 hot pepper, chopped
1 onion, grated
1/3 cup chili sauce

Place all ingredients in container. Mix thoroughly and put in jar to store in refrigerator.

Lucy Dunn McCotter (Mrs. Charles K.)

HERB BUTTER

1/2 cup butter, softened
1/8 teaspoon thyme
Dash of garlic powder
1/8 teaspoon oregano
1/8 teaspoon basil

Mix ingredients altering herbs as taste dictates. May be used on breads, vegetables or baked potatoes.

HONEY-LEMON DRESSING

2 tablespoons honey, strained
2½ tablespoons lemon juice
¾ cup salad oil
Dash cayenne pepper and salt
1 (3-ounce) package cream cheese
½ lemon rind, grated

Gradually add honey and lemon juice to cream cheese; blend until smooth. Add lemon rind. Add oil slowly, beating well after each addition, season to taste. Add additional lemon juice if a more tart dressing is desired.

Margaret Whitehead Wall (Mrs. Lawrence D.)

LEMON-SHERRY DRESSING

Delicious with fresh fruit such as apples, pears and bananas or oranges, grapefruit and grapes.
Make early in day

2-3 lemons
⅓ cup sugar
¼ cup dry sherry
¼ teaspoon salt*

*Omit salt if using cooking sherry
Through a strainer, over a measuring cup, squeeze lemons to make ½ cup fresh lemon juice. Add sugar, stirring until dissolved. Add sherry and salt. Chill.
Yield: ¾ cup dressing.

Ruth V. Miles (Mrs. Daniel M.)

RAISIN SAUCE FOR HAM

1 cup raisins
1 cup water
¼ cup vinegar
¼ cup brown sugar
1 teaspoon mustard
1 teaspoon Worcestershire sauce
½ teaspoon salt
1 tablespoon flour
1 tablespoon butter (optional)

In a saucepan cook raisins and water for ten minutes over medium heat. Mix together all other ingredients and add to tender raisins. Cook until thick and add butter, if desired.

Sylvia Hunt Cotton (Mrs. Lawrence M.)

WINE SAUCE FOR BARBECUED CHICKEN

½ cup butter, melted
1 cup white wine or sherry
Green onions, chopped
1 teaspoon Worcestershire sauce
1 teaspoon salt
Dash pepper
Juice of 2 lemons
½ teaspoon garlic salt

In large skillet with lid, mix all ingredients for sauce and simmer over low heat a few minutes until well-blended. Add chicken; cover and continue to heat until chicken is tender, about 45 minutes. While chicken is heating, prepare barbecue grill. When chicken is tender, place on grill to brown. Grilling is at a minimum as the chicken is already cooked.

Carole Beasley McKnight (Mrs. Thomas J.)

BARBECUE SAUCE

½ cup butter or margarine
¼ cup vinegar
½ cup water
2 tablespoons sugar
1 tablespoon prepared mustard
1 onion, chopped fine
½ tablespoon black pepper
½ tablespoon salt
¼ tablespoon red pepper
1 lemon, thinly sliced
½ cup catsup
2 tablespoons Worcestershire sauce

Cook all ingredients in saucepan over low heat for 20 minutes. Sauce is delicious with chicken or pork.
Yield: 4-6 servings

Margaret Hay Stallings (Mrs. Robert L.)

VALENCIA SAUCE

This is delicious with game birds.

½ cup butter
½ cup cornstarch or flour
¼ cup frozen orange juice concentrate
¼ cup frozen lemonade concentrate
¼ cup red wine
3 cups chicken stock

Melt butter in saucepan. Stir in flour. Add remaining ingredients with juices still frozen. Bring to boil; remove from heat. Use as a marinade and/or baste birds with mixture.
Yield: 1 quart

SAUCE FOR BARBECUED CHICKEN

1 fryer, cut in pieces
Flour
Salt
Pepper
Oil
⅓ cup onion, sliced
1 teaspoon salt
2 tablespoons vinegar
1 tablespoon sugar
1 tablespoon Worcestershire sauce
½ teaspoon chili powder
¼ teaspoon black pepper
½ cup catsup
¼ cup water

Dredge chicken in flour, salt and pepper and brown in oil. Do not cook completely. Mix remaining ingredients and pour over chicken which has been put in a baking dish, and bake at 350 degrees for about 1 hour.

Mary Moulton Barden (Mrs. Graham A., Jr.)

LOBSTER SAUCE

Brown sugar
Spicy brown mustard
White wine
Rosemary

Take an equal part of brown sugar and spicy brown mustard; stir to a thin consistency adding a little white wine until the mixture begins to clear. Add rosemary to taste and serve with lobster.

Elizabeth Scales Marsh (Mrs. Thomas B.)

SWEET AND SOUR SAUCE

This is delicious with cooked bite-sized shrimp or with bits of boned chicken breast which have been coated with cornstarch and fried crisp.

½ cup green pepper, chopped
½ cup onion, chopped
1 tablespoon oil
1 (8-ounce) can pineapple chunks
½ cup white vinegar
½ cup brown sugar, packed
¼ cup water
2 tablespoons soy sauce
1 tablespoon cornstarch

Sauté green pepper and onion in oil until tender-crisp. Drain pineapple *reserving* syrup. To syrup blend vinegar, brown sugar, water, soy sauce and cornstarch. Add to sautéed vegetables and cook, stirring constantly until sauce is thick and clear. Add pineapple and heat thoroughly. If desired, add cooked shrimp or fried chicken and serve over hot rice.
Yield: 1½-2 cups sauce, 4-6 servings with meat and rice

LONDON BROIL MARINADE

Easy
Do day ahead

½ cup oil
6 tablespoons soy sauce
6 tablespoons catsup
2 tablespoons vinegar
½ teaspoon sugar
½ teaspoon pepper
1 teaspoon garlic powder
Steak or roast of your choice

Mix well in 9 x 13-inch casserole dish all ingredients except meat. Place steak or roast in marinade. Refrigerate 24 hours turning several times. Grill steak over charcoal, basting with marinade as you turn. You may heat marinade and serve as a sauce with the meat.
Yield: 1⅛ cup marinade

Anna Cartner Kafer (Mrs. Oscar A., III)

MRS. LEVINE'S VERSATILE SAUCE

½ cup fresh, or dried dill weed, chopped
2 tablespoons onion juice
1-2 cloves garlic, chopped
½-¾ teaspoon salt
⅛ teaspoon black pepper
2 tablespoons olive oil
1 cup sour cream
½ cup mayonnaise

Mix dill with onion juice, chopped garlic, salt and pepper. Stir olive oil into sour cream; add mayonnaise. Whip the mix thoroughly. Add combined seasonings. Chill thoroughly and serve cold as accompaniment for both fish and meats.
Yield: 2 cups

Kathleen Winslow Budd (Mrs. Bern)

BROCCOLI SAUCE ("MOCK HOLLANDAISE")

½ cup mayonnaise
2 teaspoons prepared mustard
Juice of ½ lemon
Salt to taste

Mix all together, heat, and stir over low heat until smooth. Do not boil. Quick and easy and tasty!

Becky Elmore Clement (Mrs. Joseph M.)

PERFECT HOLLANDAISE SAUCE

15 minutes before serving

3 egg yolks
2 tablespoons lemon juice
½ cup butter or margarine, cut in thirds
¼ teaspoon salt

In top of double boiler beat egg yolks and lemon juice until well mixed with a wire whisk. Add ⅓ of the butter and cook over hot, *NOT BOILING,* water beating constantly until butter is completely melted. Repeat with another ⅓ of the butter. Repeat with remaining butter, beating until mixture thickens and is heated through; remove from heat. Stir in salt. Keep warm.

To *HOLD* sauce, discard hot water from boiler bottom and fill ⅓ full with lukewarm water; replace top. If kept too warm, sauce will thin and may curdle. *RECOVERING CURDLED SAUCE* is possible by placing a teaspoon of lemon juice and a tablespoon of curdled sauce in a bowl. Beat with whisk until creamy and thickened. Gradually beat in remaining sauce a tablespoon at a time, making sure each addition has thickened before adding the next. Yield: ⅔ cup sauce

PROCESSOR HOLLANDAISE SAUCE

Food processor

4 egg yolks
2 tablespoons lemon juice
½ teaspoon salt
Dash Tabasco
½ cup unsalted butter, melted and bubbling

Process egg yolks, lemon juice, salt and Tabasco together about three minutes. With processor still running add butter still bubbling from stove. This is very important as retained heat from butter cooks eggs.
Yield: 1 cup

Anne Fowler Hiller (Mrs. Carl J.)

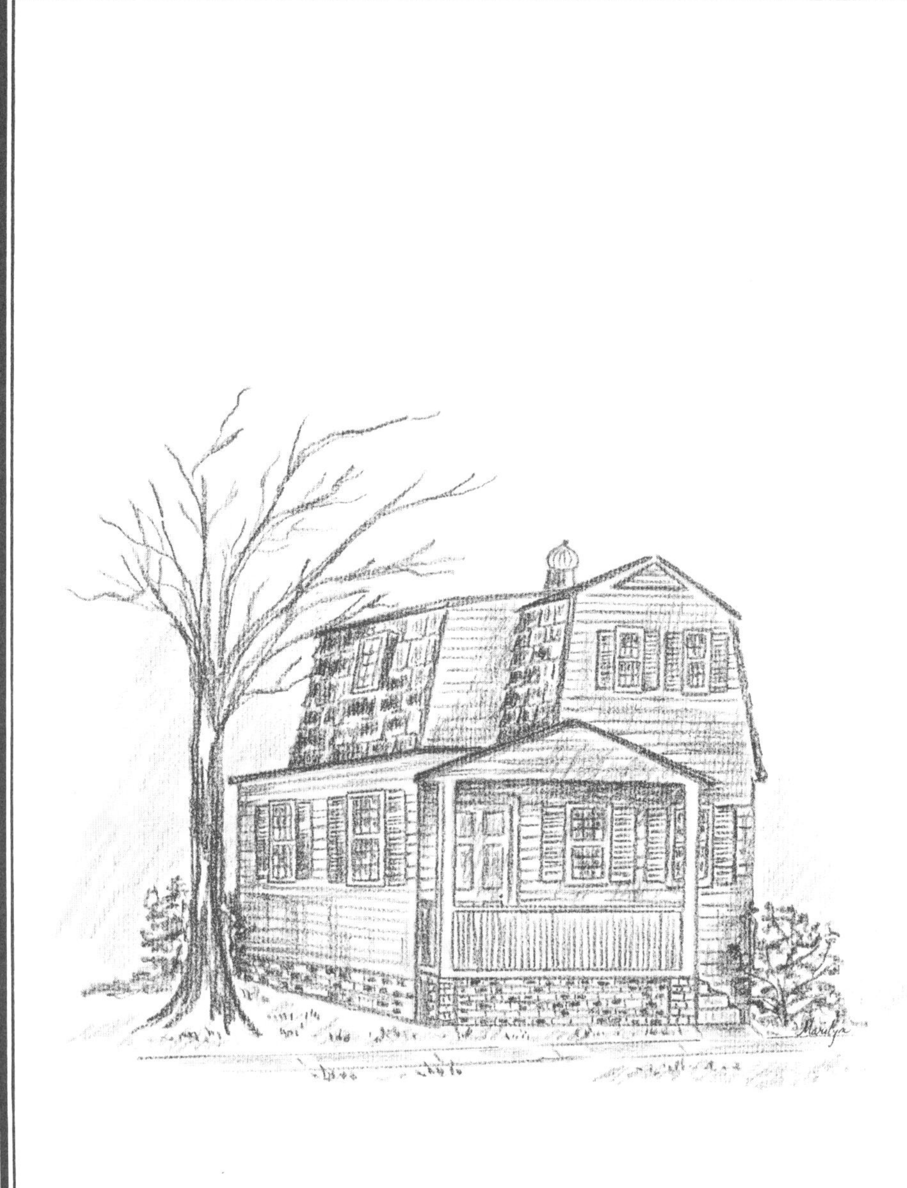

Clark House **419 Metcalf Street**

Built in the latter half of the 18th century, this Georgian house once served as a school (1789-1800). At that time it had an outside staircase by which students reached the second floor classroom. The present owner is Mrs. Elijah Taylor.

Soups, Stews, and Sandwiches

STRAWBERRY SOUP

4½ cups ripe strawberries
1¾ cups confectioners' sugar
2 cups sour cream
3 cups claret wine
3 cups cold water
8 whole strawberries

Press strawberries through a sieve. Stir in the sugar and sour cream. Add wine and water. Simmer over very low heat, stirring constantly with wooden spoon. Do NOT boil. Serve soup cold, garnished with berries and sprinkled with confectioners' sugar.
Yield: 8 servings

Freeze fruit in water in separate compartments in ice cube tray and float as a garnish in cold soups. Strawberries or raspberries are good choices for fruit soups and lemons or lime slices for vegetable soups.

COLD PEACH SOUP

Make ahead
Delicious for summer luncheon with vegetable or chicken salad sandwich

3 tablespoons quick-cooking tapioca
3 tablespoons sugar
Dash of salt
2½ cups water
1 (6-ounce) can frozen orange juice concentrate
2 pounds peaches
1 tablespoon lemon juice

Pureé peaches with lemon juice. Set aside. Combine tapioca, sugar, salt and 1 cup of water and heat to a full boil in saucepan, stirring constantly. Transfer to medium-sized bowl. Stir in orange juice until melted. Add remaining 1½ cups water and stir smooth; add pureéd peaches. Stir, cover and chill. Serve cold.
Yield: 8 servings

COLD CUCUMBER SOUP

Can do ahead

1 (10-ounce) can Pepperidge Farm Vichyssoise soup
1 large cucumber, peeled
1 green onion
Dash of lemon juice
Dill weed, salt, and pepper, to taste
Sour cream

Blend all ingredients well in a food processor or a blender. Garnish with a dollop of sour cream.
Yield: 3 servings

Alice Graham Underhill (Mrs. T. Reed)

CUCUMBER SOUP

½ cup shallots or onions, minced
3 tablespoons butter
46 ounces chicken broth
3 (8-inch) cucumbers, peeled and diced
1½ teaspoons wine vinegar
¾ teaspoon dill
4 tablespoons quick-cooking farina
½ cup sour cream (optional)
Cayenne pepper (optional)

Sauté shallots in butter. Put broth in saucepan, add shallots, cucumbers, vinegar, dill and bring to a boil. Stir in the farina and simmer, partially covered, 20-25 minutes. Pureé in blender. Put back in saucepan and heat through. Add sour cream and/or cayenne pepper if desired.
Yield: 4-5 servings

Miriam Schulman Allenson (Mrs. Andrew J.)

DELICIOUS SOUP

Will reheat often and freeze well

1 large onion, chopped
1 pound lean ground beef
2 (10-ounce) cans cream of celery soup
1 (46-ounce) can V-8 juice
2 cups carrot, grated (may grate them in blender)
Season to taste

Sauté onion and ground beef until beef is pink. Add other ingredients and cook slowly for 1 hour.
Yield: 6 servings

Betty Cleveland Livingston (Mrs. Cherry)

GAZPACHO

1 (46-ounce) can tomato juice
¼ cup dry sherry
¼ cup olive oil
¼ cup wine vinegar
1 tablespoon Worcestershire
Dash Tabasco
1 mild onion, grated
3 cucumbers, peeled and diced
3 tomatoes, peeled and diced
2 green peppers, chopped
1 teaspoon salt
¼ teaspoon pepper
1 teaspoon MSG or Accent (optional)
1 teaspoon parsley flakes
½ teaspoon basil
½ teaspoon thyme
½ teaspoon celery salt
½ teaspoon garlic salt

Combine liquid ingredients together in a large bowl. Add the spices and stir until well-blended. Add the fresh vegetables and stir. Cover and chill in the refrigerator until ready to serve, preferably 12 to 24 hours. The flavor improves the longer it sits. Serve with crackers or croutons for garnish.
Yield: 8-10 servings

Alice Graham Underhill (Mrs. T. Reed)

SUMMER SOUP

Do not do ahead
Frances Eaddy of Raleigh, N. C., who gave me this recipe, always took this soup to sick friends.

3 cups water
2½ teaspoons salt
1 cup raw carrots, sliced
1 cup raw potatoes, diced
1 pound fresh or frozen garden peas
1 cup cauliflower florets
¼ pound fresh broccoli florets
2 tablespoons flour
3 cups milk
¼ teaspoon pepper
Parsley

In large saucepan bring to boil 3 cups water and salt. Add carrots and potatoes, simmer covered 10 minutes. Add peas, cauliflower, broccoli and simmer covered 10 minutes. Blend flour with small amount of milk until smooth and add to vegetable mixture with remaining milk and pepper. Simmer 5 minutes. Sprinkle with parsley when serving.
Yield: 4 servings

Betty Simon (Mrs. Donn L.)

HAMBURGER SOUP

Freeze
Can do ahead
Do early in day
Improves with reheating

1½ pounds ground beef
1½ cups onion, chopped
¼ cup green pepper, chopped *OR* canned green chiles, seeded and chopped
1 garlic clove, minced
2 cups carrots, grated
½ pound mushrooms, minced *OR* (4-ounce) can mushrooms, drained
1 (46-ounce) can tomato juice
2 (10¾-ounce) cans cream of mushroom soup
1 teaspoon basil
1 teaspoon salt
½ teaspoon paprika
1 teaspoon cumin
1 teaspoon chili powder
¼ teaspoon pepper
1 (16-ounce) can red kidney beans, drained *OR* (16-ounce) can yellow corn, drained
Grated Cheddar cheese

Brown meat in large heavy pot until it loses its color. Drain off fat. Add onions, peppers (or chiles), garlic and mushrooms. Cook until vegetables are soft. Add remaining ingredients except cheese and mix well. Bring to boil, cover and simmer ½ hour. Adjust seasonings to taste. Sprinkle cheese on each serving. I prefer to use green pepper and corn rather than the chiles and kidney beans which give this dish a more Mexican flavor. Either makes a great soup.
Yield: 6-8 servings

Barbara Straub Stewart

BEEF STOCK OF MANY USES

1 meaty neckbone
3 quarts water

In medium-sized crockpot place neckbone and water and cook on SLOW 8-10 hours. Refrigerate and remove congealed fat. Strain broth for onion soup and use meat for vegetable-beef soup.

Nancy Scearce Deans

POTATO AND TOMATO SOUP

2 large onions, sliced
¼ cup butter
2 (10½-ounce) cans consommé
2 cups canned tomatoes
Salt
Thyme
Marjoram
Basil
2 cups potatoes, sliced
3 cups water
Parmesan cheese
Croutons

Slice and cook onions gently in butter, covering them and stirring once in a while. They must not brown. Add consommé, tomatoes, salt, thyme, marjoram and basil and cook for 30 minutes. Add potatoes and water. Simmer covered until potatoes are soft. Rub everything through a sieve adding a bit of cream if you like. Serve with Parmesan cheese and croutons.
Yield: 8 servings

Helen Cannon Mewborn

Leftovers are great for soups. Store in freezer until needed along with meaty bones.

POTATO POTAGE

4 large potatoes, scrubbed well and cut in small chunks
¼ onion, diced
1 carrot, diced
Salt to taste
Pepper to taste
6 cups water
4 tablespoons butter
4 tablespoons flour
Paprika
Fresh parsley

Slowly boil potatoes, onion, carrot, salt and pepper in water approximately 45 minutes. In skillet, melt butter over low heat. Add flour and stir continuously until browned. Be careful *not to burn*. Remove skillet from heat and gradually add one ladleful of soup liquid stirring until smooth; use a whisk if necessary. Add flour mixture and paprika to soup; stir well and bring to a boil. Serve piping hot garnished with fresh parsley.
Yield: 6 servings

Lou H. Proctor (Mrs. Jimmie C.)

MIKE WIECZERZAK'S BROCCOLI CHOWDER

1 pound fresh broccoli
2 (12-ounce) cans chicken broth
3 cups milk
1 cup light cream (half and half)
1 cup cooked ham, chopped
1 teaspoon salt
¼ teaspoon black pepper
½ pound Swiss cheese, grated
¼ cup butter

Cook broccoli, covered, in *one* can chicken broth in large kettle for about ten minutes or until broccoli is just tender. Remove broccoli from broth; cool and chop coarsely. Add remaining chicken broth, milk, cream, ham, salt and pepper to broth in kettle. Bring to a boil over medium heat, stirring occasionally. Stir in remaining ingredients and chopped broccoli; heat just to serving temperature. Caution: Do not allow to boil again.
Yield: about 2½ quarts

Grace McElven Hancock (Mrs. C. Edward, Jr.)

HOT PUMPKIN BISQUE

Serve with salad or cooked vegetables and a hot bread or sandwich. Fresh fruit may be used as dessert.

2 tablespoons butter or margarine
½ cup onion, finely chopped
½ teaspoon celery seed
2 (16-ounce) cans pumpkin
1 (13¾-ounce) can chicken broth
2 cups half and half
1 tablespoon lemon juice
2 tablespoons sugar
2½ teaspoons salt
¼ teaspoon pepper
¼ teaspoon powdered cloves
⅛ teaspoon mace
Popcorn, popped, as garnish

Melt butter; add onion and celery seed, cooking until onion is tender but not brown. Stir in remaining ingredients. Cook, stirring occasionally until soup comes to a boil. Simmer 10 minutes. Garnish each serving with popcorn, if desired.
Yield: 7 cups

Anne Haughton Hansen (Mrs. Raymond S.)

HOMEMADE ONION SOUP

From the *Slim Gourmet*
76 calories per serving, including cheese-topped toast

1 tablespoon butter or vegetable oil
6 medium Spanish onions, thinly sliced
2 quarts strained beef broth or canned beef broth or consommé
1 teaspoon salt (omit if using canned soup)
1 teaspoon MSG (optional)
10 melba toast rounds
10 teaspoons freshly grated Romano, Parmesan or Swiss cheese

Heat butter or oil in non-stick Dutch oven; add ½ onion slices. Over low-medium heat, stirring with wooden spoon, breaking into rings, heat until golden brown. Add remaining onions, broth, MSG. Heat to boiling. Cover and simmer over low heat until onions are just tender—about 5 minutes. Ladle soup in bowls or large ovenproof tureen. Float melba toast and sprinkle with cheese. Place under preheated broiler until cheese bubbles.
Yield: 10 servings

Nancy Scearce Deans

FRENCH ONION SOUP

May do ahead and warm in oven when ready to eat.
This is good for bridge lunch served with a good salad.

3 large onions, sliced
2 tablespoons margarine
1 tablespoon flour
6 beef bouillon cubes
6 cups water
6 slices French bread
8 ounces Swiss cheese, grated
Parmesan cheese
Salt and pepper to taste

Cook onions in margarine about 5 minutes. Stir in flour, salt, pepper, bouillon cubes and water. Bring to boil, then simmer, covered, for 25 minutes. Sprinkle sliced French bread with Parmesan cheese and toast in oven. After soup is cooked put in individual ovenproof bowls; put slice of toasted bread on top, then sprinkle with grated Swiss cheese and place in oven at 425 degrees for about 10-15 minutes. Remove when cheese is melted.
Yield: 6 servings

Patty Starr Willis (Mrs. A. Rexford)

CROCKPOT NAVY BEAN SOUP

Better than Grandma's!

1½ cups dry Navy beans
5 cups water
1 carrot, finely chopped
¼ cup celery, finely chopped
1 small onion, finely chopped
1 (¾-pound) ham hock
½ teaspoon salt
Dash pepper

Soak beans for 12 hours & drain.

Place all ingredients in a 2-quart crockpot or slow cooker. Cook for 15 hours on low setting. Remove ham hock and discard skin, fat, and bone. Cut meat in small pieces and place in soup. Beans can be mashed if desired.

Mary Ann Psychas Dunn (Mrs. John G., III)

A stale piece of bread or a large lettuce leaf can be used to skim fat from soups or stews.

LENTILS, MONASTERY STYLE

Do day ahead
Easy
Can double
This soup is especially good with corn muffins or French bread.

¼ cup olive oil
2 large onions, chopped
1 carrot, chopped
½ teaspoon dried thyme
½ teaspoon dried marjoram
3 cups stock *OR* seasoned water or vegetable stock
1 cup dry lentils, washed
Salt to taste
¼ cup fresh parsley, chopped
1 (16-ounce) can tomatoes
¼ cup sherry
⅔ cup Swiss or Cheddar cheese, grated

Sauté onions and carrots in oil in a large pot or Dutch oven. Add seasonings, stock, lentils and tomatoes. Cook in covered pot until lentils are tender, about 45 minutes. Add sherry. To serve, place 2 tablespoons grated cheese in each serving bowl and top with soup or vice-versa.
Yield: 4-6 servings

Carol Webb Pullen (Mrs. John S.)

SGT. BISSETTE'S CRAB STEW

Sgt. Bissette worked at Cherry Point Marine Corps Air Station and gave this superb recipe to the McCotter family when my husband, Cliff, was a fire department dispatcher at Cherry Point. It is the best stew anyone has eaten at our house. If you don't have a big canning kettle that will hold 3-3½ dozen crabs, forget it!

NOTE: You can cook the crabs separately in boiling water with about 1 cup vinegar and plenty of salt, and then add to stew. McCotters think the crabs a bit less tasty this way.

CAUTION: When thickening stew stir constantly and watch heat—this mixture sticks easily.

3-3½ dozen crabs, dressed, cleaned, claws removed
½ pound bacon, fried and crumbled (use all the bacon grease, too)
4 large onions, chopped fine
4 large potatoes, chopped fine
2 cups green pepper, chopped (more if you like)
½ cup vinegar
8 ounces catsup
12 ounces canned tomatoes
3 quarts water
Corn meal

Boil all ingredients except crabs in 3 quarts water. Cook until vegetables are done. Put crabs and claws in stew and cook until done (bright orange color—about 15 minutes). Take crabs out of stew because they mush up if you thicken stew with crabs in it. Make a paste of corn meal and water and stir into stew mixture until thickened to taste. Put crabs back in, and call your guests—roll up your sleeves!

Jean Schocke McCotter (Mrs. Clifton L.)

ROUX

The heart of a good gumbo is the roux.

8 cups flour
4 cups cooking oil

Mix flour and oil together in a heavy ovenproof container. Place on center shelf in oven which has been preheated to 400 degrees. Bake at this temperature 1½-2 hours. Stir roux every 15 minutes. Roux should be a caramel color when done. Remove from oven, cool and transfer to containers with tight-fitting lids and store in refrigerator or freezer until needed.
Yield: enough roux for 4-6 pots of gumbo

THE PROFESSOR'S GUMBO

Gumbo is the African word for okra. This one vegetable is consistently found in gumbo recipes although others may vary.

May be frozen
Part done ahead

*Denote personal choices in favor of the latter suggestion.

1 cup cooking oil
1 cup flour
8 stalks celery, chopped
3 large onions, chopped
1 green pepper, chopped
2 cloves garlic, minced
½ cup chopped parsley (optional)
1 pound fresh or frozen okra, sliced
2 tablespoons shortening
2 quarts chicken stock
2 quarts water
½ cup Worcestershire sauce
Tabasco to taste (don't use much!)*
½ cup catsup
1 large ripe tomato, chopped (canned may be used)*
2 tablespoons salt
4 slices bacon, *OR* large slice ham, chopped
1 or 2 bay leaves
¼ teaspoon thyme (optional)*
¼ teaspoon rosemary
Red pepper flakes to taste (optional)*
2 cups cooked, chopped chicken
1 or 2 pounds cooked crabmeat
4 pounds boiled shrimp
1 pint oysters (optional)
1 teaspoon molasses *OR* brown sugar
Lemon juice, if desired
Cooked rice

Heat oil in heavy iron pot over medium heat. Add flour very slowly, stirring constantly with a wooden spoon until roux is medium brown. This will take from 30-40 minutes. Add celery, onion, green pepper, garlic and parsley; cook an additional 45 minutes to 1 hour, stirring constantly. Fry okra in 2 tablespoons margarine until brown. Add to gumbo and stir well over low heat for a few minutes. Mixture may be cooled, packaged, and frozen or refrigerated for later use at this point. Add chicken stock and water, Worcestershire, Tabasco, catsup, chopped tomato, salt, bacon or ham, bay leaves, thyme, rosemary, and red pepper flakes. Simmer for 2½-3 hours. About 30 minutes before serving, add cooked chicken, crabmeat and shrimp; simmer for 30 minutes. Add oysters during last 10 minutes of simmering. Add molasses or brown sugar. Lemon juice may be added at this point, if desired. Serve over cooked rice.
Yield: 12 servings

Dorothy Oglesby Stewart

FISH CHOWDER

Always best the next day—and the next, . . . if there is any.

To Serve 6:

1½ pounds Haddock filet*
3 cups water
4 medium potatoes (½ inch cubes)
1 small onion, minced
6 tablespoons butter or margarine
***or any sweet, white fish**

6 tablespoons flour
3½-4 cups whole or skim milk
1-1½ cups cream
Salt

To Serve 50:

10-12 pounds Haddock filet*
3½ quarts water
5-7 pounds potatoes (½ inch cubes)
6-8 small onions, minced

1 cup butter or margarine
1 cup flour
5 quarts whole or skim milk
1 pint cream
Salt

In large saucepan bring water to boil, add fish and reduce heat so fish will just simmer for 20-25 minutes. Salt while cooking. Peel and cut potatoes in ½-inch cubes. Cook in salted boiling water until just tender. Drain and add potatoes to fish. Mince onion and cook slowly in butter 6 to 8 minutes. Do not brown. Add flour and 1½ cups milk. Cook until thick, stirring constantly and add to fish. Add remaining milk. Heat gently.
Yield: 6 servings, 50 servings

Alice Graham Underhill (Mrs. T. Reed)

KAY'S CRAB BISQUE

1 (10-ounce) can pea soup
1 (10-ounce) can consommé
4 tablespoons sherry

Dash curry powder
1 (6-ounce) can crabmeat

Blend soups together. Add sherry and curry powder. Mix. Add crabmeat. Heat.
Yield: 4 servings

Anne Haughton Hansen (Mrs. Raymond S.)

CLAM CHOWDER

Serve immediately
Do NOT freeze
Can double

3 large potatoes
2 medium onions
3 slices bacon
1 bottle clam juice
1 pound of fresh clams *OR* 2 (6½-ounce) cans minced clams*
Pepper and salt to taste
1 tablespoon Worcestershire sauce
2 tablespoons corn meal

*I usually use Snow's Minced Clams and find the canned clams just as tasty as the fresh ones.

Dice potatoes and onions and stew in enough water to cover until soft. While potatoes cook, fry bacon until crisp. Save bacon fat, and crumble bacon. Add bacon fat and crumbled bacon to potato mixture. Simmer one minute. Add clams, clam juice, salt, pepper and Worcestershire sauce as desired. Thicken with corn meal, stirring constantly so as not to lump. Serve for lunch or as a preface to a full meal.
Yield: 6 servings

Isabelle Schocke Taylor (Mrs. Elijah)

HOBO STEW

A favorite with teenagers!

1 cup onion, sliced thin
1 cup green pepper, coarsely chopped
¼ cup olive oil
2 pounds ground beef chuck
1 (16-ounce) can red kidney beans, drained
1 tablespoon steak sauce
1 (16-ounce) can whole kernel corn, drained
1 can (32-ounce) Italian-style tomatoes
2 (8-ounce) cans tomato sauce
Dried basil, dry mustard, salt and pepper to taste

Cook onion and pepper in oil in a large skillet or kettle until onion is golden. Add beef and cook, stirring with a fork to break up meat, until browned. Add remaining ingredients and mix well. Cover and simmer 15 to 20 minutes.
Yield: 8-10 servings

Jean Schocke McCotter (Mrs. Clifton L.)

OYSTER STEW À LA GRAND CENTRAL STATION

By the Oyster Bar—at Grand Central Station, New York City

2 cups light cream
2 cups milk
1 quart freshly shucked oysters with their liquid
2 tablespoons butter
Salt
Pepper
Paprika

Heat the cream and milk in saucepan; do not boil. Heat the oysters in their liquid with the butter in another saucepan, until the oysters are plump, and the edges curl. Remove from heat immediately. Combine the two liquids. Season. Pour into heated soup bowls, sprinkle with paprika. Serve with oyster crackers.
Yield: 4-6 servings

Gabrielle Paluzsay Lippitt (Mrs. Devereux H.)

FLY-BY-THE-SEAT-OF-YOUR-PANTS OYSTER STEW

Do NOT freeze

3-4 slices bacon, cubed
2-3 scallions, chopped, tops and all
1/8 green pepper, sliced
1 pint oysters, or more if small
Milk, enough to cover
Salt
Pepper, freshly ground
Fresh parsley, chopped
1½ cups potatoes, cooked and diced (optional)

Brown cubed bacon until crisp and reserve a little fat to sauté scallions and pepper. Add oysters and simmer about 3 minutes in bacon fat. Add enough milk to cover. Add salt and freshly ground pepper and a lot of fresh parsley which has been chopped. Simmer about 10 minutes. Add diced, cooked potatoes if desired. Yummy!
Yield: 2 servings

Marian Bartlett Stewart (Mrs. Wm. Edward)

SISTER'S BRUNSWICK STEW

Do day ahead
Time consuming, but worth the effort.
Meats can be prepared one day ahead and refrigerated.
Frozen butterbeans and corn take longer to cook than canned vegetables.
Be sure to drain canned butterbeans and corn.

1 (4-pound) boneless pork loin
2 (6-7 pound) hens *OR* 4-6 fryers
9 medium potatoes
5½ quarts tomatoes, *OR* 6 (28-ounce) cans
3 pints butterbeans, *OR* 3 (16-ounce) bags
4 pints corn, *OR* 4 (16-ounce) bags
2 teaspoons sugar
Salt and pepper to taste
½ medium onion, chopped

Cut up and salt hens and cut up pork into bite-size pieces. Cover with water; cook very slowly until it separates from bones. Remove bones and skin. Skim off excess fat. Return meat to broth, add potatoes, cut in quarters and cook on medium. When done, mash potatoes to thicken broth. Add tomatoes, sugar, salt and pepper and cook until soupy. Add butterbeans; cook on low and stir frequently. Add corn last because it may stick to bottom of pan. Cook until butterbeans and corn are done, over low heat. This recipe makes an excellent one-dish meal and freezes very well. Be sure to keep scraping bottom of pan to prevent sticking.
Yield: 12-15 quarts

Helen Jernigan Shine (Mrs. James F., Jr.)

AUNT RUBY LEE'S EASY BRUNSWICK STEW

Do day ahead
Easy
Jiffy
Can double

1 (20-ounce) can Mrs. Fearnow's Brunswick Stew
1 (12-ounce) can V-8 juice
2 (6½-ounce) cans boned chicken
1 (7-ounce) can butter beans
1 (7-ounce) can shoe peg corn
1 (10-ounce) can chicken gumbo soup
Tabasco

Mix all ingredients except Tabasco and simmer 2 hours, stirring frequently. Add Tabasco a drop at a time to taste.
Yield: 4-5 servings

Lee Thompson McIntyre (Mrs. J. Brooks

WORKING GIRL CROCKPOT BEEF STEW

Must do the night before

2½ to 3 pounds boneless chuck roast
Flour
Crisco
1 medium onion, diced
½ cup sherry
3 (16-ounce) cans mixed vegetables
1 (16-ounce) can peeled tomatoes
1 (8-ounce) package fresh mushrooms, sliced
Pepper to taste
Seasoned salt to taste

Cut meat in strips, approximately ¼-inch wide and ½ inch long. Roll pieces in flour. Pour a small amount of Crisco in an iron skillet. When oil is hot, gently place ½ of the meat in the pan and brown. Remove and place meat in a *greased* crockpot. Repeat with remainder of beef. Dice onion and add to crockpot, along with the sherry. Sip a glass of sherry yourself! Add vegetables, pepper and seasoning. Let simmer until you go to bed. Refrigerate overnight. The next day remove from refrigerator and cook on the low setting. Total cooking time should be 6 to 8 hours. This is very good with hot muffins, tossed salad and red wine. The stew you do not eat can be divided in packages and frozen.
Yield: 6-8 servings

Sarah Elizabeth Mann

PAPA MORTON'S SATURDAY NIGHT SPECIAL

Easy

2 stalks celery, chopped
2 green peppers, chopped
1 Bermuda onion, chopped
½ (14-ounce) bottle catsup
1 (16-ounce) can kidney beans
1½ pounds ground beef

Sauté celery, pepper and onions until barely done. Add meat; brown and drain. Add catsup and mix well. Add kidney beans. Heat in saucepan. Serve with garlic bread.
Yield: 4-6

Alyce Faye Tilley Grant (Mrs. David J.)

"ONE POT" DINNER (for crockpot)

A big hit, especially with men!

½-1 pound ground beef
¾ pound bacon, cut in small pieces
1 cup onion, chopped
2 (16-ounce) cans pork and beans
1 (16-ounce) can kidney beans, drained
1 (16-ounce) can butter limas, drained
1 cup catsup
¼ cup brown sugar
1 tablespoon liquid smoke
3 tablespoons white vinegar
1 teaspoon salt
Dash pepper

Brown ground beef in skillet; drain off fat and put beef in crockpot. Brown bacon and onions; drain off fat. Add bacon, onions, pork and beans, kidney beans, butter limas, catsup, brown sugar, liquid smoke, vinegar, salt and pepper to crockpot. Stir together well. Cover and cook on low 4-9 hours. If using a 2-quart crockpot, reduce recipe by half.
Yield: 8 servings

Anne Knott Branch (Mrs. S. P.)

CHILI CON CARNE

Easy
Do early in day
Stores well

1 pound ground beef
1 large onion, sliced
1 green pepper, chopped
1 (29-ounce) can tomatoes
1 large or 2 small bay leaves
1-2 tablespoons chili powder
2 teaspoons salt
⅛ teaspoon cayenne pepper
⅛ teaspoon paprika
1 (15½-ounce) can kidney beans, drained
3 whole cloves
1 stick cinnamon

Crumble and brown ground beef in heavy skillet. Add onions and green pepper; cook until almost tender. Add tomatoes and seasonings. Cover and simmer for 2 hours. Add drained kidney beans and heat through. Remove bay leaves and spices. Serve in small bowls.
Yield: 6 servings

Melanie Applegate (Mrs. Earl A.)

CHARLIE'S BEEF BURGUNDY

4 slices bacon
1½ pounds beef top round, cut into 1-inch cubes
1 (10-ounce) can cream of mushroom soup
¼ cup Burgundy wine
2 tablespoons parsley, chopped
⅛ teaspoon pepper
¾ pound small white onions
½ pound (2 cups) mushrooms, sliced
½ pound noodles, cooked

In large skillet, cook bacon until crisp; crumble. Brown beef in drippings; pour off fat. Add soup, wine, parsley, and pepper. Cover and cook over low heat 1½ hours. Add onions and mushrooms. Cover and cook 1 hour or until beef is tender. Serve over noodles. Garnish with bacon and additional parsley.
Yield: 5-6 servings

Florence Woods Christie (Mrs. Charles W.)

BOEUF BOURGUIGNON

¼ pound salt pork, diced
2 pounds lean beef, chuck, rump or round, cut in 2-inch cubes
1½ teaspoons salt
Fresh ground pepper
2 tablespoons flour
1½ cups dry red wine
1½ cups water
Herb Bouquet*
1 pound small onions
½ pound mushrooms
Minced parsley

*Herb bouquet: In a cheesecloth square put 1 carrot, a sprig of parsley, 1 bay leaf, ½ teaspoon thyme and 1 clove of crushed garlic. Tie together with string.

Prepare Herb Bouquet. Fry salt pork until crisp; drain, reserving ½ cup of drippings. In 2 tablespoons of drippings, brown beef on all sides. Sprinkle with salt, pepper and flour. Toss. Place in heavy 2-quart casserole; add salt pork. To frying pan, add wine, water, Herb Bouquet. Bring to boil; pour over meat. Cover tightly. Cook until tender, about 2 hours. Skim off all salt pork drippings. Add onions to beef; cook 30 minutes. Add fresh mushrooms; cook 10 minutes and adjust seasonings.
Yield: 4-6 servings

Melanie Applegate (Mrs. Earl)

BEER BEEF STEW

4 pounds lean beef, cut into ½-inch slices
2 pounds large onions, thickly sliced
½ cup flour
½ cup cooking oil
6 garlic cloves, crushed
3 tablespoons dark brown sugar
¼ cup red wine vinegar
½ cup chopped parsley
2 small bay leaves
2 teaspoons thyme
1 tablespoon salt
Freshly ground black pepper
2 (10½-ounce) cans beef broth (2½ cups)
2 (12-ounce) bottles of beer (3 cups)

Preheat oven to 325 degrees. Dredge beef with flour; brown them a few at a time in hot oil and put them into a large ovenproof casserole. Add onions and garlic to oil in pan and lightly brown them; put them in the casserole. Combine sugar, 2 tablespoons of vinegar, parsley, bay leaves, thyme, salt and pepper; stir once or twice. Pour off any remaining oil in the skillet. Put broth in skillet and heat over low heat, stirring to loosen all browned bits remaining in skillet. Pour over meat mixture in casserole. Add the beer. Cover casserole and bake for 2 hours. Take the casserole out of the oven and put it on top of the range. Stir in the remaining 2 tablespoons of vinegar and cook over medium heat until the sauce bubbles.
Yield: 8-10 servings

Joan Wojno Limpach (Mrs. Ralph)

TURKEY-STUFFED POCKETS

1 package Pita bread, loaves cut in half
1 (8-slice) package boiled ham slices
2 cups turkey bits, or 8 turkey slices
2 medium onions, sliced
2 cups Cheddar cheese, shredded *OR* 8 slices
Shredded lettuce (optional)
2 medium tomatoes, sliced
Salt to taste
Pepper to taste
2 tablespoons butter, melted

Stuff each half of Pita bread with turkey, ham, onion, tomato, salt, peppe and cheese slices. Spread each half with melted butter and bake in preheate 400 degree oven for 5-8 minutes or until cheese has melted.
Yield: 8 sandwiches

Marilyn Miller Smith (Mrs. Stewart H.

HERBED BEEF STEW

May do ahead
Freezes very well
Poppy-seed Almond Noodles are a perfect accompaniment for this stew.

¼ cup butter or margarine
4 pounds beef chuck roast, cut into 1½-inch cubes
1 pound mushrooms, sliced
6 yellow onions, chopped
2 cloves garlic, crushed
1 tablespoon salt
¾ teaspoon basil
1 teaspoon dill
½ teaspoon thyme
½ teaspoon savory
2 bay leaves, crushed
¼ teaspoon pepper
1 (10-ounce) can beef consommé
2 (29-ounce) cans tomatoes
1 pound small white onions *OR* canned equivalent
1 (16-ounce) package carrots, cut into 2-inch lengths
6 tablespoons flour
½ cup cold water

Brown beef in butter. Add mushrooms, yellow onions, garlic and seasonings. Sauté slowly, stirring until onions are tender. Add consommé and tomatoes. Simmer 1½ hours. Add white onions and carrots. (If canned onions are used DO NOT add until carrots are tender.) Cover and cook 45 minutes. Mix the flour with ½ cup cold water and add to stew, stirring constantly until stew is thickened.
Yield: 12 servings

Robertha Kafer Coleman (Mrs. Thomas B.)

CONFETTI SANDWICH FILLING

1 (8-ounce) package cream cheese, softened
1 tablespoon lemon juice
Mayonnaise
¾ cup carrot, grated
¼ cup cucumber, grated
¼ cup onion, chopped

Combine lemon juice with softened cheese and add enough mayonnaise to make cheese of spreading consistency. Fold in grated vegetables. Spread on bread for sandwiches. Refrigerate leftover filling.

Ann Holmes Novak (Mrs. David W.)

PIRATE STEW

Can freeze

3 pounds chuck steak, cubed
2 (15½-ounce) cans peeled tomatoes
4 (16-ounce) cans V-8 juice
1 (28-ounce) can green beans
2 (16-ounce) cans Luck's Field Peas with snaps
2 (16-ounce) cans sliced squash
2 (16-ounce) cans green peas
2 (14-ounce) cans cut okra
2 (16-ounce) packages frozen limas
3 (16-ounce) packages frozen cut yellow corn
1 (16-ounce) package frozen white corn
3 pounds onion, peeled and diced
4 pounds potatoes, chunked
1 quart water
Seasoned salt
Rosemary
Bay leaf
Curry powder
Black pepper
Thyme

Cube chuck steak and brown in oil in bottom of soup pot. Add vegetables and season to taste, using seasonings listed. Simmer all day. Remove excess fat before serving.
Yield: 36 quarts

William E. Brinkley, Jr.

SHRIMP-STUFFED POCKETS

1 package Pita bread, loaves cut in half
Boiled shrimp, chopped
Onions to taste, minced
1 (10½-ounce) can condensed cream of shrimp soup
Melted butter

Combine shrimp, onions and soup and stuff halves of Pita bread. Spread melted butter on top of each half and warm in 400 degree preheated oven 5-8 minutes, or until heated through.
Yield: 8 sandwiches

Marilyn Miller Smith (Mrs. Stewart H.)

HOT CRAB SANDWICH

1½ cup Cheddar cheese, shredded
½ cup butter, softened
1¼ cup crabmeat, picked over
⅓ cup onion, finely chopped
¼ cup green pepper, finely chopped
1 teaspoon Worcestershire sauce
¼ cup Key lime juice
3 English muffins, halved
½ cup Cheddar cheese, shredded
Paprika

Mix all of the ingredients together, except the muffins, ½ cup cheese and paprika. Spread the muffin halves with the crabmeat mixture and sprinkle shredded cheese and paprika on top. Place under the broiler for 5-7 minutes or until heated through. Serve immediately.
Yield: 3-6 servings

Nancy G. Taylor (Mrs. Harry C.)

BARBECUED HAMBURGER MIX

An original
Doubles easily
May freeze

½ cup onion, diced
½ pound sausage
1 pound ground beef
1¼ teaspoons salt
¾ teaspoon cayenne powder
1½ teaspoons Worcestershire sauce
1 (6-ounce) can tomato paste
1 tablespoon catsup
2 tablespoons molasses
½ cup celery, chopped
2 teaspoons vinegar
½ teaspoon dry mustard
⅔ cup water
12 hamburger buns

Combine first four ingredients and brown in heavy frying pan or Dutch oven over medium heat. Drain off fat. Add the remaining ingredients. Cover and simmer 45 minutes, stirring frequently. Fills about 12 buns.
Yield: 6-10 servings

Peggy Witmeyer Bernard

SKILLET BURGERS

Freezes well and kids will love these!

1½ pounds ground beef
1 large onion, chopped
½ cup catsup
1 tablespoon brown sugar
2 tablespoons mustard
2 teaspoons Worcestershire sauce
2 tablespoons vinegar
Salt and pepper to taste

Brown meat. Pour off most of the fat. Add other ingredients and simmer ½ hour. Serve on hamburger buns.

Becky Elmore Clement (Mrs. Joseph M.)

VEGETABLE SANDWICH FILLING

Good with cold fruit or vegetable soup

1 cucumber, peeled
1 green pepper, seeded
1 large half-ripe tomato
1 small onion, quartered
1 carrot, peeled
1 tablespoon Knox gelatine
1 cup mayonnaise
Salt and pepper

Grind vegetables in blender; drain off juices and save. To 4 tablespoons of juices, add gelatine and dissolve over hot water. Add mayonnaise and melted gelatine to drained vegetables. Add salt and pepper to taste. Chill. Spread on choice of bread and serve.
Yield: 1½ cups

Barbara Straub Stewart

BAMBO'S BARBECUE SANDWICH

⅓ cup vegetable oil
¾ cup catsup
⅓ cup lemon juice
3 tablespoons Worcestershire sauce
1 teaspoon salt
½ teaspoon pepper
¾ cup onion, chopped
½ cup water
3 tablespoons sugar
2 tablespoons mustard
Leftover roast, pork or chicken
Hamburger buns

Sauté onion in oil until tender. Add remaining ingredients and stir until well-combined. Add meat and heat thoroughly. Serve on hamburger buns.

Robert L. Straub

"CHEESE-ICED" FILLED SANDWICHES

Freezes well
Prepare sandwiches on waxed paper for easy clean up.
This is a wonderful lunch when the girls come for bridge!

1 (24-ounce) King-sized loaf thin-sliced bread

Using three slices of bread per sandwich, cut rounds using a 16-ounce vegetable can as a "cutter". Bread may be left square with crusts removed, if preferred.

Filling:

2 cups chicken, cooked and diced*
4 eggs, hard-boiled and chopped
¼ cup ripe olives, chopped
⅔ cup mayonnaise (or more)
Onion flakes or fresh onion, grated to taste
Dash dry mustard
Lawry's Seasoned Salt to taste
Lawry's Seasoned Pepper to taste

*I prefer to increase the amount of chicken to 3½ cups and add two additional hard-boiled eggs. Ground ham or tuna may be used in place of chicken. Combine mayonnaise with seasonings and chicken. Fill two layers of sandwiches with mixture. "Ice" with following:

Icing:

2 (5-ounce) jars Old English cheese
2 raw eggs
½ cup butter, softened

Beat ingredients together until fluffy. Spread on tops and sides of the 8 sandwiches. Refrigerate 24 hours, or prepare for freezing. Bake in preheated 375 degree oven for 15 minutes.
Yield: 8 sandwiches

Phyllis Hurtgen Harke (Mrs. Dennis M.)

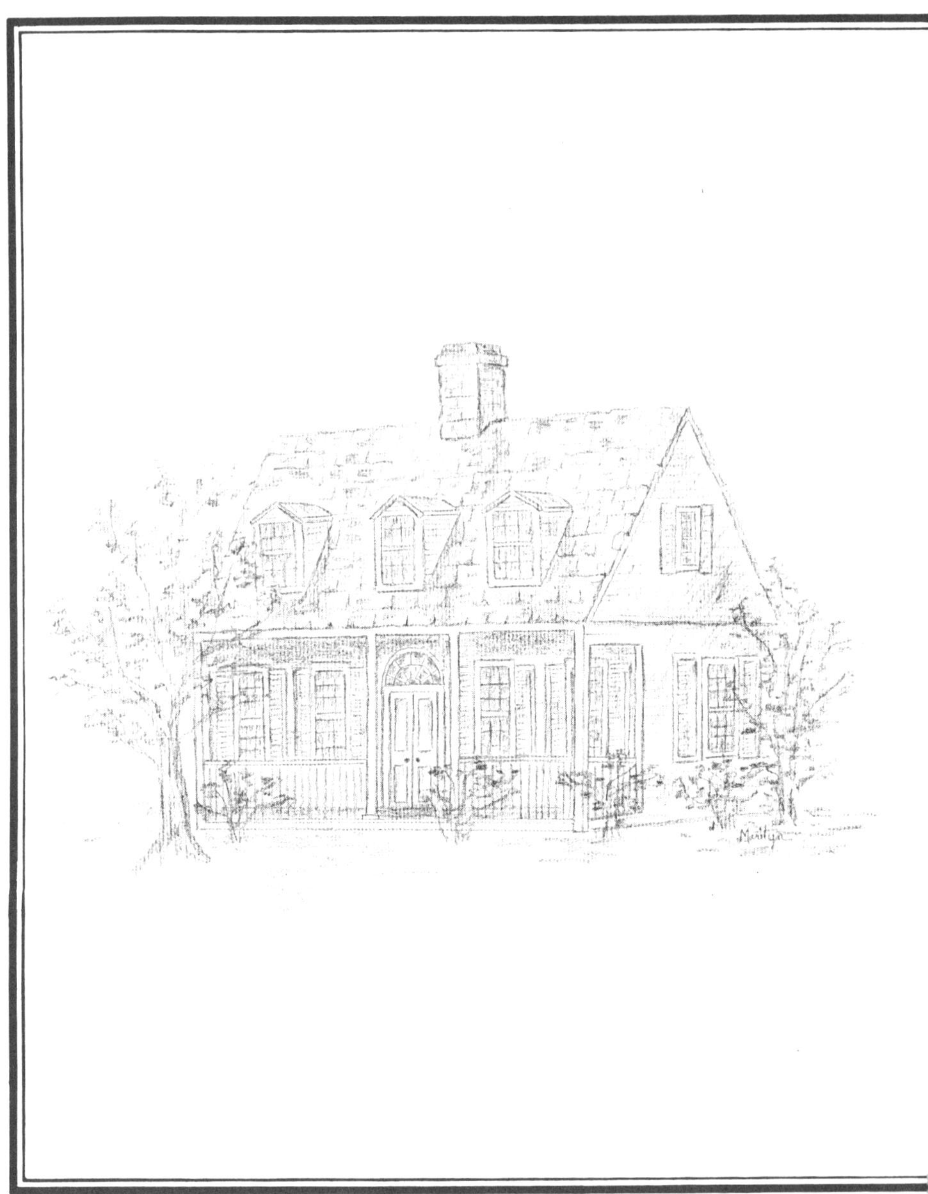

McLin-Hancock Cottage **507 Middle Street**

Like most very early New Bern homes, this elegant small dwelling cannot be precisely dated, but it was in existence by 1784. The balanced proportions of the exterior are highlighted by the graceful fanlight transome. Mr. C. E. Hancock, former warden and vestryman, and Mrs. Hancock, who has also served on the vestry, have restored and presently reside in this cottage which once was the home of Thomas McLin, a prominent 19th century coppersmith.

EGGPLANT PARMIGIANA EXPRESS

This speedy version with no "sautêing" in oil helps reduce calories.

1 medium eggplant (approximately 1½ pounds)
½ cup packaged bread crumbs
¾ cup grated Parmesan cheese
¼ cup mayonnaise
1 recipe Easy Tomato Sauce (recipe follows)
1 (8-ounce) package Mozzarella cheese, sliced

Wash and trim eggplant; cut into ½-inch slices. Combine crumbs and ¼ cup of Parmesan cheese. Spread mayonnaise thinly on both sides of one eggplant slice; dip into crumb mixture, coating both sides. Place on ungreased cookie sheet. Repeat with remaining slices. Bake at 425 degrees 10 to 15 minutes or until slightly tender. Remove from oven and lower temperature to 375 degrees. Grease a 9x13-inch shallow baking dish; arrange eggplant slices, slightly overlapping. Spread each slice with small amount of Easy Tomato Sauce; cover with slices of Mozzarella. Sprinkle half Parmesan over; spoon remaining Parmesan. Bake at 375 degrees for 15 minutes or until cheese is melted.

Susie Warren Ward (Mrs. John A. J.)

EASY TOMATO SAUCE

1 (6-ounce) can tomato paste
1½ paste cans water
¼ teaspoon basil
¼ teaspoon oregano
1 teaspoon brown sugar
¼ teaspoon salt
Dash pepper

Combine in small sauce pan and heat 10 minutes.
Yield: 4-6 servings

Susie Warren Ward (Mrs. John A. J.)

ARTICHOKE-SPINACH CASSEROLE

Economical
Do day ahead
Do not freeze

3 (10-ounce) packages frozen chopped spinach, cooked and drained
2 (3-ounce) packages cream cheese
4 tablespoons margarine
Salt and pepper to taste
1/8 teaspoon nutmeg
Grated rind of 1 lemon
1/2 cup bread crumbs
1 (16-ounce) can artichoke hearts

Preheat oven to 350 degrees. Grease casserole dish. Arrange drained artichoke hearts on the bottom of the dish. Blend cooked spinach and cheese and 2 tablespoons margarine then add spices. Pour on top of artichokes. Refrigerate at least 45 minutes. Blend crumbs with remaining margarine and add to top before baking. Bake for 25 minutes.
Yield: 4-6 servings

Nancy McDaniel Lewis

SUPERB ASPARAGUS CASSEROLE

3 eggs, hard-boiled and sliced
2 (14-ounce) cans asparagus spears
1 (8-ounce) can water chestnuts, drained, sliced
1/2 cup milk
6 tablespoons flour
1/4 cup butter or margarine
1/2 teaspoon salt
1/4 teaspoon pepper
1 cup sharp cheese, grated
2 tablespoons pimiento, diced
2/3 cup fresh bread crumbs

Preheat oven to 375 degrees. Measure 1 1/2 cups of the vegetable liquids. Put milk and flour in jar and shake until smooth; add vegetable liquid. In saucepan combine liquid mixture from jar with butter, seasonings and cheese and cook over low heat until thick. Add pimientos. Put the asparagus in a buttered casserole; top with chestnuts; cover with egg slices. Pour sauce over all and top with crumbs. Bake 30 minutes.
Yield: 6-8 servings

Jean Schocke McCotter (Mrs. Clifton L.)

ARTICHOKE FLAN

1 (9-inch) pie shell
1 egg white, unbeaten
1 (9-ounce) package frozen artichoke hearts *OR* 1 (12-ounce) can, rinsed
3 eggs
1½ cups heavy cream
1½ cups Swiss cheese, grated
½ teaspoon salt
¼ teaspoon thyme
Dash red pepper

Preheat oven to 375 degrees. Brush pie shell with egg white. Set aside to dry. If using frozen artichokes, cook according to directions and drain well, (or rinse and drain canned ones). In medium bowl, beat eggs with cream and stir in Swiss cheese, salt, thyme and pepper. Pour into pie shell. Arrange artichokes over surface. Bake at 375 degrees for 45-60 minutes, or until knife inserted in center comes out clean.
Yield: 6 servings

Genevieve Tolson Dunn (Mrs. Mark S.)

BARBECUED BAKED BEANS

Not your ordinary beans!

Great with barbecued pork

1 (16-ounce) can pork and beans
1 (16-ounce) can kidney beans, drained
1 (16-ounce) can green lima beans, drained
1 large onion, chopped
1 clove garlic, minced
1 tablespoon Worcestershire
1 teaspoon ground cumin
2-3 tablespoons strong cold coffee
¼ cup brown sugar
½ cup catsup
Pinch oregano
Pinch sweet basil
Dash Tabasco
3 strips bacon

Combine all ingredients in a 13x9-inch baking dish. Place bacon strips on top. Cover with foil and bake at 350 degrees for 1 hour. Remove cover and continue baking 15 additional minutes.
Yield: 10 servings

Penny Johnson McCaughan (Mrs. Mark R.)

BRANDY BEANS

My version of an old favorite

2 (16-ounce) cans pork and beans
3 slices bacon
1 large onion, sliced thin
½ cup Tang orange drink mix
2 tablespoons cider vinegar
1 jigger brandy

Mix all ingredients together except bacon slices and brandy. Put in bean pot or casserole and top with bacon slices, cutting up if necessary to cover the top. This can be refrigerated a day ahead, if necessary. Bake in very slow (250-300 degree) oven for 1-1½ hours. Longer will not hurt. Just before serving add 1 jigger of Brandy and stir casserole up from the bottom to mix. Your friends will try to detect the secret ingredients.
Yield: 8 servings

Dorothy Lee Taylor Jernigan (Mrs. Curtis D.)

GREEN BEANS SUPREME

Can be done early in day
Can be doubled

3 (16-ounce) cans French-style green beans
Bacon drippings
2 tablespoons onion, chopped
1 green pepper, chopped
½ cup pimiento, chopped
2 tablespoons margarine
1 (10½-ounce) can cream of mushroom soup
1 (2-or 4-ounce) can mushrooms
½ pound Velveeta cheese
¼ teaspoon Worcestershire sauce
1 cup Ritz crackers, crushed
Butter

Preheat oven to 375 degrees. In a saucepan cook beans long enough to season with bacon drippings and then add chopped onion. Drain. Place beans and onions in a 2-quart casserole. Sauté green pepper and pimiento in margarine. Add mushroom soup and mushrooms, cheese and Worcestershire. Cook until thick. Pour over beans in casserole. Sprinkle with crushed Ritz crackers and dot with butter. Bake until top is brown and heated thoroughly, about 30 minutes.
Yield: 8 servings

Mary Sue Price Pelletier

SWEET AND SOUR GREEN BEANS

Prepare day ahead

3 (16-ounce) cans whole green beans, drained
1 large onion, thinly sliced
½ cup vinegar
½ cup sugar
½ cup bacon drippings

Mix beans and onions together. Bring to a boil the vinegar, sugar and bacon drippings. Pour over onions and beans. Marinate in refrigerator at least 24 hours. Stir about four times while marinating. Heat in oven at 350 degrees for 40 minutes just before serving.
Yield: 8-10 servings

Anna Cartner Kafer (Mrs. Oscar A., III)

SAVORY BEETS

3 tablespoons vinegar
2½ cups cooked sliced beets (1 jar beets, drained)
¼ teaspoon ground cloves
½ teaspoon salt
¼ cup sugar
1 slice onion
2 tablespoons butter

Put the vinegar, ½ cup beets, cloves, salt, sugar, onion and butter in blender, cover and blend until smooth. Pour over remaining beets in saucepan. Simmer, stirring frequently, about 20 minutes.

BRUSSELS SPROUTS AND GREEN PEPPER

1 medium green pepper, cut into strips
½ cup celery, sliced
¼ cup onion, sliced
1 small clove garlic, pressed
2 tablespoons olive oil
2 (10-ounce) packages frozen Brussels sprouts, thawed and halved
2 tablespoons pimiento, chopped
1½ teaspoons salt
⅛ teaspoon pepper

In skillet sauté green pepper, celery, onion and garlic in oil until crisp-tender. Add Brussels sprouts, pimiento and seasonings. Cover and cook 5 minutes until Brussels sprouts are tender, stirring occasionally.
Yield: 6-8 servings

Anne Haughton Hansen (Mrs. Raymond)

BUFFET VEGETABLE BAKE

Can make ahead

2 (10-ounce) packages frozen mixed peas and carrots
1 (10-ounce) package frozen whole green beans
1 (5-ounce) can water chestnuts, drained and sliced
1 (3-ounce) can broiled mushrooms, sliced and drained

Cook peas and carrots with beans until just barely tender; drain. Combine with water chestnuts and mushrooms. Preheat oven to 350 degrees. Grease a 2-quart casserole and set aside.

Sauce:
1 (10½-ounce) can cream of mushroom soup
4 tablespoons cooking sherry
1 teaspoon Worcestershire sauce
Dash Tabasco
2 cups sharp American cheese, shredded
¼ cup rich round cracker crumbs

Combine all ingredients for sauce except for cracker crumbs. Toss with the vegetables. Turn into prepared pan and bake uncovered 40-45 minutes until hot and bubbly. Stir occasionally. Sprinkle with crumbs just before serving.
Yield: 8-10 servings

Henrietta Sherman Mitchell (Mrs. Alexander S., Jr.)

CABBAGE CASSEROLE

Easy
Economical
Stores well

1 head of cabbage
1 (10½-ounce) can celery soup
1 (10-ounce) package Cheddar cheese, grated

Cut up cabbage and layer it in a 8x11-inch casserole dish with celery soup and grated Cheddar cheese. Bake at 325 degrees for 35 minutes. Serve immediately.
Yield: 6-8 servings

Laura Hall Courter (Mrs. Kim)

BROCCOLI AND WILD RICE

1 to 1¼ pounds fresh broccoli cut in 1-inch pieces
1 (6¾-ounce) package long grain and wild rice
1 envelope sour cream mix
1 single-serving envelope of beef mushroom soup mix
½ teaspoon salt
2 cups milk
¾ cup soft bread crumbs
1 tablespoon butter, melted
¼ teaspoon paprika

Preheat oven to 350 degrees. Cook broccoli stem pieces, covered in boiling salted water about 5 minutes. Add broccoli flowerets and cool. Meanwhile, prepare rice according to directions. Combine dry package mixes and salt; gradually stir in milk. Combine cooked rice and sour cream mixture; fold in broccoli. Turn in 2-quart casserole. Combine bread crumbs, butter and paprika; sprinkle on top. Bake uncovered at 350 degrees for 20 to 25 minutes or until thoroughly heated.
Yield: 8 servings

Phyllis Hurtgen Harke (Mrs. Dennis M.)

A teaspoon of lemon juice can liven up canned vegetables or store bought salad dressings.

SKILLET CABBAGE

Part done ahead

2 slices bacon, fried and crumbled
4 cups cabbage, shredded
1 cup celery, sliced thin
1 cup carrots, shredded
1 green pepper, sliced thin (optional)
2 fresh tomatoes, cut in pieces *OR* 1 (16-ounce) can and half the juice (optional)
1 onion, sliced thin
Salt to taste
Pepper to taste
Sugar to taste

Fry bacon and crumble. Use grease left for cooking vegetables. Return bacon and all ingredients to pan. Cook about 20 minutes or longer until vegetables have cooked down. Serve immediately. I generally omit the green pepper and tomatoes. They give an entirely different taste to the basic recipe, if included.
Yield: 4-6 servings

Betty Simon (Mrs. Donn L.)

CHEESE SCALLOPED CARROTS

Make ahead
May freeze

12 carrots, peeled and sliced lengthwise
1 small onion, chopped
¼ cup margarine
¼ cup flour
1 teaspoon salt
¼ teaspoon dry mustard
2 cups milk
⅛ teaspoon pepper
¼ teaspoon celery salt
½ pound Velveeta cheese, sliced
Bread crumbs

Cook carrots in salted boiling water until "almost" tender. Drain. Simmer onions in margarine; add flour, salt and mustard; add milk and cook until smooth. Add pepper and celery salt. In a 2-quart casserole arrange a layer of carrots, then cheese and repeat layers until carrots and cheese are gone. Pour sauce over top and sprinkle bread crumbs over sauce. This may be covered and refrigerated or frozen until needed. Bake at 350 degrees 15-30 minutes depending on how cold the casserole is. If baking frozen, add an hour to the baking time.
Yield: 8 servings

Barbara Straub Stewart

BAKED CELERY AU GRATIN

Can do ahead

2 cups celery, cut in ¾-inch pieces
2 tablespoons butter
2 tablespoons flour
1 cup chicken broth
1 cup milk
Salt
½ cup Parmesan cheese, grated
½ cup blanched almonds, slivered

Blanch cut celery in boiling water 8 minutes; drain and set aside. Melt butter and blend in flour. Stir over low heat until smooth. Add chicken broth and milk and cook, stirring, until mixture thickens. Taste for seasoning and add salt if necessary. Combine celery and sauce in shallow buttered baking dish. Sprinkle with Parmesan cheese and almonds. Bake at 350 degrees for ½ hour or until brown and bubbly. If doing ahead, do not add the sauce until you are ready to bake as the celery will lose water and dilute the sauce.
Yield: 4-6 servings

Jane Ingraham Ashford (Mrs. Charles H., Jr.)

COMPANY CORN PUDDING

Quick
Easy to make

1 (8½-ounce) package corn muffin mix
1 (16-ounce) can cream-style corn
½ cup sour cream
3 eggs, slightly beaten
1 teaspoon salt

Preheat oven to 350 degrees. Combine all ingredients and pour into a greased casserole. Bake for 40 minutes.
Yield: 8 servings

Margaret Manning Preston (Mrs. Ronald A.)

CORN PUDDING

Easy
Can double

2 cups drained whole-kernel corn, canned, frozen or fresh
1 teaspoon sugar
1 teaspoon salt
¼ teaspoon pepper
2 eggs, well-beaten
1 cup milk
1 tablespoon butter, cut into small pieces
2 tablespoons cracker crumbs, finely crushed
2 tablespoons green pepper, minced

Heat oven to 350 degrees. Mix ingredients thoroughly. Pour into a greased 1-quart baking dish. Bake for 40-45 minutes, or until done.
Yield: 6-8 servings

Nancy Samuel Everhart (Mrs. Charles L.)

Variation:
Using cream-style, rather than whole-kernel corn, follow preceding directions until butter is added. Instead of butter, cracker crumbs and green pepper add 1 tablespoon flour, dash of red pepper and sprinkle with bread crumbs. Bake 20-30 minutes.

Cecelia Chrismon Hudson (Mrs. Forrest M.)

CORN AND SPINACH PARMESAN

¼ cup onion, minced
2 tablespoons butter or margarine
1 (16-ounce) can cream-style corn
1½ cups chopped spinach, fresh, canned and drained, or frozen and thawed
1 teaspoon vinegar
½ teaspoon salt
¼ teaspoon pepper
¼ cup fine bread crumbs
2 tablespoons grated Parmesan cheese
2 tablespoons butter or margarine, melted

Sauté onion in 2 tablespoons butter in a small skillet. Combine corn, spinach, vinegar, salt and pepper with sautéed onion. Turn into lightly-greased shallow baking dish. Blend together bread crumbs and melted butter with cheese. Sprinkle over vegetable mixture. Bake at 400 degrees 15-20 minutes or until bubbly.
Yield: 4-6 servings

Anne Haughton Hanson (Mrs. Raymond)

SCALLOPED EGGPLANT

1 large eggplant, diced (about 4 cups)
⅓ cup milk
1 (10½-ounce) can mushroom soup
1 egg, slightly beaten
½ cup onion, chopped
¾ cup packaged herb-seasoned stuffing

Cook diced eggplant in boiling salted water until tender, 6-7 minutes; drain. Meanwhile gradually stir milk into soup and blend in egg. Add drained eggplant, onion and stuffing and toss lightly to mix. Turn into greased baking dish. Sprinkle with cheese topper.

½ cup packaged herb-seasoned stuffing
2 tablespoons butter, melted
1 cup sharp processed American cheese, shredded

Finely crush stuffing and toss with melted butter. Sprinkle over casserole. Top with cheese and bake at 350 degrees for 20 minutes or until hot.
Yield: 6-8 servings

Caroline Dunn Ashford (Mrs. Charles H.)

MEATLESS MOUSSAKA

Do day ahead
Can double

Base layer:

½ cup raw brown rice, cooked to equal 1½ cups
⅓ cup dry soybeans, cooked, seasoned and puréed to equal 1 cup
Oil as needed
1 large eggplant, peeled and sliced
2 tablespoons butter
1 large onion, finely chopped
3 tablespoons tomato paste
½ cup red wine
¼ cup parsley, chopped
⅛ teaspoon cinnamon
Salt
Pepper
½ cup bread crumbs
½ cup Parmesan cheese, grated

Have rice and soybeans ready. Sauté eggplant in oil after salting and peppering to taste. Set aside. Sauté onion in butter. Add beans, rice, tomato paste, wine, parsley, cinnamon, salt and pepper to onion; mix well. In casserole layer eggplant and bean-rice mixture. Sprinkle bread crumbs and Parmesan cheese over all.

Top custard:

4 tablespoons butter
3 tablespoons whole wheat flour
2 cups milk
2 eggs
1 cup ricotta or cottage cheese
Nutmeg

Preheat oven to 375 degrees. Make a cream sauce by melting butter and blending in flour with a wire whisk. Add milk into flour mixture stirring over low heat until thick and smooth. Remove from heat. Cool slightly. Stir in eggs, ricotta and nutmeg. Pour sauce over all and bake about 45 minutes until top is golden and knife comes out clean from custard. Remove from oven and cool 20-30 minutes before serving. Cut into squares. Note: flavor is improved by standing one day. Reheat before serving.
Yield: 6 servings

Carol Webb Pullen (Mrs. John S.)

EGGPLANT EVANGELINE

May be doubled
May be prepared in advance

1 medium eggplant, peeled and diced
3 tablespoons butter, melted
3 tablespoons flour
2 cups canned tomatoes, chopped*
1 green pepper, seeded and chopped
1 small onion, peeled and chopped
1 teaspoon salt
1 tablespoon brown sugar
½ bay leaf (optional)
2 cloves (optional)
Bread crumbs
Butter
Grated cheese

*Whirl tomatoes in blender for an easy way to chop.

Grease a 7x11-inch baking dish and set aside. Preheat oven to 350 degrees, if eggplant is to be baked now. Cook diced eggplant in salted, boiling water for 10 minutes or until fork-tender. Drain. In a large skillet, melt butter and stir in flour. Add tomatoes with juice, green pepper and onion. Add salt, brown sugar, bay leaf and cloves. Simmer 5 minutes. Pour over eggplant. Top with bread crumbs and dot with butter or grated cheese. Bake 20-30 minutes until bubbly. If to be baked later, cover and refrigerate until baking time. Remove from refrigerator 30 minutes prior to baking and preheat oven to 350 degrees. Bake 20-30 minutes.
Yield: 6 servings

Jane Johnson Straub (Mrs. Robert L.)

RAYMOND ANDERSON'S ORIGINAL OKRA SUPREME

½ pound okra, cut into ½-inch rounds
1 small onion, chopped
1 medium tomato, chopped
2-3 Ritz or Saltine crackers, crushed
1 egg
Bacon drippings
½ cup Cheddar cheese, grated

Using medium heat, sauté okra and onion in small amount of bacon drippings until crisp-tender. Add chopped tomato; stir, cooking about 5 minutes. Sprinkle on crushed crackers. Blend lightly. Cook about 5 minutes. Reduce heat. Break egg onto the mixture. Blend lightly until egg begins to congeal. Shape into a flat mound. Sprinkle grated cheese on top and slip under broiler until cheese melts.
Yield: 2-3 servings

Emma Anderson (Mrs. Raymond F.)

To appease a hungry husband when dinner is late, start frying an onion.

CREAMED PEAS AND MUSHROOMS ÉLÉGANT

4 slices bacon
1 tablespoon onion, chopped
2 tablespoons flour
1 cup milk
¼ teaspoon salt
Dash of pepper
1 (17-ounce) can green peas, drained
1 (4-ounce) can mushrooms, drained
1 tablespoon pimiento, chopped
1 tablespoon butter
6 patty shells (optional)

Fry bacon until crisp. Remove from skillet. Drain and crumble. Add onion to drippings in skillet. Sauté until tender. Pour off all but 1 tablespoon of drippings. Blend in flour. Add milk, salt and pepper. Cook and stir until mixture thickens. Stir in drained peas. Sauté mushrooms, and pimiento in butter; add to peas. May be served in patty shells.
Yield: 6 servings

Anna Cartner Kafer (Mrs. Oscar A., III)

PERK SPEER'S MUSHROOMS AND WINE

1 pound mushrooms, cleaned
1 tablespoon marjoram, chopped
1 teaspoon chives, minced
½ cup butter, melted
½ cup chicken bouillon
½ cup dry white wine
1 teaspoon salt
Ground pepper

Preheat oven to 350 degrees. Combine all above ingredients and bake covered for 20 minutes.

Pat Best Woodward (Mrs. J. Arthur)

QUICK MUSHROOM STUFFING

½ pound mushrooms
1 cup carrots, shredded
1 cup celery, diced
¾ cup onion, diced
½ cup powdered milk
1 tablespoon parsley, chopped
¼ teaspoon sage
½ teaspoon kelp (optional)
½ teaspoon marjoram
⅛ teaspoon cayenne

Chop mushrooms and place in saucepan over low heat until liquid appears. Add remaining ingredients and simmer 15 minutes. Serve hot as a side dish or stuff chicken or fish with it. Do not freeze.
Yield: 3 cups

Peggy Witmeyer Bernard

CHEESY POTATOES

6-8 medium potatoes
¼ cup butter
Milk
1 (8-ounce) package cream cheese
American cheese

Preheat oven to 350 degrees. Prepare potatoes for mashing and add butter and milk in quantity sufficient for smooth consistency. While still hot, add cream cheese and blend well. Pour potatoes into baking dish and cover with strips of American cheese. Bake 10-15 minutes or until heated through and cheese is melted.
Yield: 8-10 servings

Phyllis Gaskins Carpenter (Mrs. Gary H.)

BATTLETOWN INN YELLOW SQUASH

7 small yellow squash, sliced
1 small onion, diced
½ cup cream or half and half
¼ cup saltine cracker crumbs
2 tablespoons butter

Boil squash in salted water until tender. Drain and mash. Grease a 1½-quart baking dish and set aside. Preheat oven to 350 degrees. Sauté onion in butter; add cream and cracker crumbs. Mix with squash and pour into casserole. Top with additional crumbs and dot with butter. Bake 30-45 minutes or until top browns.
Yield: 4 servings

Eugenia Hofler Clement (Mrs. Robert L.)

To cook fresh pumpkin, cut the pumpkin in half, but don't peel it. Remove the seeds and stringy part. Place the cut pieces in a baking pan, cut side down. Add enough water to cover the bottom of the pan. Bake at 350 degrees until the pulp is tender all the way through, about 30-45 minutes. When cool, scoop out the pulp. To purée, put the pulp through a sieve, food mill or a blender. If it is too thin, cook it on top of the stove until it is the consistency you want. Put the purée in freezer containers and freeze. This will keep one year.

COMPANY SQUASH

You'll get compliments every time you serve this dish.

2 pounds squash, uncooked, sliced
2 eggs
1 medium onion, sliced
2 cups thick white sauce
½ pound sharp cheese, grated
Salt to taste
Pepper to taste

Cook sliced squash and onion in boiling salted water until tender. Drain cooked squash well and mash. Add all other ingredients to the squash and mix well. Pour into top of double boiler and cook for 1 hour. Pour into a 2-quart casserole dish and brown at 375 degrees about 20 minutes. After browning, remove from oven and allow it to set about 20 minutes to make the texture firmer.

Debbie Brown Bonner (Mrs. John H.)

SUMMER SQUASH CASSEROLE

2 pounds yellow squash, sliced, cooked and drained
2 small onions, cut fine
1 (8-ounce) package Pepperidge Farm Herb Dressing
½ cup butter
1 (10½-ounce) can cream of chicken soup
1 (5-ounce) can water chestnuts, sliced thin
1 (2-ounce) jar pimiento, cut fine (optional)

Melt butter and stir into dressing. Divide and place half onto bottom of 8x12-inch baking dish. Combine squash, onions, soup, chestnuts and pimientos and pour over dressing. Cover squash with remaining dressing and bake at 350 degrees for 30-40 minutes.
Yield: 12 servings

Doloris Collins Thomas (Mrs. James J.)

TARRAGON SNAP BEANS

1 pound fresh green beans *OR* 1 (16-ounce) can French-style beans, drained
2 tablespoons salad oil
1 clove garlic, minced
½ onion, chopped
2 tablespoons tarragon vinegar
½ tablespoon brown sugar
1 large fresh tomato *OR* 1 (16-ounce) can tomatoes, drained
Salt to taste
Pepper to taste

Cut beans, if fresh, in one-inch slices and cook until tender. Drain. Set aside. Put oil in skillet over moderate heat and add garlic and onions. Cook slowly and stir ten minutes. Cut tomato in small pieces and add to skillet with vinegar, sugar, salt, and pepper. Cook five minutes more, stirring frequently. Add beans; mix well until beans are heated thoroughly.

Patricia Byrum McCotter (Mrs. C. Kennedy, Jr.)

HUNGARIAN LAYERED POTATOES

Easy and economical
Stores well; delicious reheated
Do day ahead or last minute
Can be doubled

6-8 potatoes
6 eggs, hard-boiled
1 pint sour cream
¼ cup butter
Bread crumbs
4-6 ounces pepperoni, sliced*
Salt
Paprika

*Pepperoni may be substituted with ground or cubed ham or freshly sliced tomatoes.

Butter a deep casserole. Boil potatoes in their skins. Cool and peel potatoes and eggs. Cut into thin round slices. Arrange a layer of potatoes, next egg slices. Sprinkle with salt and paprika. Spread with sour cream; top with pepperoni. Alternate layers ending up with potatoes. Top with buttered bread crumbs. Bake in 325 degree oven for 1 hour.
Yield: 6-8 servings

Gabrielle Paluzsay Lippitt (Mrs. Devereux H.)

PEG'S POTATOES

Serve immediately

4 large Irish baking potatoes, peeled and thinly sliced
4 large onions, sliced
2 cups Cheddar cheese, grated
6 tablespoons butter, sliced into pats
½-¾ cup milk
Salt
Pepper

Grease a 2- or 3-quart casserole dish. Layer potatoes, onion, cheese and butter pats alternately with a generous amount of salt and pepper in baking dish. Pour milk over layers and top again with pepper. Cover and bake until potatoes are tender. Add additional milk if necessary. Bake at 375 degrees until potatoes are soft, about 1 hour.
Yield: 4 servings

Marilyn Miller Smith (Mrs. Stewart H.)

SWEET POTATO BALLS

Looks like you worked all day!

Make ahead

1 (20-ounce) can sliced pineapple, drained
1 (28-ounce) can sweet potatoes or yams
1 cup brown sugar
2 tablespoons margarine, softened
¼ teaspoon lemon extract
Cinnamon to taste
Nutmeg to taste
10 red cherries
2 cups Corn Flakes, crushed
3 tablespoons brown sugar

Mix crushed Corn Flakes and 3 tablespoons brown sugar in shallow dish and set aside. Spray cookie sheet with Pam. Place 10 slices of pineapple on cookie sheet. Drain sweet potatoes. Mash them with a fork. Add 1 cup brown sugar, lemon extract, cinnamon, nutmeg and margarine. Beat with electric mixer until fairly smooth. With your hands form 10 balls of the sweet potato mixture and roll in Corn Flake mixture, coating well. Place ball on pineapple slice and top with cherry. Refrigerate until ready to bake. Dot with extra butter and bake at 350 degrees for 25 minutes.
Yield: 10 servings

Linda Mayes Tipton (Mrs. Maurice E., Jr.)

SWEET POTATO PUDDING

2 cups sweet potato, grated
¼ cup brown sugar
2 small eggs, beaten
½ teaspoon cloves
½ teaspoon allspice
⅓ teaspoon cinnamon
½ cup milk
⅓ cup orange juice
⅓ cup butter, melted

Butter baking dish and preheat oven to 350 degrees. Combine all ingredients and pour into dish. Bake 1 hour.

Rosa Hardison Winfree (Mrs. Charles)
Louise Johnson Lee (Mrs. Clyde B.)

BRANDIED SWEET POTATOES

Can be marinated all day, then baked

2½ pounds sweet potatoes
½ cup butter or margarine
½ cup light brown sugar
1 teaspoon cinnamon
¼ teaspoon nutmeg
½ teaspoon salt
½ cup brandy or sherry (cream or regular)

Grease shallow baking dish. Boil potatoes or yams *in the skins* until soft. Remove and cool. Peel and slice in crosswise slices about 1½-inches thick. Place in baking dish and dot with butter or margarine. Combine sugar, nutmeg, cinnamon and salt and sprinkle over potatoes. Pour brandy or sherry over all and bake at 375 degrees for 30 minutes.
Yield: 6 servings

Kay Best Burrows (Mrs. Charles)

STEWED TOMATOES AND APPLES

Truly unique and different!

Delicious with holiday turkey

2 quarts canned tomatoes, (drain and save juice for use while baking)
1 quart apples, peeled and chopped
1 cup sugar
3 tablespoons butter

Preheat oven to 300 degrees. Drain the liquid from the tomatoes, reserving the liquid for use while baking. Mix all the ingredients together and place in a greased casserole. Cover and bake slowly for 3 hours. Stir often and add tomato liquid as it bakes.
Yield: 4-6 servings

Alyce Faye Tilley Grant (Mrs. David)

TOMATO-ARTICHOKE SCALLOP

1 (35-ounce) can whole plum tomatoes
1 (14-ounce) can artichoke hearts
½ cup onion, finely chopped
2 tablespoons shallots, finely chopped
½ cup butter or margarine
½ teaspoon leaf basil
1-2 tablespoons sugar
Salt to taste
Pepper to taste

Preheat oven to 325 degrees. Grease shallow earthenware dish. Drain tomatoes and artichokes; rinse artichokes in water and quarter. Sauté onions and shallots in butter until tender. Add tomatoes, artichokes and basil. Heat 2 or 3 minutes, stirring. Season with sugar, salt and pepper. Turn into prepared casserole and bake for 10-15 minutes or until vegetables are tender.
Yield: 6-8 servings.

Alyce Faye Tilley Grant (Mrs. David J.)

FRIED RICE

6-10 slices bacon, cut up
2 cups white rice, cooked*
½ cup spring onions, chopped
½ cup carrots, grated (optional)
½ cup frozen green peas, cooked and drained
1 teaspoon Accent
3 tablespoons soy sauce
1 egg

*Leftover rice may be used.
Fry bacon in skillet. Add rice. Pour soy sauce over rice and stir. Add onions, carrots and peas. Sprinkle with Accent; stir. Break egg over rice and mix well. Serve immediately.
Yield: 4 servings

Margaret Manning Preston (Mrs. Ronald A.

GREEN RICE

1 cup dry rice, cooked as directed
½ cup oil
1 cup parsley, chopped
1 green pepper, chopped
1 bunch green onions, or 2 medium onions, chopped
2 eggs, slightly beaten
2 (5-ounce) glasses Old English Sharp Cheese
1 (13-ounce) can evaporated milk

Preheat oven to 350 degrees. Beat eggs, add oil. Soften cheese and add. Add rice, milk, parsley, green pepper and onions. Season to taste. Bake one hour.

Margaret Whitehead Wall (Mrs. Lawrence D.)

DOT'S RICE

1 cup rice, rinsed
1 (10¼-ounce) can onion soup
1 (10¼-ounce) can beef bouillon
¼ cup butter
Dash salt

Spray 2-quart casserole dish with Pam. Mix all ingredients well and pour into dish. Bake at 350 degrees for one hour stirring once midway through cooking time.
Yield: 8 servings

Elizabeth Allen Summerell (Mrs. E. W.)

EXQUISITE RICE

3 tablespoons butter
1¾ cups chicken stock
1⅓ cups rice
½ teaspoon salt

Combine stock, salt and butter in saucepan and bring to a boil. Add rice and reduce heat. Simmer 20 minutes tightly covered or until all moisture is absorbed. Serve with Exquisite Shrimp.
Yield: 6-8 servings

Nancy Springett Wetherington (Mrs. John S.)

RED RICE

1 ham hock (very meaty)
2 cups long-cooking rice
3 cups stock
1 (15-16 ounce) can tomatoes
1 (10½-ounce) can tomato soup

Cover ham hock with 3 cups water and simmer for 30 minutes or until meat is easy to remove from bone. Drain into colander saving stock. Thirty minutes before serving combine 3 cups stock and rice. Cook until water is absorbed. Add ham bits, tomatoes and soup and cook until excess moisture is gone. Serve with salad and French bread.
Yield: 6 hearty servings.

RICE CONSOMMÉ

½ cup raw rice
1 (10-ounce) can consommé
1 cup onions, finely chopped
1 cup New York State cheese, grated
¼ cup butter

Combine in 1½-quart casserole and bake 45 minutes at 325 degrees.
Yield: 6 servings

Susan Jones Collins

TURNIP CASSEROLE

Make ahead
Can freeze

3 pounds yellow turnips
¼ cup butter or margarine
1½ tablespoons sugar
1½ teaspoons salt
Pepper
1½ teaspoons lemon juice
3 eggs
1 cup bread crumbs

Pare and cut turnips into small slices. Boil until tender; drain and mash hot turnips adding butter, sugar, salt, pepper. Beat with electric mixer until blended. Add eggs one at a time and beat until fluffy. Stir in bread crumbs and lemon juice. Pour into 1½-quart casserole. Cover and refrigerate until baking time. Bake at 375 degrees for 50 minutes.
Yield: 8 servings

Jane Johnson Straub (Mrs. Robert L.

ANNE RUSSO'S SPINACH CASSEROLE

1½ pounds frozen spinach
4 eggs, hard-boiled and chopped
2 tablespoons onions, chopped
1 clove garlic, minced
1 pound fresh or canned mushrooms
½ cup butter or margarine
¼ cup flour
2 cups milk
2 teaspoons salt
⅛ teaspoon pepper
4 ounces American cheese, chopped

Grease 2½-quart baking dish. Steam spinach; drain. Sauté onion, garlic and mushrooms in butter. Add flour; blend. Add milk and cook, stirring until thickened. Add salt and pepper. Put spinach, cheese and chopped eggs into sauce mixture. Pour into prepared baking dish. Bake at 350 degrees 20-30 minutes.
Yield: 6-8 servings

Anne Bratton Allen (Mrs. H. Eldridge)

DEETER'S SPINACH CASSEROLE

2 (10-ounce) packages frozen chopped spinach
½ cup evaporated milk
2 tablespoons butter or margarine
1 tablespoon flour
1 (8-ounce) cloverleaf package Kraft process cheese food
½ teaspoon garlic salt
Dash cayenne pepper
Salt to taste
Pepper to taste
¼ teaspoon celery salt
¼ cup onions, chopped and sautéed
½ cup reserved spinach water
Bread crumbs

Grease 2-quart casserole dish. Cook spinach according to package directions in unsalted water and reserve ½ cup of the spinach water. Make a white sauce with flour, butter and milk. Stir in remaining ingredients, except bread crumbs, adding spinach last. Pour into prepared casserole. Top with bread crumbs and bake at 350 degrees for 30 minutes.
Yield: 6-8 servings

Lindy Allmond Emory (Mrs. Robert R., Jr.)

SPINACH AND CARROT CASSEROLE

Can double
Do day ahead
Stores well

1 (10-ounce) package frozen carrots
1 (10-ounce) package frozen leaf spinach
1 onion, chopped fine

Cook carrots and onions together in boiling salted water; drain. Cook spinach; drain well. Set aside to cool while making sauce.

Sauce:
3 tablespoons butter
3 tablespoons flour
1½ cups milk
1 (8-ounce) package Velveeta cheese
¼ teaspoon salt
½ cup bread crumbs *OR* Pepperidge Farm Herb Dressing

Melt butter in saucepan. Stir in flour and gradually add milk. Stir constantly until sauce has thickened. Add cheese and salt. Layer carrots, sauce and spinach in casserole dish. Sprinkle top with bread crumbs. May be refrigerated until ready to bake. When ready to bake, remove casserole from refrigerator; preheat oven to 350 degrees. Bake 30 minutes or until hot and bubbly.
Yield: 4-6 servings

Ann Harris Bustard (Mrs. Victor W.)

BAKED ACORN SQUASH

3 acorn squash
Grated nutmeg or ground ginger
Salt
Freshly ground black pepper
3 teaspoons brown sugar
6 teaspoons butter
6 teaspoons sweet sherry (optional)

Preheat oven to 325 degrees. Split squash into halves and scoop out the fibers and seeds. Sprinkle the cavity of each half with nutmeg, salt, pepper, brown sugar and a teaspoon of butter. Bake 30-45 minutes or until flesh is tender. Five minutes before serving, add a teaspoon of sherry to each cavity.
Yield: 6 servings

Ruth V. Miles (Mrs. Daniel M.)

PARMESAN HOMINY

Speedy side dish

2 slices bacon
2 tablespoons onion, chopped
2 tablespoons green pepper, chopped
1 (20-ounce) can hominy, drained
Seasoned salt to taste
Parmesan cheese

Dice bacon and fry until transparent. Add onion and pepper. Fry until tender. Add drained hominy and season to taste with seasoned salt. Heat thoroughly. Serve topped with with Parmesan cheese.
Yield: 3-4 servings

Anne Haughton Hansen (Mrs. Raymond S.)

GRATIN OF ZUCCHINI SOUFFLÉ

Easy
Part done ahead
Serve immediately
Do not freeze

3-6 zucchini (about 2½ pounds)
1 teaspoon salt
⅓ cup flour
4 large eggs
1 cup heavy cream
1 cup Swiss cheese, grated
1-1½ teaspoons salt
½ teaspoon freshly ground white pepper

Butter a 6-cup gratin dish or casserole. Boil unpeeled zucchini with salt for 6-8 minutes. Drain. Purée in blender. Sprinkle flour on top and mix well. Add remaining ingredients and mix. Pour zucchini mixture in casserole. Place in oven on cookie sheet. Bake 45 minutes at 350 degrees. If not browned at end of cooking time, place under broiler for several minutes. Let set for 10 minutes before serving.
Yield: 6-8 servings

Ann Harris Bustard (Mrs. Victor W.)

SAUTÉED ZUCCHINI AND TOMATOES

1 large zucchini, julienned
1 large tomato, chopped
Butter
⅓ cup Parmesan cheese
Salt and pepper

Melt a small amount of butter in a large skillet and sauté the zucchini until it is soft but not browned. Add the chopped tomato and salt and pepper, cooking until it is heated. Remove from the heat and add the Parmesan cheese, stirring well. Serve immediately. Zucchini does better if you let it sit before cooking in a colander lined with a paper towel for about 15 minutes and then press out the extra juice.
Yield: 4 servings

Jane Ingraham Ashford (Mrs. Charles H., Jr.)

JACK'S COLORADO VEGETABLES

Serve with steak or roast beef, or as was done in Colorado, with beaver tail elk or "ba'r" meat!

2 large green peppers
2 large onions
½ pound fresh mushrooms
¼ cup butter or margarine
½ teaspoon salt (or more)

Remove seeds and membrane from the peppers and cut in bite-sized pieces Peel onions and cut in bite-sized chunks. Wash and cap mushrooms and slice if larger than bite-sized. Melt butter in heavy frying pan and sauté peppe and onion until crisp-tender. Add mushrooms and sauté for another two o three minutes. Sprinkle with salt to taste.
Yield: 4-6 servings

Dora Winters Taylor (Mrs. John T., Jr.

COLACHE

This dish was made by the Spanish in early days in California. They made liberal use of seasoning so it was a hot and peppery vegetable stew. It goes very well with chicken dishes.

4 small zucchini, cut in ½-inch slices
2 tablespoons butter
2 tablespoons bacon drippings
1 large onion, thinly sliced
2 green peppers, seeded and cut in julienne strips
4 peeled whole tomatoes, fresh or canned
Salt
Freshly ground black pepper
Cayenne
3 ears fresh corn *OR* 1 (10-ounce) package frozen white corn

Melt butter and bacon fat in a large skillet such as an electric fry pan. Sauté zucchini until partly browned. Add onion and green peppers. Fry a bit and add tomatoes. Season well with salt, pepper and cayenne to taste. Add corn and cook 30 minutes. Do not over cook. Vegetables should retain some crispness.
Yield: 6-8 servings

Carole Beasley McKnight (Mrs. Thomas J.)

Pasta and Hot Fruit

FETTUCCINE FREDDE ALLA PRONTO (COLD PASTA)

Cold pasta and fresh bread makes a light summer lunch, served with a light, fruity red wine.

6 tablespoons olive oil
2 cloves garlic, finely minced
2 ounces pignoli nuts (pine nuts)
1 cup tomatoes, skinned, seeded, roughly chopped
1 pound fresh fettuccine
1 cup Italian-style tuna, in chunks*
½ red pimiento, cut into thin strips
6 black olives, pitted and roughly chopped
1 tablespoon fresh parsley, chopped
2 tablespoons red wine vinegar
Salt to taste
Freshly ground pepper to taste
Parsley for garnish

*An equal amount of chicken or cold boiled shrimp may be substituted for the tuna.

Heat olive oil in skillet, add garlic, pine nuts and sauté over low heat five minutes, or just until garlic turns translucent and pine nuts golden. Add tomatoes; cook a few seconds. Turn into a large bowl and cool. Cook fettuccine in a large pot of rapidly boiling, salted water 8-10 minutes, or until firm to the bite. (6-7 quarts water for one pound pasta.) When pasta is al dente (medium), add a glass of cold water to stop boiling. Drain. Add cooked pasta to bowl containing the oil, garlic, pine nut mixture. Toss gently to coat. Add tuna chunks, pimiento strips, black olives, parsley and red wine vinegar. Turn with two large spoons to blend. Season with salt and freshly ground pepper. Sprinkle extra parsley on top and serve at room temperature. Grated cheese is NOT served with this dish.
Yield: 4 servings

Anne Norman Taylo

POPPY SEED ALMOND NOODLES

2 (8-ounce) packages wide noodles
1 cup butter
1½ cups blanched almonds, chopped
½ cup poppy seeds
¾-1 teaspoon salt

Cook noodles according to directions on package and drain. Meanwhile melt butter slowly so it does not brown. Add almonds and sauté slowly until golden. Stir in poppy seeds and salt. Pour butter mixture over noodles and mix lightly.
Yield: 12 servings

Robertha Kafer Coleman (Mrs. Thomas B.)

SPINACH LASAGNE

1 (16-ounce) carton ricotta or small curd cottage cheese
1½ cups Mozzarella cheese, shredded and divided
1 egg
1 (10-ounce) package frozen spinach, thawed and drained
1 teaspoon salt
⅛ teaspoon pepper
¾ teaspoon whole oregano
2 (15½-ounce) jars spaghetti sauce
1 (8-ounce) package lasagne noodles, uncooked
1 cup water

Preheat oven to 350 degrees. Combine ricotta cheese, 1 cup Mozzarella cheese, egg, spinach, salt, pepper and oregano in a large mixing bowl. Stir well. Spread ½ cup spaghetti sauce in a greased 13 x9 x 2-inch baking dish. Place ⅓ of the lasagna noodles over sauce and spread with half the cheese mixture. Repeat layers. Top with remaining noodles, spaghetti sauce and ½ cup Mozzarella cheese: pour water around edges; cover securely with aluminum foil and bake for 1 hour and 15 minutes. Let stand 15 minutes before serving.
Yield: 8 servings

Lindy Allmond Emory (Mrs. Robert R., Jr.)

FETTUCCINE ALLA ROMA

4 ounces narrow noodles or fettuccine
1 egg, beaten
1/3 cup light cream
1/4 teaspoon dried parsley
4 tablespoons butter
1/4 teaspoon salt
1/4 teaspoon garlic salt
1/8 teaspoon (or less) pepper
1/4 cup Parmesan cheese, freshly shredded

Cook noodles in boiling salted water until barely tender. Drain. Meanwhile in a bowl combine egg, cream, parsley. In a skillet melt the butter over low heat. Add the egg mixture, salts, pepper and Parmesan. Continue stirring until mixture is creamy and warm. Add noodles and mix until well coated.
Yield: 2 servings

Jane Kinnison Millns (Mrs. Dale T.)

Add a cup of cold water to boiling pasta to stop boil.

FETTUCCINE AL MARCO

An easy dish that can be done at the last minute. It is not as rich as Fettuccine al Fredo, but has fewer calories and is higher in protein. Must be served immediately.

1/2 pound fettuccine
1 1/2 cups ricotta or cottage cheese
1/2 cup yogurt
1 egg
1/4 cup Parmesan cheese
1/2 cup parsley, chopped
2 cups fresh spinach leaves (optional but adds color)
Salt and pepper to taste
Sliced black olives as garnish

While the pasta is cooking, blend cheeses, yogurt, egg, salt and pepper until smooth. Add the parsley, spinach leaves (optional). Toss the mixture with the drained, hot pasta. Garnish with sliced black olives.
Yield: 4 servings

Cece Lippitt Snow (Mrs. James Byron, III)

COUNTRY NOODLE CASSEROLE

This is an easy recipe that complements any meat if the bacon is omitted. With the bacon it can be served as the main dish with a crisp salad.

1 pound thin egg noodles (vermicelli)
3 cups cottage cheese
3 cups sour cream
¼ teaspoon powdered garlic
2 onions, minced
2 tablespoons Worcestershire sauce
⅛ teaspcon Tabasco sauce
4 teaspoons salt
3 tablespoons ground horseradish
1 cup grated Parmesan cheese
½ cup sour cream
Meaty bacon, fried crisp and crumbled (optional)

Preheat oven to 350 degrees. Cook noodles in slightly salted water five minutes, until barely tender (al dente). Drain well. Butter a large casserole and mix directly in it, the noodles, cottage cheese, 3 cups sour cream, garlic, onions, Worcestershire sauce, Tabasco, salt and horseradish. Spread on top the Parmesan, ½ cup sour cream and bacon. Bake about an hour or until thoroughly heated.
Yield: 6-8 servings

Kathleen Winslow Budd (Mrs. Bern)

ORANGE HALVES

Do early in day
Do Not Freeze

6 oranges
6 apples, chopped
1 (8-ounce) can crushed pineapple
1 cup sugar
½ cup nuts, chopped
Butter

Preheat oven to 350 degrees. Cut oranges in half; remove sections and prepare shells for filling. Combine orange sections, apples and pineapple in saucepan. Add sugar and cook until thickened. Fill orange halves with mixture. Add chopped nuts and a pat of butter to each orange half. Put in pan, cover with foil and heat thoroughly for 15 to 20 minutes. Good and tasty.
Yield: 12 servings

Frances Mason Clement (Mrs. Donald H.)

BAKED APPLES

Wash and cut core out of top and bottom of apples. Stick sides with knife.
Fill apple with sugar, top with nutmeg and cinnamon and butter.
Fill baking dish halfway with water.
Place in oven at 350 degrees until apples are soft.

Anna Gilliken Lamm (Mrs. Ronald B.)

HOT FRUIT CASSEROLE

1 (16-ounce) can peaches
1 (16-ounce) can pineapple chunks
1 (16-ounce) can pear halves
1 (14-ounce) jar apple rings
2 tablespoons cornstarch
½ cup brown sugar
½ cup sherry
¼ cup margarine or butter

Drain fruit; save juice from peaches, pineapple and apple rings to make 2 cups. Add cornstarch, sugar, sherry and butter to juice and cook until thickened. Arrange fruit attractively in a long casserole. Pour thickened sauce over all and bake in a 350 degree oven for 20 minutes. Serve with any meat.
Yield: 6-8 servings

Betty Cleveland Livingston (Mrs. W. Cherry)

CURRIED FRUIT

Delicious with ham, lamb or poultry!

1 (16-ounce) can peach halves
1 (20-ounce) can sliced pineapple
1 (16-ounce) can pear halves
5 maraschino cherries
¾ cup light brown sugar
4 teaspoons curry powder (or less)
⅓ cup butter or margarine

Early in the day: Preheat oven to 325 degrees. Drain fruit and dry on paper towels. Arrange fruit in 1½-quart casserole. Melt butter; add brown sugar and curry; spoon over fruit. Bake uncovered for 1 hour; refrigerate. 30 minutes before serving, reheat casserole in 350 degree oven for 30 minutes. Serve warm.
Yield: 12 servings

Marea Kafer Foste

BAKED PINEAPPLE

Delicious side dish with meats, such as ham or turkey!

1 (16-ounce) can crushed pineapple, drained
3 eggs, beaten
¾ cup sugar
4 tablespoons cornstarch
Butter
Cinnamon

Preheat oven to 350 degrees and use a 1-quart baking dish. Combine pineapple with eggs. Mix the sugar and cornstarch together and add to the eggs and pineapple mixture. Mix well. Pour into baking dish. Dot with butter and sprinkle with cinnamon. Bake 45-60 minutes or until firm and brown.
Yield: 6 servings

Margaret Heath Cayton (Mrs. A. C., Jr.)

MAXINE'S BREADED PINEAPPLE

Delicious accompaniment to ham!

1 (15-ounce) can of crushed pineapple, drained
½ cup sugar
2 tablespoons flour
3 eggs, beaten
4 slices bread, cut into cubes
½ cup butter or margarine, melted

Preheat oven to 350 degrees. Spray 8x8-inch pan with Pam. Mix sugar, flour and beaten eggs. Add pineapple and pour into baking dish. Toss bread cubes in melted butter and sprinkle on top of pineapple mixture. Bake 40 minutes.
Yield: 6-9 servings

HOT SHERRIED FRUIT COMPOTE

4 ounces dried pitted prunes
8 ounces dried apricots
1 (15-ounce) can pineapple chunks with juice
1 (11-ounce) can mandarin oranges, drained
1 can Comstock Cherry Pie Filling
¾ cup of sherry wine

Preheat oven to 325 degrees. Layer in order given above. Make holes in top and pour sherry wine over all. Bake uncovered for 45 minutes.

Pat Best Woodward (Mrs. J. Arthur)

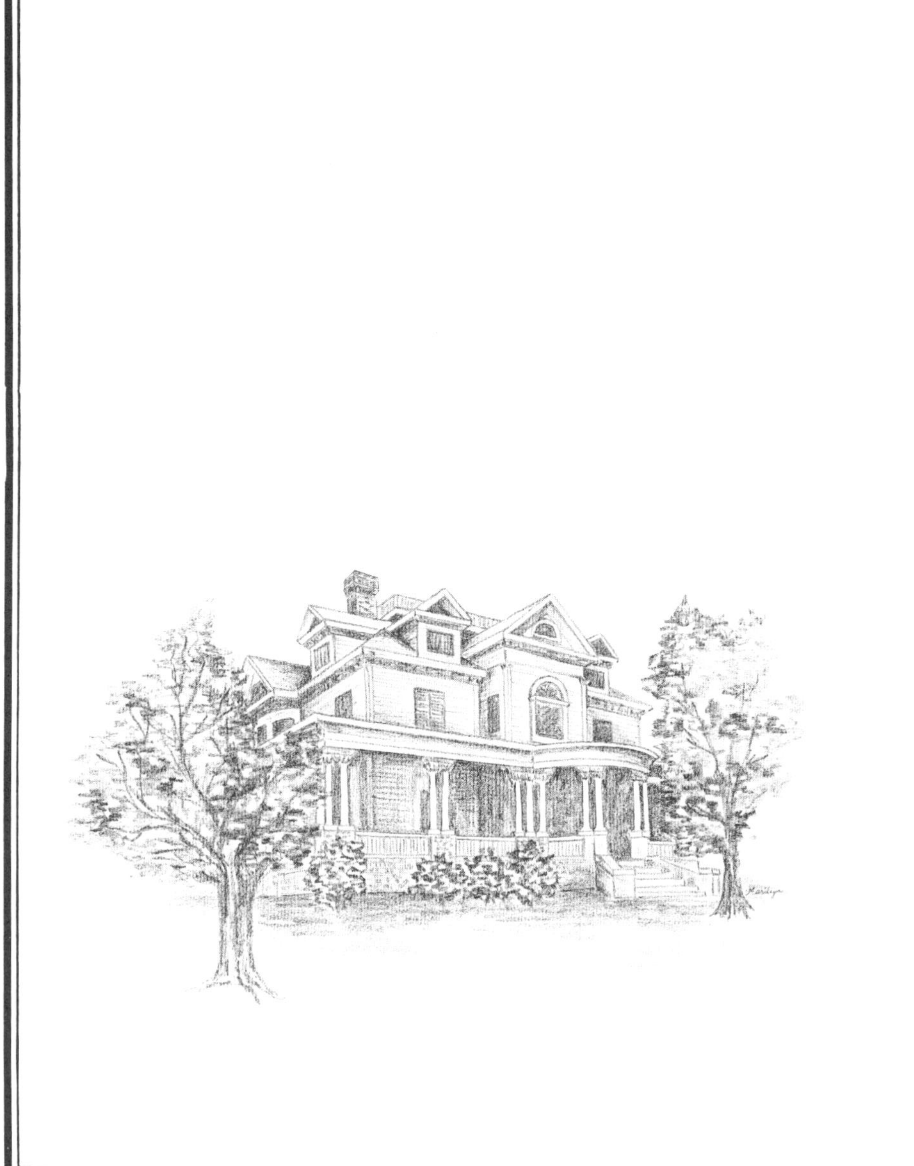

Coor-Bishop House **501 East Front Street**

James Coor, a Revolutionary War Patriot, built this Georgian House in 1767. A later owner, the immensely wealthy George Pollock, was host here in 1819 to President Monroe and Secretary of State John C. Calhoun. Early in this century Mr. E. K. Bishop, who served on the Vestry of Christ Church for over 50 years, had the house turned from New Street to face the Neuse River and made many exterior and interior changes. The house served as Christ Church Rectory from 1963 to 1970. It is the present residence of Dr. and Mrs. Raymond Houghton.

Pickles and Preserves

MANGO CHUTNEY

Must do ahead

2 dozen very firm mangoes, not ripe
1½ quarts wine or cider vinegar
5 pounds granulated sugar
1 pound raisins
1 pound dates, pitted and chopped coarsely
3 cloves garlic
2 teaspoons crushed dried red pepper
¼ pound fresh or crystallized ginger root, grated or minced
2 teaspoons salt
2 teaspoons ground cloves
2 teaspoons ground allspice
2 teaspoons ground cinnamon
Juice of 3 limes
½ cup brown sugar, well-packed
Kumquats, lemon and orange peel, optional

Peel and slice mangoes about ¼-inch thick, add vinegar, and cover. Refrigerate mangoes and marinate 2-3 days, stirring 3 times daily. When ready to assemble chutney, add white and brown sugars to mangoes and vinegar in a large pot and bring to a boil, stirring until all sugar is dissolved. Add all other ingredients and cook at a low boil 2-4 hours, stirring frequently. Mangoes should look clear along edges. Put in clean glass jars sealing properly. Mixture thickens as it cools. I usually cut this recipe in half.
Yield: 16 half-pints

Alice Graham Underhill (Mrs. T. Reed)

7-DAY CUCUMBER PICKLES

When I tried this recipe I borrowed from Betty Nobles, I won second prize at the County Fair.

Day 1—Wash 24 cucumbers and cover with boiling water. Let stand.
Day 2—Drain and repeat day 1 instructions.
Day 3—Drain and repeat.
Day 4—Drain and repeat.
Day 5—Drain, slice and cover with boiling syrup:
8 cups sugar
2 tablespoons pickling spices
15 teaspoons salt
4 cups vinegar
Day 6—Let stand on day 5 and 6.
Day 7—Bring all to a boil; simmer 10 minutes. Put into hot jars and seal. Keeps indefinitely.
Yield: 10 pints

Billy Ruth Stewart Sudduth (Mrs. W. Douglas)

CRYSTAL PICKLE CHIPS

5 small white onions, peeled and thinly sliced
1 large green pepper
4 large firm cucumbers, thinly sliced
1 large clove garlic, peeled
¼ cup salt
2 quarts cold water
14 ice cubes
3½ cups sugar
1½ cups white vinegar
1 tablespoon mustard seeds
1 teaspoon celery seeds
1 teaspoon ground turmeric

Core and seed green pepper; put through coarse blade of meat grinder. Put green pepper, cucumber, onion and garlic in large bowl; sprinkle with salt. Add the cold water and ice cubes; let stand 2 hours. Remove garlic; drain vegetables. Mix sugar, vinegar, mustard seeds, celery seeds and turmeric in large kettle; add vegetables. Bring just to a boil on high heat. Remove from heat; pack into sterile jars. Work out bubbles by pressing down firmly with a spoon; seal.
Makes 3 pints

Margaret L. Scott (Mrs. James H.)

COUNTRY-STYLE SWEET PICKLES

Worth the effort!

7 pounds cucumbers, sliced round and not too thin
2 tablespoons lime
1 cup salt
2 tablespoons alum
½ (1.25-ounce) box pickling spices
2 quarts vinegar
4 pounds sugar

Soak cucumbers in water to cover to which lime has been added. After 12 hours of soaking, drain and cover with water to which salt has been added. Soak in salt-water for 4 hours. Drain; soak in clear water 2 hours. Drain and bring to boil in water to cover to which alum has been added. Drain; rinse with hot water. Mix in a large kettle, pickling spices, vinegar and sugar. Bring to a boil. Add cucumbers and simmer 15 minutes. Pack into sterile jars. Seal.

Genevieve Tolson Dunn (Mrs. Mark S.)

SQUASH PICKLES

8 cups sliced squash
2 cups onion, sliced
1 tablespoon salt
½ cup green pepper, diced
1 cup cider vinegar
1¾ cups sugar
½ teaspoon celery seeds
½ teaspoon mustard seeds

Combine squash and onions; sprinkle with salt and let stand one hour. Combine green pepper, vinegar, sugar, celery seeds and mustard seeds. Bring to a boil. Add squash and onion and return to a boil. Pack pickles into hot, sterilized jars; cover with vinegar mixture and seal.
Yield: 2 quarts

Mary Ann Southern (Mrs. Thomas L.)

OKRA PICKLES

5 pounds young tender okra
1 cup water
8 cups vinegar
¾ cup salt (not iodized)
1 tablespoon mixed pickling spices*
1 pod hot pepper per pint jar
1 garlic clove per pint jar
Two heads dill per pint jar
¼ teaspoon alum per pint jar

*Pickling spices should be measured into a piece of cheesecloth and tied with a string for easy removal from syrup.

In sterilized jars place dill, garlic, hot pepper. Pack in whole washed okra. Heat vinegar, salt, water, spices to boiling. Pour over okra to fill jars leaving ¼-inch head space from top of jar. Add alum to each jar. Seal immediately. Let stand 8 weeks before using.

Elizabeth Scales Marsh (Mrs. Thomas B.)

WATERMELON PICKLES

2 pounds watermelon rind, peeled and cubed
¼ cup pickling salt (*not* iodized)
6 cups water
1 teaspoon powdered alum
2 cups white vinegar
2 pounds sugar (4 cups)
1 lemon, thinly sliced
1 stick cinnamon
12 whole cloves
1 teaspoon allspice

When peeling rind be sure to leave some of the pink meat on. Make a brine with salt, 4 cups water and alum. Soak rind in this mixture overnight. Drain, rinse, and cook slowly in water until barely tender. Do not overcook or pickles will be soft. Drain. Bring to boil 2 cups water, vinegar, sugar, lemon and spices which have been tied in a cloth bag. Remove spice bag and pour hot syrup over rind. Let sit overnight. Drain and reheat syrup for three mornings and pour over rind. On the fourth morning, drain and reheat syrup and pour over rind which has been packed in sterilized pint or half-pint jars. Seal.
Yield: 3 pints

Elizabeth Scales Marsh (Mrs. Thomas B.)

HOT DOG RELISH

Excellent with most meats as well as hot dogs

½ cup salt
Water
1 quart cucumbers
1 quart onions
2 bunches celery
3 sweet red peppers or pimientos
1 head of cauliflower

Chop all vegetables and place in large kettle with salt and enough water to cover vegetables. Let stand overnight. Drain.

5 cups white vinegar
6 cups sugar
2 tablespoons mustard seed
⅔ cup flour
4 tablespoons dry mustard
1 tablespoon turmeric
Paraffin

In kettle bring vinegar, sugar and mustard seed to a boil with drained vegetables. Thicken with flour, dry mustard and turmeric. Bottle in sterilized jars; cover with paraffin wax and store.

Ann Harris Bustard (Mrs. Victor W.)

BREAD AND BUTTER PICKLES

3 medium onions, sliced
30 (6-inch) cucumbers, sliced
5 tablespoons salt
1¼ tablespoons alum
6½ cups vinegar
5 cups sugar
3 teaspoons celery seed
2½ teaspoons mustard seed
1½ teaspoons turmeric
2½ teaspoons ginger

Slice onions and cucumbers. Sprinkle salt and alum over cucumber and onions. Let stand 1 hour. Drain in colander; set aside. Make syrup of vinegar, sugar, celery seed, mustard seed, turmeric and ginger in large pot and bring to boil for 5 minutes. Pour drained cucumbers into syrup. Put into hot, sterile jars immediately. Seal. I put the jars in water and bring to a boil before filling so they will be hot enough to seal.
Yield: 6 pints

Julia Woodson Hudson (Mrs. John S., Jr.)

CHOW CHOW

Delicious with meats and beans!

2 large cabbages
1½ pounds green sweet peppers
4 green tomatoes, medium-sized
4 medium onions
4 teaspoons salt
1½ pints vinegar
½ cup water
4½ teaspoons salt
2½-3 cups sugar

Chop cabbage; add 4 teaspoons salt. Work with hands, mixing and squeezing until a bit of juice comes from cabbage. Add cut up peppers and tomatoes. Work a bit more; add chopped onions. Make syrup of vinegar, water, salt and sugar. Put chopped ingredients into cold syrup and bring to a boil (a good boil in the center of the pot). Cook about 5 minutes after boil begins. Begin to put into hot, sterile jars from center of pot. Do NOT let cook too long or syrup will cook away. Seal.
Yield: 8 pints

Judith Branch Blythe (Mrs. Charles B.)

ARTICHOKE RELISH

4 quarts artichokes, cut up
2 pounds cabbage, sliced thin
2 pounds onions, sliced thin
6 green peppers, chopped
1 gallon water
2 cups salt
1 (6-ounce) jar prepared mustard
½ gallon vinegar, (reserve 1 cup)
1 tablespoon turmeric
1 tablespoon black pepper
¾ cup flour
1 tablespoon white mustard seed
5 cups white sugar

Mix artichokes, cabbage, onions, and green pepper together in large pan. Soak overnight in 1 gallon water and 2 cups of salt. In morning, drain off water. Make a sauce of the flour, mustard, vinegar, turmeric, black pepper, mustard seed and sugar. Then add the reserved cup vinegar to sauce and boil 5 minutes, stirring constantly. Add vegetables to sauce and warm thoroughly. Then fill sterilized jars.
Yield: about 8 pints

Elizabeth Morris Hodges (Mrs. C. W., Jr.

MIXED CORN RELISH

18 ears ripe yellow corn, kernels removed
1 head green cabbage, chopped
8 white onions, chopped
6 green peppers, seeds and membranes removed
6 small hot red peppers, seeds and membranes removed
2 teaspoons mustard seed
2 teaspoons celery seed
2 quarts cider vinegar
¼ cup salt
2 cups sugar
½ cup pimiento, minced

In a large saucepan, combine celery seed, mustard seed, vinegar, salt, sugar and pimiento. Combine corn, cabbage, onions and peppers and add to saucepan. Heat just to boiling point and simmer relish for 35 minutes. Place in sterile jars, seal and process 15 minutes in boiling water.
Yield: 10 pints

Isabelle Schocke Taylor (Mrs. Elijah)

GREEN TOMATO PICKLES

7 pounds green tomatoes
2 gallons water
3 cups pickling lime
5 pounds sugar
3 pints vinegar
1 tablespoon ground cloves
1 tablespoon ground ginger
1 tablespoon ground allspice
1 tablespoon celery seed
1 tablespoon ground mace
1 tablespoon ground cinnamon

Slice green tomatoes not too thin. Dissolve lime in water and pour over tomatoes; soak for 24 hours stirring often. Wash tomatoes in fresh water, and soak in fresh water for 4 hours changing water every hour. Boil sugar, vinegar, spices; pour over tomatoes and let stand overnight. Next day boil 1 hour. Seal in hot sterilized jars.
Yield: 8 pints

Annie Shipp Shields (Mrs. John)

BLUE RIBBON SAUERKRAUT

Make six weeks before using

5 pounds cabbage, shredded finely*
3½ tablespoons salt
Sterilized glass jars, lids and bands
Water

*Use good sound heads of mature cabbage.

Remove outside green and dirty leaves. Wash well and quarter heads; drain. Shred cabbage. Put cabbage into large pan or bowl; add salt mixing thoroughly with hands. Pack solidly into jars; pack down with spoon. Fill jars with cold water to within ½-inch of jar top. Put on jar lids, screwing bands as tightly as you can by hand. This will ferment for several days. When fermentation ceases, wipe off outside of jars; tighten screw lids if loose. Store jars without processing. Kraut will be ready for use in six weeks. If stored in cool, dark place will keep for many months. I have kept some of mine for two years. This is delicious in corned beef sandwiches (Reuben), hot dogs, hamburgers or cook it and serve with pork.

Yield: 5-6 pints

Elizabeth Scales Marsh (Mrs. Thomas B.)

DILLED BEANS

Prepare two weeks before using

2 pounds green beans, trimmed
1 teaspoon cayenne pepper
4 cloves garlic*
4 heads dill
2½ cups water
2½ cups vinegar
¼ cup salt

*or ⅛ teaspoon minced garlic per jar

Pack beans lengthwise into hot jars, leaving ¼-inch head space. To each pint, add cayenne pepper, 1 clove garlic, and 1 head dill. Combine remaining ingredients and bring to a boil. Pour boiling hot over beans, leaving ¼-inch head space. Adjust caps. Process pints or quarts 10 minutes in boiling bath. Let beans stand 2 weeks before tasting to develop flavor.

Yield: 4 pints

Diane Gough Fowler (Mrs. Phillip L.)

CONNIE'S SWEET AND SOUR PICKLES

Can be made any time of the year

1 gallon sour or dill pickles
1 extra gallon jar
5 pounds sugar
1 (1.25 ounce) can of pickling spices (McCormick, if available)
2 cups cider vinegar
2 sticks cinnamon
Cheese cloth

Divide spices in half and place in two cheese cloth bags. Drain the sour pickles and slice them about ½-inch thick. A crinkle knife makes a pretty sliced pickle. Heat the sugar, vinegar, and spices to boiling, stirring often; reduce heat and cook until all the sugar is completely dissolved, usually about 30 minutes. Put half of the pickles in each jar and divide the sugar and vinegar mixture between the two jars. Let the pickles marinate for two weeks, shaking well each day. Place in jars of desired size and refrigerate.
Yield: 1 gallon delicious sweet pickles

Connie Graham Brooks (Mrs. Berry)

PICKLED BEETS OR EGGS

1 can whole small beets, drained *OR* hard-boiled eggs
1 cup sugar
1 cup vinegar
1½ teaspoons cinnamon
¼ teaspoon cloves
¼ teaspoon allspice

In a saucepan combine sugar, vinegar, cinnamon, cloves and allspice. Simmer 15 minutes. Pour over beets or eggs; cover and let marinate for a day or longer. Make sure eggs stay submerged.

Diane Gough Fowler (Mrs. Phillip L.)

HOT PEPPER JELLY

Easy
Can be doubled

1½ cups green pepper, chopped *OR* 1 cup green pepper and 1 cup red pepper
¼-½ cup hot pepper, chopped
6-6½ cups sugar
1½ cups vinegar
1 (6-ounce) bottle Certo
Green food coloring (optional)

*Longer boiling yields a firmer jelly.
Seed and chop peppers. Peppers may be pulverized in blender if desired. Combine sugar, vinegar and peppers in a large pot. Bring to rolling boil 1-6* minutes. Take off heat and skim foam. Add Certo and food coloring. Pour into sterilized jars. Be very careful during boiling time or jelly will boil over.
Yield: 6-7 half-pint jars

Karen Brannock Askew (Mrs. M. H. III)
Becky Melton Kafer (Mrs. C. William)

HAVELOCK CRAB APPLE BUTTER

Free crab apples may be the secret of this recipe!

4 quarts crab apples*
Water
3 cups sugar
¼ teaspoon cinnamon
¼ teaspoon nutmeg
2 drops red food coloring (optional)

*Crab apples picked from public places, such as Main Street, Havelock, North Carolina seem best for this recipe.

Quarter and core crab apples. Cover with cold water. Bring to a boil and simmer until tender. Put through food mill. To the pulp (4 cups) in a shallow kettle, add sugar. Boil rapidly, stirring constantly and as butter becomes thick, reduce heat to prevent spattering. Have plenty to do in the kitchen, because this can take over an hour to get thick enough. Add spices and food coloring. Continue cooking until butter is thick enough to your taste.
Yield: 4 cups

Pat Moore Parker (Mrs. Joseph F.)

NO-COOK BLUEBERRY JAM

To be frozen

2 pints fresh blueberries
6 cups sugar
2 tablespoons lemon juice
1 (6-ounce) bottle liquid pectin (Certo)

Wash and drain blueberries. Crush with a potato masher or wooden spoon until smooth. Add sugar and lemon juice. Stir until sugar is dissolved. Add liquid pectin and stir for 3 minutes. Pour into sterilized jars. Will keep for several months in refrigerator or 1 year in freezer. Must be refrigerated or frozen. Powdered pectin (Sure Jell) may be substituted for liquid. Mix 1 box Sure Jell with ¾ cup water; boil for 1 minute, stirring constantly.
Yield: 4 cups

Jo Simmons Aiken (Mrs. Hovey E.)

REFRIGERATOR STRAWBERRY JAM

2 cups large firm strawberries
6 tablespoons Sweet 'N Low

Wash and hull strawberries. Measure. Place a layer of berries in kettle and sprinkle with Sweet 'N Low and continue layering until all are used. Allow to stand overnight. Place over heat; bring to boil and boil for 10 minutes. Pour into bowl and let stand until next day. Fill jelly glasses and seal. Keep in refrigerator.
Yield: 1-1¼ cups

Elizabeth Scales Marsh (Mrs. Thomas B.)

FIG PRESERVES

3 cups figs, chopped
3 cups sugar
½ cup lemon juice
2 (3-ounce) packages strawberry Jello

In a saucepan combine figs, sugar and lemon juice. Boil 15 minutes stirring occasionally. Remove from heat and add Jello. Return to stove and boil 5 minutes. Pack into sterile jars.

Sherry Piner Salter (Mrs. David C.)

KUMQUAT PRESERVES

Nice accompaniment to fowl!

1 quart kumquats
1½ cups water
1½ cups sugar

Wash fruit; slit bottom of each kumquat in a cross. Put fruit in saucepan and cover fruit with water. Bring to a boil over medium heat. Drain off water. In another saucepan combine water and sugar. Over medium heat, bring to a boil and simmer 5 minutes on low heat. Add drained fruit; simmer about 1 hour. Pour into sterilized jar.
Yield: 1 pint

Alice Smith Flood (Mrs. Robert)

CRANBERRY MARMALADE

1 pound cranberries
2 oranges
1 lemon
½ cup water
⅛ teaspoon baking soda
6½ cups sugar
½ (6-ounce) bottle Certo Fruit Pectin

Wash cranberries and set aside. Cut oranges and lemon in half and remove seeds. Grind in meat grinder or food processor. Put ground lemon and oranges in saucepan; cover with ½ cup water and baking soda. Simmer, covered 20 minutes, stirring occasionally. Add cranberries to lemon-orange mixture. Cover and continue to simmer 10 additional minutes. Add sugar to fruit and increase heat to high. Bring to a boil and boil 1 minute. Remove from heat; add Certo and stir. Skim off excess foam and spoon into sterilized jars.
Yield: 5 pints

Gretchen Deichmann Speer (Mrs. Howard)

MINCEMEAT

This is an old family recipe!

Two weeks aging time needed
May be frozen

3 pounds lean beef (round steak) boiled
1 pount suet
2 pounds seeded or seedless raisins
½ pound citron
Juice and grated rind of 1½ lemons
Juice and grated rind of 1½ oranges
½ peck apples (6 pounds)
Salt to taste
1 pound white sugar (2 cups)
1 pound brown sugar (2¼ cups)
1¼ quarts apple cider
½ teaspoon pepper
½ tablespoon ginger
½ tablespoon cinnamon
½ tablespoon cloves
½ tablespoon allspice
½ tablespoon nutmeg
New York State Sherry to taste

Grind cooked lean beef, suet, raisins, citron. Place in large pan or tub. Add lemon and orange juice and rind. Clean grinder before grinding and adding peeled and cored apples. Catch juice which may drip from grinder. Add salt, sugars, cider, pepper and spices. Mix well. Add ½-1 cup sherry according to taste. Cover and place in cool (50 degrees) place to "age." Allow at least 2 weeks to "age," checking daily the temperature and adding sherry to suit your own taste. When "aging" is complete, package in quart containers in refrigerator or freezer until ready to make into pies. Begin shortly after Thanksgiving to make and your mincemeat will be ready in time for Christmas pies. Yield: filling for 6-8 pies

Helen Jernigan Shine (Mrs. James F., Jr.)

ROSE GERANIUM JELLY

Great Christmas gift!

Tart apples
Water
Sugar
Rose geranium leaves
Red food coloring
Paraffin

Select sound, tart apples. Wash and cut off blossom end. Do not remov peeling. Cut into quarters and barely cover with water. Cook until fruit tender. Strain juice through a jelly bag (an old pillow case without holes great). Measure juice. Bring to boiling and add ¾ cup sugar for each cu strained juice. Boil rapidly to jelly stage*; when almost done immerse 2- rose geranium leaves into boiling jelly. The leaves wilt quickly and give c their flavor. Remove leaves after they have wilted. Tint rose color with foo coloring. Pour into sterilized jelly glasses. Cover with ⅛-inch melted paraffi Affix lids.

**How to judge the jelly stage:* After boiling juice rapidly for about 5 minute test by the following: to one teaspoon juice, add one teaspoon grain alcoho Stir slowly. (Wood or denatured alcohol may be used but DO NOT TAST as they are poisonous.) Juices rich in pectin will form a large amount gelatinous material. Continue cooking rapidly until large amount of gelatinou material is formed when tested. Then pour into jelly glasses. Tart apples w always have enough pectin to make jelly. The alternative to this method to use a jelly thermometer which should read 220-222 when jelly stage ha been reached at sea level.

Elizabeth Scales Marsh (Mrs. Thomas B

PEAR CONSERVE

4 quarts pears
3 oranges, seeded
2 lemons, seeded
1 (20-ounce) can crushed pineapple, undrained
5 pounds sugar
1 cup nuts, chopped
1 (6-ounce) jar maraschino cherries

Slice, peel, core and cut pears into small pieces; measure to make 4 quar Remove seeds of oranges and lemons and grind together using rind, pu and juice. Drain and cut cherries into pieces. Mix pears, oranges and lemo pineapple and sugar in a saucepan and cook, stirring frequently until cle and thickened. Add nuts and maraschino cherries and cook 15 minu longer. Pack into sterile jars and seal.

Virginia Hall (Mrs. Charles H.,

TUTTI-FRUTTI

Alcohol or strong brandy (½ cup per pound of fruit)
1 pound strawberries and/or cherries and/or peaches and/or raspberries and/or pears and/or grapes
Sugar (2 cups per pound of fruit)

Prepare jar or crock by washing well. Combine 1 pound of fruit with two cups sugar. Add to this ½ cup alcohol or brandy. Put into jar and cover tightly so that all air is excluded. (The fruit is the earliest fruit to ripen in your area, perhaps the strawberries.) As other fruits ripen, add to jar and repeat measurements of sugar with ½ cup brandy. Cover jar after each addition. When last of fruits, possibly grapes, are added, the jar is left to stand sealed until Christmas. This should start with strawberries, then pitted cherries, then peaches, then white seedless grapes etc. Originate your own with this as a guide.

Elizabeth Scales Marsh (Mrs. Thomas B.)

MOTHER'S PEACH PICKLES

Time consuming; plan to work on these pickles 9 days! This recipe has been handed down for four or five generations in my family.

10 pounds fresh peaches, ripe but firm
5 pounds sugar
5 cups vinegar
2 ounces stick cinnamon
2 ounces whole cloves

Place cinnamon and whole cloves in small cloth bag tied with string. Peel peaches, leaving pits in peach and place in a 2- or 3-gallon earthenware crock with a lid. In a large pot combine sugar, vinegar, and spices. Bring to a rolling boil. Pour over peaches and quickly cover with lid to retain heat. Strain off liquid each morning *or* evening and boil again. Pour over peaches as on first day. On the 9th day, bring syrup to boil and add peaches, but do NOT boil. Put into quart jars and seal. Place jars upside-down while cooling. Store in cool place.
Yield: 6 quarts

Helen Jernigan Shine (Mrs. James F., Jr.)

BRANDIED PEACHES

2 (16-ounce) cans peach halves
⅓ cup brandy

Drain peaches thoroughly and RESERVE syrup. Boil all peach syrup in a saucepan until it is reduced to less than a cup; about 15 minutes. Remove from heat; stir in brandy. Pack drained peaches into wide-mouth 1½ pint jar; add brandy mixture to fill the jar. Cover tightly. Refrigerate. Allow to mellow at least overnight before serving. Will keep much longer in the refrigerator.
Yield: 1½ pints

Elizabeth Scales Marsh (Mrs. Thomas B.)

PEAR RELISH

1 gallon ground pears
8 cups ground onions
8 sweet green peppers, chopped
2 hot red peppers, chopped
2 quarts white vinegar
2½ teaspoons salt
3 tablespoons dry mustard
6 teaspoons allspice
2 teaspoons ground cloves
2 teaspoons ground cinnamon
2 teaspoons turmeric
4 cups sugar

Mix all ingredients together and bring to boil. Simmer 15 minutes. Pack into sterilized jars and seal at once.
Yield: 7-9 pints

Elizabeth Scales Marsh (Mrs. Thomas B.)

PEAR PICKLES

24 pears
5-6 cups sugar
1 piece ginger root
2 sticks cinnamon
1 tablespoon allspice
1 tablespoon cloves
3 cups vinegar
2 cups water

Peel pears and cut into quarters or eighths. Mix sugar, spices which have been tied in a bag, vinegar and water. Boil until sugar dissolves. Cover pears with hot water and simmer 10 minutes. Drain. Add to vinegar mixture; heat slowly to boiling. Remove from heat. Let stand 12 to 24 hours in a cool place. Drain. Boil syrup. Pack pears in hot sterilized jars. Cover with boiling syrup. Seal. Process 10 minutes in boiling water bath.
Yield: 7-9 pints

Elizabeth Scales Marsh (Mrs. Thomas B.)

SEASONED SALT

6 tablespoons salt
½ teaspoon thyme leaves
½ teaspoon marjoram
½ teaspoon garlic salt
2¼ teaspoons paprika
½ teaspoon curry powder
1 teaspoon dry mustard
¼ teaspoon onion powder
⅛ teaspoon dill seeds
½ teaspoon celery salt

Combine all ingredients in small jar; cover and shake until well-blended. Use in salt shaker.
Yield: about ⅓ cup

Elizabeth Scales Marsh (Mrs. Thomas B.)

BONNIE'S MAPLE SYRUP

1 cup sugar
1 cup water
1 teaspoon maple flavoring
Corn syrup

Boil sugar and water 2-3 minutes. Stir in maple flavoring and a little corn syrup, if desired.

Lindy Allmond Emory (Mrs. Robert R.)

ANNA'S HOMEMADE SWEETENED CONDENSED MILK

Easy and economical. Can be used for any recipe calling for sweetened condensed milk....lots cheaper and less fattening.

cup instant nonfat dry milk
/3 cup sugar
/3 cup boiling water
3 tablespoons butter or margarine, melted

Combine all ingredients in electric blender container. Process until smooth. Store in refrigerator until ready to use.
Yield: 14 ounces

Becky Melton Kafer (Mrs. C. William)

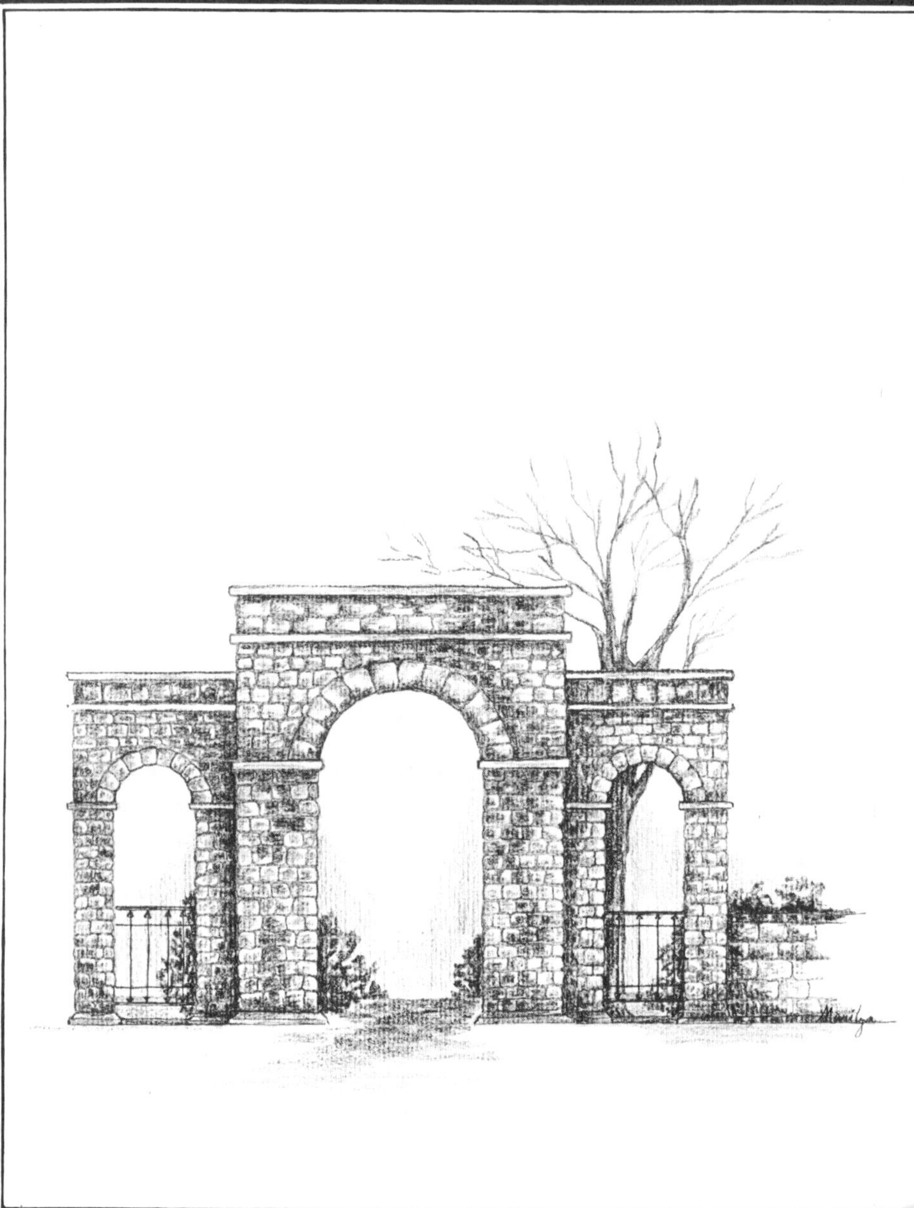

Cedar Grove Cemetery **602 Queen Street**

Christ Church established Cedar Grove Cemetery in 1800 probably because of the numerous burials in the church yard due to the yellow fever epidemics. On December 12, 1853, the cemetery was transferred to the city by the church. Moisture is held by the handsome "Weeping Arch" entrance of porous coquina stone, and a superstition has long been that if water drops on anyone passing under the arch he will be the next one carried there in a hearse.

Kids Can Cook Too!

PEAR SAUCE

1 (29-ounce) can pears, drained
Cinnamon
Nutmeg

Put the pears in the blender. Push the button and blend it up. Shake in as much cinnamon and nutmeg as you like. Serve with pork chops or on top of cottage cheese.
Yield: 4-6 servings

Katherine Culpepper

ROASTED PUMPKIN SEEDS

A three-year-old can do this with a little help!

2 cups pumpkin seeds
2 tablespoons butter *OR* 1½ tablespoons vegetable oil
1 teaspoon salt

Preheat oven to 250 degrees. Wash seeds in a colander. Drain them and pat dry with a paper towel. In a large skillet, sauté the seeds in the butter and salt. Stir 3 minutes until all seeds are coated with butter. Bake 30 minutes. If not roasted enough, bake 15 minutes more or until browned. Drain on paper towels. Eat them, shell and all.

Berleen Bryant Burnette (Mrs. Norman)

PURPLE COW SHAKES

1 (6-ounce) can frozen grape juice concentrate
1 cup milk
2 cups vanilla ice cream

Pour the juice concentrate and milk into blender container. Scoop in 2 cups ice cream. Cover and blend on high speed for 30 seconds. Serve right away. Yield: 3-4 shakes

Susan Patrick Thomas

WINNIE-THE-POOH CEREAL

4 cups quick-cooking rolled oats
2½ cups wheat germ
1 tablespoon cinnamon
2 tablespoons brown sugar
1 cup coconut (optional)
½ cup honey
⅓ cup salad oil
1 tablespoon vanilla
Nuts
Raisins or chopped dates (optional)

Preheat oven to 300 degrees. Mix dry ingredients, add honey, oil and vanilla. Mix well. Spread on a cookie sheet and bake 20 minutes, stirring occasionally. Store in an airtight container.

Diane Gough Fowler (Mrs. Phillip L.)

KATHY'S GRANOLA

¼ cup butter
¼ cup honey
1½ teaspoons cinnamon
½ teaspoon salt
1 cup flaked coconut, frozen or canned
1 cup nuts, chopped
3 cups quick-cooking rolled oats

Preheat oven to 350 degrees. Melt the butter in a 13 x 9-inch baking pan. Add honey and all remaining ingredients, mixing all together thoroughly. Spread evenly in pan and bake for about 30 minutes or until lightly browned and crispy. Keep an eye on the mixture during the baking, stirring occasionally to prevent burning. When cool, store in a tightly covered container. Serve as a cold cereal, snack, or a yummy topping on ice cream.

Paulette Cardillo Culpepper (Mrs. George V.)

FRENCH TOAST

2 eggs
½ cup milk
¼ teaspoon salt
6 slices day-old bread or raisin bread
Confectioners' sugar

Preheat griddle over medium heat or electric griddle to 375 degrees. Beat the eggs, milk, and salt in a bowl with a fork until blended. Grease the hot griddle with a thin layer of butter or margarine, using a pastry brush. Dip 6 slices of bread, one at a time into the egg mixture. Cook on the hot griddle until golden brown, about 4 minutes. Left an edge and peek. Turn with a pancake turner and cook 4 minutes on the other side. Serve with confectioners' sugar.
Yield: 6 servings

Susan Patrick Thomas

FUNNY FACE SANDWICH

1 frankfurter, split in half lengthwise
2 slices bread
1 cheese slice
Mayonnaise (optional)
Melted butter
Catsup

Preheat oven to 400 degrees. Make a cheese sandwich. Cut with a round cutter. Wrap frankfurter halves around sandwich and fasten with toothpicks. Place on a buttered cookie sheet or one sprayed with Pam. Brush bread and frankfurter with melted butter. Let the child create a face with catsup from a dispenser. Bake for 5 minutes.
Yield: 1 sandwich

Helen and Oscar Kafer

MONKEY'S DELIGHT SANDWICH

2 slices whole wheat bread
Peanut butter
Honey
1 banana, sliced into "banana pennies"

Spread 1 slice of bread with peanut butter and the other with honey. Arrange "banana pennies" on top of the peanut butter, put the two slices together into a sandwich and enjoy!

Hart Askew

ONE, TWO, THREE SOUP

1 (10-ounce) can tomato soup, diluted with 1 can water
1 (10-ounce) can green pea soup, diluted with 1 can water
1 (10-ounce) can beef consommé, not diluted
1 teaspoon chives

Empty all soup and water into a saucepan. Heat until hot, stirring constantly. Sprinkle with chopped chives before serving.
Yield: 4 servings

Anna Cartner Kafer (Mrs. Oscar A., III)

Put ½ pint whipping cream into a jar; cover tightly and let everybody shake the jar. Makes good butter!

HONEY CRUNCH PEANUT SPREAD

⅔ cup Quaker Quick Oats
1¼ cups smooth peanut butter
½ cup honey
Raisins (optional)
Crisp bacon (optional)
Celery, carrots, apples, or pears

Preheat oven to 350 degrees. Toast the oats in an ungreased shallow baking pan for 15-20 minutes. Cool and combine with the peanut butter and honey. Spread on celery, carrots, apples or pears for a good-tasting, nutritious snack.

Lisa, Jason and Bryan Ward

PEPPERMINT SNOWBALLS

1 quart vanilla or chocolate ice cream
2 cups peppermint candies, crushed
Chocolate sauce

Form ice cream into balls, roll in the candies, and serve with chocolate sauce. These may be done ahead of time and placed in the freezer after rolling in the candies until ready to serve.

Caroline Smith, Jr.

ORANGE JUICE-SICLES

1 (6-ounce) can frozen orange juice concentrate
1 juice can cold water
1 egg white
2 tablespoons honey

Mix all ingredients together in a blender. Remove foam and freeze it for use later in fruit shakes. Pour the blended juice mixture into paper cups or plastic popsicle cups and freeze. If using paper cups, let the mixture become semi-frozen before inserting sticks. When ready to serve, run the plastic form under tap water to make it easier to remove.
Yield: 12 small pops or 6 large ones

Josh and Karen Tayloe

FROZEN CHOCOLATE "DIRT"

6 small clay pots
1 quart vanilla ice cream
1 (2-ounce) chocolate bar
6 children

Plug hole in bottom of each pot with aluminum foil. Pack ice cream in each one. Grate chocolate bar over top. Freeze until you round up 6 lively children. Decorate with a flower in each pot and serve with spoons for "trowels"!
Yield: 6 servings

Berleen Bryant Burnette (Mrs. Norman)

BANANAS ON A STICK

6 bananas, ripe and peeled
12 wooden lollypop-type sticks
1 cup semi-sweet chocolate morsels
1 tablespoon butter

Cut bananas in half lengthwise. Insert a stick at one end of each banana half and freeze. Melt chocolate and butter together in top of double boiler. When bananas are frozen, dip each piece in chocolate mixture. When cold has glazed chocolate, wrap each banana in aluminum foil and store in freezer until ready to serve.
Yield: 12 servings

David Matthew Stewart

PEACH SNOW CREAM

1 (16-ounce) can peaches, undrained
1 (13-ounce) can Eagle Brand milk
Large bowl of snow

Mash peaches with a potato masher. Add milk and mix well. Add snow to desired consistency.

Virginia King Sharp

Shaving cream tinted with tempera powder makes super fingerpaint.

Use a styrofoam egg carton as a paint pallet.

KNOX BLOX

4 envelopes Knox geletine
3 envelopes flavored Jello
4 cups hot water

Mix Knox gelatine and Jello together. Add hot water and stir until dissolved. Put in 9 x 13-inch dish in refrigerator. Cut in squares or with cookie cutter when set.

Ginny McCott

HAYSTACKS

2 (6-ounce) packages butterscotch bits
1 (5-ounce) can chow mein noodles
1 (6-ounce) can peanuts

Melt butterscotch bits in a heavy pan or double boiler. Stir in nuts and noodles. Drop onto waxed paper with a teaspoon. Cool and eat.

Stephen Novak

MOON BALLS

Perfect for children to make

1 cup nonfat dry milk
½ cup honey
½ cup peanut butter
½ cup granola-type cereal, crushed

Mix dry milk, honey and peanut butter together until well-blended. Chill. Form into balls the size of marbles and roll in cereal.
Yield: 3 dozen

David Matthew Stewart

CRICKET COOKIES

Quick and easy
Great for a rainy day

½ cup wheat germ
1½ cups peanut butter
1½ cups honey
3 cups nonfat dry milk
¾ cup graham cracker crumbs

Mix all ingredients together. Butter hands and shape into balls. YUM! This is a jiffy children's recipe which gives them protein along with fun. But watch out—you'll find the adults eating just as many as the children!
Yield: 5 dozen

Peggy Witmeyer Bernard

MAMA'S HELPER CHOCOLATE CANDY

2 squares German sweet chocolate
1 can Eagle Brand condensed milk
1 teaspoon vanilla
1 cup pecans, chopped

Melt chocolate; add condensed milk. Stir constantly cooking 20 minutes until bubbly. Add vanilla and pecans. Drop on waxed paper to cool.

Jane Elizabeth Stewart

Cotton swabs with long sticks (such as those used for throat cultures) are super paint brushes.

PEANUT BUTTER CANDY

1 cup crunchy peanut butter
½ cup honey
1 cup uncooked Old Fashioned Quaker Oats
4 cups dry powdered milk

Stir together peanut butter and honey. Stir oats and milk together. Then combine wet and dry ingredients, shape into small balls in the palms of your hands. (Kids love to help.) Keep covered and refrigerated. If desired, cut small squares of waxed paper and individually wrap the candy pieces. It's a great pick me up snack.

Reed, Laura and Graham Underhill

PEANUT BUTTER BALLS

1 cup powdered milk
1 cup peanut butter
1 cup light Karo syrup
1 cup chocolate chips
Crushed Rice Krispies

Mix equal parts of milk, peanut butter, Karo syrup and chocolate chips. Shap into balls and roll in the cereal. Kids love these!

T. Reed Underhill,

CAKE IN A CUP

1 package Comet Ice Cream Cone Cups
Your favorite cake mix recipe

Fill Comet Cups ¾ full with mix. Place on a baking sheet. Bake in preheated 350 degree oven 30 to 35 minutes. Cool and frost.
Yield: 2 dozen

PUMPKIN-EATER PUMPCAKES

Mix in bowl:
1 (18-ounce) spice cake mix
1 cup pumpkin
⅔ cup water
2 eggs
1 (6-ounce) package chocolate chips
Whipped cream

Mix as directed on cake package. Stir in pumpkin and chocolate chips. Fill muffin cups ⅔ full. Bake 15-20 minutes. Cool 5 minutes. Garnish with whipped cream.

Paula Russell Vaughan (Mrs. Ross L.)

CHRISTMAS WREATH COOKIES

½ cup margarine
30 large marshmallows
1 teaspoon green food coloring (or more if deeper green color is desired)
1½ teaspoons vanilla
4 cups Corn Flakes
Red cinnamon candies

Melt the margarine and marshmallows in a large pot over medium heat, stirring constantly. Add the green food coloring and vanilla. Remove from heat and add the Corn Flakes. Stir until well-coated. Drop by tablespoonfuls onto a sheet of waxed paper and decorate with the red candies. Children adore to both make *and* eat these.
Yield: 14-16 large cookies

James Graham Underhill

EASTER EGGS

½ cup margarine or butter at room temperature
1 teaspoon vanilla
1 (16-ounce) package confectioners' sugar, sifted

Cream margarine or butter and vanilla; gradually add sugar until a stiff mixture forms. Divide into desired parts (small or large) and shape into eggs with palms. Place in waxed paper-lined airtight container. Chill in refrigerator or freeze before covering with chocolate and decorating.

Chocolate covering:
12-ounces semi-sweet chocolate morsels
2 teaspoons paraffin

Melt in double boiler. Dip eggs into chocolate with long fork. Dry and decorate with homemade or purchased decorator icing.

Alice Graham Underhill (Mrs. T. Reed)

Plastic jugs such as Clorox or dishwashing detergent come in can be thoroughly washed, softened and cut into shapes to make nametags. Write on plastic with a permanent magic marker.

AGGRESSION COOKIES

2 cups quick-cooking rolled oats
1 cup light brown sugar
1 cup butter or margarine, softened
1 cup flour
1 teaspoon baking soda
Chocolate chips or M&M's (optional)
Butter
Granulated sugar

Mix all ingredients together, except for the granulated sugar. Knead and squeeze until you feel better and there are no lumps. Form dough into small balls not as big as a walnut. Place on an ungreased cookie sheet. Butter the bottom of a small glass. Dip into granulated sugar and press balls out. Preheat oven to 350 degrees. Bake 10 to 12 minutes. Remove when lightly browned and cool on a rack. Dough will keep well if stored in tight container in the refrigerator.

Stephen Novak

PEANUT BUTTER DIPS

2½ pounds confectioners' sugar
2 cups margarine
1 (18-ounce) jar peanut butter
1½ (12-ounce) packages chocolate chips
½ (4-ounce) block paraffin

Mix sugar, margarine and peanut butter together until well-blended. Form into olive-sized balls. Melt chocolate chips and paraffin in a double boiler. Insert toothpicks in each ball and dip in chocolate mixture. Place on buttered waxed paper and remove toothpicks. Patch toothpick hole with a drop of chocolate. Chill in refrigerator before removing from waxed paper.
Yield: 200 balls

Susan Patrick Thomas

CHOCO-PEANUT-MALLOW CANDY

2 tablespoons margarine
1 (6-ounce) package semi-sweet chocolate morsels
1½ cups crunchy peanut butter
36 large marshmallows

Arrange marshmallows in an 8x8-inch pan in rows of 6. Melt margarine over low heat in a heavy saucepan or a double boiler. Add chocolate pieces and peanut butter and stir until melted and blended. Pour mixture over marshmallows and refrigerate until firm. When ready to serve, let stand at room temperature for 10 minutes. Cut between marshmallows and serve.
Yield: 3 dozen pieces

Stephanie and Erin Fowler

MISS CORBETT'S FAST OATMEAL CANDY

2 cups sugar
1 teaspoon vanilla
¼ cup cocoa
1 pinch salt
½ cup margarine
½ cup plain milk
½ cup crunchy peanut butter
3 cups quick-cooking or instant oatmeal, uncooked

Mix sugar, cocoa, milk, and margarine and put on medium heat. Bring to boil. Remove from heat and cool one minute. Add vanilla, salt, peanut butter, oatmeal. Stir well. Drop by teaspoonfuls onto waxed paper. Let cool.

Laura Helen Underhill

TURTLES

8 ounces soft caramels
2 tablespoons heavy cream
1 cup pecan halves

Melt caramels in heavy cream in top of double boiler. Arrange pecans in groups of five (a head and 4 legs). Spoon caramel in a small mound in the middle of the nuts to make the body. The caramels should partially cover the nuts to keep them in place. Let stand until hard. Coat body, head and legs with dipping chocolate.

Dipping Chocolate:
1 pound semi-sweet chocolate

Melt chocolate in top of double boiler. Stir with spoon while chocolate is melting. Be careful not to drip any water into chocolate. One drop of moisture in chocolate makes it "tighten" and become unsastisfactory for dipping. Spoon melted chocolate over body, head and legs of turtle.

John S. Stewart

POM POMS

1 cup graham cracker crumbs
1 cup coconut
1 cup nuts, chopped
4 heaping tablespoons peanut butter
1 cup margarine, melted
1 teaspoon vanilla
2-3 ounces paraffin
3 cups chocolate chips

Combine the crumbs, coconut, nuts, and peanut butter together, blendin well. Shape into bite-sized balls. Melt the paraffin and chocolate chips togethe in a double boiler or heavy saucepan. Dip each ball into the chocolate an place carefully on waxed paper to harden.

Beth Popajoh

"CANDIED" APPLE

1 apple
1 popsicle stick
Honey
Nuts, chopped
Wheat germ

Insert stick into top of apple. Dip apple into a bowl of honey, coating evenly. Hold apple over bowl until excess honey has dripped off. Do not rush this step. Roll apple in chopped nuts or toasted wheat germ. Serve immediately or refrigerate until ready to serve.

Berleen Bryant Burnette (Mrs. Norman)

POPCORN CHRISTMAS TREES

Centerpiece or favors for child's holiday party.

2½ cups sifted confectioners' sugar
1 egg white, unbeaten
1 teaspoon water
Green food coloring
6 ice cream cones
½ cup popcorn, popped
Cinnamon candies

Combine sugar, egg white, and water to make smooth icing. Tint delicate green and blend until uniform in color. Spread over outside of ice cream cones, covering completely, about 2 tablespoons each. While icing is soft, press about ½ cup popped corn all over surface. Dot with candies here and there between kernels of corn. Children love to look at these and also eat them!

Elizabeth Scales Marsh (Mrs. Thomas B.)

MINTS

1 (16-ounce) box confectioners' sugar
¼ cup butter, softened
1 tablespoon Karo syrup
Dash of salt
2-ounces water
Oil of peppermint to taste

Mix by hand, pat out to ¼-inch thick and cut with little cutters or shape into flat circles. Put on cookie sheet and freeze. Store in freezer in covered container. May use food color to color mints in mixing stage.

Paula Russell Vaughan (Mrs. Ross L.)

DOGGIE BISCUITS

Your dog will love these!

2½ cups whole wheat flour
½ cup dry powdered milk
½ teaspoon salt
½ teaspoon garlic powder
6 tablespoons shortening or meat drippings
1 egg, beaten
½ cup ice water
1 tablespoon brown sugar

Preheat oven to 350 degrees. Combine flour, dry milk, salt, sugar and garlic powder. Cut in shortening until mixture resembles corn meal. Mix in egg and add enough water until mixture forms a ball. Make small balls and flatten for bite-sized biscuits or press dough ½-inch thick and use a cookie cutter. Bake 25-30 minutes or until done.

Kathie Fowler (Mrs. Mark)

PLAY DOUGH

½ cup flour
¼ cup salt
½ cup water
½ tablespoon oil
1 teaspoon cream of tartar
Food coloring

Mix all ingredients in pan. Heat over low heat. Stir constantly until mixture forms a ball. While warm work together with hands into a ball. Keep in covered container and will keep indefinitely.

Susan Turner
Lisa Kafer

PEANUT BUTTER PLAY DOUGH

Can be eaten!

1 cup powdered milk
½ cup peanut butter
¼ cup honey

Combine all ingredients and mix well. Use for play dough and then eat. does not keep very well, so make only as much as you need.
Yield: enough for three kids

Paula Russell Vaughan (Mrs. Ross L

Index

Index

N

O

ILLUSTRATIONS

To Order **Pass The Plate**:

Please send______ copies @ $19.95 (U.S.) each $__________

Plus postage/handling @ $6.00 for one book $__________

and $1.00 for each additional book $__________

Texas residents add sales tax @ $1.60 each $__________

Check or Credit Card (Canada-credit card only) **Total** $__________

Charge to my ❑ MasterCard or ❑ VISA

ccount #______________________________

xpiration Date__________________________

gnature_______________________________

Mail or Call:
Cookbook Resources
541 Doubletree Dr.
Highland Village, Texas 75077
Toll Free (866) 229-2665
(972) 317-6404 Fax

me____

dress____

y______________________________State__________Zip_________

ne (day)__________________________(night)_________________

— — — — — — — — — — — — — — —

Order **Pass The Plate**:

Please send______ copies @ $19.95 (U.S.) each $__________

Plus postage/handling @ $6.00 for one book $__________

and $1.00 for each additional book $__________

Texas residents add sales tax @ $1.60 each $__________

Check or Credit Card (Canada-credit card only) **Total** $__________

ge to my ❑ MasterCard or ❑ VISA

unt #______________________________

ation Date__________________________

ture_______________________________

Mail or Call:
Cookbook Resources
541 Doubletree Dr.
Highland Village, Texas 75077
Toll Free (866) 229-2665
(972) 317-6404 Fax

____

s____

______________________________State__________Zip_________

(day)__________________________(night)_________________